From the Tigris to the Tiber
an introduction to ancient history

Fourth Edition

TOM B. JONES
University of Minnesota

Wadsworth Publishing Company
Belmont, California
A Division of Wadsworth, Inc.

Cover photo: ALINARI/ART RESOURCE, NY
    Battle of Issus, detail of Alexander (National Museum of Naples)

© Richard D. Irwin, Inc., 1969, 1978, 1983, and 1989

Sponsoring editor: Casimir Psujek
Project editor: Karen Smith
Production manager: Ann Cassady
Cover design: Diana Yost
Compositor: Compset Inc.
Typeface: 10/12 Palatino
Printer: R. R. Donnelley & Sons Company

LIBRARY OF CONGRESS
Library of Congress Cataloging-in-Publication Data
Jones, Tom Bard, 1909–
    From the Tigris to the Tiber : an introduction to ancient history
/ Tom B. Jones.—4th ed.
        p.   cm.
    Bibliography: p.
    Includes index.
    ISBN 0-534-11015-0 (previously ISBN 0-256-03666-7)
    1. History, Ancient.   I. Title.
D59.J64   1989
930—dc19   88–17611
                                                            CIP

Printed in the United States of America

2 3 4 5 6 7 8 9 0 DO 5 4 3 2 1 0 9

From the Tigris to the Tiber
an introduction to ancient history

Preface

At first glance it may seem paradoxical that we can *update* the past, but the fact of the matter is that we know comparatively little about what happened or what life was like five thousand or even one thousand years ago. Therefore it is not surprising that archaeological discoveries or re-examinations and revisions of older views periodically yield a harvest of new perceptions of bygone eras. These in turn must be added to our store of knowledge, a process that culminates in new editions—even of textbooks!

This fourth edition of a book first published in 1969 incorporates new material along with a revised bibliography that includes recent books of importance and eliminates others now outdated or no longer available. It will also be apparent that there has been an amplification of the text, particularly in those sections devoted to Greece and Rome. The addition of several maps especially designed to illustrate certain events or developments should also be mentioned.

One hopes that these changes will not obscure the original purpose of a book that was intended to outline the origin, growth, and climax of a great civilization that began in the ancient Near East and spread westward to Mediterranean lands, where its elaboration created a magnificent cultural heritage that we now call the Classical Tradition.

Tom B. Jones

Contents

List of Maps and Illustrations

MAPS

ILLUSTRATIONS

Chapter One

By Way of Introduction

On the morning of the 15th of March in the year 44 B.C., a lean, balding, middle-aged man entered the chamber of the Roman Senate and sat down as presiding officer in his accustomed place. Soon he was approached by a group of more than a dozen senators, one of whom presented a petition which the lean man read and abruptly rejected. As if responding to a signal, the senators bared weapons which they had concealed in their garments, set upon their chief, and stabbed him to death.

So died Julius Caesar, thought by some to be the ablest Roman of his time.

Political assassination was not new in Rome. For nearly a hundred years, opponents of political change had been accustomed to eliminate would-be reformers in this decisive manner. The whole era of violence had begun when two well-born brothers, each professing to champion the less privileged classes of society, had been struck down one after the other. Once launched, the carnage went on for decades. Even the brutal slaying of Caesar was not its climax, for Rome was again plunged into the bloody tide of civil war from which she had been rescued only temporarily by Caesar himself.

In the earlier stages of the spreading chaos, years before Caesar had been born, there had been much talk about democracy and about familiar issues: equal rights and full citizenship for all. In Caesar's childhood the underprivileged, tired of waiting on due process, had won a semblance of equality in the course of a sanguinary two-year revolution; but the sword once drawn could not be sheathed nor the tradition of violence broken. The protective wall of orderly constitutional practice was breached, the Republic within was sacked, and the dream of democracy fell—one of the first victims of the slaughter. Caesar himself had always paraded his connection with the popular faction and emphasized his devotion to the welfare of the people, yet once in power he deliberately sought reform and the restoration of order through the establishment of a permanent and comprehensive dictatorship. By his day, of course, hope for democracy was long dead, and time had run out even for class rule by a wealthy minority, the normal aspect of republican government at Rome. Caesar's murder neither saved this kind of polity nor served the interests of those who killed him. In the end, Rome bought peace at the expense of political freedom, submitting to a new governmental organization that was at best only a thinly disguised modification of the autocracy envisioned by Caesar.

The story of the death throes of the Roman Republic is as absorbing and breathtaking as a novel of adventure. Moreover, it exemplifies one of the age-old attractions of history, its narrative interest, which for many people has provided a sufficient reason to delve deeply into the past.

Going beyond this, however, it is undeniably thought-provoking to follow the march of events at Rome, a circumstance that exposes another and more serious facet of historical study. Often, familiarity with earlier times has been thought to offer a frame of reference helpful in comprehending the present. It goes without saying that no judicious, thinking person would jump to the naive conclusion that developments in ancient Rome must necessarily repeat themselves in our own age. Rather, one may experiment by setting the past and present side by side and examining them carefully for comparisons and contrasts in the hope that this may lead to a better understanding of our situation now. As a matter of fact, the reader may immediately or at some later time choose to reject absolutely the interpretation of the last century of the Roman Republic outlined above, but he or she can do so in complete honesty only after coming into possession of the facts about the past and having thought seriously and deeply about the present.

Now if Julius Caesar had been assassinated *this* morning, we might ourselves have witnessed the event on television, or someone present might have recorded it on film. As it is, we have only the story as told by several ancient writers, none of whom were eyewitnesses, and since all of our informants acquired their data at second hand, our certainty regarding the affair is pretty well confined to the fact that Caesar was killed on March 15. The day itself, fortunately, is confirmed by the letters of Cicero, a contemporary who was careful *not* to be present in the Senate for the bloodletting, and there is known also a commemorative coin issued by Brutus, one of the assassins, which displays two daggers, a liberty cap, and the inscription EID. MAR. (the Ides of March, or March 15). On the other hand, even if the crime had been committed this morning and we ourselves and others had witnessed it, there would still be much about the affair that would require months and years of investigation to discover, and some details would always remain matters of controversy.

All this reveals something more about history: that the past is obscured from us and must be reconstructed on the most tentative basis from fragmentary evidence. The examination and weighing of historical evidence and the formulation of hypotheses to interpret events and developments in the past constitute useful and instructive exercises for the intellect. From this discipline we learn that truth is illusive and that certainty is hard to achieve. The researcher soon discovers that little can be taken for granted and comes early to appreciate the prudence of keeping an open mind.

It should be understood that history is not cut and dried and that the recovery of the past is an ongoing process. This is especially true for the early history of the Near East, Greece, and Rome because our sources of information are not as complete as those for later periods. An archaeological find, the discovery of a lost manuscript or a new inscription, or the decipherment of an unknown script may contribute significantly to our fund of knowledge or sometimes force us to abandon as erroneous what we *thought* we knew. The past is the mirror of the present in the sense that we can interpret it only on the basis of our own experience. Consequently, a new situation or experience can lead to a different or even novel explanation of an episode in the past.

One should also be aware that, for at least 4,000 years, historians and other persons with special interests have struggled with the problems of chronology. In general, the greatest success has been in constructing *relative* chronologies: that "this came before that" or that the two were contemporary. An *absolute* chronology is much more difficult to establish since it aims at setting precise dates: "So and so died in 2607 B.C." or "began his reign in 374 A.D.," and so on. The many different systems of timekeeping used in antiquity are hard to reconcile and combine into one system, and as one goes farther and farther back in time, the amount of evidence progressively diminishes. No dates previous to 1500 B.C. given by modern compilers are undisputed, and by no means *all* those for periods after that. This is not to say that there are *no* fixed precise dates, since the batting average of the chronographers markedly improves for the years following 750 B.C.

Nevertheless, beginning students of history must keep in mind that dates are the pegs on which chronology is hung, and *some* need to be fixed in the memory. For generations, tyrannical schoolmasters felt it necessary to harass their students in the most sadistic manner by forcing them to memorize hundreds of dates, many of which were later found to be incorrect. This savage and inhumane species of torture has been discarded, *but* we cannot go to the other extreme and throw out the baby with the bath!

Cicero once said, "To be ignorant of what happened before you were born is to live the life of a child forever." It is unfortunately true, but quite beside the point, that Cicero's ignorance of history was exceeded only by his lack of interest in the subject. In fact, the pious sentiment quoted above was very likely one that Cicero had noted in the course of his voluminous reading and jotted down for use on an appropriate occasion. Nevertheless, Cicero—or his source—came close to the mark, and the quotation itself may serve to introduce a final comment on the study of history.

As the twentieth century A.D. grinds on, each passing year seems to bring new problems of increasing magnitude. We can, however, derive some slight comfort from two demonstrable facts: that there is a more widespread and general concern with regard to these matters than ever before and that the practitioners of a number of the relatively new social, behavioral, and natural sciences have developed previously unknown and highly sophisticated ways of studying or even alleviating some of these problems. This is all on the credit side of the ledger, but it is also true that, under the pressure of the here and now, and with the necessity of diagnosing trouble as quickly and directly as possible, people have tended to forget that one way to discover what something is today is to find out what it was in the beginning and to trace the course of its evolution and elaboration to the present. This cannot always be done in a satisfactory manner, of course, but it is often worth a try. In other words, the historical approach to current questions is seldom employed even when it might conceivably be of use.

If we seek to understand the modern world fully we must appreciate, among other things, the reality that the dominant and most complex civilization of the twentieth century is the one we call "Western," which was for centuries the possession of Europe and parts of the New World but which has now been diffused over the entire globe and is affecting vitally other civilizations and cultures. No one in this cosmopolitan age would argue that we can afford to be ignorant of "non-Western" or "Third World" history and culture, but if the question of priority of importance is raised, there can be no doubt of the choice to be made. It is an essential part of one's education to first learn something of the history of Western civilization and the manner of its evolution.

And the logical and appropriate place to begin is at the beginning, not in the middle or near the end. The first acts in the drama of Western civilization were played in succession on the stages of the Near East, Greece, and Rome, and it is with these origins that this little book is concerned.

Chapter Two

Before History

Zoologically speaking we are animals but, in our own way, unique. Clearly we differ from other animals in certain details of physical appearance and structure. We are mammals, though not whales, elephants, or sheep; primates, though not lemurs or tree shrews; anthropoids, though not monkeys or baboons; hominoids though not gibbons or gorillas or even chimpanzees. We are, in fact, the sole *hominids*, although fossil bones testify that once there were other varieties on this planet.

We could have said that gorillas are unique, too. We might have said about them all the things we have said about ourselves except that gorillas are *pongidae*, not *hominidae*, and they are not the sole survivors but have the company of the other great apes.

So what is unique about us? The essence of uniqueness in this case is not a matter of degree—that the human animal differs physically from other animals and has a larger brain and greater mental capacity. It is rather a difference of *kind* that sets us off from the rest of the animal kingdom, for our species is unique in that it alone is the creator and possessor of culture.

Culture has been defined as "the sum total of ways of living built up by a group of human beings, which is transmitted from one generation to another." Culture is the aggregate of all that the hands and brain of our species has produced: materials and material things; concepts and institutions—political, social, religious; artistic creations including music, literature, and the like; customs, traditions, and superstitions, to name only a few of the manifold categories of culture.

TRANSMISSION OF CULTURE

Imitation

Unlike our physical characteristics, culture cannot be genetically inherited but has to be acquired by each individual after birth. Cultural and physical transmission, therefore, differ with respect to the means by which they are accomplished. Culture is transmitted in two ways: by imitation and through communication by means of symbols. Imitation is especially important in the acquisition of physical skills. Most of us learned how to hit a baseball or a golf ball by watching and then imitating someone else; children, for example, are almost universally fascinated by the ways in which their parents care for an infant, and it is not long before they mimic these parental actions as they play with their dolls and toys.

Communication

Communication by means of symbols is accomplished in a variety of ways: gestures, pictures and signs, speech, and writing. With the possible exception of a few blatantly obvious gestures and exclamations, the assorted kinds of symbols that we use for communication are comprehensible to us only because each of us individually has learned the conventional meaning that has been—for the most part—arbitrarily assigned to each symbol. A driver unacquainted with traffic signals could hardly be expected to know the meaning of red or green. The sound of the word "dog" does not suggest a dog to anyone accustomed to calling a dog a "Hund" or a "chien"; even "bow-wow" does not conjure up a dog in the mind of everyone. What does "ur" mean? Is it a place name? Does it mean "primitive"? Either is admissible: the one if you have read the Old Testament, the other if it occurs in a German context. If, however, 5,000 years ago the Sumerians had used our alphabet, they would have spelled their word for dog like this: "ur."

The Brain

Now, our capacity for imitation and symbolization is so much greater than that of any other animal that it is almost impossible to discuss the matter on a comparative basis. "Monkey see–monkey do" is true to a certain extent, yet "the ape will monkey, but will not ape" comes closer to the facts of the matter. Dogs and cats, for example, learn to react to certain gestures and commands or exclamations. The author was once the proud possessor of a bilingual dog who infallibly responded with great spirit to "Voulez-vous dog biscuit?" The edge of this startling bit of testimony is somewhat blunted, however, by the reluctant admission that the gifted canine in question could somehow never manage to solve a simultaneous linear equation.

The conspicuous reason for our great ability to imitate and to communicate through symbols is that the human animal is the possessor of mental equipment far superior to that of any other animal. Little children learn to understand and to use the spoken word or to "read" highway signs at a very tender age. Animals never do this!

The Hands

So much for the brain—at least for the moment. However, we should not forget our hands. It is not without significance that the adjective "handy" has a variety of meanings: skillful, useful, and versatile. While admitting that nearly everything we are going to say in the rest of this paragraph could also be said of the primates as a whole, for the sake of convenience we are now going to treat only the human animal. Human hands are prehensile, can be used for grasping and holding, but so are the corresponding members of some other animals, as well as their feet and even their tails, in some cases. Our hands are nevertheless more specialized than this, for they are equipped with the "opposable thumb," which provides a built-in set of pliers. True, it is bad enough when one's fingers are "all thumbs," but it would be much worse if our thumbs were all fingers. Directed by the human brain—the "power" of which distinguishes us from the other primates—and assisted by binocular or stereoscopic vision, which gives to our ocular perception a depth not shared by all animals, human hands can perform wonders of manipulation and manufacture beyond the capability of any other creature.

Although we are the only creatures in the whole universe known to us who have created culture, we should not, as the readers of science fiction are well aware, rule out the possibility that some other creature has devised or might devise a culture. Unless, however, this hypothetical being had physical characteristics like those of the human animal, it is not likely that the culture thus created would resemble ours in many respects; what is most probable is that it would be utterly different. Why? Suppose the creature had no hands and lacked binocular vision. Would its tools resemble ours, and how would they be manipulated? What sort of a material culture would be produced? Suppose the creature lacked the vocal mechanism that would permit articulate speech. How would the creature's culture compensate for this deficiency in view of the fact that for the human animal a great volume of communication at certain levels is conducted by speech alone?

Up to this point our discussion has been mainly about the human animal today, but now it is time to review at least in outline the story of how our present form and capabilities were attained and how our fore-bears became the only animals to acquire culture. Enough has been said already to suggest that our culture is based primarily on two things: We are habitual tool-users and, in addition, we have the ability to symbol-ize. These in turn stem from our manual dexterity, superior mental equipment, and to some extent from the ability to speak articulately. All these qualities—and some others, too—might never have attained their present stage of development if our ancestors had not ages ago become bipeds and assumed the habitually erect posture.

HUMAN PHYSICAL EVOLUTION

Like other living things on the earth today, our species is a product of physical evolution. The details of how or why Man became Man are shadowy and vague despite the concentrated study devoted to the sub-ject during the last hundred years and more. Quite a few details relating to the story of cultural evolution seem to be lacking or muddled, too, so that the most prudent course to adopt here is to summarize what ap-pears to be the current thinking of scholars acknowledged as experts in such matters. Five years ago something very different would have been said at this point; five years hence, it is almost certain that some of what follows will have to be scrapped. The fragmentary nature of the evi-dence for physical and for early cultural evolution necessitates the for-mulation of hypotheses that are tentative in nature and often temporary in duration. The discovery of new bits of evidence, even if few in num-ber, may force the abandonment of one theory and the adoption of an-other.

Prehensile Abilities

Millions of years ago the remote ancestors of apes and hominids lived in the trees. Tree dwelling, getting around in the trees, had already enhanced their prehensile abilities, promoting also a specialization of function in the case of hands and feet. A consequence of this was the adoption of hand feeding, somewhat in the manner of squirrels, which allowed a reduction of the snout, permitted binocular vision, and en-couraged the priority of sight over smell as a means of sensory percep-tion. This, in turn, led to the development of new areas of the brain.

Beginning of Erect Posture

Later, an era of increasing dryness brought a diminution of forest areas and a spread of grasslands. Perhaps pushed out of the forests by the great apes, the ancestors of the hominids moved onto the grasslands and, instead of going back down on all fours, began more and more to adopt an erect posture. Then came the onset of the glacial period, with preliminary stages beginning perhaps 3 million years ago. The ancestors of both apes and humans were forced southward: Hominid fossils have been found in Africa dating from at least 3 million B.P. (before the present). In Tanzania in East Africa, two varieties of fossil hominids have been discovered: *Australopithecus*, a distinct genus not ancestral to humans—who scientists may ultimately give back to the apes; and *Homo habilis*, probably the first tool-user and some sort of an ancestor or relative of ours.

Parenthetically, the uncertainty of all this is well illustrated by the discovery of "Lucy" and her relatives at Hadar in northern Ethiopia in 1974. Lucy *(Australopithecus afarensis)*, a tiny predecessor of the Tanzanian creatures, has been tentatively dated at 3.75 million years B.P. It has also been suggested that she is ancestral to both *Australopithecus* and *Homo habilis*, but this is hotly debated, and we shall have to wait for a final decision based on agreement of expert opinion or new fossil discoveries.*

User of Tools

Homo habilis was a hunter of small game and a scavenger. It is suspected that *Homo habilis* killed the Australopithecines, and possibly ate them as well. It is inferred from the bones of *Homo habilis* that he had the true power grip, the opposable thumb. Yet, if the guesses of the physical anthropologists fall anywhere near the mark, *Homo habilis* did not have much of an edge, mentally, over *Australopithecus*—or a gorilla. The cranial capacity of *Homo habilis* is estimated at 680 cubic centimeters (cc.); *Australopithecus*, at 600 cc.; gorillas run around 584 cc. Our own species, incidentally averages 1,700 cubic centimeters.

Homo habilis, whose interest in Hegel, Haydn, or Hogarth might be on the dim side, was nevertheless the first cultured animal, the original handyman. How *Homo habilis* came to be a maker of tools, simple pebble choppers, can only be guessed. We can observe the antics of apes, who occasionally use sticks and stones as tools or weapons, and we can imagine that the predecessors of *Homo habilis* had been doing the same thing for a long time. The difference was, however, that with *Homo habilis* the use of sticks and stones had not only become *habitual* instead of

---

*For the details of this, see D. Johanson and M. Edey, *Lucy, The Beginnings of Human-kind* (New York: Simon & Schuster, 1981); or the condensed version in *Reader's Digest*, September 1981, p. 49 ff.

For a convenient, well-illustrated summary of these matters, see the *National Geographic*, vol. 168.5, November 1985, pp. 560–629.

desultory, but also *Homo habilis* had passed through a stage of *choosing* the sticks or stones most suitable for the purpose at hand to the ultimate level of the deliberate *manufacture* of elementary tools and weapons. The key word is "deliberate" because it implies planning, thinking ahead, something that apes do not seem accustomed to do. So culture was born. *Homo habilis* had become an habitual tool-user and toolmaker, and sometimes it is said that the brain is "handmade," implying that the use of the hands in toolmaking influenced the development of the brain.

Expansion of Brain Size

With the passage of time, the human animal finally assumed a truly erect posture. This, too, promoted an increase in mental capacities because erectness allowed the head to change its form, become less prognathous, and so gave room for the brain to expand in size. When we come to *Homo erectus* (500,000–100,000 years ago), whose remains have been found in Java and China, cranial capacity averages 950–1,050 cc. *Homo erectus* knew how to make fire, and, with only slightly improved weapons, was a hunter of big game. The debris from camp sites is evidence of this, and something else: *Homo erectus* may have been the first to pick the brains of other people—literally, however, since presumably he ate them as a delicacy.

PROGRESSIVE ELABORATION OF CULTURE

Culture has been expanded and elaborated in many ways. We have evidence of this in artifacts, mythologies, and increasing technologies such as the use of fire.

Varieties of Tools and Weapons

As we have seen, the earliest implements were made of wood and stone; eventually, there was an increasing use of bone and horn. Flint was a favorite material for tools and weapons, which were fashioned by flaking and chipping techniques. Considerable skill was required for this method of manufacture, but the rewards were in sharp points and good cutting edges. The progressive elaboration of culture can be deduced from the appearance of ever-increasing varieties of tools and weapons. Implements were designed for special tasks: for hunting, for cutting, for scraping, for perforating. An important and intellectually significant step was the introduction of hafting. For early humans, as for some of us today, it might take some doing to put two and two together, or even one and one as in the case of the haft and the blade.

Possession of Fire

The ancient Greeks had a myth that their culture-hero, Prometheus, stole fire from heaven and brought it down to humans. This symbolized the founding of civilization. Fire seemed to the Greeks a divine living force that transmuted materials: It made pottery out of clay and transformed ores into metals. The possession of fire must have raised the spirits of primitive people, too. It helped to ward off dangerous animals; it made it possible for people to warm themselves during the bitter cold of the glacial period; fire could almost turn night into day, and it could transform into food some substances previously not edible. Thus, diet was enriched as the potential food supply was increased.

Articulate Speech

We do not know when articulate speech began. It was possible for *Homo erectus*, whose physical development would have permitted articulate speech. A very plausible explanation for the origin of speech is that people first began to communicate by means of gestures; after this, particular sounds came to be associated with the gestures until finally the sounds more or less replaced the sign language as a means of communication. This last stage is believed by some scholars to have been reached only after our species had appeared on the scene.

Belief in Magic and the Supernatural

Homo habilis and Homo erectus lived during the great Ice Age in the last phase of which (well after 100,000 years ago) we encounter our own species, *Homo sapiens*. Strictly speaking, "modern Man" as known today cannot be traced back for more than 40,000 years from the present, but it will not be surprising if earlier evidence is soon disclosed. Nowadays, the tendency is to class the Neanderthals who go back 70–80,000 years or longer, as *Homo sapiens,* or at least as *Homo praesapiens,* and more or less to admit them as associates if not full members of our exclusive club. Since the Neanderthalers buried their dead, we are entitled to infer that they had evolved a belief in the supernatural.

Beginning about 25,000 years ago and continuing for roughly 10,000 years after that, abundant evidence for a belief in magic and supernaturalism is to be found in the so-called "cave art": carvings, drawings, and paintings on the walls of those caves, mostly European, which were inhabited or frequented by humans in the closing years of the Ice Age. Some of this art is truly beautiful, much is admirable in execution, and all of it is fascinating. Whatever esthetic pleasure or satisfaction through self-expression the cave artists derived from their compositions was nevertheless secondary in importance to the basic purpose of their work: to achieve religious or magical objectives. It is doubted today that the depiction of animals in cave art was solely or even fundamentally a form of hunting magic designed to ensure a kill or plenitude of game. Many curious figures on the cave walls once thought to represent weapons or the like have now been shown to be male or female symbols, just as the animals depicted were in many cases intended to typify one sex or the other. Whatever the purpose or meaning of cave art, however, it broadcasts loud and clear the message that the use and manipulation of symbols was expanding, a sure indication of increasing mental activity.

CULTURE AND HUMAN SURVIVAL

In recapitulation, we may say that by the end of the Ice Age, Man as Man, our species, was in existence; and culture, growing ever more elaborate and complex, had come to stay. The glaciers were in retreat; the "fossil men" had become extinct; *Homo sapiens* alone survived. Without question, survival was facilitated by a culture which had attained a depth and proportion of such magnitude that only *Homo sapiens* with a new brain could take advantage of it to the fullest extent. Survival was the purpose for which culture had been created; culture aided these people in the struggle for food, shelter, and protection from enemies, not only the real ones—other people and animals—but also the imaginary supernatural foes with which the imagination had now peopled the universe. It was culture that gave our species the adaptability to ride out climatic changes or adjust to new environmental situations; thus, they were able to continue to live in whatever place they chose to inhabit, or they were able to migrate and so populate all parts of the world, both Old and New, just as they did (with the exception of the polar regions) before the glacial period had ended.

As the glaciers retreated, there were changes in climate, changes in vegetation, and consequent alterations in the kind of game available as food. To cite one example, in northern and western Europe *Homo sapiens* had come to depend for subsistence upon the great reindeer herds and had organized the entire culture and manner of life with herd-hunting as its core. When the climate changed and grazing areas were reduced by the spread of forests, the reindeer became scarce and people were obliged to develop a new way of life. In such regions they met the problem by developing different hunting techniques and new weapons which allowed for successful preying on individual animals rather than herds. They also began to supplement the diet with fish and other seafood, something that involved the creation of other implements and techniques.

IMPACT OF THE AGRICULTURAL REVOLUTION

While our ancestors were effecting these changes in Europe, developments of even greater consequence for the future were taking place in the Near East, an area which we shall now consider in some detail.

First, however, it is necessary to emphasize that, up to this time, the beginning of the postglacial age, the human animal—with or without culture—had been a food collector or food gatherer. This was the basic and traditional form of the economy. Thus, except for the increased efficiency in food gathering afforded by the implements for hunting or fishing, the human animal had continued to exist on the same ecological stage as the other animals.

A great alteration in most phases of human existence occurred, then, when people became *food producers* by virtue of the domestication of plants and animals. This was the so-called Agricultural Revolution that had its beginnings in the Near East about 7000 b.c. and spread during the next few thousand years to many regions of the Old World.

Oasis Theory

Since it had long been known that the first civilizations had grown up in the great river valleys of the Near East, it used to be thought that the Agricultural Revolution must have begun there, too. The theory was that with more arid conditions after the Ice Age, and when the great deserts of the Sahara and Arabia commenced to expand, men and animals were forced to live in close quarters where water was still available: namely, on the oases and in the river valleys where plants also survived. Desperate for food, people resorted to the expedient of domestication. Thus, instead of hunting and gathering their food, they would produce it and always have sustenance at hand.

A serious and ultimately fatal objection to this theory was that it was unsupported by evidence. Indeed, it flew in the face of the archaeological testimony available when the idea was first proposed. At a date previous to any demonstrable occupation of the river valleys by humans, domestication was known to have been an accomplished fact in certain other regions. Worse than that, the very plants and animals assumed to have been domesticated by the riverine peoples were not indigenous ones; it was unlikely that people would have brought the wild plants and animals to the river valleys and subsequently tamed them.

Contradictory to the "oasis" theory was the plain fact that up to about forty years ago the earliest known peasant villages, those with an economy based on domesticated plants and animals, were located in a great arc stretching from the fringes of the Delta in Egypt through Palestine, Syria, northern Iraq, and on into Iran. All could be dated at least 1,000 years before the earliest known settlements in the Nile Valley or those of the lower Tigris-Euphrates area. The remains of these peasant villages revealed the details of peoples' lives and culture *after* the Agricultural Revolution had taken place: houses, storage facilities for grain, burials, pottery, implements of bone as well as chipped or ground stone, carbonized remains of domesticated barley, the bones of domesticated sheep and goats. Unfortunately, even the earliest levels of occupation in the peasant villages gave no hint of the first steps toward domestication, nor were the plants and animals of the villagers indigenous ones.

Chronology of the Agricultural Revolution

Where and when had the Agricultural Revolution begun? A link was missing from the chain of cultural evolution. One could follow developments from the peasant villages to the beginnings of civilization in the river valleys just as one could follow the elaboration of culture from the initiation of tool-using to the end of the glacial period. As a matter of fact, the final link in the earlier chain was thought to have been found in the form of a culture called Natufian which had been discovered in the caves of Mt. Carmel in northwestern Palestine. Two thousand years, it seemed, before the earliest known peasant villages, the people who lived in the Mt. Carmel caves had supplemented their hunting economy by harvesting *wild* grains and catching young *wild* animals which they kept in pens until they were ready to eat them. Thus, the Natufian people were on the verge of domesticating plants and animals; domestication was incipient, or, to put it another way, the Natufians were in a terminal food-gathering stage.

If a link could be found to close the gap between the Natufians and the peasant villagers, the chain would be complete, and since World War II much has been accomplished in this direction. Settlements earlier than the well-established peasant villages have been found. They are distinguished by a more limited assemblage of culture traits, more primitive houses, and the absence of pottery in their lowest levels, but the evidence for domesticated plants and animals is plain enough. Roughly, the sequence of events in the Near East might be summarized in the following chronological table:

Tentative Chronology of Events

Era	Evidence Found	Exemplified by
9500–8000 B.C.	Terminal food gathering	The (related) Natufians at Mt. Carmel
8000–6000 B.C.	Domestication in progress	The early villages
6000–3000 B.C.	Agricultural Revolution completed	The peasant villages

Other Conclusions

It should be emphasized that the so-called Agricultural Revolution was more of a process than an event. It was something that did not happen overnight. On the contrary, it took place gradually over many centuries, but it did nevertheless begin in the Near East, from which the new way of life was diffused to other areas: By 6000 B.C., for example, it had reached the Balkans. The domestication of plants and animals did not occur simultaneously; animals may have come first. It is possible that the process began in the foothills of northern Syria. There the wild ancestors of our sheep and goats grazed on the wild grasses that were the ancestors of our barley and wheat. Wherever it was, people began to capture and tame (raise in captivity) the wild animals and to harvest the wild grains which they later learned to plant.

The Agricultural Revolution was a turning point in human history almost as significant as Man's primary acquisition of culture. Since the change from food gathering to food production augmented and ensured the food supply, a population increase naturally followed. In a hunting economy, a square mile of territory might be required to support one person, whereas in an agricultural community several persons might live off a few acres. Thus, the population not only increased in size but also in density. The farmers could not be like the nomads who roamed with the animals on which they preyed. Farmers were settled folk, with fixed habitations. They congregated in villages where social and political organization inevitably grew in complexity. Man's activities and attitudes were changed by the demands of his new economy. The farmers must plan for the future, do their work at the proper season, and make their food stretch from one harvest to the next. For farming, a whole new set of tools had to be devised; some tools were best for certain purposes if made by grinding stone instead of chipping it. The religion and magic of the hunter now had to be altered to serve the farmer's needs. There was also a growing specialization of activity. In a given community most people might be farmers, but some were herdsmen, and a few remained hunters or fishermen. In addition, there were artisans who made tools and weapons, and there were embryonic traders who brought from afar the flint and salt that the farmers did not have time to secure for themselves. These specialized activities were interdependent; each specialist exchanged services or products for whatever was lacking that the others could supply.

A New Morality

Between 6000 and 3000 B.C., hundreds of permanently settled peasant villages were established throughout the Near East. From a material and institutional point of view, the new culture of the villages was much more complex than that of the food gatherers. Since agriculture was now the focus of activity and thought, the principal religious ceremonies were those of the fertility cults, the purpose of which was to secure a bountiful harvest. A new morality had come into existence, one which equated the cardinal virtues with the attributes of a successful farmer: hard work, thrift, orderliness, sobriety. Aesop's fable of the "Ant and the Grasshopper" typified what was now considered appropriate—and what was not. People must cooperate and work together for the welfare of the community. This took precedence over everything else, and thus everyone must conform to the approved modes of behavior in order that the supernatural powers might not be offended and bring disaster on the whole village.

UNFINISHED BUSINESS

In the three decades following the conclusion of World War II, the Agricultural Revolution was a subject of major interest for archaeologists and anthropologists as well as for specialists in the related fields of geology, palaeontology, and palaeobotany. The first order of business was to find the archaeological remains of a community or several communities representative of the period between the last cave dwellers on Mr. Carmel and the earliest known peasant villages in the Fertile Crescent. Jarmo, a primitive village site in the foothills of Iraq near Kirkuk, was discovered in 1948. It seemed to meet all the necessary conditions as a place where the great revolution might have begun since its lowest levels of occupation testified to the domestication of barley, two varieties of wheat, and sheep and goats; moreover, these levels were aceramic, showing no trace of pottery manufacture. The absence of pottery seemed particularly significant as an indicator of early date because it had always been thought that pottery making had begun simultaneously with the domestication of plants and animals. The apparent priority of Jarmo, however, was soon challenged (1952) by the discoveries at Jericho, an oasis in the Jordan Valley just north of the Dead Sea. While the earliest date that could be assigned to Jarmo was 6750 B.C., the larger and more sophisticated (but also aceramic) settlement at Jericho, built on top of a Natufian shrine, seemed to date from almost as early as 8000 B.C. Complications ensued. The early date for Jericho was disputed, but since Jericho was an oasis the old "oasis theory" was revived. Then, within ten years, the whole matter was thrown into confusion by the combined evidence from two sites in southern Anatolia, Hacilar and Çatal Huyuk, where an aceramic sequence was said to have begun about 7000 B.C. and blossomed into a rich culture that the excavator suggested had later been diffused to Jericho.

Was one of these sites representative of the true beginnings of the new age? Could the three each represent a separate and independent center of origin? Or would new and better qualified candidates for a single original site be discovered?

Single-Site Theory Discarded.   In the end it was realized that the quest for a single site of origin was futile. As many more early villages were found, the differences in their characteristics multiplied. Zawi Chemi, near Jarmo and dated about 9000 B.C., had domesticated sheep but no domesticated plants. Hacilar (ca. 7000 B.C.) in Anatolia had domesticated plants but only wild animals. Suberde, nearby, was an early village inhabited by hunters who had neither domesticated plants nor animals. Çatal Huyuk, redated to 6400 B.C., had domesticated barley, emmer, and einkorn but no sheep or goats; yet it possessed the earliest known domesticated cattle. To cap the climax, the Natufians, as early as 8000 B.C., were found scattered in villages throughout Palestine, where they hunted wild animals and harvested wild grain while their cave-dwelling relatives on Mt. Carmel were revealed as backward hillbillies left behind by their more progressive neighbors.

New Questions Asked.   As the single-site theory was discarded, new questions began to be asked. *Where* the Agricultural Revolution had originated gave way to inquiries about *why* and *how* it had occurred. Over the years, various answers have been proposed, but no general agreement has been reached. To begin with, it is clear that in the centuries immediately preceding the Agricultural Revolution there were certain areas in the Near East in which a plenitude of wild game to be hunted and wild cereals to be harvested maintained an "affluent society" of hunters and gatherers who could supply themselves with an abundance of food with comparatively little effort and who thus enjoyed a leisure later denied to the farmers and herdsmen of the succeeding period. So what happened to end this idyllic existence? Was there a climatic change that affected the flora and fauna of the well-favored regions? Or was there a growth of population that forced people to search for food in areas less affluent in which they had to domesticate plants and animals to provide additional and assured food supplies? Climatic change and population pressures are the two basic explanations now offered by the theorists, but there are many variations on these themes, and a consensus is lacking. It is not possible to say at the moment whether a final decision will be reached or whether the whole matter will be left in abeyance.

This rather extended discussion has been included here because it is typical and illustrative of many similar problems that arise when one tries to recreate the past. There is much we do not know. Some aspects may be cleared up by future discoveries and further investigations; others may remain obscure forever. In attacking any problem, one must decide the proper questions to be asked, and often the answer to one question may reveal new questions for consideration. In the case of the Agricultural Revolution and also that of "Lucy," we have already seen two examples of this, and we shall encounter others as we go along.

IN CONCLUSION

Much of this chapter has been concerned with the long era of *pre-history*, the first phase of hominid life as an animal with culture, a period for which we have no written records. By 5000 B.C., however, peasant villagers had started to move into the great river valleys where 2,000 years later they began to write—both figuratively and literally—new chapters in the story of culture. On the banks of the Nile, the Tigris and Euphrates, and the Indus, civilization was inaugurated, and one of the features of this great accomplishment was the invention of writing, which in turn marks the beginning of the *historic* period. It is therefore to history and civilization that we shall henceforth devote our attention.

Chapter Three

The Riverine Civilizations

Civilization, like culture, is hard to define. The word is often used in such an arbitrary or capricious manner that no definition is universally applicable. Civilizations are distinguished by their great cultural complexity; they possess an assemblage of culture that contains not only many traits found among the food-gathering and food-producing peoples, but also innumerable others that were developed, discovered, or invented at a later time. Nevertheless, the difference between the culture of a civilized group, on the one hand, and that of the farmers or the food gatherers on the other, is a difference of degree and not of kind. There is no great revolution like the change from food collecting to food producing that marks the advent of civilization, yet there does exist a distinction that can be sensed more easily than it can be expressed. Perhaps the one characteristic common to most civilizations is that trade and industry have attained a development and an importance in the economy rivaling that of agriculture instead of being subordinate to it, as in a simple peasant village. This elevation of trade and industry may either promote or be the result of an improvement as well as a proliferation of technology. It is frequently true that, in a given civilization, its technology may have grown to the point of providing people with a greater control over their environment than they would have in a farming community. Civilizations tend to be more populous, to involve more people, than the farming or hunting societies; the units of human concentration, the "towns," are also larger. Urbanization, however, is not a feature associated with all civilizations, and it seems to be conspicuously lacking in the earliest ones. Many thousands of people may be concentrated in an area of a few hundred acres, living cheek by jowl, and there may be enough people grouped in such a way that a big town, on the basis of its population size, may be technically classed as a city, but it may lack many of the characteristics that we associate with urbanization today. Generally speaking, complex forms of government and social organization will be found in a civilization; art and architecture and associated creative activities will exist on a grander and more self-conscious level than in simpler cultures; writing, recordkeeping, and literature are present in most civilizations; and more often than not, there will have been an attempt to organize "knowledge" in a formal way, classifying it into theology, science, and the like. Still, there have been civilizations without writing, without an advanced technology, without cities, or without one or another of the seemingly common characteristics enumerated above.

THE PRIMARY CENTERS

Ancient civilization, and consequently "Western" civilization, began in the Near East in three primary centers of origin and diffusion. All three were situated in great river valleys and came into existence within a space of about 500 years, roughly 3000–2500 B.C. The primary phase in each case lasted until about 1800–1500 B.C., by which time all three civilizations were either in a temporary slump or in the final stages of decay. The three primary centers were not isolated but enjoyed a certain degree of mutual contact which provided opportunities for cultural interaction, stimulation, and growth. The Mesopotamian center, being in the middle geographically, was the chief beneficiary of interaction; it had contacts with both Egypt and the Indus, while the relations of the latter two with each other were indirect and for the most part negligible.

Adaptation to Environment

The peasant villagers who came to settle the river valleys after 5000 B.C. brought domesticated plants and animals and other components of their cultural assemblage to their new homes, but what had been devised for one environment required modification in another. For one thing, in Egypt and lower Mesopotamia the rainfall was insufficient to support agriculture. It was therefore necessary to resort to irrigation and bring to the soil the waters of the Nile or the Tigris and Euphrates. Irrigation also demanded new methods of planting and cultivation. Further, some species of plants that grew well elsewhere were not suited to the new environment; the cultivation of some had to be abandoned, although in most cases it was possible to develop new strains that were hardy and productive. In lower Mesopotamia, wheat was one of the casualties; it was grown in very limited quantities in the historic period, while barley on the other hand proved adaptable and became the major cereal crop. Pasturage for the animals was another problem in Mesopotamia; the numbers of cattle had therefore to be kept at a minimum, but it was possible to maintain great flocks of sheep and goats by driving them to summer pastures in the mountains.

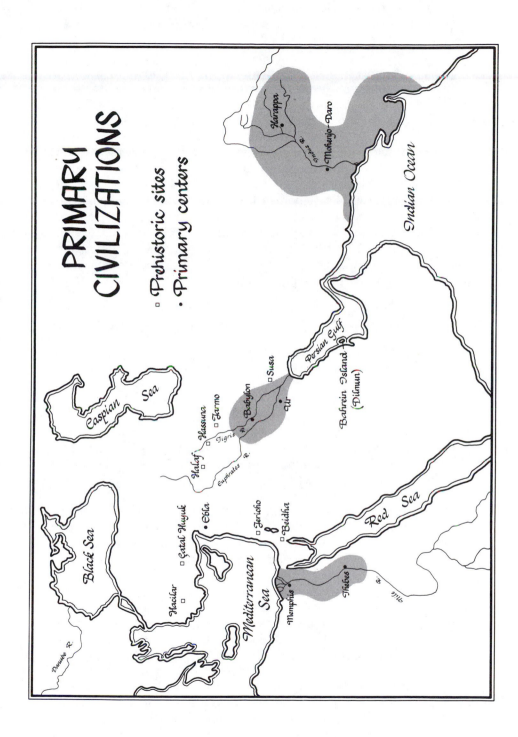

PRIMARY CIVILIZATIONS

□ Prehistoric sites
• Primary centers

Caspian Sea

Black Sea

Danube R.

Hacilar □

Çatal Hüyük □

Mediterranean Sea

Ebla •

Jericho □

Beidha □

Halaf □

Hassuna □

Jarmo □

Tigris R.

Euphrates R.

Babylon •

Susa □

Ur •

Persian Gulf

Bahrein Island (Dilmun) •

Red Sea

Memphis •

Thebes •

Nile R.

Harappa •

Mohenjo-Daro •

Indus R.

Indian Ocean

21

Expansion of Trade and Industry

Once adjustments had been made to the environment, the great fertility of the new lands brought agricultural yields far exceeding those possible elsewhere, and increased productivity encouraged a spectacular growth of population so that villages soon became towns and even cities. Although they were rich in land, the peoples of the river valleys were far from self-sufficient; their valleys lacked much that they needed or wanted: wood for building and fuel in Egypt and Mesopotamia, stone in Mesopotamia, metals in all three valleys, as well as many other necessities and luxuries. These demands had to be met by an expansion of trade, while at the same time it was necessary to develop industries to produce commodities that could be exchanged for the imported materials. Specialization of labor thus grew apace of, and along with, the development of town or city life and it promoted greater complexity in political, social, and economic organization.

Common Characteristics of the Primary Civilizations

Civilization was incipient or had actually begun in Egypt and Mesopotamia before 3000 B.C.; the Indus Valley was not too far behind with an initial date of perhaps as early as 2900. Although our knowledge of the Indus is somewhat limited, it is safe to say that the three primary civilizations had a number of common characteristics. With the provision that some of the generalizations that are made here will have to be qualified when we come to describe individual cases, we may enumerate as follows the traits which the Indus, Nile, and Tigris-Euphrates civilizations seem to have shared:

Agriculture.   Agriculture continued to be the main economic activity, with the cereals, particularly barley, as the most important crops. Barley gave people bread and beer, the latter more of a food than a leisure-time beverage in this period. Barley might also be fed to the animals when forage was scarce. Associated with this cereal culture were the herd animals: cattle, sheep, and goats. While in part a source of food—meat, milk, and cheese—these animals were more important for other reasons: Cattle were useful as draft animals and for their hides, and sheep and goats for their wool that made possible the predominant industry, the manufacture of textiles.

Planned Economies.   Agriculture was, as we have seen, dependent upon irrigation, and irrigation in turn required the mobilization of manpower for the construction and constant repair of canals and irrigation ditches. In Mesopotamia, irrigation could be managed as a community affair; in Egypt it required organization on a national basis. In Mesopotamia, on the other hand, flood control was a serious problem with which only a complete territorial organization and direction from the top could cope. In both Egypt and Mesopotamia, and probably in the Indus as well, agricultural production and associated activities were ultimately managed by a planned economy that overlooked no detail, large or small, even to the point of assigning plots of land to the cultivators and specifying the crops to be grown.

Theocracies.   The mobilization and direction of the labor force was the function of a powerful centralized government organized in theocratic form. In such a "god-ruled" state, the king was regarded either as a god on earth or as the earthly representative of the gods, chosen by them as their viceroy. Palace and temple, "church and state," were thus combined, and the result was a government with virtually unlimited, and usually unquestioned, authority. Power came down from on high. The god's will must be done, but the god was usually just; in return for obedience and homage, the god's servants would be protected and their storehouses filled with food.

Social Classes.   A concomitant of theocracy was the development of a priestly class organized in a religious, and sometimes a political, hierarchy that might serve as a bureaucracy, but which always dominated religious thought and usually other phases of intellectual endeavor. At the other end of the scale were slaves, who were not classed as human beings at all but as "things" or chattels. The earliest known slaves were captives of war; then came debt slavery along with the breeding of household slaves. Slavery may have grown out of a need for manpower but, once established, the institution persisted throughout all antiquity, and the few who questioned its validity were consistently branded as subversives, and enemies of society. Between the priests and the slaves was the great mass of the common people, mostly farmers and artisans, and sometimes in the upper echelon with the priestly class was a landed nobility or a warrior class. In general, class distinctions became more sharply marked with the passage of time.

Industry.   In the primary societies, so far as our present knowledge goes, industry was more developed and better organized than commerce. Along with pottery making, woodworking, and brewing went the manufacture of leather, perfumes and cosmetics, flour, and vegetable oils, but the making of textiles and metal working were most important. Copper, silver, and gold had come into use just before civilization began, while during the third millennium B.C. the technique of making bronze, an alloy of copper and tin, had been discovered.

Bronze, harder than copper, might be said to have been the equivalent of our steel throughout most of antiquity; it replaced stone as a material for many tools and weapons. The metals, particularly, had to be imported from the outside world, and their procurement, along with that of wood, stone, spices, aromatic gums, ivory, and semiprecious stones, was the responsibility of the traders, about whom we know very little until nearly the end of the primary phase.

Architecture.   Characteristic of the riverine civilizations was their monumental architecture, consisting mainly of huge temples and associated structures. In theocracies, this emphasis was to be expected; the buildings and monuments served religion. Moreover, with the resources and manpower at the disposal of the theocracy, great building projects were possible. The development of sculpture and painting was also under theocratic auspices, and there is no question that the stimulus for these arts was largely religious.

Writing.   All three primary centers developed systems of writing. The initial purpose of the new invention was recordkeeping, but it soon came to serve as a means of communication and as an aid to memory in the preservation of the growing corpus of ritual texts. A religious literature of rich and varied content was ultimately developed in Egypt and Mesopotamia—we do not know about the Indus. Moreover, rulers began to commemorate in writing their piety and their glorious accomplishments in war and peace. This was a way of communicating with the gods, and the great display inscriptions on stone or metal were thought to "preserve the name" and contribute to the immortality of the ruler.

Organization of Knowledge.   By and large, literacy in the primary civilizations was confined to the priests and the scribes, both receiving their training in temple schools. It was also the priests who undertook the formal organization of what passed for knowledge. They systematized theology and composed treatises and "textbooks" on medicine, astronomy, mathematics, calendrical studies, astrology, and divination. Knowledge was empirical, built up through generations of experience, observation and recordkeeping. It was not idle curiosity that brought the priests to research and scholarship. They were expected to be healers; a knowledge of drugs and surgery would do more to beef up the priestly batting average than several carloads of spells and incantations. The priests also determined the proper time for staging the great ceremonies that inaugurated the major divisions of the farmer's year: the plowing, planting, and harvest. This called for a calendar which had to be based on astronomical and mathematical studies. Geometry (land measurement) and the various calculations involved in planning the monumental works of architecture also contributed to the development of mathematics.

Although the riverine, primary civilizations had much in common, there were also important individual differences, mostly environmental in origin. They are deserving of careful consideration, and therefore we shall now survey each of the primary civilizations in turn, not only because they are individually interesting but also because this approach may suggest something about the anatomy of culture.

MESOPOTAMIAN CIVILIZATION: SUMER, AKKAD, AND BABYLONIA

The primary civilization of Mesopotamia originated in the lower Tigris-Euphrates valley where, stretching in a northwesterly direction from the Persian Gulf to a point a little above Baghdad, there was a habitable area comprising about 10,000 square miles. The southern section of this region was called Sumer in ancient times; the northern came to be known as Akkad. Toward the end of the primary period, when Sumer and Akkad were united under the leadership of a dynasty having its capital at Babylon, the whole territory was called Babylonia, and this was the name ordinarily applied to it throughout the rest of antiquity.

Early Human Occupation

The earliest known human occupation of the area in question was in the south, in Sumer, possibly as early as 5000 B.C. Several successive cultural phases can be distinguished in the stratified remains of the millennium and a half that followed, and it is also clear that during this time the gradual settlement of the northern section was effected. In the final phase, sometimes called the Protoliterate (ca. 3500–3100 B.C.), many features characteristic of Mesopotamian civilization had already appeared: Towns were large enough to be called cities; there was a rudimentary system of writing; metal working had begun; and temple architecture had reached monumental proportions. It is customary to say, however, that the next period, the Early Dynastic (ca. 3100), is the first civilized era.

The Sumerians

The creators of civilization in lower Mesopotamia were the Sumerians. They were not the first settlers of the region, and we cannot say where the Sumerians themselves originated or precisely when they arrived in Sumer although it was certainly before the Protoliterate period. To add to the mystery, the Sumerian language is unique and cannot be related to any other known language, living or dead. Sumerian, as a

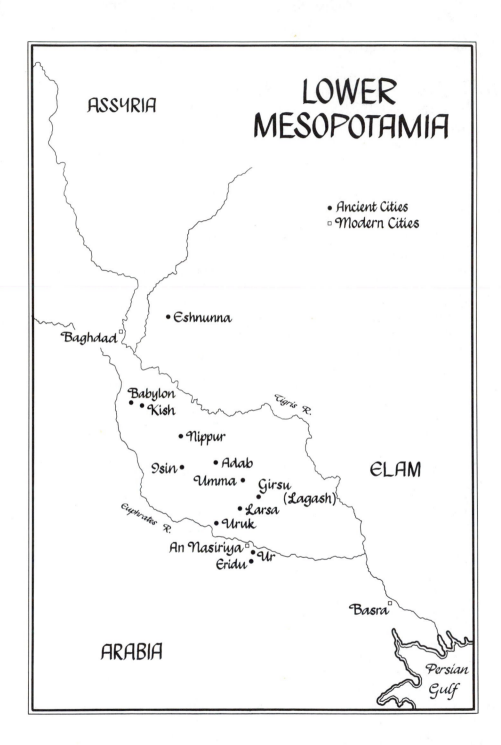

LOWER
MESOPOTAMIA

ASSYRIA

• Ancient Cities
▫ Modern Cities

• Eshnunna

▫ Baghdad

Babylon
•   • Kish

• Nippur

Isin •   • Adab
Umma •   • Girsu
          (Lagash)

• Larsa
• Uruk

Tigris R.

Euphrates R.

ELAM

An Nasiriya ▫ • Ur
Eridu •

Basra ▫

ARABIA

Persian
Gulf

spoken tongue, became extinct 4,000 years ago, but documents written in Sumerian have survived in great abundance. By a long and painful process, scholars have learned to read these texts, and thus we have written as well as archaeological evidence with which to reconstruct at least in outline the history of the Sumerians.

Although descendants of the first settlers (non-Sumerians) may have remained an element in the population into the historic period, and although desert peoples speaking a Semitic language were certainly living in the lower valley from an early date, the Sumerians continued to be dominant in the area after the Protoliterate period and onward to about 2350 B.C. Politically, the region was divided among a number of little city-states. These independent units were ruled by "kings" who often fought one another over land and water rights. As time passed there was an increasing tendency on the part of the victors to join the territory of a defeated enemy with their own. This embryonic imperialism took a more concrete form when the Semites, who constituted a major element in the population of the northern section, overcame the Sumerian kinglets and forced a semblance of unity upon the whole country (ca. 2350 B.C.).

Sargon of Akkad

Sargon, whose name means True King, was the conqueror of the Sumerians. He established the capital of his empire in a northern city called Akkad, a place which now gave its name to the whole upper region while the south continued to be known as Sumer. Sargon of Akkad, the first "personality" in history, is nevertheless a shadowy figure. He set up inscriptions, some in Sumerian and some in his own Semitic language (Old Akkadian), boasting of his conquests not only of the Sumerians but also of outlying territories, although we may suspect him of some exaggeration. In a later age, Sargon became a legendary figure and was given credit for things he could not possibly have done so that it becomes difficult to discover what is true about the True King. He did, however, establish a dynasty that reigned over an empire of sorts until about 2200 B.C. In the end, Akkadian power fell before the attacks of barbarians from the north after it had been weakened from within by resurgence of independence among the cities of Sumer.

Third Dynasty of Ur

About 2100 B.C. a new and theoretically "Sumerian" empire took up the heritage of Sargon. For better than a century there was a Sumerian "renaissance" under the leadership of the kings of the Third Dynasty of Ur. From their capital in the old Sumerian city of Ur in the south, rulers who were at best half-Sumerian and half-Semitic slowly gobbled up city after city over a period of about fifty years until they could claim with truth that they were "Kings of Sumer and Akkad." A series of raids beyond the lower valley itself brought tribute from, and a measure of control over, Elam to the northeast, Assyria to the north, and some towns on the middle Euphrates. Royal governors with the title of *ensi* (once read *patesi*) represented the king *(lugal)* in each of the old city-states; these officials served at the king's pleasure and were moved by him periodically from one city to another. While earlier rulers in Meso-potamia, with the exception of the Sargonid dynasty, had been priest-kings, representatives of the gods, the last kings of the Ur III period proclaimed themselves to be divine, as had some of the descendants of Sargon. We may wonder whether this was a Semitic trend, whether the Ur III kings were aping the Sargonids, or whether this apotheosis was the natural consequence of empire. At any rate, Ur was a large and handsomely built city under the Third Dynasty. The ornamentation of the capital began with Ur-Nammu, the founder of the line, who also promulgated a law code, the earliest one known at present.

By the Ur III period the Mesopotamian civilization created by the Sumerians had been in the process of formation and development for 1,000 years, and the reign of Ur-Nammu and his successors was to mark the climax of the Sumerian contribution. Although, in the centuries to come, certain aspects of culture would be modified and a few radically changed, the Sumerians had established something more than the foun-dations for a way of life in Mesopotamia that would endure. In addition, elements of Sumerian culture were borrowed by peoples living beyond the borders of the lower valley; some features would be adopted by civ-ilizations yet unborn and even survive to be incorporated into the civi-lization of the twentieth century A.D.

Our Sources of Information.   From the remains uncovered by the archaeologist and from texts inscribed on stone, metal, and clay, we can reconstruct some of the details of Sumerian history and learn much about Sumerian civilization. Architecture, sculpture, metal work, pot-tery, jewelry, tools, weapons, cult paraphernalia, modes of burial, and the like are revealed by archaeology, while the texts provide historical narratives, religious compositions, government documents, and eco-nomic records. The evidence is not equally full for all periods nor evenly distributed from the geographical point of view, so that now and then, or here and there, we get only a glimpse or a hint of the state of affairs. On occasion, generalizations based on such bits and pieces can be mis-leading since what may be characteristic of one site may not hold for another.

ARCHITECTURAL EVOLUTION

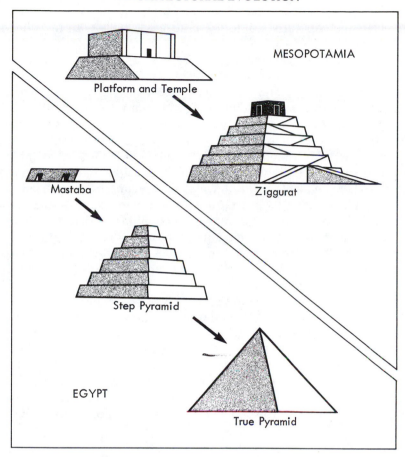

Architecture.   Lacking wood and stone, which had to be imported at some labor and expense, the Sumerians were forced to build mostly with sun-dried bricks; they also made use of reed matting for some features of domestic construction. The custom of building with bricks restricted the size of rooms and limited the height of structures to one or two stories; a large building would thus occupy a big area. The chronic danger of floods taught the Sumerians to place their temples on high platforms. Moreover, once a temple had occupied a particular site, the tendency in rebuilding was to use the same hallowed spot again. The result was that successive temples on a given site were erected on the ruins of their predecessors, and so in time the buildings became considerably elevated above the ground level. Painted stucco and colored glazed bricks were employed for architectural decoration; sometimes, huge clay nails were driven into the mud-brick walls with their heads forming a mosaic pattern.

The tallest structure erected by the Sumerians was the *ziggurat*, consisting of a series of platforms, decreasing in size as they were placed one on top of another, and crowned by a small chapel at the highest level. The great ziggurat at Ur built by Ur-Nammu measured 200 by 150 feet at its base and had at least three platforms; even in decay, it is 60 feet in height. The ziggurats were ascended by flights of steps set at such an angle that a person standing at the foot of the incline might feel that the stairway went right up to heaven itself. Simulating a mountain, the ziggurats were planted with flowers, shrubs, and trees; the Hanging Gardens built by Nebuchadnezzar in Babylon many centuries later and the legendary Tower of Babel were ziggurats. Situated adjacent to a temple and within a complex of religious structures, the ziggurat towered above the priestly compound and the houses of the town and provided an admirable stage for the performance of certain religious ceremonies.

Sculpture.   Because of the shortage of stone, Sumerian sculpture in that medium remained crude and tentative for a long time. Even after a considerable period of evolution, it never compared with Egyptian sculpture in technical proficiency. Working in metal or clay, however, craftsmen achieved impressive results. The handsome objects found in the royal graves of the First Dynasty of Ur, dating from the twenty-sixth century B.C., are convincing testimony of the ability of the Sumerians to work with gold, silver, bronze, lapis lazuli, and semiprecious stones.

Clay Tablets.   The importance and utility of written documents in reconstructing the past can be persuasively demonstrated when one turns from the difficult and unrewarding task of describing the prehistoric period to the welcome assistance afforded by the records of a literate civilization which offer a wealth of testimony with regard to events, procedures, and institutional organization as well as thought and belief. This is certainly true of the historic period in Mesopotamia. The royal inscriptions of Sumer and Akkad tell of military campaigns and the building of temples; from the archives of the priests come prayers and proverbs, hymns and myths, incantations and mathematical texts; there are law codes and records of judicial decisions; and there are administrative documents that disclose the workings of the bureaucracy and the organization of the economy. We emerge gratefully from the dark, untidy basement of prehistory into the bright, well-ordered mansion of Clio, the Muse of History.

Cuneiform Writing.   Clay was used extensively by the Sumerians not only for building, but also as a material to receive writing. Most of the records we now possess from ancient Mesopotamia were written on clay tablets in the cuneiform script, which was a Sumerian invention. The wedge-shaped characters of this system of writing evolved from simple sketches of objects—a pottery vessel, a fish, an ear of grain— incised in the wet clay of the tablet with reed stylus. As time passed, the characters were conventionalized, and, using a stylus equipped with a triangular or square point, the scribes began to make the signs not by line drawing but by massing the wedge and crescent impressions made by the stylus as it was pushed into the clay. The characters at first were elementary pictographic (iconographic) signs which represented a man, or an animal, or the like, and there were also characters representing numbers. The original texts of the Protoliterate period consisted of pictographs and numbers: They were merely records of so many sheep brought in or disbursed, and so on. Now, a pictograph generally represents a thing, a noun, but the Sumerians soon passed on to a second stage of writing in which characters were used ideographically, in large part to represent action (verbs). By way of illustration, let us suppose that we used this kind of writing, and we drew a sketch of an automobile. Pictographically, this would stand for "motor car," but the same sign as an ideograph might mean "to travel," or "take a vacation," or "have an accident." A final development was phonetic writing, using the sound associated with the character to "spell out" words. Thus, a sign standing for "ocean" or "sea" might be combined with pictographic characters for man and woodtick; phonetically, by writing sea + man + tick, we would have "semantic." Again, we could have a character which pictographically represented something repulsive and ideographically meant to be "disgusted." We could then combine this with two ocean signs and so write "seas-ick." In Sumerian, or in Egyptian writing for that matter, the same sign could be used as a pictograph, an ideograph, and as a phonetic character. If we had a sign which stood for a building that housed a financial institution, we could use this character four times in succession—twice as a phonetic sign, once as an ideograph, and once as a pictograph—and read: "(Mr.) Banks–banks (in)–(the) bank."

Administrative Documents.   As for the content of the Sumerian documents of various kinds, it is not difficult to imagine the kind of information that a royal inscription, or a priestly composition, or a law code might provide, but it will be worthwhile at this point to say something about the value of the administrative documents, or "economic texts" as they are sometimes called. Texts of this kind were the first to appear, as we have already seen, in the Protoliterate period, but as time passed they paralleled in content the increasingly elaborate and comprehensive activities which they recorded. The volume of the known texts varies from period to period; for some eras none at all, for others a few hundred, but for the Ur III period we have tens of thousands. Consequently, it is possible to describe certain aspects of life in this age in great detail.

The Ur III texts are administrative records of the imperial government, of the great temples, and possibly in one instance of a city. Most are accounts and lists, and they reveal an elaborate accounting system: There are records of single transactions; there are daily, monthly, and annual summaries; some texts even record transactions over a period of several years. Some documents have to do with the receipt or disbursement of commodities; some deal with both income and outgo, thus disclosing an embryonic double entry system of bookkeeping. There are accounts of sacrifices, of ration payments to workers, of milling and weaving, of metal working, of boat building, and of beer making. There are records of flocks and herds: the shearing of sheep, the use of oxen for plowing, the transport and use of the animals for religious purposes and for food.

Tablet Archives.   For the most part the tablets we now have come from several great archives which were uncovered by archaeological excavation or as a result of clandestine digging by Iraqi natives, who then sold the tablets to antiquities dealers in Baghdad and elsewhere. Each archive had a different purpose or function so that the content of the texts varies from one archive to another. The palace records from Ur, for example, are by no means carbon copies of those from the temple archives of Lagash. At Ur we learn about the activities within the palace: daily sacrifices to the gods; rations paid to priests, officials, workers, and slaves; the palace industries—metal working, weaving, leather working, and the like; the receipt of royal income in the form of foodstuffs; raw products; and manufactures. From Lagash, on the other hand, the records are those of the priestly corporations that had managed the economy of the city for centuries and had just been subordinated to imperial control. Again the distribution of rations and the records of manufacture by temple artisans are numerous, but the tablets pertaining to agricultural activity bulk even larger in the Lagash archives. Here is something of what they reveal about Sumerian agriculture:

Agriculture.   Preparation of the soil and planting of the grain, mostly barley, was done in the fall. The fields were plowed by oxen; workers broke up clods of earth with pickaxes, and then the fields were

SUMERIAN CLAY TABLET (actual size)

harrowed. The seed was thickly sown in widely spaced rows so that it could be efficiently irrigated. When the harvest came in the spring, everyone in the city turned out to help, along with migrant workers hired from the hill tribes—farmers, priests, artisans, slaves, women, and children all participated. In the case of barley, the average yield was 36-fold, somewhat less than the figure given by Herodotus or modern "scholars" who have not understood or have not read the texts; thus, a good crop of barley would run 25-30 bushels an acre. After the grain was cut with bronze sickles, it was taken to a threshing floor to be trodden by animals or beaten by people with sticks; winnowing was done with wooden forks or branches used to toss the grain into the air and thus separate it from the chaff.

The arable land of Lagash was divided among more than a dozen great priestly corporations that were responsible for working it. More than 100 square miles were sown in barley each year, and a normal yield was over 2 million bushels. About half of this amount was absorbed by production costs: payment to cultivators and harvesters, food for the animals, and the seed grain that had to be kept back for the following year's planting. A fourth of the yield was paid to the imperial government at Ur as tax or tribute, and the remaining quarter fed the priests, workers, and slaves of the temples themselves. Grain was stored in warehouses and paid out during the course of the next year; some was transported to milling and brewing establishments to be made into flour and beer.

Bureaucracy.   Each temple had a staff for business administration; officials who managed the fields, the flocks, and herds; and the manufacturing enterprises of the corporation. Annual tables of organization listed the numbers of scribes, managers, surveyors, supervisors of workers, and other functionaries assigned or allotted to each temple. Each year budgets were prepared; everything was estimated and planned at the beginning of the Sumerian fiscal year, which came right after the harvest. At that time, for example, the fields would be surveyed and divided into plots for cultivation; the crops to be grown on each plot were specified, the seed allotted, and the plots assigned to specific farmers. All this was completed three or four months before the fall plowing and planting. We do not need additional evidence to see that this was a planned economy of the most thoroughgoing sort.

Social Classes: Freemen and Slaves.   From the law codes and texts of the kind just discussed, it appears that there were only two social classes: freemen and slaves. The latter were used in the workshops and fields, while the freemen were the priests, officials, artisans, and farmers. On the basis of personal names appearing in the Ur III texts, Semites seem to have been almost as numerous as Sumerians, and there were also people with non-Sumerian, non-Semitic names who had been drifting down from the hills to the north and east. There were Semites who were officials and in the army; they were also numerous in the crafts—textile and metal working in particular.

Religion.   The Sumerians were polytheistic—to put it mildly—for we know the names of several hundred deities worshipped during the Ur III period. There were craft gods, local civic gods, gods with various specialized functions, and a kind of Olympic pantheon of major deities recognized throughout the length and breadth of the land as "national" gods. The city of Nippur, located near the dividing line between Sumer and Akkad, was the great religious center for the country as a whole. At Nippur the chief deity was Enlil, the creator of heaven and earth and the one who directed the activities of the other gods. Major Sumerian deities tended to be connected with the heavenly bodies, something that may have given rise to the study of both astronomy and astrology as the priests observed carefully the "behavior" of the sun, moon, and visible planets, ultimately associating astronomical phenomena with events on earth. For the Sumerians, the sun god was the source of law; the moon god's province was wisdom and astronomy; there was an earth god, Enki, and a god of the underworld, Nergal. Important among the goddesses was Inanna. A goddess of fertility, Inanna was also a deity of love *and* war. Associated with Inanna was her consort, a young god named Dumuzi. Each year Dumuzi was believed to die as the hot summer came on and the vegetation withered away, but he was born again with the autumn rains and the start of the growing season. In appearance, behavior, and intellect, the Sumerians thought that human beings resembled the gods; the distinction between them and the gods was that the gods enjoyed immortality, something denied to mankind. When people died, they descended to the underworld, the "Land of No Return," a cold dark place where they existed but did not live.

Literature.   Sumerian priests set to writing myths that explained how things came to be and why things are as they are. There was a creation story, a tale about how Inanna stole civilization from Enki and brought it to man, a flood story that was somewhat like the one in the Old Testament, and many other tales of a similar kind. The majority of these literary works were couched in poetry that used difficult and complex meters which are just beginning to be understood by modern scholars. Proverbs, fables, and other didactic literary types are known; now famous is the so-called *Farmer's Almanac*, a short treatise on the best methods of farming. There were also a number of ballads dealing with the adventures of Gilgamesh, a hero and strong man somewhat like Samson, Heracles, and Theseus.

Sumerian literature was studied in the temple schools where boys were trained as scribes and priests. Many clay tablets have survived that illustrate the "textbooks" and the practice exercises of these students as they learned to read and write and do simple arithmetic. The *edubba*, the temple school, had a literature of its own. From one composition that describes a day in the life of a Sumerian schoolboy and the methods of instruction, we learn that teachers were anything but permissive; on the contrary, they were stern, often given to tongue-lashing, and not at all reluctant to deal out physical punishment.

Rise of Old Babylonia: Elamites and Amorites

About 2000 B.C., the Third Dynasty of Ur was terminated by attacks from two directions. The Elamites, who lived in the northeast, declared their independence, sacked Ur itself, and carried off Ibbi-Sin, the last of the Ur III kings. The Elamite success was made possible, however, by new Semitic attacks from the west as a people called the Amorites (Westeners) moved down the Euphrates and occupied the Ur III kingdom in the area around Babylon. Continued Amorite pressure detached Nippur and other towns from the empire until little more than Ur itself remained to Ibbi-Sin when the Elamites swooped down to destroy the capital and put an end to the dynasty and Sumerian dominance as well.

After a period of disunity in Mesopotamia in which the lower valley was divided into three kingdoms—Amorite in the north, Elamite in the south, and a semi-Sumerian state in the middle—the Amorites moved southward from their capital at Babylon to gobble up Isin, the middle kingdom, and wrest Larsa, the southern state, from the Elamites. Thus, lower Mesopotamia was unified once more, with the Amorite, or Old Babylonian, kingdom having approximately the same boundaries as those of the empire of the Third Dynasty of Ur.

Hammurabi and His Code.   The leader of the Amorites who restored unity to the southern plain was the famous Hammurabi, the sixth king of his line to reign in Babylon. The precise dates of Hammurabi's reign are in dispute, but he certainly ascended the throne in the eighteenth century B.C. and ruled for forty-three years. The greatest of the Amorite kings, Hammurabi was a master strategist, a capable administrator, a notable reformer, and an inspired leader whose name was remembered and revered for generations. Hammurabi not only made Babylon the political and economic center of the southern plain, but his capital also became a cultural center of enduring prestige in Mesopotamia. Although having to outwit and outmaneuver powerful enemies—the Elamites to the east, the Assyrians to the north, and a rival Amorite kingdom, Mari, to the west on the middle Euphrates—Hammurabi weakened his foes with a succession of feints and darting attacks, drove the Elamites from the south, and finally captured Mari. We have on clay tablets some of the administrative correspondence of Hammurabi from which we can judge his broad concern for the welfare of the kingdom and his incisiveness in making decisions. His famous law code, though somewhat dependent on earlier compilations, did "modernize" the law to permit a fusion of Sumerian and Semitic customs and to make provision for the changed economic and social conditions that prevailed after the Amorite conquest. To legitimize his rule, Hammurabi sponsored a revision of Mesopotamian theology which substituted his deity,

Marduk, for the old Sumerian god, Enlil. This involved rewriting the Sumerian creation epic in order to show that it was Marduk who brought order out of the primeval chaos, then created plants and animals, and finally mankind. With Marduk established at the head of the pantheon, Hammurabi could claim that Marduk had chosen him to rule and to promulgate a new law code.

Although Hammurabi is no longer distinguished as "the first lawgiver," his code of laws remains the most complete to be discovered, and without it we could understand little about either its predecessors or successors. The laws cover a broad range of criminal and civil matters. Among the topics with which they deal are physical injury, social offenses (adultery, incest, etc.), theft, contracts, inheritance, slavery, trade, agriculture, transportation, wages, and prices. The usual form of a law is, "If a man does such and such, the penalty is so and so." Penalties were harsher than in Sumerian law and involved capital punishment for many offenses. The basic principle invoked in the case of injuries was the *lex talionis*, the law of retaliation: "an eye for an eye." The laws tell us much about social and economic organization; they suggest a further stratification of society and a new kind of agricultural economy, as well as a great development of trade.

Private Records of Agriculture and Trade.   More precise information about agriculture and trade can be gleaned from the economic texts. From this period come many private records as opposed to the palace and temple accounts of the Ur III epoch. The majority of the personal names appearing on these tablets were Semitic ones, while Sumerian names became rarer as time went on. Even though Sumerian survived as the language of religion, most documents were now couched in Old Babylonian (Akkadian), the Semite dialect of the conquerors. The temples no longer bulked large in the economy, and, although the government gradually took more and more leadership in organizing agriculture and trade, the texts of the first half of the Old Babylonian period disclose an era of private enterprise.

Private Enterprise and Trading.   New canals, government-sponsored, brought an expansion of the area under cultivation. The documents tell us of many small plots of land owned and worked by families or individuals; these plots were bought and sold, as were houses and town lots. Before the Old Babylonian period ended, there was a tendency for the land to become concentrated in large estates owned by nobles and palace officials. The small landholders were gradually crowded out, and many of them ended up as renters and sharecroppers on lands their forebears had once owned.

Trade was in the hands of individuals, families, and partnerships.

The operations of some of the trading firms became complex and widespread. Prosperous merchants, who had amassed capital, became "moneylenders" and collected interest on their loans. They did not themselves go out on trading expeditions, but rather they financed other traders whom they supplied with silver or trade goods and with whom they shared the profits of a trading venture. Branch establishments were maintained in foreign towns; careful estimates and projections were made of local prices so that buying or selling might take place when the profits would be greatest. The caravans of the traders went out in all directions by land, and there was trade by sea down the Persian Gulf. Textiles, metal work, vegetable oils, and other manufactures were exchanged for the products of foreign lands: stone, wood, bitumen, copper, tin, silver, gold, pearls, and semiprecious stones. By the middle of the Old Babylonian period, the traders in the big towns of Babylonia were being brought together into loose corporations and their activities were controlled and directed more and more by the central government.

Writing, Science, and Literature.   The Amorites, like the earlier Semites of Akkad, adopted the cuneiform system of writing, but they simplified the script by reducing the numbers of pictographic and ideographic characters and depended largely on the phonetic signs which stood for syllables. At first, Sumerian words and phrases were used in legal, mathematical, and astronomical texts, but these were gradually supplanted by Old Babylonian equivalents. In like manner, there was a growing tendency to translate the Sumerian religious literature into Old Babylonian. These people who had succeeded the Sumerians were, however, not slavish imitators. Mathematics and astronomy in the Old Babylonian period reached heights far above those attained by the Sumerians.

From arithmetic, the newcomers advanced to algebra, and amazing developments took place in astronomy. A tradition of mathematical and astronomical studies was established which grew richer with the passing centuries, and much later Babylonian knowledge was to provide the basis for similar studies initiated among the Greeks.

Literature did not lag behind mathematics and science. The Semites had a poetic tradition of their own, and one of the great achievements of the Old Babylonian period was the composition of the *Epic of Gilgamesh* which utilized the old Sumerian ballads about Gilgamesh to create an artistically unified and very lengthy epic poem. The magnitude and excellence of the Gilgamesh epic were such that in later Babylonia the poem came to occupy a position comparable to that of the *Iliad* and *Odyssey* among the Greeks and Romans.

Older than the Gilgamesh epic but definitely a product of the Old

Babylonian period is the *Atrahasis,* which provided a model for the flood story in *Gilgamesh.* "When gods like men" is the opening line of the *Atrahasis* poem, which begins the story of the creation of mankind and the problems it caused both gods and human beings. In brief summary the essence of this epic is that originally three major gods drew lots and divided their responsibilities. Anu received the heavens, Enlil the earth, and Enki (Ea) the waters. All the minor deities were obliged to labor in order to support this great triad. After forty years of hard work the minor gods revolted and picketed the house of Enlil, much to his consternation. In this crisis the major gods consulted one another and decided to create man to relieve the minor gods of their burden, but after 1,200 years mankind had multiplied to a point at which "the earth bellowed like a bull" and the noise was unbearable. Therefore a plague was sent to eliminate humanity but Enki, always the friend of mankind, warned Atrahasis (the all-wise) and suggested that the plague deity should be won over by special homage. This stopped the plague, but after another 1,200 years the situation once more got out of hand and the gods enlisted Adad, the rain god, to create a drought. Again Enki came to the rescue by advising special treatment for Adad. At last, goaded to extreme measures, the gods commanded a universal flood that would wipe out the human race. Enki, however, felt he must save Atrahasis, so he warned him of the impending flood and advised the building of an ark that would accommodate all the animals and the family of Atrahasis. The flood came. Without the labor of mankind, the gods were soon reduced to cannibalism. Then the survival of Atrahasis was discovered, and Enki was in trouble for having circumvented the will of the gods. In the end it seems that a compromise was reached. The gods could not exist without the labor of mankind, but henceforth the overpopulation of the earth would be limited by an increase in infant mortality and other means. The essential elements of the flood story thus appear in the *Atrahasis*—the displeasure of the gods, the great flood, the good man who is spared, and the final compromise and repopulation of the earth. It is possible, even probable, that the Sumerians had a flood story, but the oldest Sumerian composition (found long ago at Nippur) is of the Old Babylonian period, though written in Sumerian.

All in all, the Age of Hammurabi has been thought to be an important period in Mesopotamian history. The land now came under nearly permanent domination by the Semites. The mingling of Semitic and Sumerian culture gave Mesopotamian civilization the form that it retained for many centuries, and it was this civilization, vitalized by the fusion of peoples, that was to be borrowed and adapted in regions of the Near East and in Greece as well. Its effect upon the Hebrews and Greeks was particularly important since through them it was transmitted to the west and ultimately to us today.

New Horizons: The Western Semites

Before we can conclude our survey of the "riverine" phase in Mesopotamia, describe the fall of the Old Babylonian kingdom, and then go on to the early history of Egypt, we should consider the possible implications of some rather recent discoveries in Syria and parts of Mesopotamia lying to the west of the Tigris-Euphrates Valley.

For nearly a century after the first excavations revealed the glories of ancient Assyria and led to further archaeological investigation of the lower Tigris-Euphrates area, interest was concentrated on Assyria and Babylonia. Once the cuneiform script could be read and thus disclosed more and more about the history and civilization of this part of the Near East, research was intensified at the expense of seemingly less important matters. Then the Sumerians were identified, and a whole new early culture came to light. Further excavation and the study of Sumerian texts provided a wealth of information that is still being digested. Therefore, it was only natural for people to assume that Sumero-Babylonian civilization was the primary source of development in that region as well as in areas farther west. Consequently, the great cultural burst in the Old Babylonian period might be explained as a stimulus derived from a fusion of two elements: that of the older Sumero-Babylonian sparking a response from the "simpler" culture of other invading Semitic groups.

This seemed a reasonable interpretation of the phenomenon until, beginning in the 1930s, a series of excavations in the west showed that Sumerian influence was widespread outside the lower valley at an early date, as a matter of fact even before Early Dynastic times (prior to 3100 B.C.). The French excavations at Mari on the middle Euphrates, when combined with what had already been learned about the Old Assyrian traders in Anatolia and the economics of the Old Akkadian (Sargonid) period, indicated that the Semites had a culture of their own that was more sophisticated than previously supposed. At Mari, contemporary with the Hammurabi period, the great palace with its many rooms and novel wall paintings, the extensive archives of diplomatic correspondence and administrative records, and the presence of a score of temples devoted to Semitic and a few Sumerian deities gave a glimpse of a mature culture that also contained information lacking from Hammurabi's Babylonia.

Now, as early as the days of Sargon of Akkad, mention began to be made of four states: Mari, Ebla, Emar, and Urshu. For a long time they were assumed to lie west or northwest of the lower valley. Urshu has still to be found, but the other three are now known to be more to the west than to the north. A look at the map suggests that the path of diffusion from the lower Tigris-Euphrates Valley followed the course of the Euphrates instead of the northern caravan route just south of the mountains. The former would take us to Mari, Emar, and Ebla, and probably Aleppo, a major site that has not been excavated due to the dense modern population of the city. Could Aleppo have been Urshu? We may never know.

Ebla.   A short distance south of Aleppo is Tell Mardikh, a large mound containing the remains of Ebla, once the capital of an important Syrian kingdom. Excavated by Italian archaeologists beginning in 1964, the site was positively identified as that of Ebla four years later. Like Tell Hariri (Mari), Tell Mardikh covers more than 100 acres, and its stratified levels date all the way back from the Hellenistic Age to a protohistoric stratum (3500–3000/2900 B.C.). Best known today is Level IIB1 (2400–2250 B.C.) that corresponds in date to Sumerian Early Dynastic III and to the Old Akkadian period when Naram Sin, a successor of Sargon, is thought to have, or claimed to have, devasted Ebla.

As is the case with any big tell, complete excavation of the site may never be accomplished, partly because major discoveries at one level often engage the full attention and energies of the archaeologists for some time. This has been the experience at Ebla as a result of the discovery (in 1973–74) of the Royal Palace and other structures along with the cuneiform archives yielding 15,000 texts (if one includes the fragments that account for 80 percent of that total). The tablets fall into several categories: administrative (economic), literary, lexical and school texts, and some diplomatic and legal. Some features of this material are noteworthy, even startling:

1. The script is an early form of Sumerian writing characteristic of Early Dynastic III (2500–2300 B.C.) when the first known Sumerian literary texts appear at Sumerian sites.

2. Many texts duplicate already familiar Sumerian lists of personal names, names of professions, birds, fish, plants, and so on, previously found in Sumer itself.

3. Other tablets are syllabaries for learning Sumerian. They are bilingual in the sense that the pronunciation of the Sumerian words is spelled out in syllables and each meaning is rendered in the Eblaite dialect, also spelled syllabically.

4. Other texts, identified as administrative, legal, or diplomatic, seem to be in Eblaite using mostly syllabic characters and few logograms which are common Sumerian signs that stand for ox, sheep, and the like but would be read as Eblaite just as we in English would read the ox sign as the "ox," while the scribes of Ebla who were Semites would read it as "alpu" or something similar.

These finds tell us that the Sumerian *edubba* (temple school) and its methods had already been adopted at Ebla and that syllabic writing for a Semitic language (in which the vocalization was different from Sumerian) had been created. Before these finds at Ebla, it had been thought that the development of syllabic writing began with the Sargonid period which follows Early Dynastic III, and by the beginning of Old Babylonian times its evolution had reached an extreme form in which logograms were rarely used by the Old Assyrian traders in Anatolia.

Most perplexing is the identity of the Eblaite dialect and its relation to other Semitic languages. Unfortunately, this question has been confused by premature and extravagant claims that Eblaite was an early form of Canaanite, possibly even Hebrew, and thus a valuable addition to Old Testament studies. The early identification of personal and place names as "biblical" has now been discredited, and the many popular articles and press releases in the late 70s and early 80s have little value except to discourage the acceptance of wild speculations by irresponsible angels who dash in where others fear to tread.

Ebla is beyond question a very important site and more will surely be found when a peaceful political situation permits further excavation, as well as exploration of several large mounds in the same general neighborhood. At present these three things seem highly desirable:

1. Continued excavation at Ebla in the newly discovered Levels IIIA and IIIB, embracing the period 2000 to 1600 B.C. If recovered, the archives of this age should give much needed information about relations with Ur III and the Old Babylonian dynasty and perhaps supplement the finds from Mari.

2. The Eblaite dialect must be properly identified. Recent opinion is that it is related to Amorite but more closely resembles some other West Semitic dialects of that time, for IIB1 is much too early to suspect Amorites already in residence at Ebla. By Ur III, however, messengers from Ebla who appear in Sumerian administrative texts do generally have Amorite names.

3. It would be highly desirable to excavate Emar and other large mounds in that part of Syria to learn whether the finds might resemble those of Ebla.

In summary, these "new horizons" have suggested that the early Semites in the west did indeed borrow elements of culture from the lower Tigris-Euphrates Valley, yet by the time of Hammurabi and even before that they possessed a very respectable culture of their own that was more influential than we have supposed in shaping the civilization that developed in the Old Babylonian period.

Decline of Old Babylonia

Strange to relate, Hammurabi's empire was no more lasting than that of his Sumerian or Akkadian predecessors. The kings who came after the great Babylonian were not able to arrest the decline that began soon after Hammurabi's death. Although the Old Babylonian kingdom continued to exist until perhaps 1550 B.C., its trend was always down-hill. Part of the trouble was that the techniques of imperial government had not been mastered, but even more crucial was the perennial problem of the openness of Babylonia to invasion. This had proved the undoing of the early Sumerian states, the Sargonids, and the kings of Ur III. Unfortunately, no solution to this problem could be found by the Old Babylonian kings. New barbarian invasions terminated the dynasty in the sixteenth century B.C.

It was not entirely a case of history repeating itself. The world was changing; in fact, a new world was in the making. Indo-European speaking tribes, which had long ago left their homes in north-central Europe, were now appearing on the fringes of the civilized world. In the course of our narrative, we shall meet these people often. About 1600 B.C., the Hittites, centered in Anatolia, had staged a great raid that reached Babylon. The Hittites, loaded with plunder, withdrew, but after them came the Kassites, who rode out of the Armenian mountains to overcome the last of Hammurabi's line and establish themselves as a ruling minority in Babylonia (ca. 1550 B.C.). Kassite kings ruled the land until about 1200 B.C., contributing little to its culture and finally being absorbed to the point of extinction. Yet, the Kassite invasion ended the primary phase in Mesopotamia. Babylonia was reduced to the status of a second-rate power. The center of political gravity ultimately shifted to the north, and that is where we shall pick up the thread of the story later on.

EGYPTIAN CIVILIZATION

Habitable Egypt in ancient times comprised an area of about 10,000 square miles. This approximates the figure already given for Babylonia, but here the similarity of the two regions abruptly ends. Egypt was more arid and yet more fertile than Babylonia. The latter could have supported a small human population even without its rivers; lacking the Nile, Egypt would have been as barren as its surrounding desert. The shape of Babylonia was roughly rectangular, but Egypt, as a glance at the map will show, consisted of two parts: the triangular delta in the north and then, running southward from it, the long crooked line of the valley. In length, Babylonia was about 165 miles; Egypt stretched more than 600 miles from the Mediterranean sea in the north to the first cataract of the Nile in the south. The width of the Babylonian rectangle was perhaps 60 miles; the valley of the Nile, a deep trench cut through the desert by the river, was only a few miles across at its widest point.

The earliest peasant villages known in Egypt date from shortly after 4500 B.C. A thousand years later two kingdoms were in the process of formation: one in the Delta (Lower Egypt), and the other in the Valley (Upper Egypt). According to later Egyptian tradition, intermittent warfare between the two states came to an end about 3000 B.C. when Upper and Lower Egypt were united by Menes, the first pharaoh, who reigned sixty-two years and was killed by a hippopotamus.

Civilization and Culture

The distinctive, and in some ways peculiar, civilization of ancient Egypt had already begun to take shape before Menes' reign and continued to evolve after it, but by the beginning of the Pyramid Age (2700 B.C.) its basic form had been established. Some Egyptologists believe that cultural development in Egypt was influenced by borrowing from Mesopotamia; this could have occurred as a result of a diffusion of culture, or perhaps it was the consequence of an invasion and the settlement in Egypt by Semites who had been in contact with the Sumerians. At any rate, several things suggest Mesopotamian influence before the Pyramid Age: certain architectural forms and art motifs, seemingly foreign religious concepts, the sudden appearance of a fully developed system of writing, and the adoption of two culture traits characteristically Mesopotamian—the custom of naming the year after an event and the use of cylinder seals.

Old and Middle Kingdoms

Nevertheless, by 2700 B.C. when the formative period ended, Egypt was under the control of a powerful, highly centralized, theocratic, definitely native Egyptian government, and her cultural independence was firmly established. The primary phase of this great riverine civilization stretched over the next 1,000 years, during which there were two periods of marked prosperity and cultural advance: the Old Kingdom (2700–2200 B.C.) and the Middle Kingdom (2000–1800). After the Middle Kingdom, a gradual decline was climaxed by a foreign invasion about 1700 B.C. Like the coming of the Kassites to Babylonia, the invasion of Egypt by a people called the Hyksos concluded the primary period.

Comparisons and Contrasts with Babylonia.   Partly because environmental conditions were not the same in Egypt and Babylonia, the two countries differed in their history and culture. Mesopotamia lay open to invasion from all sides, while Egypt tended to be isolated and protected by her natural boundaries: the Mediterranean sea in the north, the cataracts of the Nile in the south, and the desert on the east and west. The effects of invasion upon Mesopotamia were disruptive, though sometimes culturally stimulating as in the case of the Amorite conquest. A unified Egypt could ordinarily defend her frontiers and re-pel would-be invaders, with the result that an indigenous civilization developed that for long periods was rarely subject to foreign influence. This had its good and bad aspects. Egyptian culture was perfectly adapted to the Egyptian environment; the various lines of development were followed to a logical conclusion. On the other hand, an evolution-ary plateau was reached very early, and Egyptian civilization tended to become static without the benefit of stimulating contacts with the out-side world until the Hyksos invasion and the subsequent Egyptian Em-pire (New Kingdom).

Agriculture.   Egyptian agriculture was dependent upon irrigation, as was the case in Babylonia, but we have already remarked that in the latter country irrigation could be handled on a local basis, whereas in Egypt it had to be a national affair. The early Egyptians had to drain the swamps along the Nile and then learn to control the river itself. The Nile flood occurred annually at the beginning of summer; it covered the land and, when it receded, it left behind a rich deposit of soil that made the use of fertilizer unnecessary. Yet, the Nile flood, if uncon-trolled, could be as disastrous as the raging waters of the Tigris and Euphrates. Canals, ditches, embankments, and catch basins had to be built and kept in perfect repair so that the flooding Nile could be tamed and some of its waters stored up for the long dry months ahead.

Transportation.   In Babylonia, transportation was dependent upon boats and wheeled vehicles. Boats were floated down the rivers and towed back up again; they were also towed along the canals. In Egypt, land transportation in the narrow valley was out of the question. The Nile was the only highway; it was ordinarily broad and sluggish, but with reliable winds, so that the Egyptians could navigate up and down the river in sailboats, and there was much barge traffic. Wheeled vehi-cles, on the other hand, were rare in Old and Middle Kingdom times.

Architecture.   Like the Babylonians, the Egyptians lacked wood and made considerable use of mud bricks for domestic construction, but they could bring wood from Lebanon by sea, and they had an abun-dance of stone that could be employed for public buildings and sculp-ture. Metals, too, were procured with relative ease: gold from the eastern hills and Nubia as well as copper from Sinai. The comparative self-sufficiency of Egypt meant that foreign trade was slow in developing. The effect of this, in turn, was that since production was geared to local needs there was no large-scale industry; no large cities appeared for a long time; the absence of a trading class was certainly one reason why Egyptian law was not codified at an early period.

Sculpture.   The availability of stone in Egypt led to the early development of stoneworking techniques and proficiency in sculpture. Colossal figures, rare in Babylonia, were common in Egypt. Building in stone, the Egyptians used the column and lintel. Moreover, the architectural use of stone ordained that Egyptian structures would differ from the brick buildings of Babylonia. Egyptian monumental architecture tended toward long, narrow buildings with a succession of columned rooms and open courts; the narrowness was a consequence of the difficult problem of roofing a stone structure. The brick palaces and temples of Babylonia were, as we have seen, low complexes of small rooms. The exteriors of buildings in lower Mesopotamia were decorated with glazed bricks when they were embellished at all, but the Egyptians made great use of high-relief sculpture on exterior blocks of stone; these blocks were also painted in bright colors to ensure greater contrasts for the high relief in the bright sunshine of Egypt. This close relationship between sculpture and painting affected the latter in that painting always remained two-dimensional, even on the flat surface of interior walls. Moreover, there was no attempt to achieve perspective.

Writing.   Many of the same pictographs were used in early Sumerian and Egyptian writing, but the physical forms of the characters diverged markedly later on as the systems of writing developed. This was owing to the fact that different materials were used to receive writing. The skill of the Egyptian stone carvers resulted in the creation of the familiar hieroglyphic script frequently applied to building exteriors for ornamental and magicoreligious purposes, but the invention of a kind of paper made from the papyrus plant was responsible for the evolution of a cursive script (hieratic) as the scribes began to use papyrus for written documents of all kinds.

Other Distinctive Features.   It should be noted that fish were very important in the diet of people in all three riverine civilizations, but Egypt and Babylonia differed in that wheat was the major cereal in Egypt as opposed to barley in Babylonia; Egypt also seems to have had more cattle and poultry available for food. With regard to materials for textiles, one associates flax with Egypt, wool with Babylonia, and cotton with the Indus civilization. Finally, it seems to have been a fact that slavery was not common in Egypt under the Old and Middle Kingdoms and that the Egyptians enjoyed greater social mobility than the Babylonians. In the first instance, infrequent foreign contacts and the absence of large-scale industry may have kept slavery to a minimum, while in the second, the bureaucratic establishment in Egypt was preeminently scribal in membership—a good scribe, even of humble origin, could move up to a position of importance.

Dynastic Chronology.   The Egyptians periodized their history with reference to dynasties, or families of rulers. This is not the most convenient arrangement that could be imagined, partly because on many occasions the only change to be observed in passing from dynasty to dynasty was that one family had succeeded another, and partly because sometimes dynasties were contemporary with each other and not chronologically successive; in one case, the twenty-fourth Dynasty lasted longer than the twenty-fifth so that the successor of the twenty-fourth Dynasty was the twenty-sixth. Egyptologists, however, have chosen to retain the traditional practice, and thus we have little choice but to follow them in this matter. Menes, then, was the first king of the first Dynasty. The Old Kingdom included Dynasties III–VI, and the principal dynasty of the Middle Kingdom was the twelfth.

Theocratic Government.   The government of Egypt was theocratic in form. All power was concentrated in the person of the pharaoh who was called "the good god" and addressed as the son of whatever deity happened to be regarded as supreme in Egypt in that age. After death, the pharaoh was worshipped as a deity, but some Egyptologists like to qualify the usual statement that the ruler was actually regarded as a god on earth during his lifetime; it is perhaps most correct to say that he ruled by divine right. Whatever the truth may be, it can be said with assurance that the peak of pharaonic authority was attained under the Old Kingdom. By this time a completely planned economy had come into existence. There was a regular census of the national resources. Moreover, as a result of generations of careful observation the Egyptians knew from measuring the flood stage of the river at the first cataract how much of the land of Egypt would be flooded that year, and thus they were able to estimate the national income from agriculture weeks before the flood reached the land downriver and months before the sowing and the harvest.

Achievements of the Old Kingdom

The Old Kingdom was noteworthy not only for its efficient, centralized national government, but also for advances made in literature, astronomy, arithmetic, geometry, and medicine. The three greatest achievements in the cultural field were, however, the development of an accurate calendar, the construction of the pyramids, and the firm establishment of a belief in immortality.

Solar Calendar.   In very early times people tended to use a lunar calendar, one based on the phases of the moon. Since a lunar month averages between 29 and 30 days, 12 lunar months total less than 360 days, several days short of the solar year of approximately 365¼ days. The Sumerians used a lunar calendar which they more or less kept in phase with the solar year by adding a thirteenth month every three years. The Egyptians, too, had employed a lunar calendar, but by the twenty-eighth century B.C. they had discovered something better. It had been observed that the annual flood always began about the time of the summer solstice and coincided with the heliacal (dawn) rising of the Dog Star, which they called Sothis. The length of the solar year and the period of time between one dawn rising of Sirius (the Dog Star) and the next are almost identical. The Egyptians had stumbled upon a means of approximating the solar year, and their discovery was going to be helpful to astronomers later on in antiquity who wished to devise a solar calendar. On the other hand, what the Egyptians did with their new find was something a little less satisfactory. They introduced 12 new months of 30 days each and added 5 intercalary days at the end of each 12-month period to make a year of 365 days. Since this was a quarter-day less than a solar year, the new Egyptian calendar diverged from the solar one at the rate of twenty-five days, nearly a month, a century. The result was a cyclic arrangement: once every 1,460 years the first day of the first month of the new calendar would coincide with the dawn rising of Sirius. Then, there would be ceremonies and rejoicing in Egypt, and a new era would be said to have begun.

Pyramids.   It is tempting to think that the discovery of the Sothic cycle may have been the work of that great and wise man, Imhotep, who was the principal adviser of Zoser, the second Pharaoh of the third Dynasty. Imhotep's reputation as a physician, wonder-worker, and purveyor of wisdom endured for centuries. Moreover, as an architect he was responsible for planning and building the famous Step Pyramid, which was a series of platforms like a ziggurat and rose to a height of over 200 feet. The pyramids were the tombs of the pharaohs. Their evolution had begun in the time of the first Dynasty when the underground chambers in which the kings "rested from life" were covered by low benchlike mounds; these tombs were called *mastabas*. Zoser had simply piled one bench or platform on top of another to make his step pyramid. The true pyramid with its sloping sides came with the fourth Dynasty when the largest of these royal monuments were constructed.

The Great Pyramid of Cheops (Khufu) covered an area of 13 acres at its base and rose to a height of nearly 500 feet. Around its base was a complex of temples devoted to the cult of the dead ruler, who was identified with the sun god after his demise. For the Egyptians, the pyramid was a sun symbol; for us today it epitomizes the wealth and power of the fourth Dynasty pharaohs. The construction of a pyramid was the work of many years; it required the employment of a large proportion of the manpower of Egypt during the summer months when the Nile was in flood and covered the land so that no field work could be done. Even for a ruler as wealthy as the Egyptian pharaoh, the construction of a pyramid must have been hideously expensive and a considerable drain on the royal treasury.

Belief in Immortality.   Eventually there was an extension of the idea that the ruler was of divine origin and immortal. It came to be felt that his associates, the nobles, were entitled to immortality also, and shortly after the Old Kingdom there was a "democratization" of belief so that the privilege of life after death was allowed to everyone. Whether the next life was lived in an underworld that was the exact replica of the Nile Valley, or whether one enjoyed an existence among the stars, it was agreed that the soul was immortal if the proper ceremonies were performed and if the physical identity of the body was preserved intact through skillful mummification—or, as a backstop, by means of sculptured or painted effigies.

Disintegration of the Old Kingdom

About 2200 B.C., the Old Kingdom disintegrated after a gradual decline. It is most likely that a series of low Niles may have terminated the earlier prosperity, or possibly a succession of weak rulers may not have been able to meet the challenge of the great nobles who governed the two-score provinces (*nomes*) into which Egypt was divided. To say that the pharaohs went bankrupt building the pyramids is a jest that contains an element of truth, since it may have been the burgeoning of the funerary cult that toppled the throne of the Old Kingdom pharaohs. Lands and revenues were increasingly devoted to the service of the dead, not only deceased kings but nobles as well, and the substance of living kings may have reached the vanishing point when more wealth and land and labor were expended on the dead than on the living.

The Old Kingdom succumbed to anarchy. For 200 years (2200–2000 B.C.) Egypt was in turmoil, disorganized and weak. Under the eleventh Dynasty a slow revival commenced that reached a climax with the twelfth Dynasty in the second great period of Egyptian history, the Middle Kingdom (2000–1700 B.C.).

EGYPTIAN SCULPTURE

(Courtesy of Aramco World.)

Differences in the Old and Middle Kingdoms

The Middle Kingdom was unlike the Old Kingdom in several respects. Memphis, at the junction of Upper and Lower Egypt, had been the capital of the Old Kingdom, but under the Middle Kingdom the pharaohs ruled from Thebes, several hundred miles upriver. With the ruler residing in Upper Egypt, a major representative of the king was needed to govern Lower Egypt. Moreover, the throne itself was none too secure, and the continuation of the dynasty through orderly succession had somehow to be guaranteed. The answer to all these problems was found in the introduction of a system of co-regencies. The pharaoh took his intended successor as co-ruler with himself and appointed him to govern Lower Egypt. When the pharaoh died, kingship did not lapse because it was already in the possession of his colleague. Another difference between the Old and Middle Kingdoms was the apparent decline in royal prestige. The pharaoh seemed to be on the defensive, frequently calling attention to his justice and good works as if he needed to reassure people that he was doing a good job. Moreover, he must tread gingerly among the great nobles who governed the nomes; without their support and cooperation, the regime would collapse. Pyramids were still being constructed, but they were small compact models, poor copies of the large uneconomy size of the Old Kingdom. Contacts with the outside world were more frequent now. The Egyptians traded with and exerted some cultural influence in Syria, and to the south they pushed down into Nubia to raid and to establish defensive fortresses against reprisal. Sinai was intensively exploited, and trade opened up also with the Red Sea coast.

Art and Literature.   The Middle Kingdom was an important period in art and literature. Portrait sculpture developed; new types of temples and public buildings appeared. This was the age of literary classics: the *Story of Sinuhe* and the *Tale of the Shipwrecked Sailor*. The *Rhind Mathematical Papyrus* is a Middle Kingdom product, and there are several medical papyri from this period also. The canons, classic forms of sculpture and literature, established in the Middle Kingdom set the standard for future ages.

The Legacy of Egypt.   In Egypt, as in Mesopotamia, though both were subjected to some modification, the primary civilization provided basic patterns that endured and influenced other peoples. Much later, the Greeks were to borrow their arithmetic from the Egyptians and their algebra from the Babylonians; the Sothic cycle enabled the Greeks to devise a solar calendar, but Babylonian astronomy was the foundation from which the Greeks proceeded in that field; in both sculpture and painting the Egyptians were the teachers of the Greeks, while in religion the Greeks borrowed from both primary civilizations. Egyptian litera- ture was to rival that of Babylonia in its influence on Syria and Palestine. The Egyptians possessed a marvelous poetry that was employed for re- ligious and secular purposes, while in prose there were narratives, folk tales, meditations, prophecies, and didactic writings. Borrowings from Egypt have been demonstrated in the case of both Psalms and Proverbs in the Old Testament.

Religion.   It was religion that inspired Egyptian art and literature, just as it did in Mesopotamia. The ancients thought that the Egyptians were the most religious people in the world. Indeed, visitors to Egypt discovered there a multitude of cults. The chief national deity was al- ways the sun god who was worshipped under different names and guises in various periods; some aspect of the sun was supreme whether the deity in the ascendant was Horus, Amon, Re, or Aten. Very impor- tant was Osiris, the king of the dead, connected with the fertility cult and beliefs in immortality. Osiris was believed to have been a king in Egypt who died and came to life again. His cult was influential in its emphasis on morality and in introducing the idea that a man's actions would be judged in the hereafter.

It should be noted that our understanding of Egyptian religion is imperfect, a fact well illustrated by the conflicting opinions of present day "authorities" on the subject. Egyptian religion was not static; in the course of 3,000 years it was bound to change periodically—and it did! If Herodotus had visited Egypt in the twenty-fifth century B.C. instead of the fifth, his account of the religious practices would not have been the same in many aspects. As it was, he found that the priests of the various cults did not agree in what they told him. Nor were the beliefs and practices of the common people ever the same as those of the educated nobility and the priests of the major cults. Among the people there were regional differences as, for example, the basic totemism in the nomes varied from one of these districts to another where the sacred animal worshipped might be a bull, a cat, a crocodile, or a hippopotamus. In addition, it is baffling to discover that an Egyptian was capable of ac- cepting several differing, even contradictory, beliefs at the same time without being disturbed by the contradictions involved. Extinct religions that have to be reconstructed on the basis of surviving monuments and fragmentary texts defy our full comprehension. Egyptian religion is no exception to this universal rule.

Decline of the Middle Kingdom

After the twelfth Dynasty, the Middle Kingdom declined. Unity could not be maintained, and such weakness resulted that the Delta was invaded and occupied by foreigners for a whole century (1670–1570 B.C.). The invaders were the Hyksos, "Rulers of Foreign Lands," who were mostly Semites entering Egypt from the direction of Palestine. Hyksos kings ruled the Delta, but a succession of Egyptian dynasties managed to survive in the Valley. Eventually, the national spirit of Egypt revived, the Hyksos were expelled, and a great new period was inaugurated in 1570 B.C. with the coming of the eighteenth Dynasty and the New Kingdom.

THE INDUS CIVILIZATION

It is the fate of some peoples and some civilizations to be forgotten, while the recollection of others is preserved through the medium of history or legend. Our twentieth century has witnessed the rediscovery of several "lost" civilizations, the existence of which had been unsuspected until archaeology took a hand. Egypt and Babylonia had never passed from the memory of man, but the finding of a third primary riverine civilization about fifty years ago came as a real surprise.

Resemblances to Egypt and Mesopotamia

Stretching throughout the length and breadth of the Indus valley and reaching 500 miles down the west coast of the subcontinent of India itself, the Indus civilization covered an area ten, or possibly twenty, times greater than that of Egypt and Lower Mesopotamia combined. Yet these three civilizations were contemporaries, and that of the Indus resembled the other two in a number of ways: It was riverine; its agriculture was based on the production of cereal crops and the raising of herd animals; irrigation was developed, and there were problems of flood control; trade and industry had attained significant proportions; there were towns big enough to be called cities; monumental architecture, writing, and metallurgy had been introduced.

Lack of Written Documents

Since this was a literate civilization, it may have had a literature, and there may have been a formal organization of knowledge as in Egypt and Babylonia, but we can only guess about this because no documents corresponding to the papyri of Egypt or the clay tablets of Babylonia have been found. Our knowledge of the writing comes from the impressions of stamp seals on which the Indus script occurs; presumably in each case a seal inscription gave the name or title of the owner of the seal. If only we could read the script, which has not been deciphered as yet, we might get some clue as to the language and therefore the identity and even the origin of the creators of the Indus civilization. As matters now stand, however, we cannot write the history of the Indus region in this period, and nothing illustrates better than this situation the importance of written documents in historical reconstruction. We are forced to deal with this epoch as if it were prehistoric, although on the analogy of Egypt and Babylonia we can, if we dare, make some assumptions about characteristics the Indus civilization may have possessed: It might have had a theocracy, a priest class, social stratification, a planned economy as well as the literature and organized body of knowledge already mentioned.

Differences from Egypt and Mesopotamia

On the other hand, the Indus civilization differed from its contemporaries in certain respects. Not only was a uniform material culture spread over a huge area, but the Indus cities were built on a common plan with broad streets intersecting at right angles, thus forming an overall gridiron pattern. This suggests that the cities were planned before they were built; they did not grow from simple origins to something more complex, as in Egypt or Mesopotamia. The towns themselves were unwalled, but their citadels, always located on the western side, were strongly fortified, or, as some people have suspected, built up on artificial heights to protect them from floods. Nearby were huge granaries for storage, and on the citadels were tanks for ceremonial bathing and buildings that served a religious purpose. The association of governmental and religious structures suggests a theocracy, while town planning and grain storage are probably indicative of a highly centralized government that maintained a planned economy. Considerable use of kiln-baked bricks in building can only mean that the Indus people, unlike the Mesopotamians or Egyptians, had ready access to wood for fuel; and, it should be remarked, they made greater use of wood as a building material also.

The Indus people cultivated wheat, barley, vegetables, and fruit. Their textiles were manufactured from wool and cotton. Domesticated animals were cattle, sheep, goats, as well as the water buffalo and zebu, and perhaps the elephant. Jewelry was made of precious metals and semiprecious stones. They had bronze which was used for tools and weapons, and in sculpture bronze and stone were employed; figurines were also made of clay and terra-cotta. However, with the exception of their handsome painted pottery, the artistic achievements of the Indus people are not as impressive as those of Egypt or Babylonia.

Trade

From seaports on the Indian Ocean, the Indus people traded with lower Mesopotamia by a route that led up the Persian Gulf. Trade objects from the Indus have been found in Mesopotamia, and Sumerian artifacts appear in the Indus Valley. The Sumerians spoke of products coming by sea from Magan and Meluhha; of these, the latter may have been the Sumerian name for the Indus Valley. In Babylonian times the trade continued, but it was no longer direct since Indus and Babylonian traders seem to have met on Bahrein Island in the Persian Gulf to exchange their wares. For their internal commerce, the Indus peoples used boats on the great river and its tributaries, and some land transport had recourse to wheeled carts.

Towns and Cities

The sites of dozens of Indus towns and cities have now been identified, but the largest population centers known are Harappa in the north and a site called Mohenjo-daro in the south. The latter has been excavated extensively because it is better preserved than Harappa. The interesting thing is that Harappa and Mohenjo-daro are 400 miles apart, yet both enjoyed the same culture. We do not know whether one of these was a capital city, whether they were separate capitals, or if neither was a governmental center.

Decline of the Indus Civilization

The creators of the Indus civilization may have been invaders. Much of their culture does not appear to have developed from preceding cultures in the area; it has also been found that some of the older pre-Indus sites were destroyed and subsequently occupied by people having culture traits which we associate with the Indus civilization. In its final stages the Indus civilization seems to have been in decline. The reason for its disappearance may have been a foreign invasion, but it is perhaps most likely that difficulties in controlling the Indus river, its floods and the wandering course of the river which might shift direction and leave a river port without access to the stream, may be nearer the truth. It has been suggested that by deforestation the Indus people encouraged erosion and floods and "wore out" their land. Because of soil deposited by the river, the level of the plain kept rising in relation to the foundations of the towns and cities; this meant also a rising level of subsoil waters so that towns might be drowned out. A recent hypothesis envisions changes at the delta of the Indus which caused the river to back up and virtually inundate the lower valley. Any of these causes would render the area uninhabitable.

For whatever reason, then, the Indus civilization ceased to exist about 1700 B.C. No certain trace of its influence on subsequent cultures can be demonstrated, and we cannot be sure that reference to the civilization existed in later folk tale or legend. It was truly "lost."

Why do we mention the Indus civilization at all? The answer to this question is that it not only illustrates something about historical research—the importance of documents, or their inaccessibility—but also it is important to keep in mind that future discoveries may change the picture quite radically. In view of the trade contacts of the Indus and Mesopotamia, it is inconceivable that there was not a cultural exchange. Given the complexity and widespread nature of the Indus civilization itself, it is not likely that it had no effect upon subsequent cultures in this part of India. The last word has not been said about the Indus civilization. On the basis of experience with other ancient civilizations during the past century and a half, with new discoveries constantly changing our ideas about them, it is simply not reasonable to imagine that our present view of the Indus culture will remain unaltered.

Chapter Four

From Amosis to Zoroaster:
The Ancient Oriental Empires

If the founding of the primary civilizations constitutes one chapter in the story of antiquity, its appropriate successor is an account of Near Eastern events and developments during a millennium or so beginning in the middle of the sixteenth century and ending about 500 B.C. The period opens with the recovery of the civilized world from the effects of the invasions that terminated the primary phase, and it closes with the political unification of the Near East that came with the establishment of the Persian empire.

MAJOR THEMES OF THIS ERA

The major themes of this era of 1,000 years are those of diffusion, expansion, and consolidation. Indeed, until the apex of cultural development in ancient times was reached seven centuries later in the days of the Roman empire, these trends were the characteristic ones. It is true that there were fits and starts, periods of growth and contraction, but despite minor interruptions, the current of civilization moved in what might be called a positive direction.

Cultural Diffusion

It is not an oversimplification but rather a statement of something basic and valid to say that in ancient history there was a process that was repeated again and again in various periods and in different areas. What happened was that culture traits from civilized areas tended to be diffused into adjacent regions where culture was less complex. Such diffusion was accomplished through trade, conquest, or the movement of peoples. Reactions to diffusion varied with the complexity of culture enjoyed by the recipients, the utility to them of the culture traits available through diffusion, and the distance of the receiving area from the civilized one. A nearby people with a less complex culture might simply be engulfed by the neighbor civilization. A group farther away in a different environment could pick and choose elements it needed at the time and reject others for which no use could be found. Frequently, a culture trait would be borrowed and then adapted to new conditions, or it might be combined with some element in the receiving culture to create a new item. Eventually, the borrowers themselves became civilized, and their country might begin to function as a center from which their own brand of civilization would be diffused to new adjacent areas. Diffusion was not a one-way process. The older centers picked up traits from their neighbors, usually only a few at a time. The transfer of European culture to the New World in the sixteenth century A.D. illustrates very well what we have been discussing: Not only was a more complex culture imposed upon cultures less complex, but the Europeans adopted a number of American Indian culture traits—one has only to think of the importance to Europe of the introduction of tobacco and potatoes. As we survey the growth of ancient civilization in this and later chapters, we shall be able to see many examples of the action and consequences of diffusion.

It now seems that, before the end of the primary period, there had been a massive diffusion of culture from Egypt and Babylonia into Syria and Palestine so that the receiving areas had become civilized by 1800 B.C. or even earlier. Babylonian culture had also profoundly affected northern Mesopotamia, as well as parts of Anatolia and Iran. Diffusion from Syria and probably Anatolia brought about the rise of civilization in Crete, a new adjacent area, after 1800 B.C. What did the adjacent areas borrow from the primary civilizations? In the main, they borrowed technology, business methods, standards for weights and measures, writing, art motifs and techniques, literary forms and themes, and religious ideas. The transmission of things literary and religious from the primary to the new secondary cultures was especially direct because it took place in the new scribal schools established in secondary culture centers; in such schools the scribes not only learned to use the cuneiform or the Egyptian scripts but they also studied the associated languages and literary works. It is quite possible that the methods of instruction already developed in the primary centers were borrowed wholesale by the new schools.

Trade Expansion and Transportation Revolution

The territory controlled by the kingdoms of the primary period had been pretty much confined to the river valleys. In the new age we are about to consider we shall discover much larger states and empires no longer limited to the river valleys but even existing outside them. Part of the explanation for this is that the expansion of trade had created economic unities that could be transformed into political ones. Another factor that affected both the expansion of trade and the appearance of large territorial states was a revolution in transportation. The development of large cargo vessels which were reasonably seaworthy brought expanded use of the sea lanes of the Mediterranean; bulky goods that would play no part in trade by land could now be moved by sea. Commerce grew in volume, and the character of the trade objects changed. New areas could be reached by sea, developed, and in some cases politically controlled. A more startling change occurred on land with the introduction of the domesticated horse. This was the contribution of the invaders who had toppled the primary civilizations. The horse meant to that age what the radio or telegraph and the airplane have meant to our own. Transportation and communication were speeded up so that the world seemed smaller than before. It was now easier to hold a large empire together. Warfare changed with the introduction of the horse-drawn chariot; in some areas the chariot warriors constituted a new social class.

Political Unification

The growth of trade, the spread of civilization, and the creation of larger and larger empires were productive of a final result that was anything but surprising. Despite local differences and variations, the Near East tended to become an economic and then a cultural unity, and the logical conclusion to all this was the political unification of the whole accomplished by the Persians in the last half of the sixth century.

CHRONOLOGICAL SUBDIVISIONS (1570–500 B.C.)

The Age of Empires (1570–500 B.C.) has three major chronological subdivisions. In the first (1570–1100 B.C.), the Near East was dominated by the Egyptian empire, the Hittite kingdom, and that of the Mitanni in northern Mesopotamia; the Kassites in Babylonia played some part in international intrigue, but they constituted a second-rate power. This first subperiod was terminated by a new wave of barbarian invasions (1200–1100 B.C.) that destroyed some empires and weakened others to the level of impotency. The second subperiod covers roughly three and one-half centuries (1100–750 B.C.). During this time there was gradual recovery from the barbarian invasions, but no major power held the stage so that this was a period of local independence in which small states rose and fell and fought among themselves. The last phase (750–500 B.C.) opens with the rise of the great Assyrian empire which was to spread over Babylonia, Syria, Palestine, and Egypt before it declined and was finally destroyed in 612. After a couple of generations in which the Near East was divided among four major kingdoms, the Persians, on a tide of militant nationalism, overcame the four kingdoms one after another (550–525 B.C.) and emerged the rulers of the largest empire the world had yet seen.

EGYPTIANS, HITTITES, AND MITANNIANS

The most powerful state in the Near East between 1570 and 1370 B.C. was Egypt. In 1570 the Egyptians had united under a great leader, Amosis, to drive the Hyksos from the Delta. Through his victories and the reunification of Egypt, Amosis, the first pharaoh of the eighteenth Dynasty, was to inaugurate a new and major period which we call the New Kingdom or Empire (1570–1100 B.C.); included in the New Kingdom were Dynasties XVIII–XX.

Egypt: The New Kingdom Era

It was the achievement of Amosis to restore the prestige of the ruler and diminish that of the great nobles in the nomes who were his potential rivals. The military success of Amosis made possible the development of a strong national army, and young nobles were quick to sense the career possibilities that lay in serving the king. The expulsion of the Hyksos generated a kind of crusading fervor among the Egyptians that was soon extended to "Asiatics" in general so that the successors of Amosis had no trouble in mounting invasions of Palestine and Syria for revenge, plunder, and finally conquest. Before 1400 B.C., Syria and Palestine had been brought under Egyptian control and made tributary to the pharaohs.

The empire thus acquired brought great wealth into Egypt as well as changes on the Egyptian scene. Thousands of captives of war were brought back by the conquerors, and slavery assumed unwonted proportions in Egypt. New ideas came from abroad; other new concepts evolved as the Egyptians left their narrow land and became acquainted with the outside world.

Architecture, Art, and Culture

Characteristic of the new era and its wealth are the great temples built by the New Kingdom pharaohs and the huge obelisks which honored the rulers. An obelisk is a single block of stone terminating in a pyramidal top and inscribed with hieroglyphic characters advertising the might of a pharaoh; weighing many tons and when erect rising 30

(Courtesy of Aramco World.)

to 50 feet, an obelisk was and still is today an impressive monument—the Washington Monument is not monolithic, of course, but it is an obelisk in form. The pyramid as a tomb had now been superseded by underground chambers cut into living rock; in such rock-cut tombs in the Valley of the Kings west of Thebes, the New Kingdom rulers were laid to rest in rooms overflowing with treasure and with sprightly painted scenes of daily life decorating the walls. This was a great age of Egyptian painting, and sculpture did not lag behind. In poetry and prose, in hymns, narratives, and folk tales, the New Kingdom was a match for its predecessors, the Old and Middle Kingdoms. What one does notice, however, is that the joy of living and the optimism expressed in the literature and painting of the eighteenth Dynasty are replaced by a gloomy preoccupation with death and the next world as the nineteenth and twentieth Dynasties wear on. All this seems to correspond with the success and growth of Egypt under the eighteenth Dynasty and the gradual decline that followed it.

Records of War and Diplomacy

Since war and diplomacy bulked large on the international scene in New Kingdom times, we are fortunate in having records that help in reconstructing the march of events. There are archives of diplomatic correspondence from Egypt and other states; there are narratives and annals which tell us about battles and conquests—in Egypt some of these were inscribed on temple walls and illustrated with relief sculpture; and some treaties survive in which the contracting parties were the major powers of the age. In outline, here is the story.

Mitannian Kingdom

When the Egyptians pushed up into Syria in the sixteenth century B.C., they found the region controlled by the Mitannian kingdom which had its center in northern Mesopotamia. This state existed for roughly two centuries, 1550–1350 B.C. As in Kassite Babylonia, control of the kingdom was vested in a minority of recent invaders, in this case of Indo-Aryan (eastern Indo-European) linguistic stock. The population ruled by the Mitannian kings was mixed: The two most important linguistic groups were the Semites and the Hurrians. The Semites had entered the upper Tigris region before 2000 B.C. In this area they had created the Assyrian Old Kingdom that was contemporary with, and hostile to, the Old Babylonian Kingdom. Then, about 1800 B.C., a new people had begun to drift down from the Armenian hills. These were the Hurrians, a distinct linguistic group unrelated to the Semites, Sumerians, or Indo-Europeans. Subsequently, the Hurrians had spread

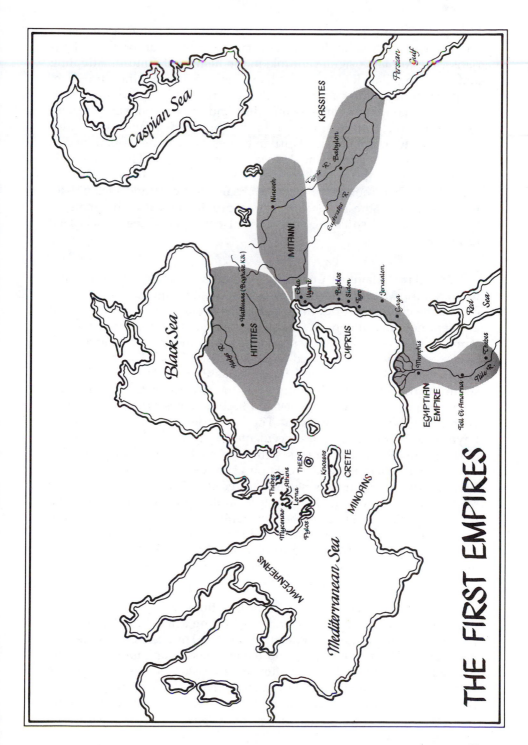

THE FIRST EMPIRES

Caspian Sea

Black Sea

Persian Gulf

KASSITES

Nineveh
Tigris R.
Babylon
Euphrates R.

MITANNI

Hattusas (Boghaz Köi)
Halys R.
HITTITES

Ebla
Ugarit
Byblos
Sidon
Tyre
Jerusalem
Gaza

CYPRUS

Red Sea

Memphis

Thebes
Nile R.
Tell El Amarna

EGYPTIAN EMPIRE

Knossos
THERA
CRETE
MINOANS

Thebes
Athens
Lerna
Mycenae
Pylos

MYCENAEANS

Mediterranean Sea

over Assyria and to the west across northern Mesopotamia into Syria and even into Palestine. Never important as a political force, the Hurrians were to play a significant role in the history of culture. Adopting and adapting Babylonian civilization, they employed the cuneiform script for writing their own language, but what was more important, they borrowed Babylonian religious ideas and were responsible for communicating much of this material directly to the Hebrews and Hittites and indirectly to the Greeks. Hurrian deities came to be worshipped in the area through which the Hurrians spread; even Hurrian words were borrowed—the word for "gold" in Greek may have a Hurrian etymology. Our knowledge of the Hurrians is recent and incomplete. With a little luck, the archaeologists may provide us with more material in the future and so change our present concepts of the period 1800 to 1600 B.C.

Egyptian-Mitannian Coalition.   At any rate, in the sixteenth century B.C., the Mitannians, along with the Kassites and others, had penetrated the civilized world. In possession of the domesticated horse and a potent new instrument of warfare, the horse-drawn chariot, the Mitannians took over the old Assyrian kingdom and then extended their holdings westward to the Mediterranean. They clashed with, held off, and then retreated before the Egyptians pushing up into Syria from the south. By the late fifteenth century B.C. the two contestants had found it advantageous to end hostilities and become allies against a common enemy, the Hittites of Anatolia. The now friendly relations between Egypt and the Mitannians were cemented by a succession of marriages of state with Mitannian princesses entering the harems of the pharaohs.

The Mitannian-Egyptian coalition gave the allies a feeling of security, and the Hittite danger seemed to recede. About 1400 B.C., in the reign of Amenophis III, the grandest of all eighteenth Dynasty pharaohs, Egyptian prestige reached its zenith. Kassite kings and minor princelings courted the favor of Amenophis and sent their daughters to his harem; letters of friendship came from Hittiteland. It was an era of glorious peace and prosperity that promised to last forever.

Fall of the Mitannians.   Within less than fifty years, the happy illusion had vanished. The Assyrians, revolting against the Mitannians, reestablished their independent kingdom. The Hittites went on the warpath, drove Egypt from Syria, and made a vassal kingdom of what remained of the Mitannian state after the secession of Assyria. No later than 1335 B.C., a revolution in Egypt itself had overthrown the eighteenth Dynasty and brought the country under a military dictatorship.

Akhenaten, "the Heretic."   It is customary to ignore the inherent weakness of the Mitannians, their precarious position as a ruling minority; to overlook the potential and ambitions of the Hittites who were on the way up; and to minimize the possibility that the regime of Amenophis III may have become soft and superannuated and was already treading a downward path when the old king finally died after a reign of nearly forty years. Instead, ancients and moderns have preferred to lay the burden of blame upon the narrow shoulders of a poor, probably diseased, unfortunate who just happened to be pharaoh when the proverbial roof caved in. This was Amenophis IV, better known as Akhenaten, the "heretic," and we are sometimes told that he was a religious reformer, a visionary, a fanatic, or the "first monotheist."

Atenism.   Our sources of information about Akhenaten are really quite limited, and much less is known about him than some novelists and historians have led the general public to believe. He was the son of Amenophis III. He tried to promote the cult of Aten, a sun god, as the official state religion. Since this involved a demotion for older established cults, their priesthoods cannot have been pleased by the prospect. Did Akhenaten aim at an official monotheism? It is possible but proof is lacking. Aten was never represented by anthropomorphic statues or paintings but merely by a symbol: the sun disk with its rays extending downward and terminating in hands. It is probably safe to say that the conception of Aten was that he was not an exclusively Egyptian deity, but a universal god. Surviving hymns and prayers addressed to Aten suggest a highly ethical religion. Praise of the god, thanksgiving for his goodness to man, and an insistence upon truth as the supreme virtue may be the keys to Atenism. It is certainly true that in Akhenaten's reign many of the artistic conventions of Egyptian sculpture and painting were abandoned for a lively, naturalistic style and a portraiture that strove to show people as they were and not idealized as they ought to be. It is also true that Akhenaten abandoned Thebes as his capital and moved the court to a new city, Akhetaten, which was consecrated to Aten. The site, in the valley about halfway between Memphis and Thebes, we know today as Tell el-Amarna, and its excavation has given us most of the information we have about Akhenaten.

Akhenaten's Diplomacy.   At Tell el-Amarna was found a portion of the diplomatic archives of Akhenaten's government. These consist of the correspondence with rulers and officials in Syria, Palestine, Mesopotamia, and Anatolia. The internal problems of the Mitannians, the intrigues of the Hittites as they encouraged Syrian princes to revolt against Egypt, and the desperation of loyal subjects as the Hittites advanced all emerge from these letters. People assume that Akhenaten made no effort to save his empire, that he was interested only in promoting religious reform at home, but the letters we have are all from the incoming basket, and we do not have what the Egyptians wrote in reply.

The End of Ateniam.   About midcentury, Akhenaten died. His name was soon excised from monuments, his portraits systematically defaced, and his capital city deserted. His short-lived successors, Smenkhkare, Tutankhamen, and "Father Ay," strove ineffectually to make their peace with the powerful and grievously offended Amon priesthood which demanded the extermination of Atenism and a return to the "true faith."

"King Tut."   Very little is known of these last three shadowy pharaohs of the eighteenth Dynasty. The first two were members of the royal family, possibly brothers of Akhenaten, but all three based their claims to legitimacy as rulers on marriages to one or another of the daughters of Akhenaten. Tutankhamen, a child of nine at the time of his accession and probably not more than eighteen when he died, was rescued from obscurity in November 1922 A.D. when his virtually unplundered (and thus unique) tomb was discovered by Howard Carter and Lord Carnarvon. The fabulous wealth and beauty of the objects from the tomb can only encourage the wildest speculation regarding the opulence that might have been found in the undisturbed tomb of a major pharaoh.

Recantation did not save the eighteenth Dynasty from extinction, nor were the efforts of the military regime which then came into power successful in winning back Syria from the Hittites. In fact, it was a plague decimating the enemy that alone prevented an invasion of Egypt itself.

Egyptian-Hittite Treaty of Friendship

Efforts to regain Syria were continued by the rulers of the nineteenth Dynasty which was established about 1319 B.C. Even the great warrior-pharaoh, Rameses II (1299–1232 B.C.), could not win back the lost territory, but neither could the Hittites capture Palestine. The stalemate was finally recognized about the middle of the thirteenth century B.C.; Egypt and the Hittites concluded a treaty of friendship and alliance, agreeing that the former would keep Palestine and the latter, Syria.

Hittites and the New Empire

Who, then, were the Hittites, and why were they important? Invaders from the north, like Kassites and Mitannians, the Hittites had occupied central Anatolia in the nineteenth century B.C. The Hittites

EGYPTIAN CARVED RELIEF SCENES AT KARNAK
FROM THE TIME OF TUTANKHAMEN

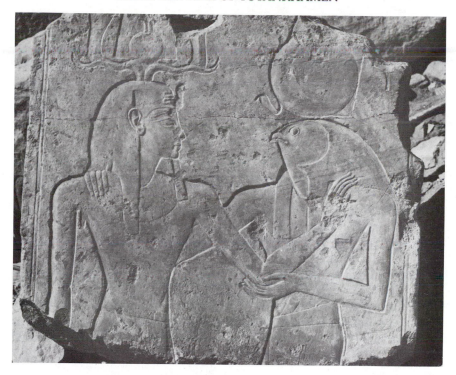

(Courtesy of O.S.)

Top: Tutankhamen and Khonsu, the Theban moon god.
Bottom: Foreign warriors, spearmen and bowmen, "Asiatics," and Nubians.

spoke an Indo-European language which occupied a position in that language family about midway between the eastern (Indo-Iranian) and western (Greek, Latin, Germanic, etc.) branches. Their traditional institutions, many of which they soon abandoned, seem to have been much like those of the early Greeks and Romans, a matter reserved for later discussion. The Hittites overcame the Anatolian natives and imposed themselves upon the population as a ruling minority. At first organized in a number of small independent kingdoms, a semblance of unity was briefly achieved in the formation of a feudal empire in the seventeenth century B.C. After a temporary setback, by 1450 B.C. the Hittites had achieved a strong and more centralized government, the New Empire, which was to last until about 1200.

Expansion.   From their capital at modern Boghaz-Köy in the Halys river basin in central Anatolia, the Hittites extended their control westward virtually to the Aegean Sea and then moved southward over the Taurus mountains into Cilicia. Under the leadership of Suppiluliumas (1375–1335 B.C.), the greatest of all Hittite kings, the Hittites gained possession of Syria and northwestern Mesopotamia as the Mitannian kingdom weakened and Egypt seemed unable to retain the loyalty of the Syrian princes. This was the high point of Hittite expansion, and eventually the Hittites had to come to terms with Egypt, as we have seen.

Civilization.   Starting with their own less complex culture, the Hittites borrowed from Mesopotamia and the Hurrians and finally created a distinctive civilization of their own. The cuneiform system of writing, the form of the Mesopotamian law code, and religious concepts and ceremonies were among the borrowings, but the different environment of Anatolia militated against the adoption of many Babylonian culture traits. The land of the Hittites was agriculturally self-sufficient without irrigation, but it also admitted the development of a diversified economy. With plenty of wood, stone, mineral resources, and a country where the grapevine and sheep, goats, cattle, and horses flourished, the Hittites could engage in metal working, textile manufacture, and viniculture. Trade had reached respectable proportions even before the arrival of the Hittites, since the civilized world had long sought the copper and silver resources now controlled by the New Empire, but there was an added attraction because the Hittites were the first to manufacture iron. Controlling the iron deposits, and with plenty of wood for fuel, the Hittites long enjoyed a monopoly of iron production and fixed prices to their own considerable advantage. Since it was also used for weapons and armor, iron was a strategic commodity which the Hittites were not inclined to distribute too liberally or cheaply to their enemies. It should be noted, however, that the prosperity of the Hittites was circumscribed by a transportation problem: Their goods had to be brought out of the country by land over long and difficult routes, and this limited the volume of trade as well as the kinds of goods that could be profitably exported.

Architecture and Art.   The availability of wood and stone meant that the Hittites would certainly not imitate Babylonian architecture and that they could develop an individual kind of sculpture. Neither were they greatly affected by Egypt because direct contacts were few and infrequent. The remoteness of Hittiteland also contributed to the development of a distinctive style of art works in metal.

Literature.   On the other hand, we can see the effect of the traditional scribal school among the Hittites as elsewhere. Although Hittite religious literature has much that is Hittite, the effects of borrowing from the Babylonians and Hurrians are very clear. The yield to the archaeologist of cuneiform literary texts from Boghaz-Köy has been rich, and the finds continue. The literary types include ritual texts, myths, legends, religious epics, and annals and narratives relating to the exploits of the Hittite kings.

Collapse of the Hittite Empire.   About 1200 B.C. the Hittite empire collapsed under the impact of barbarian tribal migrations, which in turn triggered a massive movement of Anatolian peoples southward both by land and sea. The island of Cyprus was attacked, many towns in Syria and Palestine were devastated, and about 1190 B.C. the Egyptians just managed to repel a gigantic sea raid. Rameses III, great pharaoh of the twentieth Dynasty, beat off the sea peoples, but the effort contributed to a growing exhaustion in Egypt. By 1100 B.C. the country had fallen into a profound weakness from which it did not recover for some 400 years.

Overseas Neighbors

Thus far in this chapter we have dealt with the major states on the mainland of the Near East: Egyptian, Mitannian, and Hittite. By the second millennium, however, civilization had spread from the river valleys to other continental areas in addition to Hittiteland in Anatolia, to the large islands in the eastern Mediterranean, Cyprus and Crete, and to the European mainland in southern Greece. Discussion of the Minoan civilization in Crete and its Mycenaean successor in east-central and southern Greece is usually presented as an introduction or prologue to Greek history, yet Near Eastern elements can be identified in both cultures, and archaeology bears testimony to extensive commercial relations linking Syria and Egypt with Crete and Greece. Cyprus, of course, had come within the Near Eastern orbit earlier because of its copper mines, and even before its colonization by the Mycenaeans about 1300 B.C. it played a part in Near Eastern diplomacy. If we were dealing solely with the history of the Near East in this volume we should proceed to a description of the Minoan and Mycenaean cultures at this point, but to adhere to the traditional order of presentation in an "ancient history" we are obliged to postpone that subject to the beginning of Chapter 5.

THE CANAANITES AND THEIR NEIGHBORS

Throughout the centuries, Syria and Palestine have known little peace and less freedom. In antiquity, this long, narrow strip of territory between the Arabian Desert and the Mediterranean was the main highway connecting Egypt and Mesopotamia, and the land echoed to the tramp of marching warriors obeying the commands of pharaohs and alien kings. To these shores also came people from the sea, eager to trade or raid. Truly dark and bloody soil, a region fragmented by topography and even more divided by the varied and irreconcilable groups that called it home, it was a land that could fulfill promises to no one.

Yet, there was a time between the fall of the early empires and the rise of Assyria when Palestine and Syria enjoyed a measure of local independence. Once they had dug out from the debris of the great raid of 1200 B.C., the people found a measure of prosperity if not peace, and an age of accomplishment ensued. These were the days of David and Solomon—and Elijah.

Syro-Hittites and the Philistines

At the beginning of the first millennium B.C. the population of Syria and Palestine was predominantly Semitic, yet there were notable exceptions. In the north, scattered across Cilicia, upper Syria, and northwestern Mesopotamia, were the Syro-Hittites who perpetuated many elements of the old Hittite culture. Actually, these people were Luwian in speech, descendants of the pre-Hittite population and possible relatives of the Minoans; their peculiar syllabic script, called Hieroglyphic Hittite, had much in common with the earliest kind of Minoan writing. Possessing a distinctive style of architecture and sculpture, the Syro-Hittites ruled over a varied Semitic population in a number of small independent kingdoms.

In the far south, on the coast of Palestine, were the Philistines, the survivors of a group of sea raiders driven off from Egypt by Rameses III. Iron-users, the Philistines employed their technological superiority to dominate the native population. The rulers of five independent city-

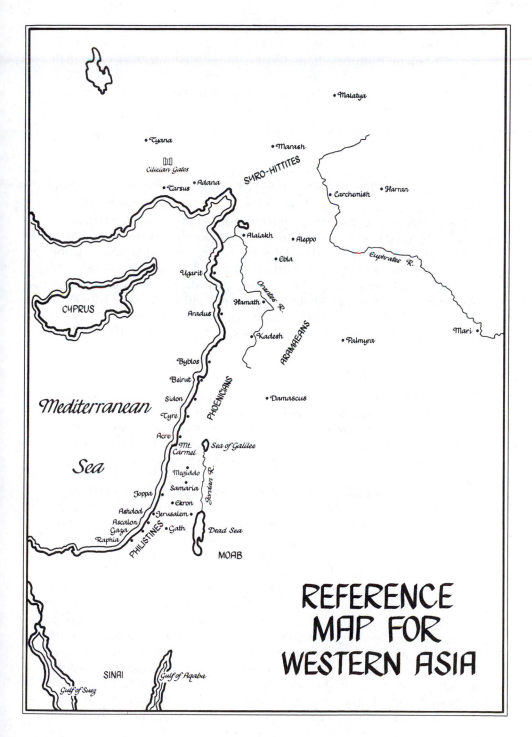

REFERENCE
MAP FOR
WESTERN ASIA

states along the coastal plain—Gaza, Ascalon, Ashdod, Gath, and Ekron—these invaders from the sea maintained themselves as a distinct group for many centuries. In material culture, the Philistines had much in common with the Minoans and Mycenaeans, but their precise identity and their language are unknown. It may be guessed that they, like the other sea raiders, came from southern Asia Minor.

Aramaeans

On the eastern side of the Syrian mountains, from Damascus northward to the region of the great bend of the Euphrates, lived the Aramaeans, a linguistic group of Semitic origin. Never politically unified, the Aramaeans had two things in common: They spoke Aramaic, and they were prominent as caravaneers who dominated trade by land. They were to be found in city-states in the area specified above, some ruled by Aramaean princes and others by Syro-Hittite kings. Because of the widespread trade of the Aramaeans, their dialect was diffused and later employed by people distributed over a wide area from Babylonia to Egypt. In New Testament times, it was the language spoken in Judaea, for example, and therefore the tongue of Jesus and his disciples.

Canaanites

By far the most numerous Semites in the Syria-Palestine area were the Canaanites, another linguistic group which had begun to penetrate the region as early as 1800 B.C. The Hebrews and Phoenicians were Canaanites important after 1000 B.C., but they had distinguished predecessors, particularly the inhabitants of Ugarit, modern Ras Shamra.

The First Alphabet.   Ras Shamra is on the Syrian coast just opposite the Island of Cyprus. The site of a peasant village earlier, it grew into a town in the third millennium, and then a city under the Canaanites after 1800 B.C. Although ruled by a native Canaanite dynasty, it was a vassal state, successively, of the Mitannians, Egyptians, and finally the Hittites. It was destroyed and abandoned after the great raid of 1200 B.C. The most prosperous period at Ugarit came in the century between 1450 and 1350 B.C. A composite culture including Canaanite, Egyptian, and Mesopotamian elements produced some interesting results. Ugaritic scribes were trained to use both the cuneiform and the Egyptian system of writing; moreover, they studied Akkadian, Sumerian, Hurrian, and Egyptian and became familiar with not only the languages but also the associated literature. In the fifteenth century B.C. they wrote their own Canaanite dialect, Ugaritic, in a unique script, a cuneiform alphabet. This is the first appearance of the alphabet in history, unless one is willing to accept the dubious opinion that the Sinai inscriptions of 300 years earlier are alphabetic.

Literacy and Religion.   When the Ugaritic cuneiform alphabet was deciphered in 1930, and the clay tablets on which it was written began to be read, it became clear that the religious literature of Ugarit was of great importance. Epics, hymns, and prayers told much about Canaanite religion, but just as significant was the fact that these compositions provided something that had been lacking before: actual examples of Canaanite literature. The content of these writings, the poetic forms, and the Ugaritic dialect itself have all contributed to a greater understanding of the Old Testament, the supreme achievement of the Canaanites in literature. Nor was this all, for at some time, either in the Mycenaean period or 500 years later when Greek merchants came again to the Syrian coast, the Greeks borrowed ideas from this area. Just to cite one example, the gods of Ugarit were believed to dwell on the top of a nearby mountain; the name of this Ugaritic Olympus was Mt. Casios. El, the principal Ugaritic deity and father of the gods, was known as Zeus Casios when the Greeks came to inhabit this region in the Greco-Roman period.

Trade and Industry.   The prosperous city of Ugarit in the second millennium derived its wealth from trade and industry. It was a terminus on the Mediterranean for the overland trade from Mesopotamia, and the main north-south routes led through the town also. To the port came the copper ore of Cyprus to be smelted at Ugarit, and there was a flourishing woodworking industry. Minoan, and then later Mycenaean, traders maintained residences and warehouses at the port and the town; some died and were buried there. A meetingplace where the men of many nations came together to exchange goods—and inevitably ideas— Ugarit has much to tell us if we can ask the right questions.

Phoenicians

The Phoenicians, who flourished in the first millennium B.C., were closely related to the people of Ugarit in both language and culture. A string of harbor towns along the coast just above the Palestinian border—Arvad, Byblos, Tyre, Sidon, and Beirut—constituted independent city-states ruled by Phoenician kings. As it evolved in the tenth century B.C., Phoenician prosperity was based upon a virtual monopoly of seaborne trade in the Mediterranean. This consisted mostly of an exchange of the manufactures of Phoenicia for the raw products of the Mediterranean littoral. The Phoenicians produced metal work, textiles, glass, ivories, and the famous Tyrian purple dye made from a local shellfish,

A PAGE OF SCRIPTS

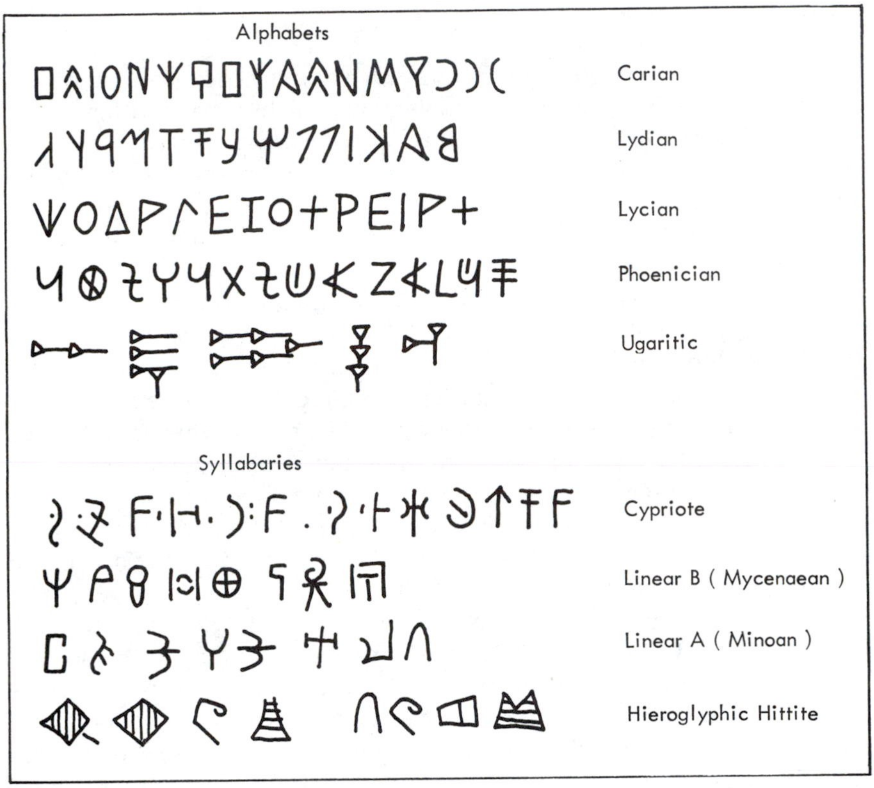

Alphabets

□𐤀IONY𐤒O𐤉A𐤀NM𐤉))(Carian

𐤀Y𐤒𐤐T𐤅Y 𐤅77I𐤊A𐤁   Lydian

VOΔ𐤛𐤔EIO+PEIP+   Lycian

𐤉O⊗Ƶ𐤉𐤉X⼕𐤅𐤊 Z𐤊L𐤉𐤅   Phoenician

(Ugaritic cuneiform characters)   Ugaritic

Syllabaries

(Cypriote syllabic characters)   Cypriote

(Linear B characters)   Linear B (Mycenaean)

(Linear A characters)   Linear A (Minoan)

(Hieroglyphic Hittite characters)   Hieroglyphic Hittite

the murex; in return, they got metals, foodstuffs, and slaves. The urban dwellers of Phoenicia lacked sufficient land to produce their own food, but they had other resources that more than compensated for the deficiency: the murex, the cedars of Lebanon, and a special sand essential for glassmaking.

Economy.   The Phoenicians provide a striking, if not unique, example of cultural growth. Unlike the people of the river valleys, they could not base their economy on agriculture. In fact, until the Near East had reached a certain stage in its evolution, Phoenicia could support neither a large population nor a complex civilization. By the first millennium B.C., however, conditions were favorable for the growth of an economy based almost entirely on trade and industry. The Greeks, in a similar situation later, developed their economy in much the same way.

Culture Carriers.   The Phoenicians borrowed rather than created culture, and their importance in the history of civilization, though con-

PHOENICIAN SHIPS

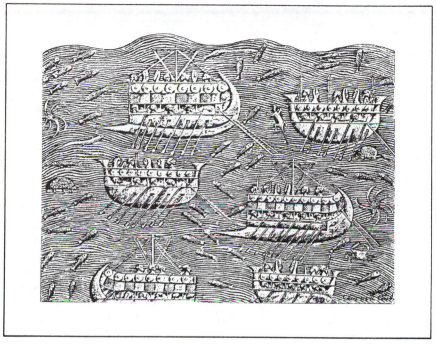

(After Layard, Nineveh)

siderable, was based on the fact that they were carriers of culture who transported elements of Near Eastern civilization to the lands around the Mediterranean Sea. It was the Phoenicians who brought the alphabet, the Babylonian weights and measures, Mesopotamian astronomy, Near Eastern business methods and art motifs, and countless other culture traits from Egypt, Babylonia, and the rest of the ancient Orient to Greece, Italy, Spain, and the western shores of North Africa.

Navigation. We cannot be sure that it was the Phoenicians who invented or developed the Semitic alphabet, though they used it, but they were great navigators, ship builders, and explorers. Their ships were copied by the Greeks who also borrowed Phoenician navigational techniques and relied on their geographical knowledge. The Phoenicians sailed out into the Atlantic and found the route to the Tin Islands (Britain); they explored the eastern and western coasts of Africa, and some people said that they had circumnavigated the Dark Continent. For purposes of trade, and later to relieve overpopulation at home, the Phoenicians established colonies in Cyprus, North Africa, and Spain.

Carthage, the greatest of all Phoenician colonies, was to challenge the Greeks and later the Romans for the control of the western Mediterranean.

THE BIRTH OF A WORLD RELIGION

It was in Palestine that a new group, wanderers who had undoubtedly been influenced by the culture of the lands through which they had passed, settled and established a new religion—Judaism—which became the source of two other major world religions—Christianity and Islam.

Israelites

It may have been in the thirteenth century B.C. that a horde of Semitic invaders pushed westward across the River Jordan and into Palestine. According to tradition, after they had attacked and destroyed Jericho and other towns, they settled down to live on the land. Among these invaders was an embryonic national group called the Israelites. Their ancestors had once been numbered among the Habiru, a class of caravaneers and nomadic brigands that wandered back and forth along the edge of the desert from the great bend of the Euphrates in the north to the region of the Negev in the south. Contacts with the Amorites and the Hurrians had resulted in a borrowing of certain elements of Mesopotamian culture, and some of these wanderers had indeed sojourned in Egypt where they had acquired other culture traits. In Palestine, living side by side with their Canaanite relatives who were already civilized, the Israelites were exposed to other influences.

Solomon.   Without much skill as artisans, the Israelites lived at first in Palestine as farmers and herdsmen. When the Philistines came after 1200 B.C. they subjugated the Israelites along with the rest of the population, but after several generations, a struggle for freedom was begun that finally unified the Israelites under the leadership of Saul—and then David. King David (1005–965 B.C.) captured the Canaanite fortress of Jerusalem and made it his capital. The Philistines were confined to their coastal cities, and Solomon (965–925 B.C.) brought the new kingdom to the height of its prosperity and power. Solomon promoted trade by land and sea; he made friends with the Phoenicians of Tyre and so shared in Mediterranean commerce; he also established a port on the Gulf of Aqaba from which he traded down the Red Sea, exporting thither the copper of Sinai. The accumulated wealth from these ventures allowed Solomon to maintain a brilliant court and to beautify Jerusalem, which also became a religious and cultural center; it was Solomon who built the Temple.

Fall of Israel and Judah.   After Solomon died, there was internal dissension, and the kingdom split into two parts: the Kingdom of Israel, with its capital at Samaria in the north, and the Kingdom of Judah, which remained centered at Jerusalem. The fierce hostility that characterized future relations between Israel and Judah would have been debilitating enough, but it put them even more at the mercy of more powerful kingdoms in Syria and the reviving strength of Egypt and Mesopotamia. At best, Israel and Judah must join the larger contestants as inferior allies and hope that they had picked the winning side. They were not allowed the option of neutrality. Furthermore, they got small benefit from the victories of their superiors; the only consolation was that they would have suffered more if they had joined the losers. At last, Samaria was captured by the Assyrians in 722 B.C.; the Kingdom of Israel ceased to exist as its people were dispersed as captives throughout the Assyrian empire. Disaster came to Judah in 586 B.C.; Nebuchadnezzar carried off the Jews to their Babylonian captivity, and only a pitiful remnant came back to Jerusalem under Persian auspices two generations later.

Judaism

In the history of civilization, the political importance of the Hebrews, Israelites, or Jews is small in comparison with the story of their religious evolution, for Judaism became a mighty and enduring faith as well as the source of two other major world religious, Christianity and Islam. The basic facts seem to be these:

At least as early as the time of Abraham, perhaps 1800 B.C., that patriarch and his descendants seemed to have arrived at a "monotheism that was practised without being defined." The existence and power of other gods was not denied, but they gave their allegiance to the "God of Abraham," a tribal deity with whom a covenant had been made. In return for the exclusive protection of God, the people would obey him and worship no other deity.

The Covenant.   As the Israelite nation evolved during the Exodus, Moses transformed the tribal covenant into a national affair. According to the traditional story as told in Exodus, at Mt. Sinai Moses was instructed that if the Israelites would obey God and keep the Covenant they would be the "Chosen People" and a "holy nation." After the elders and the people agreed to the pact, Moses received the Ten Commandments which defined the moral responsibilities that the Israelites must assume in order to keep the covenant they had made.

It was one thing for a simple nomadic people to make an agreement in the wilderness, but it was something else to keep to the bargain as they prospered in Palestine and their culture grew in complexity and sophistication. The proximity of the great civilization of Egypt, along with the even closer daily contact with Canaanite culture, smothered cultural creativity and even prevented the Israelites from adapting what they were forced to borrow. By the time of Solomon, the primitive uniformity of Israelite society had disappeared; a wide gap separated rich and poor. New social and economic circumstances forced an elaboration of the law and its codification and then recodification. Religious ceremonies became grander and more formal, augmented by borrowing from the Canaanites; the mere existence of a temple invited a ritual of greater splendor and complexity than that which could be performed in the open air or in a tent. It was not surprising that palace and temple began to contest for supremacy with extravagant claims.

The Prophets.   With the divided kingdom and political decline, the ancient religion faltered and might have disappeared if it had not been for the prophets. Beginning with Elijah in the ninth and continuing on through the fifth century B.C., a remarkable succession of great preachers appeared to remind kings, priests, and commoners alike of the Covenant and the duties of the people to their God. The tribulations of both Israel and Judah were proof enough that God was not bound to prosper and protect his people if they would not live up to their part of the bargain. They must remain steadfast in their worship in form and fact, and they must adhere to the Law in their relations with one another. All men were equal before the Lord; all were entitled to the same justice; there could be no distinction between the rights of the rich and the poor.

Failure to Keep the Covenant.   The meaning of the destruction of Samaria and the fall of the Kingdom of Israel was clear enough. The people had failed to keep the Covenant. This demonstration of the validity of prophetic message made its impression, for in 621 B.C. King Josiah of Judah tried to avert a similar catastrophe from his realm by radical reforms. A book of the Law was discovered in the temple, probably an early version of the Book of Deuteronomy; it was read to the people, and all swore to renew the Covenant. Foreign cults were uprooted, unfaithful priests executed, and the unlawful shrines destroyed. An official and compulsory monotheism was instituted with the ceremonies of the worship of the deity confined solely to Jerusalem itself.

But it was too late, said Jeremiah, and he was right. Josiah was foully murdered by the Egyptians; Jerusalem was twice captured by the Babylonians. Then came the Babylonian captivity, the suffering that tempered the steel of Judaism, and, with the return to Jerusalem, a new phase of religious development was ready to begin.

The Torah.   By the time of the Restoration in the late sixth century B.C., the concept of the Chosen People, fostered by the prophecies of Ezekiel and the Second Isaiah, had been clarified. The Jews returned to Jerusalem to become uncompromising monotheists dedicated to a faith that demanded ritual and ethical purity. The new order envisioned a closed society in which mixed marriages (between Jews and Gentiles) were prohibited. A theocracy was established under the High Priest of Judah at Jerusalem. Its constitution was the Torah, the Law of Moses as found in the Pentateuch, the first five books of the Old Testament. Popularly ascribed to Moses himself, these books were introduced to the people by the priest, Ezra, about 400 B.C.

The Old Testament.   This was the beginning of the formation of the sacred book, the Old Testament. Oral traditions and actual written accounts dealing with cosmology and historical events had already been in existence for a long time. In both Israel and Judah materials had begun to be committed to writing as early as the ninth century B.C. Later, the two separate traditions were combined and reconciled in the books of the Pentateuch, Kings, and Chronicles. The publication of the Pentateuch by Ezra, however, was the start of a collection of writings that about A.D. 100 attained its final form in the Old Testament as we know it today. To books of law, cosmology, and history were added the collected works of the prophets, the psalms, proverbs, and so on. As a work of literature, and in its ethical content, the Old Testament is supreme among the writings of the ancient Near East. It is indeed the Book of Books.

In the light of modern knowledge, it is clear that the Old Testament is complex in origin and indebted to many sources. Merely by way of illustration, we may note that it contains a Mesopotamian flood story, several proverb compilations of Egyptian origin, and psalms based on both Egyptian and Mesopotamian models. From what we know about Ugaritic poetry, it is manifest that the poetic forms used in the Old Testament are Canaanite. This list could be extended to considerable length, but enough has been said here to remind us that civilization itself and many of the individual culture traits of which it is composed are complex structures built of materials derived from varied sources.

THE GREATEST EMPIRES

By the end of the sixth century B.C. the countries of the Near East were at last combined into a single political unit. This had been a development foreshadowed by the spread of the Assyrian empire (750–612 B.C.), then interrupted by the fall of Assyria and the temporary division of the Near East among four large kingdoms, and finally realized in the formation of the Persian Empire after 550. Political unity was preceded and made possible by a trade revival that created a great economic and cultural entity upon which a single government could be imposed.

Assyrian Empire

We have already met the Assyrians, a Semitic people who had lived in Mesopotamia in the upper Tigris region since before 2000 B.C. An early Assyrian kingdom, established about the same time as the Amorite kingdom in Babylonia, had later become subject to the Mitannians, but it regained its independence in the fourteenth century B.C. It was not until the ninth century B.C., however, that Assyria emerged as the major state in the Near East. Under vigorous royal leadership, a national militia composed of hardy Assyrian peasants won many victories over fierce barbarian tribes that menaced Assyria from the mountains north and east of the plain. Then came a series of campaigns or raids against the Syro-Hittite and Aramaean principalities in the west. Sometimes an expedition for plunder would carry the Assyrians all the way to the shore of the Mediterranean, and in the ninth century B.C. the first contacts were made with Israel and Judah. Shalmaneser III, one of the Assyrian warrior kings, erected the famous Black Obelisk which shows King Jehu, "son of Omri," of Samaria, paying homage and bringing tribute to the victorious Assyrian ruler (842 B.C.).

External and Internal Problems. Between 800 and 750 B.C., however, a succession of weak kings, city rivalries in Assyria, a plague, and an eclipse of the sun (763 B.C.) temporarily eclipsed Assyria, too. Furthermore, it had not been merely internal difficulties but also external problems that had weakened the Assyrian power. Abroad, the chief thorn in the side of the Assyrians was the Armenian kingdom called Urartu, which had tasted the fruits of Mesopotamian civilization and posed a threat to the northern frontier of Assyria; the situation worsened as the Urartians cut off the customary sources of copper and other metals from Mesopotamia. To compensate for this loss, a revived Assyria after 750 B.C. drove in earnest toward the west to secure the copper of Cyprus, the cedars of Lebanon, and the silver of Cilicia. Mere raiding

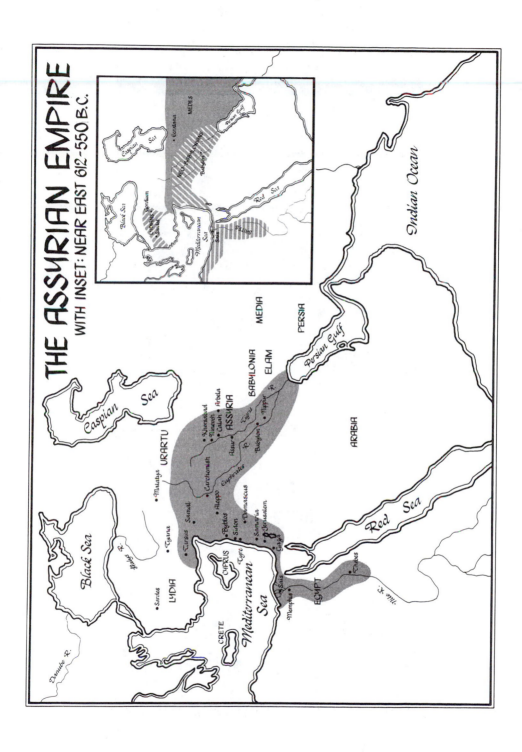

THE ASSYRIAN EMPIRE
WITH INSET: NEAR EAST 612–550 B.C.

Caspian Sea

MEDES

+ Gordiana

Tigris Gulf

NEO-BABYLONIANS

Babylon

Black Sea

MEDIANS
Sardes

Red Sea

Mediterranean Sea

Memphis

Indian Ocean

Caspian Sea

URARTU

MEDIA

PERSIA

Persian Gulf

Khorsabad
Nineveh
Calah • Arbela
ASSYRIA
Assur
BABYLONIA
ELAM
Tigris R.
Babylon • Nippur

Malatya

Carchemish

Euphrates R.

Aleppo

Samal

Cyrus

Tyana

Sardes

LYDIA

Halys R.

Black Sea

Damascus

Samaria

Jerusalem

Gaza

Sidon
Tyre

CYPRUS

Byblos

CRETE

Mediterranean Sea

El Said

ARABIA

Red Sea

Thebes

EGYPT

x mi.

Danube R.

ASSYRIAN LOW RELIEF CARVING OF A "WINGED GENIUS" FROM THE PALACE OF ASHURNAZIRPAL AT NIMRUD (KALAKH) (ninth century B.C.)

(Courtesy of the Minneapolis Institute of Arts.)

would no longer suffice; only conquest and empire would ensure a constant supply of strategic materials.

Revival.   The Assyrian revival began under Tiglath-Pileser III (745–727 B.C.). The Urartians were pushed back into their mountains, Babylonia was annexed, and victories were won in the west. Shalmaneser V (727–722 B.C.) was probably the captor of Samaria, but his successor, another True King of obscure origin, Sargon II, claimed the credit for the successful siege of the Israelite capital. Sargon II founded the last and best-known Assyrian dynasty, for his successors were Sennacherib, Esarhaddon, and Ashurbanipal. By the reign of Esarhaddon (681–668 B.C.) the empire included Assyria, Babylonia, Syria, Palestine, and the Delta in Egypt. For the first time, a truly imperial system of government began to emerge, and a pattern of administration was shaped that was to be borrowed and refined by later empires: those of the Persians, Alexander and his successors, and the Romans.

Cimmerian Menace.   It was a changing world in which Sargon and his descendants lived. In the late eighth century B.C. the Urartian menace was removed by a new barbarian horde, the Cimmerians, who swept in from the north. In 705 B.C. Sargon himself was killed in battle against the Cimmerians, but the raiders were driven off and pushed westward through Anatolia where they destroyed another big kingdom in Phrygia, the realm of legendary Midas, and then they burst upon the Greek towns on the Aegean coast of Asia Minor. In the end, the Cimmerians were controlled and then dispersed by the rise of a new power in western Anatolia, the Kingdom of Lydia with its capital at Sardis. Assyrian inscriptions tell us that Gyges, the first important Lydian king known to the Greeks, was briefly an ally of Assyria.

Enlargement, Consolidation, and Decline.   After Sargon, his successors enlarged and consolidated the empire. Sennacherib (704–681 B.C.) put down revolts in Babylonia, fought off Greek attackers in Cilicia who were based in Cyprus, captured Phoenician and Philistine towns, and besieged Hezekiah "like a caged bird" in Jerusalem. Esarhaddon (681–668 B.C.) exacted tribute from the Indo-European-speaking Medes and Persians who had just begun to settle in Iran; provoked by Egyptian meddling in Syria and Palestine, he invaded and made the Delta region tributary.

Under Ashurbanipal (668–626 B.C.) the empire attained its greatest extent, but almost immediately fell into a rapid decline. It was something of a paradox that the prosperity accruing from the unification of a large area under a single government had encouraged a revival of national feeling in Egypt and Babylonia. This coincided with a diminution of the Assyrian military potential, to say nothing of the fact that the Assyrians had probably expanded beyond the limits of the territory they could effectively control. At any rate, the national militia of Assyrian yeomen was no more, for the casualties occasioned by decades of desperate fighting had virtually exhausted this source of strength. The army of the seventh century had come to be a force of mercenaries and subject levies: Philistines, Syro-Hittites, Phoenicians, and others. Such an army could not, would not, stand up against determined opponents, since men who fought for pay or had been conscripted to serve a hated ruler were no match for those who fought for home and country and independence. Egypt regained its freedom in midcentury; the Medes and Persians refused to pay their tribute; and Babylon, after an unsuccessful revolt between 652 and 648 B.C., became independent after Ashurbanipal died in 626. Following this, Assyria itself was brought under attack by the Babylonians and Medes; the destruction of Nineveh, the Assyrian capital, in 612 B.C. marked the end of the empire.

Government and Military.   Hated and feared by their subjects and their enemies, the Assyrians had nevertheless laid the foundations for a new period of cultural and economic growth in the ancient world. As contributors to civilization, they could claim novelties in governmental and military organization. Reference has been made to their development of imperial government, while it may be noted that the Assyrian army was a model of versatility with its chariotry, heavy- and light-armed foot soldiers, archers, slingers, and an engineering corps equipped with siege machinery. Assyrian kings were diligent in the preservation of the ancient culture of Mesopotamia; in great libraries they gathered together copies and made translations of the older literature and themselves developed a magnificent narrative style for recording their own achievements.

Art and Architecture.   Probably the work of subject artists and artisans rather than the native Assyrians, the art and architecture of Assyria were nevertheless impressive. Ready access to stone and wood enabled the Assyrians to develop a style of palace and temple architecture that differed from the Babylonian, which was dependent on clay bricks. The huge Assyrian palaces were decorated with relief sculpture and glazed tiles; they also used a columned portico borrowed from the Syro-Hittites. Combined with all this, there was a lavish use of cedar, cypress, juniper, and other aromatic woods. Sculpture in the round perhaps did not equal the Egyptian achievement, but Assyrian reliefs are inferior to none and particularly interesting and valuable in their exciting narrative style. The age was also notable for its fine ivories and metal work, usually attributed to "Phoenician" workmanship but very likely

ASSYRIAN WARFARE: SEIGE OF A TRIPLE-WALLED CITY

(After Layard, Nineveh)

ASSYRIAN RIVER TOWN

(After Layard, Nineveh)

the product of traveling guilds of artisans belonging to several national groups. "Assyrian" art was influential in the artistic traditions developed by Persians and Greeks, since both peoples knew it at first hand.

Rise and Fall of Four National States

Four national states flourished briefly after the fall of Assyria: the Medes in Iran and eastern Anatolia; the Neo-Babylonians in Babylonia, Assyria, Syria, and Palestine; the Saites (Dynasty XXVI) in Egypt; and the Lydian kingdom in western Anatolia. For the most part there existed a kind of balance of power among these states which enabled, or forced, them to live generally at peace with one another. These were the days of Nebuchadnezzar in Babylon, Amasis in Egypt, and Croesus in Lydia. This intermediate period of less than a century is one of the most interesting in the whole history of the Near East. This was the world that Herodotus reconstructed from folk memory a century after it had disappeared; it was an age in which the Greeks first began to become acquainted with the Near East as they entered it as traders and mercenaries.

The end, when it came, was swift if not merciful. Like dominoes the kingdoms toppled and fell in response to an impulse originating in Iran. The newest and least secure of the four states was that of the Medes with its capital at Ecbatana (Hamadan). Among the subjects of the Medes were the Persians, a group of scattered tribes in southwestern Iran. Encouraged by Babylonian intrigue, the Persians combined under the leadership of a tribal kinglet, Cyrus, later called "the Great." By 550 B.C. the Persians had not only won their independence but also overthrown the Medes and annexed their territory. Croesus, the Lydian king, either in an attempt to avenge his brother-in-law, the King of Media, or hoping to grab territory for himself, made the mistake of taking the field against Cyrus. This aggression was not only repelled, but Cyrus invaded Lydia, capturing Sardis and Croesus in 547 B.C. Aided by internal dissension in Babylonia, where the priests hated the reigning Nabonidus, Cyrus took over the Neo-Babylonian realm in 539 B.C. The Saites in Egypt were temporarily spared as Cyrus turned his attention to Bactria (Turkestan) where he died in battle in 530 B.C., but his successor, Cambyses (530–522) invaded and annexed Egypt with little trouble in 525 B.C.

Thus, in twenty-five years, the whole political map of the Near East had been altered, and in place of four kingdoms there was now one empire. It did not change the course of destiny that Cambyses died during the time of, or as a result of, a revolution in Persia, for his place was soon taken by Darius, a distant relative, who put down the revolt, en-

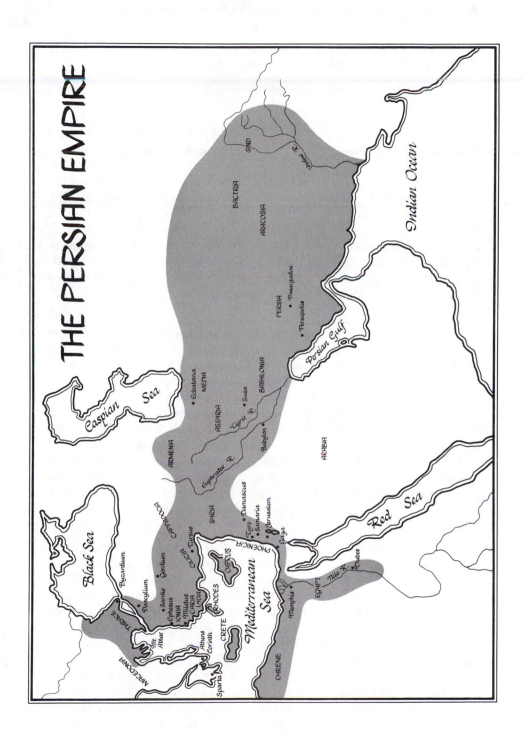

THE PERSIAN EMPIRE

SIND

Indus R.

Indian Ocean

BACTRIA

ARACOSIA

Caspian Sea

PERSIA

Pasargadae

Persepolis

Ecbatana

MEDIA

ASSYRIA

Tigris R.

Susa

BABYLONIA

Babylon

Persian Gulf

ARMENIA

Euphrates R.

ARABIA

Red Sea

CAPPADOCIA

Damascus

SYRIA

Tyre

Samaria

Jerusalem

Gaza

PHOENICIA

CILICIA

Tarsus

CYPRUS

Black Sea

Byzantium

Dascylium

Sardis

Gordium

LYDIA

Ephesus

Miletus

CARIA

IONIA

RHODES

CRETE

Mediterranean Sea

Nile R.

Pelusium

Memphis

EGYPT

THRACE

Mt. Athos

Athens

Corinth

MACEDONIA

Sparta

CYRENE

larged the empire, and established a dynasty that was to rule for nearly 200 years until its conquest by Alexander the Great.

Persian Empire

Darius the Great (522–486 B.C.) added the upper Indus Valley and what is now European Turkey to his far-flung domains, but his contribution was not so much as a conqueror as an organizer and administrator. He promulgated a law code of the Mesopotamian type; he provided the empire with a uniform system of weights and measures; and he improved communication and transportation by the construction of roads, the establishment of a royal post relay system, and the building of a canal that connected the Nile with the Red Sea. Darius also introduced an imperial coinage of gold and silver, something that shows his extraordinary grasp of the contemporary situation, for coined money was a novelty that was less than a century old.

Government.   Adapting and improving the imperial organization patterns devised by the Assyrians, the Persians divided their empire into about thirty provinces *(satrapies)*, each ruled by a royal appointee called a *satrap*. Local government was administered by native princes or by city-state authorities—we shall see later that it was typical of imperial governments in antiquity, even in the Roman period, that direct imperial control rarely descended below the provincial level. At any rate, Persian garrisons were stationed at key points to preserve order and defend the frontiers against foreign invasion. Tribute was collected in money and in kind. Annual revenues were so large in the Persian empire that over the years a huge surplus in gold and silver bullion was accumulated and stored in government treasuries.

Militant Nationalism.   Until the rise of Macedonia in the fourth century B.C., the Persian Empire had little to fear from outside enemies. The real problem was to prevent internal uprisings, particularly in Egypt or among their Greek subjects in Asia Minor. The Persians might have been able to raise a force of 50,000 from among their own nationals, but this was hardly large enough to keep their millions of subjects in line. As a result, they were forced to hire mercenaries, many of whom were used for garrison duty.

This problem of reliable and loyal soldiers limited Persian territorial expansion. The Persian fleet consisted almost entirely of Phoenician and Greek ships and men; there might be difficulties if the Persians decided to move against the free Greeks or the Phoenician colonists in the western Mediterranean. For a big foreign war, like the so-called "Persian Wars" of the early fifth century that pitted the mainland Greeks against

(After Maspero)

Top: Tomb of Cyrus.
Middle: Ahuramazda.
Bottom: Darius the Great and the Usurpers at Bisitun.

the Persians, the latter could use their own nationals, mercenaries, and small contingents of subject levies, but they could not cannibalize their permanent garrisons nor safely arm large numbers of their non-Persian subjects.

In the sixth century, the Persians with their own militant nationalism could expand rapidly because they had only to defeat ruling minorities and mercenary troops in countries where nationalism had spent its force for the time being. Later, however, as the Persians dissipated their strength over a great area, and their own national spirit had begun to decline, they themselves came to constitute a ruling minority, and the prosperity of their empire promoted a renaissance of nationalism among certain subject nations. Egypt, especially, was often in revolt against Persia. Moreover, Persian control in general was so tenuous that almost every new Persian king, as he came to the throne, had to quell revolts throughout the empire.

Architecture and Sculpture.   Culturally, the Persians were the heirs of the Mesopotamians. In architecture and sculpture they borrowed from the Assyrians. Like the Assyrians, they had plenty of stone; and, also like the Assyrians, they depended upon subject artisans to build their palaces and to carve their sculpture. A lack of wood, however, forced the builders to make great use of the column and lintel technique, as in Egypt or in Greece. Darius established in Persia a magnificent capital, known to the Greeks as Persepolis. In time, under Darius and his successors, Persepolis came to consist of a complex of palaces along with a treasury and a great audience hall. In technique, Persian sculpture in the round was superior to anything Mesopotamian in that category. The Assyrian narrative style, however, was not borrowed for relief sculpture except perhaps in the instance of the grand staircase at Persepolis. Ordinarily, relief sculpture among the Persians was decorative and subsidiary.

Language and Script.   To communicate with their subjects, most of whom did not know Persian, the conquerors had to employ a variety of traditional languages and scripts. Babylonian, Elamite, Aramaic, Egyptian, and Greek were the common languages used, the first two written in cuneiform, the Aramaic and Greek in the alphabet, and the Egyptian in demotic, the final and most cursive form of the Egyptian script. We do not know how the Persians wrote their own language for the purposes of ordinary communication, but for display purposes, a new script was devised: The characters were cuneiform in appearance, but none of the traditional characters were used, for the Persian signs had new shapes and mostly syllabic values.

CARVED RELIEFS AT PERSEPOLIS

*(Courtesy of the Oriental Institute
of the University of Chicago.)*

Top: Audience scene with Darius I (center), Crown Prince Xerxes (behind Darius),
dignitaries, and attendants.
Bottom: Persian dignitaries on the grand staircase. The lion and the bull are a royal
emblem (possibly Zoroastrian).

Religion.   Proximity to a more complex culture forced the Persians
to borrow rather than create in most instances, but they did make one
considerable contribution to civilization in their religion: Zoroastrianism. Zoroaster was a prophet and religious reformer who appeared in
Iran in the sixth century. Condemning idolatry and superstition, Zoroaster preached the worship of Ahuramazda, the god of light, truth,

and goodness. A true follower of Ahuramazda strove for the highest sort of ethical behavior and guided himself by a "Golden Rule" by "doing as he would be done by." Approaching monotheism and eschewing graven images, Zoroastrianism had some things in common with Judaism. The dualistic features of the new theology later affected both Judaism and Greek philosophy, for Zoroaster stressed the conflict of opposites: good and evil, light and darkness, truth and untruth. Ahuramazda himself was opposed by a power of darkness called Ahriman, the prototype of Satan in the later Judeo-Christian tradition. Zoroastrianism was adopted by the Persian royal family and many of the nobles; it declined after the middle of the fifth century B.C. but later revived and became an important religion in Persia and parts of India.

IN RETROSPECT

Looking back at the period of 1,000 years just described, one can see that it differed from the 1,000 or 1,500 years encompassed by the primary phase that had gone before. In the primary period, civilization had taken shape; its form largely conditioned by adaptation to life in the river valleys. In the second period, civilization was again adapted, but this time in a variety of ways to diverse environments, although whatever local form it took there was always the necessity of building upon foundations already provided.

In the second period, there were new inventions, discoveries, and developments. Some of these were much more important than others. One doubts that the conscious, deliberate imperialism, more comprehensive and ruthless than any the world had seen before, would stand very high on any list if it were not for its by-product, the organization of imperial government. The Iron Age dawned in this second period but iron did not displace bronze, and it is fair to wonder whether the important thing about iron was not its superiority over bronze, but rather the fact that iron ore was more widely distributed and thus more commonly at hand than copper deposits—tin, of course, was rare and not easy to come by. Coined money appeared at the end of the second phase, but what we should call a money economy did not develop until much later, and we shall therefore delay discussion of this matter for the present. On the other hand, two new elements of great importance should be listed here: the invention of the alphabet and the new trends in religious thought.

Foreshadowed perhaps in Atenism at the beginning of the second period, a positive development at the end of the epoch was a combination of monotheism and morality that appeared with Judaism and Zoroastrianism and continued to evolve throughout successive ages. There was a universal and personal quality in the new thought that is not easily discernible, if indeed it existed, in early periods. The individual, no matter what his station in society, could be involved in Judaism and Zoroastrianism, and this was fraught with great significance for the future.

The Semitic alphabet, an invention of scribes somewhere in the Syria-Palestine area in the latter half of the second millennium B.C., began as a stenographic device which used less than a score of characters to write the Semitic consonants. The importance of this invention was that it opened the way for a simplified system of phonetic writing when someone, presumably the Greeks, borrowed the idea and added signs for the vowels. The alphabet was a shortcut to literacy; anyone, with a little industry or a brief period of instruction, could now learn to read and write; it was not necessary to undertake the long and rigorous training required in the scribal schools to master the cuneiform or the Egyptian system.

In the last analysis, coined money, the invention of the alphabet, the new personalization of religion, and the spread of civilization were related, some directly and others less so, to the growth of widespread, more individually organized trade which also, as we have seen, brought a new phase of industry. There was an emancipation from palace and temple that made for new freedoms in activity and thought. A new era had dawned, and we shall now turn to the Greeks, who were able to capitalize on it.

Chapter Five

The Beginning of a New Tradition

THE PROLOGUE

In the middle of our nineteenth century, when George Grote, banker, liberal politician, and more than capable Greek scholar, was writing his monumental twelve-volume *History of Greece*, it was his opinion, shared by numerous others, that little or nothing could be known about Greece in the period before 776 B.C., the traditional date of the first Olympic games. It would be impossible, he thought, to sort out fact from fancy in the tangled mass of ancient Greek folk memory, myth, and legend. Although Grote did cram his first volume with a lengthy survey of this "prehistoric" material, his basic purpose was to demonstrate that history could not be salvaged from the impenetrable darkness that obscured events prior to the first Olympiad.

As it happened, not everyone concurred with Grote since this was a time when vast enthusiasm for things Greek was sweeping England. Part of this interest was due to the recent success of the Greek war of independence in which British sympathizers had participated, but equally influential was the fact that the study of the ancient Greek language had become part of the education of many people, not just those who attended the universities but also those in the preparatory schools. Homer's *Iliad* was already familiar through English translations in prose and some poetic versions, but the magic of Homer was even more exciting and compelling when one read it in the original Greek.

It seemed unlikely to the admirers of Homer that the story of Troy was solely the product of the poet's imagination. For one thing the site of Mycenae, the legendary home of Agamemnon, had long ago been identified by the ancients, so there must also have been a Troy which, if it could be found, would provide an important step toward establishing the historicity of the whole legend since there were details of the story not included in the *Iliad* that were known from other early epics by poets thought to have been contemporary with Homer.

The believers agreed that Troy was somewhere in northwestern Anatolia near the Dardanelles. Various specific sites had been suggested, but certainty was desirable. So it was that an incurable and stubborn romantic, rich enough to afford eccentricity, resolved to find Troy. This was Heinrich Schliemann, who did in the end realize a boyhood dream to his own satisfaction and that of a great many other people.

Schliemann knew that in Greco-Roman times there had been a large city called Ilium that claimed to be and was generally considered to occupy the site of Troy. It attracted many visitors in antiquity, including Alexander the Great and several Roman emperors. It was a veritable tourist trap with guides to show you where the Achaeans had beached their ships, the tomb of Achilles' friend Patroclus, and so on. Undoubtedly souvenirs were available.

Greco-Roman Ilium was not hard to identify. The ruins of the town were strewn with inscriptions and coins bearing the name of the place. Although the general topography of the locality did not coincide with Homer's description—nor have recent geological studies resolved the contradictions—Schliemann decided to excavate the citadel then known as the hill of Hissarlik which was covered by the remains of Greco-Roman temples and other structures of that date, clearly a civic center. Permission to dig was secured, and the work began in 1870.

Progress was slow at first because, as Schliemann began to clear away some of the Greco-Roman stratum, he realized that there were still other levels of occupation below it, so he conceived the then-novel idea of digging a deep trench through the mound that went right down to bedrock. When this was done, almost anyone could walk through the deep cut and make out several levels distinguished by different masonry and varied pottery types. Schliemann thought he could see at least five levels, which he labeled Cities I, II, III, and so on. In 1872 he found a stratum covered with a burned layer that seemed indicative of some kind of wholesale destruction. This was the second level from the bottom, the Second City as he called it, and when he found a great treasure of gold jewelry and silver and copper vessels seemingly once enclosed in a wooden chest which had burned atop the city wall, Schliemann was sure he had found Homeric Troy, the one captured and destroyed by the Achaeans.

Some skepticism greeted Schliemann's announcement of his discovery, and therefore, partly to justify his claim and probably eager for continued success in archaeology, he went to Greece and began to dig at Mycenae where he uncovered the spectacular remains of a civilization (we call it Mycenaean) that seemed to have many characteristics of the one described by Homer.

We can summarize the final details of Schliemann's career by noting that he soon realized that the extent and wealth of Mycenae so far ex-

TROY, 1879

(After Schliemann)

ceeded the small size and relative poverty of Troy II that it was hard to understand why the Mycenaeans bothered to attack and besiege such an insignificant place for more than a decade. Therefore Schliemann returned to Troy to search for a stratum that might contain material of Mycenaean date. He was on the verge of success in 1890 during his last campaign, but he died before he comprehended the significance of what he had found. His assistant and successor, Wilhelm Dörpfeld, a few years later found that the Sixth City contained Mycenaean pottery and other trade goods and was much larger and more strongly fortified than Troy II, and could be dated in the period already assigned to the Mycenaeans. The remaining difficulty—that Troy VI was damaged by an earthquake rather than an enemy attack—was resolved by Carl Blegen of the University of Cincinnati during his excavations in the 1930s when he found City VII-A, which was covered by a burned layer and could be dated at a time corresponding to the date the Greeks of the classical period had calculated as that of the fall of Troy.

We may not have heard the last word about Troy since several questions remain unanswered. Instead, it would seem more appropriate to give Schliemann the credit he deserves. He found "Troy" and discovered the Mycenaeans. In so doing he unwittingly became the father of prehistoric Greek archaeology by demonstrating that excavation could open doors shut tight against Grote and others who used only the literary sources. Henceforth archaeologists would explore and discover not only the pre-Mycenaean background of Greece but also fill some of the later gaps in the time between the fall of the Mycenaeans and the early horizons of Greek history proper as the classical era dawned in the eighth century B.C.

Schliemann was not an archaeologist in the modern sense. His excavation procedures would have horrified a professional archaeologist of the twentieth century, and he was not above making a good story better by a little elaboration of the truth. After all, Schliemann lived in the era of great showmen. He was a contemporary of P.T. Barnum, who also appreciated the value of publicity spiced with a hoax or two along the way. Much has been written about Schliemann, and it is fashionable to expose his departures from veracity, yet no "life" of the man is as interesting and exciting as his own autobiography, published shortly after his first successes at Troy.

In the century since Schliemann much, but not enough, has been learned about the prehistory of Greece. For a long time it appeared that Greece, unlike Italy, was devoid of human habitation in the Old Stone Age, but a few traces of late Paleolithic culture have now been found, and we also know that the Age of Agriculture (Neolithic period) began as early as 6000 B.C. Beginning about 2500 B.C. there were two and possibly three arrivals of newcomers of unknown geographical origin who introduced new types of domestic architecture and pottery. The villages of the first invaders suffered damage in the nineteenth century B.C. from a new intrusion of people who may have been the ancestors of the Mycenaeans, although the Greek-speaking Mycenaeans themselves were definitely in residence by 1550 and could represent the results of a third invasion. Scholarly opinion is sharply divided on these matters, and for our purposes we can avoid controversy and concentrate instead on the fact that civilization in Crete and Greece began with the Minoans and the Mycenaeans, whose culture we shall now describe.

Minoans

The Greeks of the historic period believed that long ago a great king named Minos had ruled at Knossos in north-central Crete. Schliemann had planned to find and excavate Knossos but unsettled conditions on the island had forced him to abandon his idea. So it was that in 1899 a British archaeologist, Sir Arthur Evans, found Knossos and excavated it. He discovered that the site had been occupied by a series of peasant villages but, in stratified layers above the village levels, Sir Arthur found a succession of palaces dating roughly (as he believed) from 1800 to 1450 B.C. The final palace was so grand that Evans called it the Palace of

Minos, and, as similar palaces were discovered elsewhere in Crete, along with many other evidences of civilization, the name Minoan was applied to the culture and the people. We still do not know what the inhabitants called themselves.

It seems likely that Minoan civilization was in large part brought to and developed in Crete by migrants who came from southern Asia Minor in the nineteenth century B.C. The imported culture contained elements borrowed from Egypt and Mesopotamia, but the system of writing, the style of architecture, and much of the technology were probably developed by the immigrants themselves before they came to Crete.

Architecture and Art.   In its material aspects, Minoan civilization deserves the adjective brilliant. The palaces were all built on the same general plan: a complex of rooms and corridors at least two stories high built around a huge central court. The principal building materials were stone, wood, and mud brick; roofs were flat. Rooms and corridors were decorated with fresco paintings in bright colors; Egyptian influence is evident in the style of painting but the Minoans were not rigidly bound by convention so that their compositions were naturalistic and much freer than the Egyptian. Animals, human beings, flowers, outdoor scenes, religious processions, and ceremonials were among the subjects portrayed. The Minoans had a handsome painted pottery that employed floral and marine motifs; fine metal work in gold, silver, and bronze; terra-cotta, ivory, and faience figurines; and stone vases carved in high relief from a soft stone called steatite which had probably been covered with gold leaf.

Industry, Trade, and Colonization.   The Minoans were engaged in agriculture and stock raising. They exported pottery, wine, olive oil, and metal work. From the finds of Minoan pottery in Egypt, Syria, Palestine, the Aegean islands, and Greece, it would appear that the Minoans dominated the carrying trade of the eastern Mediterranean to about the middle of the sixteenth century B.C. They also colonized certain islands in the Aegean, probably for trade. Long ago a Minoan palace was found on the island of Melos, and more recently (since 1967) excavations on the island of Thera at the site of Akrotiri have revealed a whole town, a kind of Minoan Pompeii, that was buried in a volcanic eruption about 1500 B.C.

Religion.   In the Cretan palaces, the presence of numerous rooms used for cult ceremonies might lead us to infer that the Minoan rulers were priest-kings, but for the most part speculation about Minoan religion has to be based on the frescoes, cult objects, and symbols. We can safely assume that there was a fertility cult, and the use of the double

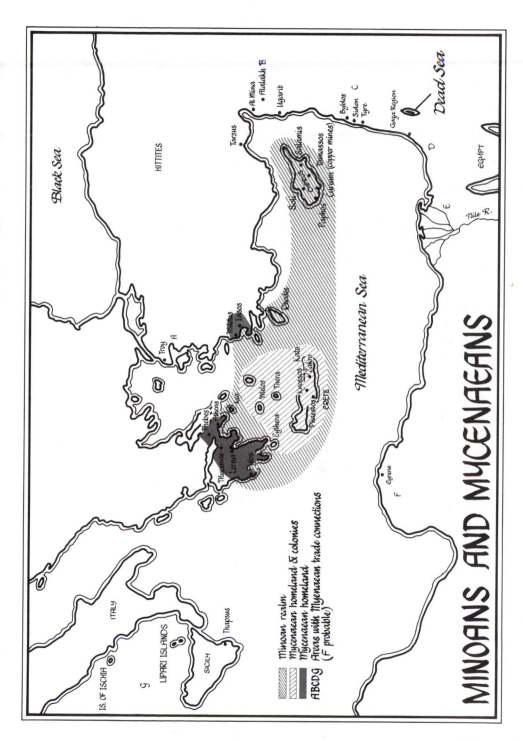

MINOANS AND MYCENAEANS

Black Sea

HITTITES

Troy

Mediterranean Sea

Tarsus

Al Mina
Alalakh B
Ugarit

Byblos
Sidon C
Tyre

Gaza Region

Dead Sea

Nile R.

EGYPT

Soli
Salamis
Curium
Tamassos
Paphos
Curium (copper mines)

Miletus
Lesbos
Rhodes

Iolkos
Thebes
Athens
Mycenae
Lerna
Pylos

Delos
Kea
Melos
Thera
Cythera

KNOSSOS
Kato Zakro
Phaestos
Knossos
CRETE

Cyrene

ITALY

IS. OF ISCHIA

LIPARI ISLANDS

SICILY

Thapsus

Minoan realm
Mycenaean homeland & colonies
Mycenaean homeland
Areas with Mycenaean trade connections
(F probable)

ABCDg

axe symbol makes it probable that the sky god of southwestern Asia Minor was worshipped. There was a stone and pillar cult; birds, snakes, and butterflies appear often in Minoan art and were probably symbolic of certain deities. The bucranium, a bull's head with horns, is also common, and reminds us of the Minotaur story which the Greeks connected with Minos and Knossos. The labyrinth in which the Minotaur was supposed to have been confined makes for interesting speculation, too. To us, the word "labyrinth" means a maze, but its original meaning was "place of the labrys," and labrys is the word for "double axe." One of the great Minoan ceremonies was bull leaping, a rite in which young men and young women, either captives of war or specially trained athletes, attempted to grasp the horns of a wild bull and do a somersault over his back; it is believed that the performance was staged in the great central court of the palace with the populace watching from the windows and galleries of the surrounding rooms.

Writing. The Minoans wrote on stone and pottery but mostly on flat clay tablets. The few texts inscribed on stone or pottery are probably dedications, but the clay tablets are accounts relating to (probably) the receipt of commodities and animals. Only a few hundred texts have been found. Minoan writing, clearly related to similar scripts of Anatolia, came in its final form to use three kinds of characters: (1) signs for numbers, (2) pictographs for objects or things (cattle, grain, vases, and the like), and (3) characters which had syllabic values. There was an early form of the script, called Hieroglyphic, and a later development which we call Linear A. The latter has been deciphered—we know most of the phonetic and other values of the signs—but the texts cannot be read because the underlying language has not been identified.

A still-later, closely related and derivative script called Linear B was found by Evans at Knossos, but the great proportion of the clay tablets we now possess were excavated at Greek sites in the Peloponnesus. Linear B, it now appears, was a late form developed in Greece and brought by Mycenaean invaders and conquerors to Crete. The script was deciphered by Michael Ventris in 1952. Moreover, the tablets can be read because the underlying language is an early dialect of Greek, related in grammar and vocabulary to the language of the Homeric poems, the *Iliad* and the *Odyssey*. The great importance of the Ventris decipherment will emerge from the following discussion.

Mycenaean Civilization

Before 750 B.C., civilization in Greece was confined in time to the period 1550 to 1200 B.C. and in space to the east-central part of Greece and the Peloponnesus, the southern peninsula. Village life had begun fairly early; after 2500 B.C. there was considerable trade, and bronze had been introduced, but, with the exception of Lerna on the Gulf of Argos where a simple palace structure has been discovered, life had not gone beyond the peasant village stage. In the nineteenth century B.C., as the founders of Minoan civilization arrived in Crete, Greece was invaded, and many of the older towns were sacked and burned. The invaders, who may have come from northwestern Asia Minor, were perhaps the first Greek-speaking people to arrive in Greece. In actual fact, the matter is disputed, and the Greeks may not have come until 1550 B.C., but it is not possible to decide the question at the moment.

At any rate, by 1550 B.C. these early Greeks constituted the ruling class in the civilization that had grown up in Greece. One of the most spectacular centers of this culture was located at Mycenae in the northeastern part of the Peloponnesus. Mycenae was traditionally the home of Agamemnon, the legendary king who commanded the besieging force at the equally legendary siege of Troy, and thus we call this early Greek civilization Mycenaean. We also call the people of the period Mycenaeans, as well as applying the term Mycenaean to the Linear B script which they used for writing.

Trade.   Borrowing from the Minoans, but adapting Minoan culture to the different environment of Greece, the Mycenaeans evolved a civilization of their own which flourished in the period 1550 to 1200 B.C. By 1550 B.C., the Mycenaeans had replaced the Minoans in the carrying trade of the eastern Mediterranean; later, they conquered the Minoans and ruled in Crete, and they also colonized Cyprus in large numbers. The extent of Mycenaean trade can be comprehended from the fact that Mycenaean pottery has been found in western and southern Asia Minor, Syria, Palestine, Egypt, and on or just off the coasts of Sicily and Italy.

Culture.   Combining the evidence of the archaeological finds and the Mycenaean tablets, it is possible to reconstruct many features of Mycenaean culture. The Mycenaean realm was divided into a number of independent kingdoms. The kings lived in great fortified palaces built on hilltops. The citadel walls were constructed of huge stones, and they resembled in outward appearance the fortified towns of the contemporary Hittites. Within the fortress was a palace consisting of complexes of rooms surrounding pillared halls *(megarons)* equipped with huge central hearths. The principal megaron was the throne room where royal audiences and possibly religious ceremonies were held. The throne room was decorated with fresco painting, sometimes in the Minoan style but more frequently in a distinctive mainland style. The palaces also included quarters for the women (harems), workshops, and store-

THE LION GATE AT MYCENAE (1875 A.D.)

(After Schliemann)

rooms. It is interesting that at the Mycenaean palace at Pylos in the
southwestern Peloponnesus, the throne room had frescoes representing
griffins, while in the so-called Queen's Megaron in the women's quarters dolphins were represented; the same thing was true of the palace
of Minos in Crete except that the throne room was very small and must
have been used for religious ceremonies rather than royal audiences.

   King and Social Classes.   The Mycenaean king was called the
wanax. This is a term that reeks of theocracy since we know that in later
times the Greeks reserved this appelation for their divinities. Mycenaean social classes included nobles (or warriors), artisans, farmers,
herdsmen, slaves, and religious functionaries. The king's estates were
large, as were those of the religious establishments. The absence of temples, with the exception of a sanctuary found on the island of Keos,
again suggests the priest-king syndrome. Royal families were laid to rest
in great "beehive" tombs of stone, built into hillsides and covered with
earth. Although most of the royal tombs, like the pyramids and rock-

GOLD FACE MASK FROM THE
SHAFT GRAVES AT MYCENAE

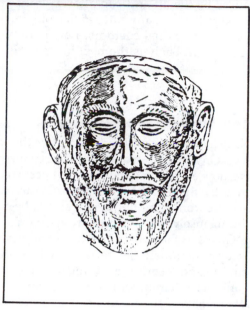

(After Schliemann)

cut tombs of Egypt, were robbed in ancient times, enough of the grave
furniture survives to tell us that the tombs were well worth robbing.

Economy.   Basically, the Mycenaean economy was not much different from that of Crete. Pottery, metal work, ivories, olive oil, wine,
turpentine, and possibly textiles were exported. The numerous words
for artisans of various kinds—weavers, carders, workers in bronze, car-
penters, goldsmiths, and the like—indicate a great specialization of activity. There is much about chariots, for the Mycenaean nobles were
chariot warriors.

Dimly reflected in the Homeric poems, this was the heroic age of
Greece. Whether there was an Agamemnon or a Nestor, whether the
Mycenaeans captured Troy, we cannot know. We do not even know
whether the Mycenaeans had direct contact with the Hittites, a people
who were in many ways very similar and certainly contemporary.

Fall of the Mycenaeans.   About 1200 B.C. many Mycenaean palaces
were attacked and destroyed. It used to be thought that this devastation
was the work of a new wave of Greek invaders from the north who

spoke the Doric dialect of Greek. The Dorians came after 1200 B.C., it is true, but they may well have been able to take advantage of the prostration of Greece caused by the hit-and-run attacks of the same sea raiders who crippled the Near East. At any rate, archaeological evidence dated just before 1000 B.C.—new burial customs, new pottery styles, and the increasing use of iron—probably is the best indicator of the time of the Dorian arrival.

REBUILDING OF GREECE

While the Near East struggled to rebuild after the raids of the thirteenth century B.C., Greece was isolated from the civilized area for many centuries, and the slow evolution of culture that occurred in Greece was largely conditioned by the Greek environment. The new Greeks who settled in Greece were iron-using herdsmen and at best part-time farmers. They imposed themselves as a ruling group upon assorted peoples, Greeks, and pre-Greeks, whom they found in the new land and then spread out to occupy the unfamiliar territory which they would soon call home. The culture and institutions of the invaders had served them well enough in another environment, but adjustments would be necessary if they were to make a go of it in Greece. Thus, between 1200 and 750 B.C., in what we may call the Greek "Dark Ages," a new culture was gradually developed.

The Greek Environment

Greece was never a rich country, even before its overexploitation by man. The soil was thin; in some places there was only bare rock. A few fertile plains could be found in Laconia, Messenia, Boeotia, Euboea, and to a lesser extent in Attica. On the west coast, where there was considerable rainfall, the forest cover was so dense that even in the classical period the region had little agriculture and a small population. On the eastern side with less rainfall the forest cover was not heavy, but as the forests were cut down to increase the arable land, a shortage of wood for building and fuel developed, and erosion set in. Furthermore, as the agricultural area was expanded to grow more wheat and barley for an increasing population, pasture lands were diminished so that horses and cattle became scarce. Beef almost disappeared from the Greek diet as the Greeks were forced to depend upon sheep and goats that could graze on the rocky hillsides and forage for themselves. The more inadequate the land became as a provider of food, the more the

Greeks sought to feed themselves from the sea. "Landlubbers" originally, they learned to sail, to fish, and ultimately to explore the north Mediterranean and Aegean coasts for copper, iron, silver, and gold.

Geographic Units and Political Unification

The rough topography of Greece naturally divides the land into small compartments: valleys and plains. In these geographic units, tiny independent states began to form. Even though the invaders had arrived in large tribal groups, whatever feeling of identity with these "nations" people had once possessed was weakened by the fragmentation that occurred when they settled down to live in one little valley or plain. They began to think of themselves as natives of such a place, separate and distinct from those who lived in neighboring compartments. Outsiders were regarded with suspicion and hostility, and this "in-group" sentiment, combined with the minute dimensions of the natural geographic divisions, brought political unification within them rather swiftly.

In some of the larger compartments, however, the change was gradual and was not completed much before the end of the Dark Ages. Such delays were often due to local rivalries. For example, one site might have become a recognized religious center where people gathered to celebrate periodic festivals; another might be a defensible hilltop, a rallying point in time of danger; still another could have been a likely marketplace or adjacent to a sheltered coastal area where ships could be beached. At any one of these sites there could be some concentration of the population in the form of a large village or even a small town. Nevertheless, in the end, either by mutual consent or by force, unification took place—the Greeks called the process *synoikismos* (setting up house together).

Thus, centers of political life, "capitals," arose, and this brings us to the subject of the Greek *polis,* a word usually translated "city-state." It is necessary to remind the reader that the Greeks used *polis* in several ways. In Athens *the polis* referred to the Acropolis where Mycenaean kings had lived and which in the classical period was the religious center of Athens; *polis* was also a word for "city," and in addition it could denote a "state." Unfortunately, in modern usage "city-state" calls up the image of some late medieval and early modern—or even Sumerian—city-states in which a city dominated the surrounding area where the country people, except for the nobility, did not have the same political rights as the citizens of the city itself. This was not the normal case in Greece. Instead, all the citizens of the *polis* (state), whether they lived in the country or the city, enjoyed equality of participation in the government, in the very least the right to attend and vote in the assembly and later in some instances to be members of the council and to hold office.

The Primitive Indo-European Monarchy

The Greeks brought to Greece a form of political organization which we shall encounter again in Italy; we may call it the primitive Indo-European monarchy. There was a king *(basileus),* a hereditary monarch who had some religious functions and might arbitrate disputes if asked to do so, although he was primarily a war leader who had few powers or duties in peacetime. The king was advised and assisted by a council of elders *(gerousia)* which represented the clans (groups of families), the principal social divisions of the populace. All adult males capable of bearing arms and having the means to provide themselves with weapons and armor could participate in an assembly of the people *(ecclesia).* The king convened and presided over the assembly. It, in turn, elected the new king and alone could confer upon him the power to rule. The assembly could discuss, approve, or reject proposals laid before it by the king. Only the assembly could issue a declaration of war, since in wartime the king was invested with special and extended powers which the people had the sole right to bestow upon him.

Land, Wealth, and Political Power

In accordance with ancestral custom, the invaders had divided up the conquered land. Equal-sized plots of farmland were assigned to each family. This family land could not be bought or sold; it was administered by the patriarch, the head of the family, who directed the labors of his sons and the family servants and slaves. The sons shared equally in the division of the family lands when the patriarch died, and each son became the head of a new family. Such progressive divisions of property soon brought problems for large families since the inherited plots would become too small to support a man and his wife and children. The result was that such an unfortunate might try to bring new land under cultivation, or abandon his farmstead and move to another place, or become a worker or tenant on a larger estate. Moreover, the family plots *(kleroi),* though originally of equal size, had not been of equal fertility. Some farms were ruined by overcropping; others located on the hillsides were damaged by erosion. Big families, poor soil, erosion—it all came to the same thing: before the Greek Dark Ages ended in 750 B.C., a few persons had most of the land, and many families had very little or none at all. Since land was wealth and wealth led to political power, the unequal division of wealth soon brought political inequality. As the poorer citizens were unable to equip themselves for military service, they lost their right to participate in the assembly. The large landholders took over the council of the elders and then began to contest with the king for authority. By progressive steps they stripped the king of his functions and at last abolished the monarchy. At the same time, as the poorer citizens were forced out of the assembly, the landholders and the tenants who were their political satellites came to have a majority in the ecclesia.

Purely economic and environmental factors thus altered governmental form as the monarchy was exchanged for a new kind of government dominated by the great landholders who now constituted a nobility. They called themselves *aristoi*, the best people, and we call this form of government aristocracy. The powers of the king were subdivided and exercised by short-term magistrates chosen from the ranks of the landed aristocrats. One official would be commander-in-chief; another would hold the principal religious authority. Still others would act as judges in cases of dispute over land ownership and similar matters; one is not surprised to learn that the common people complained that the judgments of the aristocratic officials tended to favor the landed class. As for the council, also monopolized by the aristoi, its functions and authority were greatly enlarged as it supervised the officials and decided what matters should be laid before the assembly for consideration.

Overpopulation, Colonization, and Trade

By 750 B.C. many of the Greek states along the east coast faced a serious crisis. The declining fertility of the soil and overdependence on agriculture had resulted in overpopulation. A simple agrarian economy could not sustain the Greeks in Greece any longer. With so many people sunk in poverty and seething with dissatisfaction, something had to be done to relieve pressures that might bring a political explosion. Overpopulation had to be dealt with and the Greek economy diversified. Colonization of lands outside of Greece, shipping off the surplus population, accomplished the first objective, while a gradual development of trade with the new colonies stimulated industry at home and created a diversified economy. In large part, the Greeks after 750 B.C. thus duplicated what the Phoenicians had already done in a similar situation but there was to be a difference: Somehow the Greeks became creators of culture rather than carriers like the Phoenicians. This was the "Greek miracle," a phenomenon which we shall investigate.

GREEK COLONIZATION AND ITS CONSEQUENCES

Between 750 and 500 B.C., thousands of Greeks left their homes in Greece to settle in scores of colonies established in the north Aegean, around the Black Sea, in Sicily, southern Italy, southern France, northeastern Spain, and in Cyrene just west of Egypt in North Africa. Most colonies were formally organized, state-sponsored projects. The home government would select a site for the colony, choose a leader for the expedition, and arrange for the transport of the colonists. Once founded, however, the colony was usually politically independent; it ceased to have political ties with the metropolis, or parent state, unless some military or commercial treaty was later sought by both parties.

Economic, Political, and Social Changes

Even though political connections between metropolis (mother city) and colony were rare, other bonds were not so easily severed. Kinship, common religious beliefs, and pure sentiment helped to maintain a feeling of cordiality between parent and offspring. Trade relationships developed because the colony, lacking economic self-sufficiency, tended to exchange its raw products and foodstuffs for special products and manufactures from the homeland. As trade grew and manufacturing for the colonial market was encouraged, the economy of the metropolis became diversified. A new growth of population was stimulated: States whose land was poor or limited in size could sustain only a few farmers, but they could easily accommodate many more traders and artisans whose activities made it possible to import food. Such states with converted economies flourished, and their villages grew into towns and cities.

As time passed, economic change altered phases of Greek life. The diversified economy led to the formation of a new socioeconomic class of traders and artisans which took its place between the big and small landholders. The growth of manufacturing brought an increase in slavery: Since few of the Greeks at this time were skilled artisans, great numbers of slaves were purchased in Near Eastern markets and transported to Greece to serve as metal workers, potters, makers of textiles, and the like.

New social and economic patterns necessitated change in governmental form. Of itself, the growth of the city complicated problems of government. The new "middle" class, whose interests might clash with those of the landed aristocrats, would challenge the monopoly of the great landlords and demand a voice in government. Custom and religion were bound to be affected by the alterations in economics and society. All these changes, as well as renewed contact with the outside world, would influence and stimulate developments in literature, art, and thought. Accumulation of capital from the growing prosperity would encourage patronage of culture, thus providing opportunity and support for creative activity.

Cultural Borrowing

Although colonization and its economic consequences brought Greece out of barbarism and back to civilization, the *form* that this new and complex Greek culture took was determined in large part by a renewal of contact with the Near East in the years following 750 B.C. Left to themselves, the Greeks might have developed a very different civilization, but as it was they borrowed heavily and adapted Near Eastern culture to their own needs. Economic development reached a point at which the Greeks had to make provision for a system of writing, certain business procedures, and an organized legal system. To satisfy these needs the Greeks adopted ready-made culture traits: They borrowed and adapted the Semitic alphabet, Near Eastern business methods, and the form of the Mesopotamian law codes, along with the Babylonian system of weights and measures. These things were probably borrowed directly from the Phoenicians with whom the Greeks were now trading, but the trade with the Near East was not entirely a one-way affair since the Greeks had begun to sail to the Syro-Palestinian coast and Egypt. Culture traits as well as foreign goods were brought home from the Near East; in art, literature, religion, science, mathematics, and other fields the Greeks received novel ideas and concepts from their more civilized neighbors.

The emergence of the Greeks from the Dark Ages had very nearly coincided with the economic and cultural revival of the Near East. A rebirth of trade and industry had occurred in Syria and along the Phoenician coast in the tenth century B.C. By 850 B.C., the Phoenicians were well embarked on a commercial career, conducting their growing trade with Cyprus, Asia Minor, and the western Mediterranean. It was not an accident that the so-called Asiatic or Eastern Greeks, who lived in western Asia Minor and the Aegean islands just offshore, were the first to become civilized and that the beginnings of Greek philosophy, certain types of sculpture and architecture, an "orientalizing" style of art, and a new poetry should appear in exactly those areas that were first in contact with Phoenicia.

We know too little about these Eastern Greeks. Presumably they had left the Greek mainland to settle in Asia Minor in the ninth century B.C. or perhaps earlier. As the Dark Ages ended, their situation was never as desperate as that of the Greeks back home, since the Eastern

Greeks had good agricultural land, a flourishing textile industry of native origin, and access to minerals and wood. Large and prosperous
towns—Miletus, Ephesus, Smyrna, and others—came into existence
and began to trade before comparable population centers developed in
Greece, but in the seventh century the Asiatic Greeks had come under
the control of Lydia, and with the overthrow of Croesus by the Persians
the Eastern Greeks lost their freedom to Cyrus the Great and his successors. This political misfortune proved damaging to East Greek trade
and appreciably slowed the pace of cultural development so that initiative in formulating Greek civilization was transferred to the mainland of
Greece itself.

Greek Trade

Certain island states, particularly Aegina and some of the towns of
Euboea, along with the mainland towns of Corinth, Megara, and Si-
cyon, had been affected by developments on the other side of the Aegean and had followed the lead of the Asiatic Greeks. Aegina traded
with Egypt, while Chalcis in Euboea began to trade with the north Aegean and also with the Etruscans in Italy; Corinth and Megara colonized
and engaged in commerce with the west as well as with the north Aegean and the western end of the Black Sea, beginning soon after 750 B.C.
When the East Greek towns became subject to Persia, the rival trading
powers across the Aegean simply took over their foreign trade and prospered even more.

Triangular Patterns.   Greek trade was often organized in triangular
patterns. The Greeks wanted the spices, perfumes, foodstuffs, and
other products of Egypt, but they had little of their own that was of
interest to Egyptian buyers. On the other hand, Egypt was eager for
silver and, to a lesser degree, gold. The Greeks solved this problem by
taking their own manufactures to the north Aegean where they could
be exchanged for silver and gold from the mines of that area. The precious metals were then shipped to Egypt to purchase the commodities
wanted back home in Greece. The Corinthians followed a similar procedure in their trade with the western Mediterranean: Corinthian manufactures were traded through their colonies up the Adriatic for silver
brought down from the mines of central Europe, and then the precious
metal was exchanged for foodstuffs and raw products in Sicily and
South Italy, where silver was in great demand.

Coined Money.   To facilitate this bullion trade in silver and gold,
the Greeks adopted—or perhaps were responsible for—the new invention of coined money. The precious metals, measured by weight, had

long been used in the Near East as media of exchange, and in Greece a similar practice was beginning to replace the barter economy of the Dark Ages. Gold and silver ingots, nuggets, and gold dust were familiar forms, but coins did not appear until at least the end of the eighth century B.C. and possibly later. The coin, a piece of metal of definite shape and weight, bearing the symbol of the issuing authority as a guarantee of its weight and purity, was a great convenience in trade. Coins did not need to be weighed; they could be transported easily, counted quickly, and thus exchanged with facility. Most of the coins used in the international trade of the seventh and sixth centuries were pieces of gold, silver, or electrum (an alloy of gold and silver). It is important to understand that they functioned not as money but as bullion. It was only later that coins were used as money for local transactions in the Greek states themselves; then, smaller denominations and particularly bronze coins for small change made their appearance.

Political Changes

Along with other changes, the political changes in Greece at this time led to new institutions and ways of life.

Revolution and Tyrants.   Turning now to political changes after 750 B.C., we have seen that the impending conflict between the big landholders and the impoverished small farmers in mainland Greece had been averted in many states by colonization, but the rise of a new socioeconomic class as a result of the growth of trade and industry created new political problems. When the great nobles ignored the demands of the middle class for reform and greater participation in government, revolutions sometimes occurred. Often, these uprisings against the aristocrats were led by men who were themselves of noble birth but who had chosen to join the opposing faction in order to gain power or wealth or even to satisfy patriotic impulses. Successful leaders of this type were known as *tyrants*.

Tyrannos, the Greek word for tyrant, appears to have been of Lydian origin; it originally meant "lord" or "leader" and did not have the modern connotation of "despot." The tyrants had first made their appearance among the Eastern Greeks. They were essentially dictators who seized control during periods of civil strife; some of them may have come to power in the crisis of the Cimmerian invasion of the early seventh century. Many became long-term heads of state who did not abolish the councils or assemblies but prolonged the existence of those bodies as part of the machinery of government. The tyrants promoted and gave direction to the economic development of the cities which they ruled. When the Lydian kingdom extended its sway over the East Greek towns in the late seventh and early sixth centuries B.C., the tyrants fell, but tyranny was a culture trait diffused from Asia Minor to mainland Greece, where it took a slightly different form.

In Greece, especially in the seventh and sixth centuries B.C., tyrants led the middle class, or the poor farmers, or both groups, against the entrenched aristocrats. Often, but not always, the tyrant was a political boss who did not change the constitution or hold state office but operated behind the scenes making sure that his candidates secured the magistracies and controlled the council. The great landholders were sometimes exiled and their lands confiscated. They were replaced in the government by representatives of the middle class with the frequent result that when the tyranny fell or the tyrant died, occasionally the businessmen as a class would gain more influence in politics. The mainland tyrants promoted trade and manufacturing; they also aided the poorer citizens with gifts of land or by setting up public works projects that not only beautified their cities but provided work for those who could not make a living by full-time farming. Many of the tyrants were patrons of culture; they subsidized artists, literary men, and philosophers whom they invited to come to their towns. The Greek tyrant, like the nineteenth century (A.D.) Latin American *caudillo*, or dictator, was likely to appear when a state had reached a certain point in its political and economic development. Whatever his personal aims may have been, a Greek tyrant—whether intentionally or not—often brought about the overthrow of a political monopoly and provided a measure of political stability, if not freedom, until the state in question gained sufficient economic and political maturity to get along without him.

Military Development.   The rise of the middle class to political power in Greece had been aided not only by the creation of new sources of wealth through business or by the immediate intervention of the tyrants, but also by a military development. During the Dark Ages the mainstay of the army had been the chariot warrior, with the spear-bearing foot soldier playing only a minor part. In this "Homeric" type of warfare the nobles with their horses and chariots did most of the fighting. We have already noted, however, the diminution of pasture land that brought a decrease in the numbers of cattle and horses. The shortage of horses and the consequent increase in their price made them almost too valuable to be risked in warfare. Then, in the seventh century, a new type of warfare came into Greece from Asia Minor; this was based on the *phalanx*, or packed mass of heavy-armed foot soldiers. Chariots tended to become obsolete because they were ineffective against the solid wall of the phalanx bristling with spears. The key to the phalanx was manpower. The nobles were too few to man it; consequently, the middle class whose members could afford the heavy armor and new weapons became indispensable to the state. Because of their growing numbers in the assembly and because of their value to the phalanx, the new class could not long be denied increased participation in the government. Sometimes the aristocrats were forced by military necessity to compromise and open the council and some of the offices to the businessmen; in such case, the intermediate step of tyranny could be avoided.

Timocracy Prevails.   By the sixth century B.C., aristocracy as a form of government was the exception rather than the rule, just as monarchy had given way to aristocracy at the close of the Dark Ages. The prevailing governmental form was now *timocracy*, a government in which citizens participate in proportion to their wealth. Typically, in a timocracy the richest citizens would be able to hold any of the offices of state, be members of the council, and participate in the assembly; those of more moderate means would hold minor posts, be eligible for the council, and vote in the assembly; the poorer citizens might be restricted to the assembly, and the poorest might well be excluded entirely from governmental participation. Timocracy had its origin in the development of sources of wealth other than land. Trade and industry had created new ways of acquiring wealth, and thus, according to Greek thinking, people of substance had a right to be represented in the government.

MAJOR GREEK STATES OF THE SIXTH CENTURY

As the sixth century B.C. drew to a close, mainland Greece had become the home of several states notable for political, military, or economic strength. These were Athens, Sparta, Corinth, Thebes, and Argos. All were situated on the eastern side of Greece, with Thebes and Athens in the central area and the other three in the southern peninsula, the Peloponnesus. Only about fifty miles separated Thebes, farthest north, from Sparta, farthest south, yet in this tiny cockpit the main drama of Greek history was to be played out (550–350 B.C.). Very little is known of the internal history of Thebes, and certainly not enough about Corinth and Argos. Athens and Sparta we know better because they had the leading roles in the fifth century B.C., a circumstance that led the ancient writers to deal copiously with them to the neglect of the history of the other states. Thebes was a land-locked city-state in the midst of the fertile region of Boeotia. Corinth was a great commercial and industrial state possessed of considerable naval strength. Argos, important in Mycenaean times but declining at the end of the Dark Ages, was still a force to be reckoned with. Corinth typified the new era (750–500 B.C.), while Thebes and Argos seemed backward and atavistic by comparison. Sparta and Athens, each in its own way, were atypical;

unlike Corinth, neither had followed the pattern of development already outlined for the Age of Colonization but both had arrived at greatness before the end of the sixth century B.C.

Sparta

Sparta differed from other Greek states in its size, resources, and historical development. The territory of Laconia controlled by Sparta was much larger than that of the ordinary Greek state, and it contained some of the most fertile land in Greece. It was in its political evolution, however, that Sparta could most justly claim to be unique.

Rulers and Subjects.   The ruling element in Laconia was Dorian, as it was also in Corinth and Argos. The Dorian conquerors of Laconia had taken over the most fertile land and forced the natives to cultivate the soil as *helots*, or serfs. Before the end of the Dark Ages, the inhabitants of mountain and coastal areas had been made subject to Sparta; since their lands ringed the fertile Laconian plain, these people were known as *perioeci*, "dwellers around." The perioeci had local self-government, but their foreign relations were in Spartan hands, and they had to furnish contingents for the Spartan army in time of war.

Government.   Sparta itself was a *polis*, or city-state, which controlled the surrounding area of Laconia. Spartan citizens who could perform military service participated in the assembly, or *apella* as it was called in Sparta. There was a council of the elders, composed of the senior representatives of twenty-eight noble clans. What was truly remarkable was that the monarchy had not been abolished, but even more startling and unusual was the fact that Sparta had two royal families and two kings. We may guess that this dual monarchy had been the result of some ancient compromise.

In spite of its fertility, Laconia had known land hunger. Just before 700 B.C. colonists had been sent to Tarentum in southern Italy, and in the seventh century Laconia also participated in the colonization of Cyrene in North Africa. In a less conventional move to assuage the desire for land, Spartan aristocrats had invaded and conquered a fertile plain in Messenia, just across the mountains to the west of Laconia. About 630 B.C., however, the Messenians rose in revolt, drove out the Spartans, and invaded Laconia. In this extremity, the aristocrats were forced to seek the aid of the common people. Messenia was reconquered, but the nobles had to repay the commoners by acceding to an extensive reorganization of the Spartan economy and governmental system. These reforms, once credited to a semilegendary lawgiver named Lycurgus, we now know to have been gradually accomplished over a long period of years and still in progress in the mid-sixth century B.C. Sweeping change made Sparta into a unique state dissimilar to any other in Greece. The completed arrangements may be described as follow.

Citizen Warriors.   Private ownership of land was abolished. The state controlled the land and distributed farms of equal size to heads of families, along with helots to work the land for the citizen tenants. Henceforth the adult male citizen had two responsibilities: to see that his farm maintained a certain rate of productivity and to perform what amounted to nearly lifelong, continuous military service. These citizen warriors had to be constantly alert to prevent a helot uprising or to fight off outside enemies who might wish to invade the rich country of Laconia and Messenia. The job of policing Laconia itself was not easy since the perioeci might become restive and the helots, always dangerous, outnumbered the Spartans about twelve to one. This was one reason why Spartan policy was generally isolationist; they had enough to worry about at home without getting involved in trouble abroad.

Sparta became completely militarized. Every man was a soldier, and his training, or indoctrination, began at the tender age of seven when he was taken from home and put into barracks with other boys. Until a citizen was thirty years old he continued to live in the barracks where he underwent a regimen that developed his physique, made him skilled in the use of weapons, and trained him to execute military maneuvers with the precision that was essential for the effectiveness of the new phalanx formation. This made the Spartan army practically invincible since all other Greeks were, at best, summertime soldiers.

On the other hand, political, economic, and cultural evolution ended for Sparta. Time stood still. The reforms brought Sparta a strength and security that were temporarily beneficial, but the rest of the world moved on, and the Spartans were eventually left behind. Their state was overcome in the fourth century because they had not adapted themselves to the changing times.

Ephors: Guardians of People's Rights.   The kings, the council of the elders, and the apella were left unchanged under the new system adopted after the Messenian war, but a new feature was added: this was the board of five *ephors* annually elected by the assembly. The ephors were supposed to guard the people's rights achieved by the reforms and to see that no alterations were made in the system now adopted. Possessing power superior to that of the kings, the ephors supervised the kings closely; they could even fine the kings or force them to abdicate. The ephors conducted the foreign relations of Sparta, and at home they had the responsibility to oversee and regulate every phase of public and private life.

Peloponnesian League.   Once established, the Spartan system was unchanged for nearly 200 years. Only one important addition was made: This was the formation of the Peloponnesian League which began to be organized about 560 B.C. and was virtually completed by 500. The league consisted of a series of alliances contracted by Sparta on the one hand and individual Peloponnesian states on the other; each state was bound to Sparta by a separate treaty. The alliances were defensive in intent; the treaty makers were pledged to aid one another in case of enemy attack. This created a ring of buffer states around Laconia that would reinforce the protective shell provided by the perioeci. In addition, the Peloponnesian League made the Spartans the leaders of a powerful military machine which completely outclassed the land forces of any possible enemy or combination of enemies in Greece. When the Spartans broke the power of hostile Argos by a victory in 547 B.C., they became supreme in the Peloponnesus. It was fortunate for the rest of the Greeks that the policy of Sparta was isolationist and defensive and that the forces of the Peloponnesian League could be mobilized only for defense and not for aggression. If the Spartans had turned to imperialism in the sixth century B.C., they might have subjected most of Greece to their rule.

Athens

Athens, destined to become the principal opponent of Sparta, represented the other side of the coin. Where Sparta was a land power, archaic in political institutions, and isolationist in policy, Athens was to become a sea power, attempt a daring experiment in democratic government, and embark upon a militant imperialism. Sparta completed its evolution and had attained its major characteristics by 500 B.C., while the Athens just described was to develop its salient features in the fifty years after that. The story of Athens in the fifth century B.C. will be introduced later in our narrative; for the present, we shall content ourselves with a survey of Athenian history to the close of the sixth century.

Geography.   Attica, the territory in which Athens was situated, was neither as large nor as fertile as Laconia. It possessed some arable plains, good clay, fine marble, and forest reserves that lasted until the end of the fifth century. Two possessions of value were not exploited by the Athenians before 500 B.C.: deposits of silver at Laurium and a fine harbor, the Piraeus. Attica is triangular; two sides are defined and defended by sea boundaries, but the landward side of the Attic peninsula posed some problems in antiquity. Adjoining Attica on the west was Boeotia, dominated by hostile Thebes; to the southwest was Megara, a

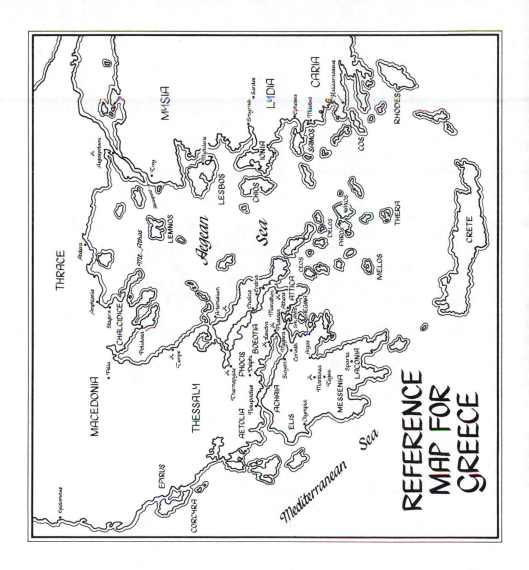

REFERENCE
MAP FOR
GREECE

117

tiny Dorian state that was not always an effective buffer between Athens and her other archenemy, Corinth.

According to recent opinion, Attica was fairly prosperous during the Dark Ages. At any rate, population pressures that promoted foreign colonization by Corinth and Megara in the eighth and early seventh centuries do not seem to have disturbed Attica until after 650 B.C., when it was too late for the Athenians to share in the colonization movement. This meant that Athens would have to solve its problems in a different way, and so, like Sparta, its history would not follow usual patterns.

From Monarchy to Aristocracy.   The march of events at Athens is obscured from us until well into the second half of the seventh century B.C. By that time the monarchy had been abolished and the functions of the king divided among several annually elected magistrates chosen from the ranks of the landed aristocrats. These officials were called *archons*. One, known simply as *the* archon, headed the administration of Athens; another was the war-archon *(polemarch)*; still another was a kind of high priest called the *archon basileus*, or king archon; by 620 B.C. six other archons, the *thesmothetai*, had been added to the list to serve as judges. A council manned by nobles was called the *Areopagus* because it met on the hill of that name just northwest of the Acropolis. All citizens able to perform military service were eligible to participate in the assembly *(ecclesia)*, but a large number of people had already been excluded from this body by reason of their poverty.

Solon.   Trouble had been brewing for some time. There had been an unsuccessful attempt to establish a tyranny, perhaps even before 620 B.C., and about that date the aristocrats had been forced to consent to an elementary codification of the law, presumably because the administration of justice had been abused by the nobles. At last, a real crisis developed, and revolution was averted only at the cost of sweeping political and economic reforms. In 594 B.C., or possibly as late as 570, the constitution was suspended, and a single lawgiver, or *nomothete*, was given the authority to make changes that would save the state from chaos. Solon, a distinguished citizen trusted by both nobles and commons, was authorized to institute the necessary reforms. Emergency legislation enacted by Solon canceled the mortgages that bound many small farmers to their own lands where they had been forced to labor for their creditors; other citizens who had been sold into slavery were redeemed and emancipated at public expense, and debt slavery in any form was henceforth prohibited in Attica.

Economic Reforms.   These measures forestalled a revolution. They were remedies for an immediate situation, but Solon realized the neces-

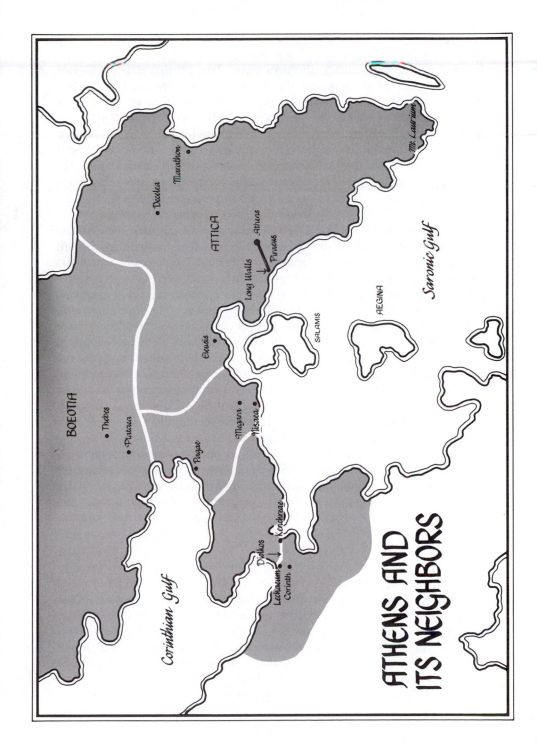

ATHENS AND ITS NEIGHBORS

Corinthian Gulf

BOEOTIA

- Thebes
- Plataea
- Pagae

- Eleusis
- Megara
- Nisaea

Diolkos
- Lechaeum
- Corinth
- Kenchreae

ATTICA

- Decelea
- Marathon
- Athens
- Piraeus
- Mt. Laurium

Long Walls

SALAMIS

AEGINA

Saronic Gulf

sity for more drastic changes in order to cure the basic ills of the country and prevent new crises from arising. Attica must be freed from her over-dependence on agriculture; the economy must be diversified. To this end, Solon sought to encourage the development of trade and industry. He promoted the production and export of olive oil, a commodity of superior quality in Attica. This would be a cash crop that could be traded abroad for food and raw materials. To stimulate industry, Solon offered Athenian citizenship to foreign artisans who would settle in Attica and produce their wares for local consumption and export. Athenians were encouraged to apprentice their sons to these artisans in order that farm boys might learn a trade and find a place in the new economy.

Constitutional Reforms: The Timocracy.   Constitutional as well as economic reforms were made by Solon. He transformed the government from an aristocracy into a timocracy by arranging the citizens in census classes according to their wealth and fixing the degree of political participation for each class. The *thetes,* the poorest citizens, were admitted to the assembly *(ecclesia)* even though they were unable to perform military service. People of moderate means were allowed to hold minor offices and perhaps be elected to the council as well as to participate in the assembly. The archonships, other offices, the council, and the assembly were of course all open to the wealthiest citizens. To forestall abuses of power by the masses, who could now outvote the wealthier citizens in the assembly, Solon bestowed upon the Areopagus the privilege of reviewing legislation passed in the assembly; the Areopagus could invalidate measures which it deemed unconstitutional. Solon also promulgated a new law code, less harsh and more comprehensive than the older one of the seventh century, and he created a court of appeal called the *heliaia.* Any citizen sentenced by a magistrate to the penalty of death, exile, or a heavy fine could appeal the case to the heliaia. The exact composition of this court is somewhat in doubt, but the evidence suggests that the heliaia was actually the ecclesia sitting as a court to hear such appeals.

Solon thus averted a revolution, liberalized the Athenian government, and reconstituted the Athenian economy. The export of olive oil stimulated the growth of a pottery industry. At first the potters made the containers in which the oil was exported, but later they also began to make and sell abroad extremely handsome painted vases used for tableware and other purposes. Other types of manufacturing developed as producers were able to exploit markets opened up by the oil trade. A middle class spawned by trade and industry soon appeared and, as elsewhere in Greece, entered the political arena.

Struggle for Political Supremacy.   It may have been a full generation before the Solonian reforms began to take effect in politics, economics, and social structure. According to tradition, there was a period of factional strife after Solon completed his year as lawgiver, but we do not have any clear view of Athenian affairs until about 560 B.C. That year found three parties locked in a struggle for political supremacy: the landed aristocrats who were trying to retain their ebbing power; a faction probably representing the new middle class; and a third group composed mainly of impoverished small farmers. The leader of this last faction was a noble named Peisistratus who established a tyranny in 546 B.C. after two previous and unsuccessful attempts. Peisistratus drove out some of the nobles and confiscated their lands, won the support of the business class, and directed the affairs of Athens until he died in 527. Cultivating close relations with states likely to increase Athenian commerce and continuing the liberal citizenship policy of Solon so that more foreign traders and artisans settled in Athens, Peisistratus built up trade and industry until his state was more than a match for its main competitor, Corinth. Some of the landless were given land; others found employment in the public works program of Peisistratus which aimed at the adornment of the Acropolis, the religious center of Athens, and other parts of the town. Peisistratus was a notable patron of culture who brought artists, poets, and philosophers to Athens. He inaugurated dramatic contests in honor of the god Dionysus; these were the forerunners of the great Athenian tragedies and comedies of the next century. Peisistratus in addition enlarged and elaborated the Panathenaic festival which honored the goddess Athena, and this gave Athens a religious pageant rivaling the Isthmian, Nemean, and Delphic games in other parts of Greece and nearly competitive in fame with the Olympic festival which honored Zeus at Olympia in Elis.

It was probably Peisistratus who introduced the first official Athenian coinage that evolved into the familiar type bearing the head of Athena on the obverse and her symbol, the owl, on the reverse along with the accompanying inscription alpha-theta-epsilon (α θ ε) that suggested Athena, the patron goddess of Athens, or Athenaioi (the Athenians themselves).

Looking at the Peisistratid period as a whole and including the years 527–510 B.C. when his sons, Hippias and Hipparchus, attempted to prolong the tyranny, we can see the emergence of many diverse currents and the evolution of certain policies that would plague the Athenians for years to come. An influx of foreigners who were offered citizenship but later denied full civic rights was a festering problem that had to be solved by the reforms of Cleisthenes after 508 B.C., although this did not remove the hostility of native-born Athenians who resented the prosperity of the aliens and often suspected them of treachery as well. Then there were long-standing feuds among the Athenian noble clans that antedated Peisistratus himself, and these would continue well into the fifth century as long as political leaders were mostly recruited from the nobility. The powerful clan of the Alcmaeonidae, buttressed by marital alliances with other clans, would be opposed by other great families, as we shall see. The Alcmaeonidae, for example, allied with Peisistratus in his second attempt at tyranny and then, responsible for his overthrow in 557 B.C., were themselves exiled when he returned to power in 546. Undaunted, they were avenged when Hippias was overthrown in 510 B.C. In discussing the years to come we shall encounter numerous Athenian leaders who were either Alcmaeonids themselves or had marital connections with the clan: Cleisthenes, Xanthippus, Pericles, and Alcibiades, to mention some of the most important. Representatives of another clan, the Philaidae, included Miltiades, his son Cimon, and his daughter Elpinice who married Callias, a cousin of Aristides. Miltiades, Aristides, and Callias were generals in the battle of Marathon. These names have been introduced here to illustrate the influential position of the nobility in Athenian politics and for future reference because they will ultimately occur in the narrative. Perhaps at this point, if just for contrast, Themistocles, a maverick of obscure ancestry whose mother was not an Athenian, should be mentioned. Though young, he is said by some to have fought at Marathon; in the first decade of the fifth century he was already a leader of some consequence and later would become the father of the Athenian navy and also contribute to the defeat of the Persians and the building of the Athenian democracy.

After the death of Peisistratus, new problems arose that did not admit of quick resolution, so it is not enough to say that the Athenians tired of tyranny and disposed of his sons, Hippias and Hipparchus, who had succeeded him in power; Hipparchus was killed in an uprising in 514 B.C., and Hippias was expelled with Spartan aid four years later. This, incidentally, was not the end of Hippias since he had left behind a considerable following of supporters in Athens who conspired for his return while he himself sought help from the Persians to accomplish his restoration; the specter of his potential return would haunt the Athenians for thirty years.

This was not the only difficulty that appeared on the horizon after Peisistratus died. For one thing the world situation changed when, after 514 B.C., the Persians moved across from Asia into Europe and gained control of the gold mines of Mt. Pangaeus in Thrace that had supported the tyranny in Athens for many years. Furthermore, while Peisistratus had maintained friendly relations with Thebes and Corinth, Theban good will was lost in 519 B.C. when the Athenians made an alliance with

Plataea just over the Boeotian border, a move that saved Plataea from incorporation into the Boeotian League headed by Thebes and gave the Athenians a vital strategic post that could block a Theban invasion of Attica. A short time later the Corinthians became alarmed as the growing trade of Athens began to threaten Corinthian prosperity. Not only that, but the friendship of Argos and Athens seemed to endanger the security of both Sparta and Corinth.

Cleisthenes. The departure of Hippias left the Athenians free to fight among themselves once more. There was a conservative faction backed by Sparta that wanted to scrap the liberal reforms of Solon and rescind the policy of giving citizenship to foreigners; the absent Hippias still had a sizable following in Athens that plotted for his return; and there was a liberal party with democratic inclinations led by a young noble named Cleisthenes. After attacks and counterattacks and interference by the Spartans, the liberals were finally victorious. In 508 B.C. Cleisthenes was given powers resembling those of Solon with a mandate to revise the constitution. Perhaps following on the heels of a military reform, Cleisthenes divided the Athenian citizen body into ten tribes—previously there had been only four. Each tribe then annually elected fifty councillors who took their places in a new council, or *boule*, called the Council of the 500; the councillors were chosen from persons enrolled in the middle and upper census classes. The old council, the Areopagus, was not abolished; it retained its power of legislative review, but henceforth its members were ex-archons. The army consisted of ten tribal regiments, each of which annually elected its own general, or *strategos*. The ten *strategoi* composed a military board which operated under the presidency of the war archon *(polemarch)*.

The new Council of the 500 was larger and more representative than the Areopagus had been. It was supposed to supervise the activities of the magistrates and other officials; it deliberated on matters of policy previous to meetings of the assembly; and it drafted legislative measures to be submitted to the assembly for enactment. The ancients believed that the Council of the 500 superseded a Council of the 400 introduced by Solon, but the matter is debatable.

Deme Membership. Perhaps one of the most important changes effected by Cleisthenes was his introduction of *deme* membership as the test or badge of citizenship. A *deme* was a small geographic division or ward in Attica, and henceforth a citizen was registered as such in his own deme so that the presence of his name in the deme rolls constituted proof of citizenship. Formerly, citizenship had been based on membership in a clan or *phratry* (brotherhood, a sort of artificial clan), and apparently many foreigners who had been granted citizenship by Solon or

Peisistratus had been prevented from acquiring full civic rights because religious or social obstacles had been set in their path by conservative Athenians who were not in sympathy with the liberal citizenship policies. Transferring the matter to the demes took it out of the realm of religion and traditional social organization and into that of the purely civic or political.

By the end of the sixth century B.C., then, Athens had achieved a diversified economy and great prosperity. Solon's timocracy had been translated into a reality when Peisistratus broke the power of the nobles, while the reforms of Cleisthenes carried the Athenian constitution one more step toward the democracy which was to be created in the fifth century B.C.

THE SOUL, THE HANDS, AND THE INTELLECT

We have called the period 750–500 B.C. the Age of Colonization, but it has other names. Art historians call it the Archaic Period. If, however, one plans to consider the Greek achievements in literature and philosophy together with the development of architecture, sculpture, and painting in this age, the Greek Renaissance would not be an inappropriate title. In fact, there are a number of similarities between the European Renaissance that followed on the heels of the Middle Ages and the lively growth of culture in Greece after the end of the Greek Dark Ages. In both instances people were stimulated to creativity by contact with an ancient civilization that was new to them; the Greeks could build upon the culture of the Near East, and the Europeans began to build upon classical Greco-Roman remains rediscovered at the beginning of their renaissance. In both cases there was a further stimulus to be derived from exploration and the discovery of new worlds. The accumulation of wealth from trade and an economy reborn in each case provided the patronage so essential to the support of creativity. These are only a few of the many parallels between the two periods that might be mentioned.

We have also spoken of the similarities between Phoenicians and Greeks. Why were the Greeks creators and the Phoenicians mainly purveyors of civilization? Perhaps because the Phoenicians were part of the Near East, too familiar with its culture and too close to the great centers of origin to attain cultural independence, whereas the Greeks were farther away, and, exposed to the novelty of a foreign culture, they were able to take various items out of context and use them differently. New culture traits are often devised by picking and choosing old elements and combining them in new ways, and this is what the Greeks had an opportunity to do.

Poetry of the Epic Style

In the Dark Ages, and perhaps even in the Mycenaean Age, the Greeks possessed poetry of the epic style, composed in hexameters and orally transmitted. The deeds of heroes provided the subject matter for these poems, and the stories were those of great campaigns: the Trojan war, the Seven against Thebes, and the like. In their original form these poems were ballads, very like the Sumerian tales of the adventures of Gilgamesh. The culmination of the epic tradition was reached just as the Greek Renaissance began, just before the alphabet began to come into common use and a written literature commenced. Two magnificent epics, the *Iliad* and the *Odyssey*, date from this transitional age. The ancients ascribed both to the authorship of Homer, although for a variety of reasons these poems seem to be the work of two separate poets.

Homer's Poetry.   The *Iliad* and the *Odyssey*, in the view of Greeks and Romans for centuries to come, represented the ultimate in poetry which no other work ever surpassed. Even today the poetic beauty, marvelous similes, and engrossing plots of these two epics have not lost their power to charm. The *Iliad* is a tragedy in the Greek sense based upon an incident at the siege of Troy—the wrath of Achilles and its consequences. Our sympathies are not with the Achaeans but with the Trojans, as they are meant to be. The stubbornness of Agamemnon or the adolescent pride of Achilles are of little consequence when set beside the tragic fate of Hector, the widowhood of Andromache, and the brutal humiliation of the aged, grief-stricken Priam when he comes to the Greek camp to beg for the body of his son. This is not the work of some ballad minstrel of a dark age—it is far too sophisticated for that.

The *Odyssey* is unlike the *Iliad* in form and purpose. A novel rather than a tragedy, it achieves unity by a combination of two separate stories: the wanderings of Odysseus and his return to Ithaca. The first weaves together a number of already ancient Oriental folk tales, while the theme of the return of the hero was a favorite of the Dark Ages. Everyone knew the story of the House of Atreus and the disastrous return of Agamemnon. The homecoming of Odysseus seems to have been deliberately modeled on this, but its novelty and the proof of its sophistication lay in the fact that it showed the other side of the coin and came to a happier conclusion.

The influence of these Homeric poems was pervasive and long-lasting. Painters and sculptors were inspired to depict the heroes and memorable scenes from the siege of Troy or the return of Odysseus. Later poets were measured by the yardstick of Homer; even prose writers were subjected to the same treatment by literary critics in antiquity. Homer was the first author to be studied when little children went to school; his verses were memorized, and grown men quoted lines from the *Iliad* or the *Odyssey* to make a point or settle an argument just as today it is customary to snatch a tag from Shakespeare or the Bible.

Hesiod's Poetry.   Another teacher of the Greeks was Hesiod, who also employed the epic hexameter and probably lived about 700 B.C. Two poems, perhaps again by separate authors, were attributed to Hesiod— the *Works and Days* and the *Theogony*. The first is a long and not particularly unified didactic treatise containing precepts of morality, a discourse on the best methods of farming, and ending with a list of taboos and an enumeration of what Hesiod considered lucky and unlucky days of the month. The *Theogony* is a cosmological poem describing the origin of the world and the genealogy of the gods. The ethical concerns of Hesiod remind us forcibly of the preoccupation of the Hebrew prophets and Zoroaster with morality, and modern scholarship has demonstrated the Near Eastern origin of many of Hesiod's cosmological concepts as well as the myths and legends he relates. Like the poet of the *Odyssey*, Hesiod was affected and inspired by the Near Eastern lore that was beginning to seep into the Aegean world.

New Poetic Forms.   As Greek life changed in the new period, as a different economy was shaped, as people became aware of the world outside of their little valleys and plains, and as the bustling tempo of the new cities and new political forms replaced older modes of existence, poetry changed, too, in order to be expressive of the new era. The epic style gave way to novel meters and forms, some of which may have been devised by the Greeks and others which were probably borrowed from Asia Minor. Among the new poetic forms were the elegy, the personal and choral lyric, and the iambic.

Recited to the accompaniment of a reed pipe or flute, the elegy was used for martial poems, or war songs; it was employed for love poetry; and Solon used the elegiac form to advocate his reforms at Athens. The iambic, sharper than the elegy and very much like speech itself, was a form adaptable to satire and some didactic purposes. Lyric poetry, on the other hand, was sung to the accompaniment of a stringed instrument. The personal lyric, recited by a single performer, was best for love poetry and drinking songs. The choral lyric was performed by groups of singers for processionals, funeral dirges, marriage songs, and hymns of victory.

With regard to this new poetry, it is worth noting that many of its first exponents were Asiatic Greeks: Callinus of Ephesus with his martial elegies, Archilochus of Paros who composed iambics, Alcaeus and the poetess, Sappho, of Lesbos, who were superb in the personal lyric, and the famous Asiatic Greek Alcman who brought the choral lyric to

Sparta. Solon and possibly Tyrtaeus (martial elegies) were Athenians and thus mainland Greeks, and this was also true of Theognis, the elegaic poet from Megara.

Second, whereas the epic had been composed and transmitted orally, the new poetry was soon written down if not originally committed to writing; some poems, in fact, were intended to be inscribed on gravestones and the like. The alphabet was beginning to have an effect on literature, and before long prose works in writing would begin to appear.

The epic continued to be popular in the seventh century B.C., but it steadily lost ground to the new poetry which had its heyday from about 650 to 500. Elegies, lyrics, and even epics continued to be composed after the end of the sixth century. The choral lyric possessed the greatest vitality; moreover, it was basic to a new form developed after 500 B.C.— the drama.

Architecture and Sculpture

When wood was plentiful and technology crude in Greece during the Dark Ages, the Greek temple had been a simple structure of wood and mud brick, and the statues of the deities within were carved from tree trunks. A shortage of wood at the end of the early period, however, brought an increasing use of stone in architecture and sculpture. In addition, the prosperity of some towns led people to build more elaborate temples and to lavish more care on the images of the gods. Contact with the Near East soon began to affect sculpture and other art forms; Oriental motifs were copied; techniques were borrowed from Egyptian and Assyrian art; and the Greeks learned the Near Eastern method of casting bronze. The transition from woodworking to building and sculpting in stone could not be made by the Greeks overnight. At first they used limestone instead of marble for temple construction because it was easy to quarry and fashion as well as being plentiful. The tools of the sculptor and his methods of carving stone must be acquired. Often foreign non-Greek artists were introduced to execute works of art and to teach the Greeks these crafts.

During the Archaic period, the plan of the Greek temple grew in complexity. The old style, with its single room, or *cella*, and simple columned portico was elaborated in various ways. A rear portico might be added to match the one at the front; the cella might be divided into two rooms; a colonnade might be constructed to surround the whole exterior of the building. In addition to the cult statue which stood in the cella, sculptured figures in the round were placed in the triangular pediments or gables over the front and rear entrances, and a frieze of relief sculptures could encircle the temple just above its colonnade. Stone temples continued to be painted in bright colors just as the old wooden ones had been. In fact, many architectural features which had been functional in the old-style wood structures were retained for decorative adornment in the stone buildings.

Doric and Ionic Architecture.   The Archaic period knew two main styles, or orders, of architecture: Doric and Ionic. The first was common in mainland Greece and the western colonies, while the second originated in Asia Minor and represented a borrowing from the Near East. The two styles differed mainly in column and frieze. The Doric column had no base and rested directly on the top step or floor of the temple. The column capital consisted of a curved block, the *echinus,* upon which was placed the *abacus,* a flat block of stone. The column itself was channeled with vertical flutes, each divided by a knife-like edge, or *arris.* The Ionic column had a base formed by two convex rings separated by a concave ring; its flutes were more numerous than those of a Doric column and were separated by a flat band of stone; the column was topped by a volute capital instead of the Doric echinus and abacus. The Ionic frieze was continuous, running all the way around the temple, and usually depicting some kind of procession. The Doric frieze, on the other hand, was episodic, consisting of alternate *triglyphs* and *metopes.* The triglyphs, blocks marked by three projections, had once been terra-cotta sheathings that protected the beam ends of the wooden temples. The metopes were blocks decorated with relief sculpture and inserted between successive triglyphs. The scenes represented on the metopes usually portrayed a series of episodes in a connected story: the labors of Heracles, or the like. Some very large temples were planned and some actually completed in this period. Peisistratus started, but failed to complete, a huge Doric temple to Olympian Zeus at Athens. At Ephesus there was an equally large Ionic temple to Artemis; destroyed by fire in the fourth century B.C., it was replaced by an even larger structure that was counted among the seven wonders of the ancient world.

Cult Statues.   Cult statues of the Archaic period were generally of two types: the standing, nude figure of a male deity *(kouros),* and the standing, draped figure of a goddess *(kore).* These two types were reproduced again and again by the sculptors who by continuous practice with the two simple forms were able to increase their technical proficiency and to work out two major problems: the representation of human anatomy and the treatment of drapery. The kouros afforded an opportunity to attack the first problem, and the kore did the same thing for the second one. Standing with left foot advanced and arms stiffly at the sides, the kouros presented a pose borrowed from Egyptian sculpture. The kore, completely draped in a single garment with only the toes

GREEK ORDERS OF ARCHITECTURE

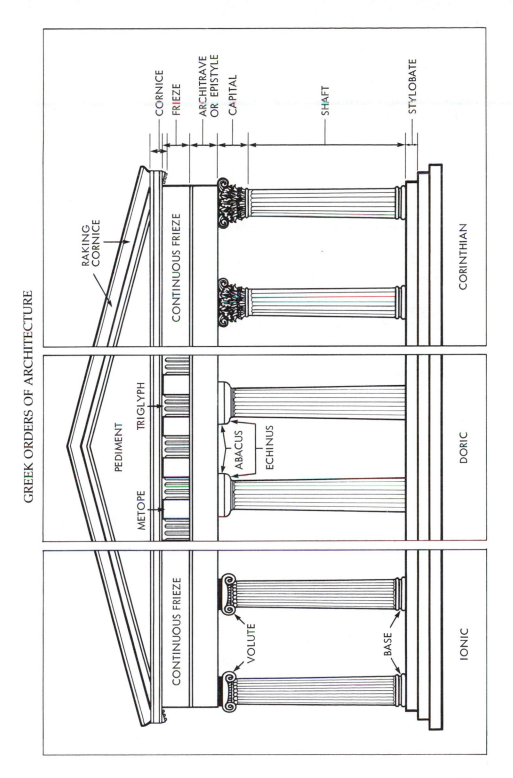

CORNICE
FRIEZE
ARCHITRAVE OR EPISTYLE
CAPITAL
SHAFT
STYLOBATE

RAKING CORNICE

CONTINUOUS FRIEZE

CORINTHIAN

PEDIMENT

TRIGLYPH

METOPE

ABACUS

ECHINUS

DORIC

CONTINUOUS FRIEZE

VOLUTE

BASE

IONIC

peeping out at the bottom, appears to have been derived from a native Greek prototype in wood which was hewn out of a log. By the sixth century, anatomical details in Greek sculpture began to show the results of careful study, and the representation of drapery became very elaborate; moreover, the introduction of various hair styles indicated the growing confidence and skill of the artists. It is worth noting that sculpture in stone, like the temples, was painted.

Painted Pottery

No examples of Greek painting have survived from this early period except for the painted vases. The attention given to human anatomy by the vase painters and their treatment of drapery not only parallels what we find in sculpture but also falls in with the tradition that these matters were the concern of the early Greek painters. The painted pottery may therefore tell us something about the art in general, but in addition the scenes painted on the vases illustrate Greek costumes, religion, customs, and mythology.

Eastern and Western Styles.   During the Dark Ages the prevailing style of painted decoration on the pots was geometric; the decorative patterns were suggestive of textile work, and figures of men and animals were composed of circles, squares, triangles, and the like. Two new styles of vase painting appeared at the end of the Dark Ages: an eastern, generally "orientalizing" style using Near Eastern motifs that were painted in outline on the light-colored surface of the clay, and a western style in which figures were painted in black silhouette. The Asiatic towns as well as island states—Rhodes, Chios, and others—just off the coast of Asia Minor were the producers of the eastern style. The western style was localized in Greece; the leading producers were Corinth, Chalcis (on Euboea), and Athens.

Black-Figured Style.   Corinthian and Chalcidian pottery was handsome and in great demand, especially in the markets of the western Mediterranean, but in time Athenian pottery surpassed in quality and outsold all the rest. The black-figured style of Athens, using a silhouette technique, was in the process of evolution during the second quarter of the sixth century B.C. and attained perfection in the period 550 to 520. Potters and painters signed their names to vases which they considered their masterpieces; at least fifty of these artists are known, their individual styles have been studied, and it is possible as a consequence to identify their unsigned works as well. Set against the orange background of the clay,, the black silhouettes had interior details incised in white; the silhouette itself was well adapted to the curved surfaces of

ARCHAIC GREEK SCULPTURE

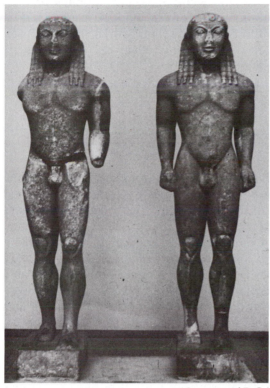

ATTIC NECK AMPHORA
IN THE STYLE OF EXEKIAS
(about 540 B.C.)

(Courtesy of B.C.)   *(Courtesy of the Minneapolis
Institute of Arts.)*

the vases. Athenian vases were exported to many parts of Greece as well as markets in the eastern and western Mediterranean. At many sites it is possible to see an increasing prevalence of Athenian wares and a corresponding decline of the Corinthian. This is dramatic proof of the effectiveness of Solon's reforms and the vigorous commercial policies of Peisistratus.

Red-Figured Style.   About 520 B.C. a new, red-figured style began to replace the black-figured style at Athens. An outline technique succeeded that of the silhouette. Now the background of the vases was painted black and the figures were drawn in red-brown and other colors on the surface of the clay itself. The outline technique gave the painters greater opportunity to follow their interest in the depiction of drapery and anatomy. The popularity of the new style lasted until the end of the fifth century, and it passed through several phases which must parallel the evolution of the art of painting for which we lack examples. For some time the painters continued to sign their works; little phrases which were sometimes added—"Euphronius never did better"—suggest a lively competition among them.

Philosophy

Along with other changes, the Greeks developed new forms of philosophy.

Ionians.   One of the best examples of the process by which the Greeks borrowed from the Near East to create something new and "Greek" may be observed in the case of philosophy. During the sixth century B.C., in Ionia in western Asia Minor, and particularly in Miletus, there flourished a group of Greek thinkers whose interests were in mathematics, astronomy, and cosmology. Their mathematical and astronomical lore was clearly derived from Babylonian sources, probably through Phoenician contacts. In later times these early Greek philosophers were credited with many discoveries, but modern scholarship has cast some doubt on this matter, and it seems likely that the Ionians actually contributed little that was new to either astronomy or mathematics. On the other hand, in their speculations regarding the origin and nature of the world, new departures were made in the sense that they attempted to explain the physical world in natural rather than supernatural terms. The theories which they evolved are interesting but the most enduring contribution which they made was not in theory but rather in method.

By rejecting the supernatural in large part and seeking natural causes to explain the phenomena of nature, the Ionians popularized among the Greeks the concept of rational, logical thought. This approach was later to be applied by the Greeks to all aspects of nature, people, society, and politics. In the Near East the priests had enjoyed a virtual monopoly of intellectual activity. The temple had provided explanations for the beginnings and nature of the world in the form of myths, which were couched in supernatural terms. The Greeks, however, did not live in a theocratic society, and they were not bound to accept the Near Eastern ideas in the form in which they were transmitted. The Ionian philosophers were not priests, but laymen. Unfamiliar with the whole body of theology in which the Near Eastern cosmology was embedded, the Greeks could take ideas out of context; they could remove the supernatural shell from a concept and use only the kernel of the idea.

Near Eastern Cosmology.   In the Near East, for example, it was commonly believed that in the beginning all was water and that out of the primeval waters a creator-god fashioned the earth, animals, plants, and humans. This is the basic idea in Babylonian and Egyptian mythology and in Genesis. In the Babylonian story, Marduk, the creator-god, representing order, overcame the dragon Tiamat, typifying disorder, and so brought order out of chaos. Marduk slit Tiamat in half; one-half of her body became the earth and the other half the dome of the sky. The earth floated on water; both earth and sky were surrounded by water so that when it rained the water leaked through the holes which Marduk had made with his spear in Tiamat's skin. An inkling of these concepts came early to Greece. Homer believed that "Ocean" surrounded the earth; Hesiod said that the world began with chaos out of which came heaven and earth, and he also thought that the earth was a flat disk floating on the surface of the water.

Thales' Origin of the World Theory.   Thales of Miletus, the first of the Ionian philosophers, who flourished about 580 B.C., thought of the earth as a kind of bowl floating on the surface of the waters; above was an inverted bowl, the hemisphere of the sky. Speculating about the origin of the world, Thales decided that in the beginning there must have been some original or prime substance from which all matter was derived, and water seemed the logical candidate for this honor. The Greeks believed, and Thales along with them, that water was living, animate stuff. Water moved: it came gushing out of springs; it flowed in rivers; there were currents in the sea. Plants needed water to grow; water must not only be alive, but it must have power to give life to other things. Combining the evidence of his senses with the commonly accepted belief in the primeval waters, it seemed reasonable to Thales to conclude that the forms of matter and living things must have evolved from water.

Anaximander's Separation of Opposites Theory.   Anaximander of Miletus did not agree with Thales. It was accepted "common knowledge" that there were four basic elements: fire, air (mist), earth, and water. Anaximander therefore reasoned that these elements must all have been derived from some undefined material which he called simply "the unlimited." This theory was that the world had evolved from the separation of opposites. Everyone knew that there were many pairs of opposites: hot and cold, wet and dry, light and dark, good and bad, and the truth and the lie that Zoroaster was to stress. Generation was accomplished by the union of male and female. It was logical; it conformed with human experience to think that creation might have been the result of the alternate combination and separation of opposites.

First, said Anaximander, hot separated from cold. The "hot" moved out from and enveloped a central nucleus of "cold." The most extreme temperatures would be found on the periphery and at the center of this mass; it would be surrounded by a sphere of flame, while the lowest temperature would be found at the center. The fires of heaven acted on the "cold" to produce a second pair of opposites: wet and dry. Land would form at the center; it would be surrounded by water; the evaporation of water produced mist which enveloped the water, while encompassing all this was fire. Anaximander thought that the first living things were generated from moisture evaporated by the sun; life must have begun in the water and then moved onto the land. The elements, said Anaximander, were continuously at war: the "hot" drew moisture upward to feed the fires above; the "cold" reclaimed moisture in the form of rain.

Anaximenes' Mist Theory.   Succeeding Anaximander, Anaximenes identified "the unlimited" with mist and maintained that the thinning or thickening of the mist produced all visible forms. This concept was important because it led to the atomic theory supported by two fifth-century philosophers, Leucippus and Democritus, who believed that all matter was uniform in substance, consisting of minute particles called atoms; any structure therefore depended for its form on the density and manner of combination adopted by the atoms.

Heraclitus' Fire as Catalyst Theory.   Heraclitus of Ephesus, who lived at the end of the sixth century B.C., stressed fire as a catalyst that changed one element into another. This again accorded with human experience: fire (cooking) altered foods; it changed clay into pottery; and so on. Heraclitus accepted the idea of the warfare of the elements and postulated continuous change, or flux. This was borrowed by Leucippus and Democritus, who thought of their atoms as being continually in motion.

Pythagoras: Transmigration and Number Magic.   Pythagoras of Samos, another sixth-century B.C. philosopher, is difficult to assess. In some way Pythagoras got hold of ideas that must have been diffused across the Persian empire from India in the closing years of the sixth century B.C. He believed in the transmigration of souls and that the soul could be purified and immortalized through contemplation. Pythagoras settled in Italy in his later years and founded a cult there in which his numerous disciples observed food taboos, lived in virtual monasteries, and devoted themselves to meditation and study. The Pythagoreans studied mathematics and acoustics, among other things, and got themselves entangled in a sort of number magic. They deemed it significant that a point could be represented by one, a line by two, a plane by three, and a solid by four. Moreover, the total of one, two, three, and four is ten. People have ten fingers and ten toes, and so on; thus they rationalized that there must be something cosmic about ten.

Pythagoras and Thales, too, became legendary figures. All kinds of feats and discoveries were credited to them by the Greeks and Romans of later ages. Pythagoras did not discover the Pythagorean theorem, neither was he the first to demonstrate it by logical proof. The Egyptians and Babylonians used the "Pythagorean" method more than 1,000 years before Pythagoras was born, and recently a cuneiform tablet of the Hammurabi period was found in which the theorem is demonstrated as well as used to solve a problem. Thales was reputed to have used trigonometry to calculate heights and distances and to have demonstrated that the base angles of an isoceles triangle are equal. We do not really know that he did these things, but it is common knowledge today that he could not have predicted the solar eclipse of 585 B.C. as he was supposed to have done.

None of this is intended to belittle the achievement of the Greeks in the period 750 to 500 B.C. Giant steps were taken toward the establishment of an important tradition which was to affect western civilization from that time to the present day. It is enough to recognize this fact. It does not need the embellishment of legend or overstatement.

Chapter Six

To Olympus and Back

The fifth century B.C. is the Athenian century. At the hub of Greek affairs, the city-state Athens dominated the political and economic life of the Aegean, while Athens, the city, was not only the capital of an empire but also the center of artistic, literary, and intellectual activity for the Greek world. In this greatest period of Greek achievement, the essence of the whole can be distilled into a single phrase: the Age of Pericles.

The glories of fifth-century Athens are truly inspiring, but they should not blind anyone to certain unpleasant yet highly instructive facts. It was, in the last analysis, the Athenian navy implementing the Athenian will to resist that won the Battle of Salamis in 480 B.C., stemmed the tide of foreign aggression, and ensured the independence of the Greeks from Persia. It was also the Athenian navy, transformed into the tool of a greedy imperialism, that shortly deprived many Greek states of their freedom and subjected them to a ruthless exploitation more direct and comprehensive than any the Persians might have imposed. It was the Athenian navy and the revenues of an empire that made possible the world's first experiment in democracy, while imperialism provided the wealth to fund a patronage that made Athens a center of culture.

In effect Pericles once said, "The good that men do lives after them; the evil is interred with their bones." So it was with Athens. She rose. She fell. No contemporary mourned her passing, but civilization was forever enriched because Athens had once been great.

THE PERSIAN WARS

A test of strength between the Persians on the one hand and the Greeks on the other was virtually inevitable. The rapid expansion of the Persian empire between 550 and 500 B.C. had been accomplished with such ease that the Persians could not gauge without some probing whether they had reached the natural limits of their empire. Already lording it over the Greeks on one side of the Aegean and with a foothold in Europe in what is now European Turkey, the Persians might well consider the annexation of the prosperous mainland Greek towns. Generally determined to resist the Persian advance and hopeful that the Asiatic Greeks might some day be liberated, the mainlanders could hardly dismiss the Persian problem as unimportant. Conflict was latent; the smouldering fires of hostility were continually fanned by the activities of exiles seeking restoration to the cities from which they had fled or been expelled: the Asiatic refugees who had come to mainland Greece, and the political exiles of the caliber of the ex-tyrant Hippias conspiring to return home with Persian assistance.

The Ionian Revolt

The two decades between 499 and 479 B.C. were crucial for the Greeks. The new century opened with a desperate revolt against Persia, which began in Miletus and spread to other Ionian towns. The early successes of the rebels, aided by contingents from Athens and Euboea, were soon canceled by defeat as the Persians rallied from their initial surprise and brought up strong reinforcements by land and sea. At the end of the revolt in 494 B.C., the vengeful Persians imposed controls far stricter and harsher than before so that the plight of the wretched Ionians was worse than ever.

The assistance given the rebels by the free Greeks could only be regarded as presumptuous meddling by Darius, the Persian king. Punitive measures were certainly in order, and in 492 B.C. a Persian force, supported and provisioned by naval units, advanced along the coast of Thrace and Macedonia with the object of invading Greece from the north. The Greeks were spared on this first occasion, however, when the Persian fleet was crippled by a storm off Mt. Athos, and the army had to turn back once its naval support was withdrawn. After this failure, the Persians adopted a different strategy. In 490 B.C. a seaborne expedition proceeded directly across the Aegean to attack Euboea and Athens. First, the Euboean town of Eretria was put under siege, and a relieving force from Athens was pinned down in Attica when the Persians established a beachhead at Marathon twenty miles northeast of Athens. As the Athenians concentrated their army on the hills above the Plain of Marathon to block any Persian advance from that direction, Athens was left undefended. Expected helped from Sparta to garrison Athens failed to arrive. Then Eretria fell, thus freeing the Persian force in Euboea for an attack on Athens. While the Athenian army was rooted to the spot by the enemy at Marathon, the main Persian force could sail from Euboea around to a landing on the Bay of Phalerum, south of Athens, and mount an attack on the capital. Goaded into action by the news of the capture of Eretria, the Athenians descended upon the Persian forces at Marathon, drove them into the sea, and marched back to Athens during the night to oppose the main enemy contingents when they sailed in from Euboea the next morning. This unexpected show of strength disheartened the Persians, who abandoned the venture and returned to Ionia.

Persian Invasion of Greece

Marathon had not been a great battle, but victory inspired the Athenians and some other Greeks with confidence to resist the Persians. Moreover, King Darius died before the enemy could put together a third expedition, and Xerxes, Darius' successor, was occupied for some time with widespread revolts throughout his empire. The next attack on Greece, when it came, was the result of several years of careful planning. In addition, Persian objectives had changed, for the offensive scheduled for the spring of 480 B.C. aimed at the conquest, not the punishment, of the Greeks.

We do not know what impelled Xerxes to take drastic action against the Greeks. The haughty Persians were not likely to forget their ignominious defeat at Marathon. Pride alone would cry out for vengeance. Furthermore, the Persian image of invincibility was endangered, and that was something the rulers of a vast and scantily garrisoned empire could ill afford. It is also possible that Xerxes, after restoring order in his realm, may have felt that he should settle the Greek question forever and put an end to the meddling in Ionian affairs by the mainland Greeks.

The Greeks themselves believed that Xerxes was pressured into the new offensive by several individuals at the court. There was Mardonius, the general who had quelled the Ionian revolt and planned the combined land and sea invasion of 492 B.C., halted by the destruction of his fleet as it rounded Mt. Athos. Disgraced and out of favor, Mardonius hoped to repair his fortunes and justify his strategy by pointing to the debacle at Marathon that demonstrated the inadequacy of mere seaborne invasion. Another advocate of invasion was the ex-tyrant Hippias, a hardy perennial who was still insisting that he had support in Athens for his restoration. He had accompanied the expedition of 490 and may have advised the landing at Marathon where his father had initiated a successful return to tyranny in 546. Sober reflection, however, suggests that, whatever the Greeks thought about Hippias, his influence on Xerxes must have been minimal by the time of the final invasion in 480. If still alive he would have been in his late sixties, and in reality his best chance to return to Athens would have been ten years earlier when we know that he still had relatives of some consequence there. The infamous shield signal flashed from shore to the Persians when they sailed away from Marathon, though blamed on the Alcmaeonidae, was always interpreted by the Athenians as an invitation for the Persians to attack Athens, and reason dictates that the partisans of Hippias were the most likely culprits.

Mardonius and Hippias were not the only agitators at the court of Xerxes after 486 B.C.. Demaratus, the ex-king of Sparta, was there, and he would accompany and advise Xerxes in the campaign of 480. The story went back a long way. In 510, when Hippias was driven from Athens, the two Spartan kings were Cleomenes and Demaratus. Cleomenes, incredibly stubborn and bullheaded, had cowed (no pun intended) even the ephors and never saw eye to eye with his colleague, Demaratus. Cleomenes had aided in the fall of Hippias and then returned to support Isagoras against Cleisthenes. This came to naught because not only Demaratus but also the Corinthians refused to send troops to Athens to assist Cleomenes in a venture that lacked their approval. Infuriated, the angry king went home and convinced the Spartans that Demaratus was not the true son of the former king and therefore was disqualified for the throne. This accomplished, Cleomenes secured the appointment of another candidate more acceptable to him personally.

To come back to Xerxes, Herodotus says that a fourth person with considerable influence at the Persian court was the famous seer Onomacritus, a former recipient of Peisistratid patronage, who had an extensive collection of oracular responses that he could produce or tailor to the occasion when necessary. Selecting those which promised Persian victory over the Greeks, Onomacritus enforced the arguments advanced by Mardonius, Hippias, and Demaratus.

For several years before the actual invasion was scheduled, the Persians made no secret of their plans if for no other purpose than to weaken the Greek will to resist. The mere rumor of the huge forces being assembled at Sardis and the great fleet that would support the attack undermined Greek confidence. The two bridges of boats by which the armies would cross into Europe and the massive collection of supplies along the land route in the north Aegean were impressive enough, but when a canal was dug behind Mt. Athos for the safe passage of the fleet no one could doubt that the venture was in earnest.

In the decade of the 480s, the devisiveness of the Greeks nearly proved their undoing. The victory at Marathon did little to remove the fear of Persian conquest from the many states in central Greece that would be imperiled by the first assault from the north. Many "medized," declared their neutrality or pledged allegiance to Persia, some thinking to escape the horrors of conquest and others (like Thebes) hoping for the destruction of Athens. There was wavering also in the south: The Spartans and their allies felt that only the Peloponnesus was defensible by fortifying the Isthmus of Corinth, while the Argives medized in the hope that Sparta would not survive.

In Athens, the main target of Persian vengeance, the majority favored resistance but "politics as usual" hampered planning for the coming struggle with Persia. The fiery Miltiades, long the object of Persian hatred even before his prominence at Marathon, had been undone by his own impulsiveness. Right after Marathon he was sent with a fleet of seventy ships to harass the retreating enemy, but he had turned aside to attack the island of Paros where pro-Persian leanings were suspected. If Paros had been taken, Miltiades would probably have been hailed as a hero. As it was, the attack failed; ships and men were lost, Miltiades was injured, and he was brought to trial on his return to Athens. Xanthippus, the father of Pericles, was his prosecutor. Although Miltiades died of his injury before the trial was completed, he was convicted and fined fifty talents of silver, a sum that was later paid by his son Cimon. This was the origin of the feud between Pericles and Cimon that dominated Athenian politics in the sixties and fifties of the fifth century.

Far more important in the eighties and seventies, however, was Themistocles, whose influence determined the history of Athens in many ways; on some occasions his policies had immediate effects and on others far-reaching consequences of long duration. In the years just before Marathon, Themistocles, along with Miltiades, had strongly advocated opposition to Persia, and after 490 B.C. he had become the acknowledged leader of a large political faction.

Themistocles rather than Cleisthenes was the inventor of ostracism. At any rate, he was the first to introduce it, in 488 B.C. when Cleisthenes was no longer alive. This curious instrument for political choice, the reverse of a popularity contest, may be described as follows.

Ostracism.   Just after the Battle of Marathon, ostracism was used for the first time. Under this novel system, each year in the sixth month the citizens were polled to determine whether an ostracism was deemed necessary; if the answer was affirmative, balloting took place in the eighth month. On an appointed day, each citizen came down to the marketplace *(agora)* and wrote on a piece of broken pottery *(ostrakon)* the name of the Athenian whom he considered most dangerous to the state. If as many as 6,000 votes were cast, the politician who received the greatest number of votes was required to go into honorable exile for a period of ten years. This arrangement worked well because ordinarily two party leaders would be advocating opposite courses of action. The people could thus eliminate the man whose views they did not favor and leave the field clear for their favorite. By a succession of ostracisms, Themistocles before 480 B.C. managed to clear out of Athens the partisans of Hippias and then most of the conservative leaders who opposed his pro-democratic ideas and his plan for a big navy.

The decision to build a powerful navy was indeed a fateful one for the Athenians. It came about with the discovery of a rich vein of silver in the Laurium mines of southeastern Attica. Some people thought that the find should be exploited and the wealth divided equally among all citizens so that everyone would be rich. With the Persian menace looming in the near future, however, wiser heads proposed that defense should have priority. Aristides, for example, argued for a bigger army, but Themistocles advocated the construction of a formidable naval force that could operate in conjunction with the sizable armies the Greeks could put in the field. A heated debate led to an ostracism in 482 B.C. in which Aristides was the loser.

When the Persian advance began in 480 B.C., it seemed irresistible. The odds did not appear to favor the Greeks. Gloomy predictions from the oracle of Apollo at Delphi undermined Greek morale, and the refusal of the Sicilian Greeks to send aid because they themselves feared an invasion by the Carthaginian allies of Persia was disheartening news. The only bright spot in the picture was that a strategy for defense had been formulated at the last moment.

Since the rough topography of Greece forced the Persians to use the main road or set of roads that led from Macedonia into central Greece, it was clear that the route to be followed by the Persians was predetermined. Along the way there were several passes that might be defended. One of these was Tempe just below the Macedonian border, and the other was Thermopylae in Locris south of the territory of Thessaly. A force was sent to Tempe, but the discovery of alternative passes led to its abandonment and a withdrawal to Thermopylae.

The site of Thermopylae was preferable to that of Tempe in many ways. Virtually on the border between northern and central Greece, it was closer and therefore more easily accessible to the forces of the major Greek states participating in the resistance. The pass itself was extremely narrow and already had a wall that could be repaired and used by the defenders. On the landward side the only alternative way around Thermopylae was a rough goat track over the heights, supposedly unknown to any except the native mountaineers, which could be held by a small force. The most serious threat to those holding the pass was that the Persian fleet could sail in from the Aegean, land behind the defenders, and so turn the position. This danger could be avoided if the Greek fleet could occupy the strait at Artemisium, a narrow passage situated between the northern tip of Euboea and the Thessalian peninsula of Magnesia. Stopped there, the Persians would have to resort to the time-consuming alternative of sailing down around the southern tip of Euboea and forcing the way through the narrow waters separating the island from the mainland.

In the subsequent struggle for Thermopylae, the Greek fleet with some luck more or less discharged its responsibilities, but the 4,000 troops sent to hold the pass were not sufficient for the purpose. The Spartans sent a token force of 300 under the command of the young king Leonidas, the successor of Cleomenes (who had become insane and finally expired). Sparta had promised more help to be sent after an important festival; at the same time their Peloponnesian allies were, they said, getting ready for the Olympic games. After a gallant defense of several days, Thermopylae was lost as the existence of the mountain road was betrayed to the Persians. Leonidas dismissed most of his army so that they might escape while he and his Spartans and a few hundred others stayed behind to face the enemy. The unreliable Thebans surrendered to the attackers, but all the Spartans (except one) and most of the others perished. War memorials were later erected to honor these heroes including a famous one for the Spartans which read:

> Go tell the Spartans, you who read:
> We took their orders, and are dead.

The fall of Thermopylae occurred in midsummer, 480 B.C. During August, the victorious Persians fanned out through east-central Greece without any significant opposition. Thebes now openly medized and other states could only follow suit. The one Persian setback came when an attempt to seize the treasure of Apollo at Delphi was foiled by a violent thunderstorm. Athens could not be defended; even Spartan help, if it had been offered, would not have saved the doomed city. As the able-bodied citizens were withdrawn to the island of Salamis or assigned to the fleet, the women and children were evacuated to towns in the Peloponnesus. Only the priests and a handful of stubborn civilians remained behind on the Acropolis to await the coming of the Persian host. Athens was taken and sacked; after a short siege the Acropolis was captured, its temples and shrines destroyed, and its defenders put to the sword.

While the Spartans and their Peloponnesian allies worked to complete the wall across the Isthmus of Corinth which was intended to halt the southward advance of the Persians, the Greek fleet was still intact and concentrated in the Bay of Salamis. Themistocles and other Athenian leaders, including Aristides, now recalled from exile, invoked a Delphic prophecy that Greece would be saved by a wooden wall, arguing that this referred to the navy and that the Persian fleet must be faced and destroyed. As the captains of Greek ships other than the Athenian showed signs of deserting and sailing home, Themistocles threatened

ATTIC GRAVE STELE,
FIFTH-FOURTH CENTURIES B.C.

THE BRONZE
CHARIOTEER
OF DELPHI

(Courtesy of the Minneapolis Institute of Arts.)   *(Courtesy of B.C.)*

that the Athenians would themselves depart and find new homes in southern Italy. The final decision was made by the Persians who reasoned that, by sealing off both sea exits from the strait separating Salamis from the mainland, they could attack and destroy the Greek fleet before it scattered in all directions. This proved to be a mistake: The Greeks were able to outmaneuver the Persians in the narrow waters between Salamis and the mainland of Attica, and the naval capability of the Persians ceased to exist. It was a battle more decisive than Marathon.

Victory at Salamis did not end the war. The huge Persian army was not withdrawn from Greece. Mardonius did leave Athens but only to go into winter quarters in Boeotia, a friendly territory where food was available. During the winter he tried to persuade the Athenians to desert the Peloponnesians and win their freedom by siding with him. This failed, so in the spring the struggle resumed.

In 479 B.C. it was army against army. Thus, the command naturally passed to the Spartans who led the combined Greek forces into Boeotia in the spring. After some marching and countermarching, Pausanias, the Spartan general, was forced to make a stand at Plataea in which the Greek phalanx proved superior to Persian tactics. Mardonius was killed, and his army began the retreat from Greece, never to return. Only a few days after the Battle of Plataea Greek forces from the fleet landed at Mycale, an Anatolian promontory just opposite the island of Samos, and won another victory that was the first step in a number of annual campaigns leading to the freedom of the eastern Greeks.

Greeks Take the Offensive

After Plataea, the Greeks took the offensive and began a series of campaigns to liberate the island cities and Greek towns of Asia Minor from Persian rule. At first these operations were conducted by combined Greek forces under the command of the Spartan general, Pausanias, the hero of Plataea, but by 477 B.C. a change had occurred. Returning to its policy of isolation, the Spartan government recalled Pausanias and pulled out of the war against Persia. Command passed to the Athenians, who had been cultivating popularity at the expense of the arrogant Pausanias and who now proposed the organization of the celebrated Delian Naval League for the purpose of continuing the war and effecting the liberation of the Asiatic Greeks.

The Delian League.   The Delian League of 477 B.C. was probably the brainchild of Themistocles, the brilliant and resourceful leader of the pro-democratic faction at Athens. Themistocles had always advocated resistance to Persia, even in the dark days before Marathon when many Athenians had favored a more conciliatory policy. It was Themistocles who had talked the Athenians into building the navy that won the Battle of Salamis. Now he proposed that the Greeks should combine in a formal and permanent organization to conduct annual attacks on the Persians until all Greeks were free. With a treasury and meetingplace on the tiny neutral Island of Delos, the league would fight under Athenian leadership with a fleet composed of Athenian vessels and additional ships provided by other member states under a quota system. If a state did not wish to send ships and crews, it might substitute a "contribution," a sum of money equivalent to the cost of its share in the year's operations.

The Greek offensive continued for nearly a decade until, in 468 B.C., a major victory over Persia ensured the independence of most of the Greeks. By this time many of the league members were tired of fighting and apprehensive of the growing strength of Athens. Many of the allies had preferred to contribute money in lieu of ships and men. Consequently, they had unwittingly fostered the growth of the Athenian navy. Athenian ships, financed by allied funds, had been built and kept in repair, while the unused vessels of the allies had deteriorated. The Athenians refused to consider disbanding the league; when some allies tried to secede, they were attacked by Athens and reduced to the status of subjects who were forced to support the Athenian navy by the payment of tribute instead of the former contribution. The Delian League was thus gradually transformed into the Athenian Empire, and many of the Greeks freed from Persia found that they had only exchanged one master for another.

The foregoing survey of the sequel to the Persian Wars has brought us down to 461 B.C., the beginning of the Periclean Age, but before we can go on to that phase of Greek history it is necessary to look at domestic affairs in Athens (479–461 B.C.).

Throughout most of the 470s, Themistocles continued to dominate Athenian politics. Not only was he responsible for the formation of the Delian League, although it was Aristides who was entrusted with assessing the quotas due from the allies, Themistocles also guided Athenian relations with Sparta. This was no easy matter because the Spartans had proposed that the buildings and monuments destroyed by the Persians should not be repaired but left as a reminder of Persian barbarism. A noble sentiment, but Themistocles realized that Athens would remain an open, defenseless city if its walls could not be rebuilt. There could be little doubt that this was the real reason for the Spartan proposal. Themistocles therefore went down to Sparta and engaged the Spartans in a long discussion while, unknown to them, the Athenians were feverishly renewing their defenses. The Spartans never forgave him for this deception, and in the end they helped to bring about his downfall.

For several years Themistocles' policies included the liberalization of the government at home, the prosecution of the war against Persia, and continued opposition to the Spartans. Eventually, however, feeling that the liberation of the eastern Greeks left further hostilities against Persia without justification, he recommended peaceful relations with the Persians that would make possible trade with their empire, something more profitable than prolonged plundering. His conservative opponents at home, who deplored his anti-Spartan stand and did not favor his domestic liberal policies, now gained support from people unreceptive to peace with Persia. In 471 B.C. the sword of ostracism was turned against Themistocles. He was exiled and hounded from Greece by the vengeful Spartans who connected him with a scandal involving the alleged treachery of their own ex-general, Pausanias.

In 471 the leader of the now-victorious Athenian conservatives was a war hero, Cimon, the son of Miltiades, who cultivated the friendship of Sparta and prolonged the war with Persia. After the Persians were soundly beaten in 468 B.C., however, the war issue declined in importance, while the pro-Spartan, anti-democratic sympathies of Cimon and his conservative friends began to receive closer scrutiny at home. In 464 Cimon persuaded the Athenians to send an expeditionary force to Sparta to help in putting down a major helot revolt. When Athenian assistance proved ineffectual, the troops provided by Cimon were dismissed and sent home with scant courtesy and little thanks by the arrogant Spartans. Athens had been exposed to insult. Popular indignation boiled over, and Cimon paid the penalty of ostracism in 462 as the liberals returned to power.

In the future the Athenians found that they could ill afford to do without the military genius of Cimon, but the legacy of Themistocles was even more influential since he had forged a connecting link between the reforms of Solon and Cleisthenes and the full-blown democracy of the upcoming Periclean Age.

THE AGE OF PERICLES

The fifth century can be divided chronologically into three nearly equal parts: the first third belongs to the Persian Wars; the second to Pericles and the flowering of the Athenian democracy; and the third to the Peloponnesian War and the fall of Athens.

In the first section of this tripartite arrangement, we have dealt with the Persian failure to subdue the Greeks and looked at strategic, imperial, and political developments stemming from the creation of the Athenian fleet.

As we now approach the second section we shall resort to a division of the material into (1) the foreign policy of Pericles and (2) his domestic program.

The ostracism of 462 B.C. that pitted Cimon against his principal liberal opponent, Ephialtes, resulted in the exile of Cimon and the prompt assassination of Ephialtes by a person or persons unknown. Presumably the disgruntled conservatives had more than a little to do with the death of Ephialtes, but they had not acted soon enough to prevent the passage of a bill that deprived the conservative-dominated Council of the Areopagus of its supervision of the chief magistrates, as well as its power to review the constitutionality of laws passed by the ecclesia and the right to negate those of which it did not approve. This meant

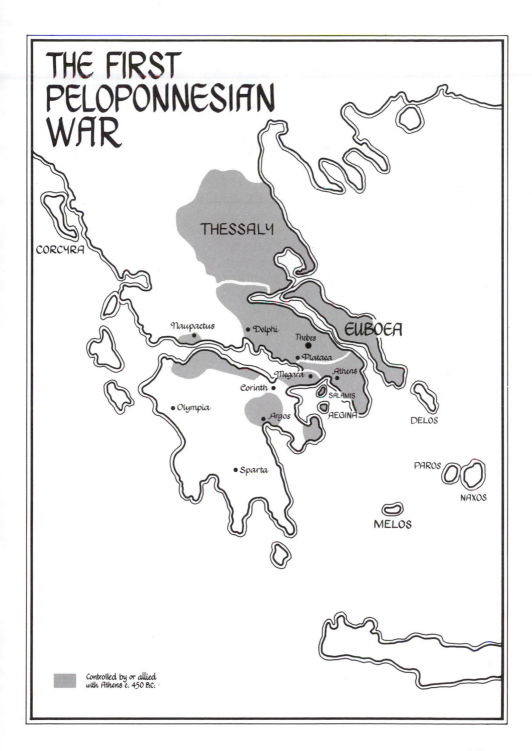

THE FIRST PELOPONNESIAN WAR

CORCYRA

THESSALY

Naupactus

Delphi

Thebes

EUBOEA

Plataea

Megara

Athens

Corinth

SALAMIS

Olympia

AEGINA

Argos

DELOS

Sparta

PAROS

NAXOS

MELOS

Controlled by or allied
with Athens c. 450 B.C.

that the future conduct of the government basically would rest in the hands of the Council of 500 and the ecclesia, both more receptive to the will of the people. Furthermore, if the opponents of Ephialtes had thought to gain from his death, they were sadly mistaken because the leadership of the liberals passed to Pericles, Ephialtes' second in command.

It is true that Pericles rode in on the full tide of democracy, but he would have been outstanding at any time. An intellectual who had profited from the best education Athens had to offer, his natural ability had helped to make him a fine orator with the good sense not to display his gift too often but only when it counted. Another asset was his wonderful Olympian dignity that set him apart from the mob and engendered respect. Not the least of his advantages was his ancestry; he was the son of Xanthippus, and his mother was the niece of Cleisthenes, the great reformer. A master of politics, Pericles had one glaring fault: he was no strategist! It was a classic case of too much education and not enough practical experience.

As an Athenian liberal of his age, Pericles was committed to a policy that was pro-democratic and anti-Spartan. Since democracy had to be financed by imperial revenues, he was bound to maintain their flow and, if possible, increase them. This entailed conquest and aggression. Therefore, between 461 and 445 b.c. Pericles attempted to add a land empire to the maritime realm Athens already possessed.

The idea of landward expansion was something tempting only to an amateur armchair strategist born too soon to learn from the bitter lessons that history would supply not only to him but also the next two generations. Aggression involved Athens in a struggle with the Peloponnesians and Thebes, but not before they were warned and then aroused by the behavior of the Athenians. Between 459 and 457 b.c. the Athenians angered Corinth by weaning away Megara from the Peloponnesian League to an alliance with Athens. This seemed to provide a buffer state on the Isthmus of Corinth. In addition, the two harbors of Megara would also give access for the Athenians, their navy and their traders, to both the Aegean on the east and the Gulf of Corinth on the west without having to sail around the Peloponnesus or use the Corinthian *diolkos* (ship road) across the isthmus. This threatened the trade of Corinth but in addition gave the Athenians in theory something we used to talk about before the construction of the Panama Canal: a two-ocean navy. About the same time, the strategic anxieties of Corinth were augmented when the Athenians annexed Naupactus at the entrance to the Corinthian Gulf and settled there the unconquered helots recently given free passage out of Laconia by the Spartans. Next, Pericles resurrected the old and discredited Peisistratid policy of alliances with Thessaly and Argos, which seemed to threaten Thebes and Sparta, and he capped this with an attack on Aegina, the "eyesore of the Piraeus" as he called it, a commercial rival and a Peloponnesian ally. By this time the fat was in the fire and, as the Athenians overran central Greece with the exception of Thebes, what might well be called the First Peloponnesian War was in progress with the Athenians having to cope with the combined strength of Thebes and the Peloponnesians headed by the now thoroughly aroused Spartans.

In the midst of the fighting in Greece, Pericles threw away any chance of victory by sending a fleet to aid anti-Persian revolts in Cyprus and Egypt, but fortune deserted the Athenians at this crucial time. Even the aid of the great admiral Cimon, now recalled from exile, and the temporary coalition of conservatives and liberals in Athens resulted in failure as Cimon died on the verge of success in Cyprus, and before midcentury two big naval task forces were destroyed by the Persians in Egypt. Athens temporarily lost control of the sea; the allies and subjects of Athens began to break away, and some were repossessed by Persia. Pericles soon had to conclude an ignominious truce with the Persians in order to concentrate on the war in Greece where the tide had definitely turned in favor of the Peloponnesians. The land empire was quickly lost, even Euboea revolted, and the enemy invaded Attica itself. In desperation, the Athenians made a separate treaty with Sparta. As the Spartans deserted their allies and withdrew from the war, the Corinthians, Thebans, and others could not continue to fight alone and unwillingly ceased hostilities. In 445 B.C., after more than fifteen years of aggression and bloodshed, Athens possessed no more territory than she had in 461. The cost in lives and money had been staggering, and it had purchased only hatred and suspicion.

The thirty-year peace agreement of 445 B.C. endured only fourteen years; in reality the arrangement was no better than a truce barely concealing a cold war just waiting to be ignited into a major conflagration.

We shall resume this part of the narrative presently, but first we must look at Athenian domestic affairs under Pericles.

Development of the Athenian Empire and Democracy

Political Power Shifts to the Masses.   The development of the Athenian empire was closely connected with domestic politics in Athens itself. In creating the navy, Themistocles had strengthened the popular party at Athens. His main supporters were the *thetes*, the poorer citizens. Admitted to the assembly by Solon's reforms, the thetes had not been able to exert much influence in politics because they could not equip themselves for army service as heavy-armed foot soldiers (*hoplites*). With the creation of the fleet, however, the thetes could be, had to be, used as oarsmen. The manpower which they provided was essential, and therefore they were in a position to demand an increased voice in the government. The whole weight of political power suddenly shifted to the masses who, in the assembly, far outnumbered the middle and upper classes, the backbone of the army. The increased importance of the navy following the Battle of Salamis led to successive changes that made the government more responsive to the popular will. Athens passed from timocracy to democracy. As the Delian League was transformed into the Athenian empire, financial support for the fleet as well as the democracy at home seemed assured. Greeks who had been helped to freedom by Athens now had to "help" the Athenians to achieve democracy.

Athenian Navy Maintains the Empire.   Themistocles had done more than create the naval force that won the Persian wars, for he had also found a way to protect Athens from her doubtful friends in Greece. Athens could not hope to compete with Sparta as a land power, but at sea it was a different matter. The Spartans were "landlubbers," and the fleet that had freed Athens from the threat of Persia could also hold the Spartans in check. The navy could conquer and maintain intact a rich tributary empire; it could guard the supply lines that brought food to the growing metropolis unable any longer to produce enough at home to feed itself; it could be turned against commercial rivals, like Corinth, to bring about their destruction when sheer trade competition failed to do the trick. In short, the navy was an offensive instrument useful in politics, diplomacy, economics, and strategy.

DEMOCRACY AT ATHENS

The Athenians were the first people in history to experiment with democracy; as a matter of fact, it was only at Athens in the Periclean Age that democracy was given a fair trial, not only among the Greeks but also among the ancients as a whole. The Athenian experiment ended in dismal failure, mainly because the Athenians lacked the experience and education essential for the success of any democracy. In antiquity it was felt that the Athenians had given democracy a bad name, but as the centuries passed and the modern period dawned, the dream of political equality typified by a legendary Athens inspired people to give democracy another try and to make a dream into a reality. We can still learn something from the Athenians about democracy, but it is their mistakes rather than their successes that are most instructive.

Timocracy, Democracy, and Ochlocracy

Timocracy was the prevailing form of government among the Greeks from the sixth century B.C. onward; even in Hellenistic and Roman times, when large territories were incorporated into great kingdoms and empires, government at the local level remained timocratic. This was only natural because a *liturgy* (performance of public service) was traditionally regarded as an honor and duty for which a man was not paid; instead, he was supposed to bear the expense of his office as magistrate or councillor as part of his normal responsibility as a citizen. This meant that ordinarily only a well-to-do person could afford to participate in governmental affairs beyond attendance at the occasional meetings of the assembly. Under such conditions, it was not surprising that government *by* the rich often resulted in government *for* the rich. The masses of the people, who might call themselves democrats, frequently became dissatisfied with the way things were handled by the oligarchs, as the wealthy ruling citizens were called. Then there were revolutions which established short-lived regimes in which "the people" were in the ascendant, usually represented by some demagogue who was the next thing to a tyrant. The oligarchs believed in class rule; they mistrusted the masses and felt that the state should be run by the "better" people. It should not be forgotten that the masses believed in class rule, too. When they talked about democracy, they really meant a government controlled by and administered for the benefit of themselves, and they intended to exclude the rich from any voice in government. It may be taken as axiomatic that democracy for the Greeks was often synonymous with ochlocracy, or mob rule. Most Greek states were too poor to support democracy as we understand it today. This is why only Athens, with her empire to foot the bill, could pay citizens for public service and achieve a kind of democracy as long as the empire lasted.

Rise of the Masses

We have already seen that the Persian wars had fostered the development of the Athenian navy and that the navy was the means by which the empire was created and maintained. The war vessels were manned by rowers from the thetes, the poorer citizens of Athens. Indispensable to the fleet, the thetes could thus demand a greater share in the government, and they could be paid for public service from the revenues of imperialism. With the introduction of ostracism about 488 B.C., the voting power of the masses could be used to eliminate any politician who opposed their will. Down to 462 B.C., the major remaining obstacle to popular ascendancy was the ancient Council of the Areopagus which had the power of legislative review and could set aside measures passed by the assembly. The Areopagus was composed of ex-archons, all men of property, and it was naturally conservative and anti-democratic in sentiment. When the conservative government of Cimon fell from power in 462 B.C., the first act of the victorious popular faction was to take away the right of the Areopagus to invalidate laws enacted by the ecclesia. Henceforth, the assembly, in which the masses were dominant by sheer numbers, was supreme. The ecclesia enacted the laws; it reviewed and determined state policy; it elected the generals; and it functioned as a high court of appeal when it sat as the heliaia.

Use of Sortition and Committees

By this time, too, other changes had been or were about to be made. With the wars and the growth of the empire, the archonships had declined in importance because they were essentially municipal offices. The *zeugitai* (middle census class) were admitted to the archonship, and the archons were no longer elected but chosen by lot from a list of citizens whose wealth qualified them for the office. The members of the *boule*, Council of the 500, were selected in the same manner. Sortition, the use of the lot, was also employed for choosing the personnel of the many boards or committees which managed the police force, the prisons, various temple and imperial treasuries, the market, the issuance of state contracts, and the collection of taxes. Most of these boards consisted of ten men, one from each of the ten tribes, and a secretary, all chosen by lot and serving for a period of a year.

Sortition and the committee were basic to the Athenian system at this time. Underlying the use of the lot was the theory that any citizen could fill any post if he could afford the time to serve. The committee system, the use of ten men to do the work of one, made it possible for more people to participate in government. Along with this went the practice of rotation in office; no man could be chosen to fill the same post twice. The Athenians also felt that a man should be reimbursed for his services, and they went as far as they could in that direction: the members of the boule and the jurymen (discussed below) were paid, but a big military budget for army and navy pay sopped up most of the revenues of the empire. Even so, if we include the military, it may be estimated that each year about one third to one half of all Athenian citizens drew some pay from the state.

LOOKING ACROSS THE RUINS OF THE ATHENIAN AGORA
TOWARD THE STOA (COLONNADE) OF ATTALUS

(Courtesy of J. M. F.)

Generalship Remains Elective

While the idea that any man could fill any post in the government
was nice in the abstract, even the Athenians knew that theory could not
safely be put into practice. The most important office, that of the generalship, remained elective. Each year ten *strategoi,* or generals, were
elected. These men were either military leaders of known competence
or major political figures. Pericles was elected general every year but
one between the time he came to power in 461 B.C. and his death in 429.
The generals commanded the army and navy, conducted military campaigns, and managed the affairs of the empire. The political leaders
among the strategoi formulated policy and frequently appeared before
the boule or the ecclesia to argue the merits of this or that measure.

Council of the 500

The Council of the 500 (boule) was essentially a big permanent committee of the assembly. The councillors, 50 from each tribe, were annually chosen by lot from the middle and upper census classes. They
drafted measures to be presented to the assembly for enactment into

law, supervised the magistrates and committees, and generally kept track of the affairs of state. By a prearranged system of rotation, the 50 councillors from each tribe in turn were on duty 24 hours a day for a whole civil month of 36 days so that, even when the whole council was not in session, a part of that body was always ready for any emergency.

The Ecclesia

The ecclesia, composed of all adult male citizens, met ordinarily from one to four times a month; in a crisis it might be convened every day. The assembly elected the generals, passed the laws, enacted all financial measures, received embassies from foreign states, and alone could confer Athenian citizenship. It was also the assembly that conducted ostracism. While the assembly could not initiate legislation, it could ratify, amend, or reject proposals submitted to it by the boule.

Jury Courts

An innovation of the Periclean Age was the system of *dikasteria*, or jury courts. Each year a panel of 6,000 jurors was drawn. Juries of anywhere from 201 to 1,001 members were then chosen by lot from this list to serve on various cases each day the courts were in session. Any case involving an Athenian citizen, as well as many cases concerning the subjects and allies of Athens, had to be tried before these juries in the city itself. Under the presidency of one of the archons, a trial must begin at sunrise and end before sunset. The fines imposed helped to pay the salaries of the jurors. The use of sortition in choosing the juries prevented the subversion of the courts by bribery, but the large size of the juries often led to a mob hysteria that made a just verdict difficult. Moreover, the jurors were not noted for their impartiality; in several known instances they favored Athenians over allies or subjects despite the weight of the evidence presented. A peculiarity of the court system was that the plaintiff or the defendant in an action had to plead his own case without the benefit of a lawyer to represent him. A man could get an expert (usually a skilled orator) to prepare his case for him, but once the trial got under way the litigant was on his own.

Administration of the Empire

The generals were charged with the supervision and defense of the empire of more than 200 states and 2 million subjects that Athens had built out of the Delian League. Although local self-government was usually allowed the subjects of Athens, there were cases in which dis-

ATHENIAN ACROPOLIS FROM THE SOUTHWEST

(Courtesy of J. M. F.)

obedient states were forced to accept constitutions modeled on that of
Athens and in which self-government was closely circumscribed. Sometimes desirable land might be taken over by the Athenians and colonized by military contingents sent out as *cleruchs* (military colonists) to
perform a kind of garrison duty. The empire itself was divided into five
tribute districts; fragments of the so-called tribute lists inscribed on
stone have been found which help to reconstruct a picture of the empire
and its finances. Because of the tribute, the cleruchy system, the tyranny
of the courts, and the tampering with local government, the Athenians
came to be thoroughly disliked by most of their subjects and many of
their allies.

Final Assessment

The Athenian democracy was pretty much at the mercy of its demagogues. As long as a popular leader provided material and immediate
privileges and advantages for the masses, he could count on their support in higher and more complicated matters of state which they did not
understand or care about. Under Pericles, the system was not perfect
although it worked fairly well, but after his death when less able or less

scrupulous men took his place, the Athenians and their leaders soon gave democracy a bad name among the Greeks, and the whole idea of popular government fell into disrepute.

THE GREAT PELOPONNESIAN WAR (431–404 B.C.)

Just as tribute from the maritime empire supported the Athenians in the luxury of democracy at the expense of their former allies, so also the control of the Aegean brought to Athens an artificial commercial prosperity. The plain fact of the matter was that Corinth rather than Athens was the natural trade center of mainland Greece. The Corinthians and the Athenians could never be friends. To prosper, or even to survive, one of these states must destroy the other, and in the complications of this not-so-simple business we may find the key to Greek affairs in the second half of the fifth century B.C.

First of all, the protagonists in the first part of the Peloponnesian war and the conflict that preceded it were not Athens and Sparta, but Athens and Corinth. The Spartans adhered to their policy of isolation all during the fifth century. They were drawn into war by treaty obligations which demanded that Sparta must support its allies who were victims of aggression. Again and again Sparta was willing to stop fighting and make a separate peace when the allies were out of danger. Much as the Corinthians or the Athenians might be spoiling for a fight, neither could initiate hostilities because of Sparta. The Athenians could not attack Corinth because aggression would bring in the Spartans and the Peloponnesian League, and this would involve a risk of defeat that the Athenians ordinarily would hesitate to assume. The Corinthians alone could not fight Athens; they could not provoke hostilities since Sparta and the League would not take the field except in a defensive war.

Athens Breaks the Peace

Bound to destroy Corinth, the Athenians had to play a dangerous game of covert aggression, avoiding open hostilities and yet trying to weaken Corinth by diminishing her trade, particularly the commerce with the western Greeks. As the years dragged on after 445 B.C., the uneasy peace developed into a cold war marked by a succession of incidents that brought Athens and her enemy closer and closer to an open break. Corcyra, a powerful island state in the Adriatic and a former Corinthian colony that controlled one leg of the triangular trade between Corinth and the west, was induced to become an Athenian ally. The Corinthians countered by sending "volunteers" into the north Aegean to aid the revolt of Potidaea, another former Corinthian colony now tributary to Athens. In 432 B.C. the Athenians went too far: By the so-called

Megarian Decree they excluded that Peloponnesian ally from the ports of the Athenian empire. To preserve the commerce that was their sole source of livelihood, the Megarians would have to desert the Peloponnesians and enter the Athenian empire. If the Megarians succumbed to this coercion, Athens would control Megara and would be able to close the Isthmus of Corinth to any north-south troop movement essential to Peloponnesian-Theban cooperation in the event of war. But the Megarians did not give in. Instead, they joined with the Corinthians in calling together the delegates of the Peloponnesian League and accused the Athenians of aggression. When the case was argued before the league members, the Spartans were convinced that Athens had broken the peace of 445 B.C., and war was declared.

Peloponnesian War Begins

The long and bitter Peloponnesian War began in 431 B.C. and finally ended in 404. The naval might of Athens was pitted against the land power of the Peloponnesians and Thebans. Neither side could meet the other on its own terms without great risk. During the summer campaigning season, the enemy could invade Attica at will, but the Athenians could take refuge behind the strong walls that welded Athens and its port, the Piraeus, into a single impregnable stronghold. Planned long ago by Themistocles and completed by Cimon, these celebrated "Long Walls" now stood Athens in good stead. While the enemy roamed the land, the Athenian fleet ruled the seas, convoyed food to the besieged, preyed upon the coasts and commerce of the foe, and permitted Athenian trade to be conducted as usual. The economic resources of Athens greatly excelled those of the enemy at the beginning of the war and remained as strong as ever, while the reserves of Corinth, Megara, and other states melted away because of the virtual blockade of the Peloponnesus maintained by the Athenian navy. Pericles had planned this waiting game designed to exhaust the enemy without much risk to Athens, and he might have been successful in his strategy if fate had not intervened. The great plague which struck Athens in 430 B.C. and carried off Pericles himself in 429, revolts among the subject and allies of Athens in 428, and defeat in land encounters forced upon the Athenians, spoiled the plan for a long defensive war that would impoverish the foe and bring them to their knees. The loss of Pericles was serious because the Athenians could find no leader with the ability to conceive and carry out long-range plans or with the prestige necessary to maintain internal unity. With various ups and downs, the war dragged on until 421 B.C. when Sparta deserted her allies and made peace with the Athenians following friendly overtures by the Athenian conservatives who had come into power once more.

As in the earlier fighting between 459 and 445 B.C., nothing had been resolved. Neither Athens nor Corinth had been destroyed, and so they must fight again. Pericles was dead and gone, but Athens did not lack for schemers. Alcibiades, the brilliant and unscrupulous nephew of Pericles, rose to leadership in the popular party. His plan to ally with Argos and other anti-Spartan states in the Peloponnesus failed in 417 B.C. and only awoke new mistrust of Athens among the Spartans. Undaunted, Alcibiades conceived a master stroke in 415 B.C. The Athenians would intervene in Sicily to protect the small states that were in danger of being swallowed up by the aggressive imperialism of Dorian Syracuse. The Athenians would appear as deliverers, destroy Syracuse, and ruin Corinth by cutting off its western trade at the source. It was a fine idea, but political treachery forced Alcibiades into exile just as the great Athenian expedition sailed for Sicily in 415 B.C. The remaining Athenian leaders bungled the enterprise, and the whole Athenian force was destroyed by the Syracusans in 413 B.C.

In the meantime the war in Greece had resumed. During this final phase of the conflict (414–404 B.C.) it was no longer a fight stemming from the rivalry of Athens and Corinth. Rather it was Sparta versus Athens with the Spartans determined to settle the matter once and for all. In the first phase of the war (431–421), with its alternating victories and reverses, there had been occasions when one side or the other had been willing to make peace, but time and time again one of the antagonists would be eager to press his fleeting advantage against the other until at last both sides were too exhausted to continue hostilities.

In the war in Sicily, Doric Syracuse had received aid from Doric Sparta, so by 413 B.C. the Spartans could reasonably expect some help from the Syracusan navy. Before that, however, Sparta had found a valuable ally in the person of the resourceful, charming, and persuasive Alcibiades. Hunted from one place to another by his implacable enemies, Alcibiades had turned up in Sparta proclaiming his hostility to Athens and suggesting a strategy that would bring the Athenians to their knees in no time at all. The Spartans, he said, should invade Attica and occupy the land on a year-around basis instead of attacking in the summer and then going home for the fall planting. This would keep the Athenians penned up behind the Long Walls. He argued that this would be demoralizing to Athens, and so it turned out. The Sicilian disaster and the new enemy gnawed at the Athenian will to fight.

In 411 B.C. a conservative revolution overturned the democracy, and the victors prepared to negotiate peace with Sparta. The conservative coup, however, had been possible because the Athenian fleet, overwhelmingly democratic in sentiment, had been absent from Athens conducting the siege of Samos, an important ally that had broken away. While the fleet seethed with indignation over the conservative action, Alcibiades appeared at Samos with a promise of Persian aid against Sparta.

This brings us back to Alcibiades, who had worn out his welcome in Sparta—it was said that he had been much too friendly with one of the Spartan queens while her husband had been away fighting in Attica. At any rate, Alcibiades, now in danger from both Athenians and Spartans, had fled to Asia Minor to cultivate the friendship of one of the Persian satraps named Tissaphernes.

Having lost none of his charm and ingenuity, Alcibiades convinced Tissaphernes that the Persians should enter the war on the side of the Athenians in order to prevent a Spartan victory. His argument was that if the Spartans won they would inevitably be compelled to try to free the Asiatic Greeks from Persia. Whether Tissaphernes meant to keep his promise we shall never know, but if he had he would have straightway regretted it because the appearance of Alcibiades and his news at Samos crystallized anti-conservative and pro-war feelings in the navy, and the thought of Persian aid when the word reached Athens was sufficient to bring about a counterrevolution that overthrew the conservatives. With the democracy restored and Alcibiades soon recalled to Athens, the war continued with some successes for the Athenians. Tissaphernes now gave his support to the Spartans, anticipating that an Athenian victory would have the same consequences as those Alcibiades had prophesied for Spartan success. Thus it was in Persia's best interest to keep the pot boiling.

The blazing star of Alcibiades set at last after one of his subordinates disobeyed orders and lost a battle at sea in 407 B.C. Alcibiades was blamed for this and once again became an exile. Hounded by Athenians, Spartans, and Persians, he was cornered and killed by the Persians at the request of Sparta; this was after the end of the Peloponnesian War and the details are uncertain. Long afterward Plutarch wrote a biography of Alcibiades, but from the bits and pieces to be found in other ancient writers some one will some day write a gripping story of intrigue based on the negotiations between Alcibiades and Tissaphernes and others of that period (412–407).

After 407 B.C. it was downhill all the way for Athens. The last major action of the war took place in the Hellespont in 405 where the Athenian navy was crushed in the Battle of Aegospotami.

Athens surrendered in 404 B.C. Her empire was taken away, her democracy was replaced by the rule of "the Thirty Tyrants," a group of pro-Spartan collaborators, and a Spartan garrison was stationed in Attica to keep the peace. Athens was finished. She might remain the cultural capital of the Greek world for the next 900 years, but her empire, trade, and industry were gone forever.

EXIT THE GREEK CITY-STATE (404–362 B.C.)

There was no victor in the Peloponnesian War. Athens was perhaps the heaviest loser, but all the Greeks lost something which they could never recover. Casualties and property damage had been heavy; lines of trade had shifted, with the western Greeks becoming economically self-sufficient, and the center of economic activity had moved away from Greece, never to return. The internal unity of many Greek states had been ruptured by the war; bitter civil conflicts between oligarchs and democrats, rich and poor, had broken out in other states besides Athens. This *stasis*, as the Greeks called it, became endemic in the fourth century B.C. Not only states but also individuals were altered by the long years of warfare; public and private morality were nearly destroyed. After the war, many participants found that they had become professional soldiers who lacked the opportunity or the desire to return to peaceful occupations. These men wandered from place to place selling their services to the highest bidders and, having chosen to live by the sword, the bones of many were left to whiten in foreign lands.

The Peloponnesian War changed even the Spartans. They abandoned their traditional isolation for a mad career of imperialism. During the Peloponnesian War the Spartans had justified themselves by saying that they were fighting for the freedom of the Greeks. Having freed the subjects of Athens, they were further committed to try to liberate the Asiatic Greeks still held by Persia. Since the Persians had helped Sparta to beat Athens, this put the Spartans in an awkward position, but they were trapped by their own propaganda and decided shortly after 400 B.C. that they must free the Greeks in Asia despite their obligation to Persia.

Greek Hostility toward Spartans

In Greece itself, the Spartans had allowed little freedom. They had continually interfered with Greek affairs after the Peloponnesian War even to the point of bullying their faithful allies, Corinth and Thebes. Hostility toward Sparta mounted in Greece. In 395 B.C., while the Spartans were fighting the Persians in Asia, the Argives, Thebans, Corinthians, and Athenians combined against the Spartans in Greece. The fact that Thebes and Corinth could cooperate against their former ally,

Sparta, and go so far as to join with their bitter enemies, Argos and Athens, showed how the Spartans had blundered in their relations with the Greeks. Before long the Spartans had to make peace and renew their alliance with Persia in order to cope with Greek affairs. When fighting reached a stalemate in 387 B.C., the exhausted participants appealed to the Persian king to arbitrate their disputes and devise a treaty that would end the war. Under the terms of the "King's Peace," as it was called, it was proclaimed that all Greeks should be free; moreover, Sparta and Persia pledged themselves to maintain this new liberty among the Greeks.

The Spartans chose to interpret the King's Peace in a novel way. They insisted that all combinations of states were in restraint of liberty. They dissolved the Boeotian League, an ancient combination headed by Thebes, and other similar alliances; they even forced religious associations of states to disband. Wherever opposition to their policies developed, the Spartans overthrew recalcitrant governments and replaced them with groups of collaborators supported by Spartan garrisons. Even Thebes was seized by treachery and occupied by a Spartan force in 382 B.C.

Spartans Defeated by Thebans

Despite Persian aid, the Spartans were neither clever nor strong enough to perpetuate their tyranny over Greece. Revolting successfully in 379 B.C., the Thebans were joined in hostility against Sparta by the Athenians after the failure of a sneak attack on Attica by the Spartans in 378. As other states rose in revolt, the Thebans reactivated the Boeotian League, and the Athenians organized a new naval confederacy in 377. At Leuctra in Boeotia in 371 B.C. the Spartans were decisively beaten by Thebes. With their army reduced to only a few thousand men and their ancient ways of life disrupted, the Spartans sank into a slow but steady decline.

The Athenian and Spartan experience had demonstrated that it was difficult to hold a land empire in Greece, given the topography and the relatively primitive forms of transportation and communication then in use. A maritime empire was possible if one had a fleet, something that the Spartans lacked, but when a great land power like Sparta could not hold interior regions, it was not surprising that Athens had failed to do the same. The ultimate defeat of the Spartans was, however, another matter. The long Peloponnesian War and the struggles succeeding it had brought changes in tactics and strategy as well as military organization, but the Spartans had not kept pace with the times. While the hoplite phalanx was still the nucleus around which an army was built, the new army of the fourth century B.C. was more versatile and maneuverable than the old. Light-armed foot soldiers, *peltasts*, had been added. A troop of them had proved their worth back in 391 B.C. when they had caught a Spartan phalanx in rough territory and cut it to ribbons. Archers and slingers had become important, too, but the real innovation of the Thebans was the introduction of a true cavalry arm. A cavalry charge could sometimes stampede a phalanx by a frontal attack although the maneuver might be costly; the better strategy was to wheel around the enemy's left wing and attack the phalanx from the rear. The only defense against enemy cavalry was to have cavalry of your own. The Spartans had no cavalry; thus, their obsolete army was no match for the Thebans.

Thebans Also Fall

After 371 B.C., it soon appeared that the Thebans had learned nothing from the failures of the Athenians and the Spartans. Led by Pelopidas and Epaminondas, two patriots who had engineered the revolt against Sparta in 379 and brought about the final defeat of the enemy in 371, the Thebans tried to build an empire in central Greece. Between 371 and 362 B.C. they enjoyed some small success and also attempted to organize some of the Peloponnesian states against Sparta. But continuous fighting meant heavy losses in manpower for Thebes. Pelopidas was killed, and along with him died many others who could not be replaced. In 362 B.C., in an effort to attack and destroy Sparta itself, the Thebans invaded the Peloponnesus. They won the great Battle of Mantinea, but their casualties were so heavy that they could not follow up their victory. Epaminondas himself was mortally wounded at Mantinea; as he expired, he pleaded with his followers to make peace and give up dreams of empire.

Greeks Exhausted

By 362 B.C. the Greeks had been fighting one another for over a century to secure a freedom that none of them could henceforth protect. The lesson of the Persian wars, when they had successfully worked together for a common purpose, had made no impression upon these people. Broken, divided, and impoverished, they no longer had the power to defend themselves against foreign aggression. The Macedonians and then the Romans would become their masters.

GREEK CIVILIZATION

It is generally considered that Greek civilization reached its full maturity between 500 and 362 B.C. Creativity was never more in evidence among the Greeks. A major period in sculpture, architecture, and painting, it was also the great age of Greek drama. Prose evolved rapidly and attained major proportions in the works of Herodotus, Thucydides, Xenophon, and Plato; philosophy came into full bloom under the tutelage of Plato and Aristotle, and there was progress in scientific thought. Although many artists, writers, and thinkers of this age were Athenians, Athens did not have a monopoly on creativity; Herodotus came from Halicarnassus in Asia Minor, Hippocrates from the Island of Cos, Aristotle from Stagira in Macedonia, Pindar from Boeotia, Polyclitus from Argos, and Scopas from Paros. Among the Sicilians were Corax, the founder of oratorical studies; Epicharmus, the comic playwright; and Empedocles, the philosopher. The city-state, the *polis*, was the key to the aims and achievements of this age; its patronage supported creative activity and even directed it into certain channels.

Civic Architecture

Architecture in the fifth century B.C. was predominantly civic. The polis had resources far exceeding those of any individual, and there was a need for the construction of council halls, law courts, and other buildings required to house governmental activities. Furthermore, the glory of the state and growing civic pride encouraged expenditures on larger and more magnificent temples. The popularity of the Doric order was challenged by the Ionic, and the latter became the most frequently used order in the fourth century.

Agora.   Athens was the scene of great building activity during the fifth century B.C. Many new structures were erected, especially in the Agora and on the Acropolis. The Agora was the center of civic life; on the west side were the council hall *(bouleuterium)* and the Tholos, a round building in which official documents were kept. Behind these on an eminence was a fine Doric temple dedicated to Hephaestus. Sometimes called the Theseum, this temple is still in a good state of preservation and constitutes one of the landmarks of the Agora.

Acropolis.   On the Acropolis, some buildings were completed during the lifetime of Pericles, while others were finished during the Peloponnesian War despite losses in revenue occasioned by the conflict. A

THE DORIC ORDER: THE THESEUM
IN ATHENS (TEMPLE OF HEPHAESTUS)

(Courtesy of B.C.)

monumental gateway, the Propylaea, stood at the entrance to the
Acropolis; just to the south was a small, perfectly proportioned, Ionic
temple to Athena Nike (Victory). The Parthenon, the largest and most
important building on the Acropolis, was truly symbolic of the Periclean
Age. The third in succession to be built on this spot, this Doric temple
to Athena, the patron goddess of Athens, was planned by the architects
Ictinus and Callicrates, and its sculptural decoration was supervised by
Phidias, the greatest sculptor of the fifth century. The two pediments of
the Parthenon were adorned with figures in the round; on the east, the
scene portrayed was the birth of Athena, and on the west, the contest
of Athena and Poseidon for the possession of Attica. The Ionic frieze
which ran around the outer wall of the cella portrayed the Panathenaic
procession in which the dignitaries and citizens of Athens marched in
honor of the goddess Athena. Within the cella was the masterpiece of
Phidias, the great gold and ivory statue of Athena herself. North of the
Parthenon on the Acropolis was an Ionic temple of unusual shape: it
faced east in the customary manner, but it had two porches at the rear,
one of which faced north and the other south. This was the Erechtheum,

MODEL OF THE ATHENIAN ACROPOLIS

(Courtesy of the Royal Ontario Museum, Toronto, Canada.)

sacred to Erechtheus who was believed to have been early king of Athens. The south porch of the Erechtheum was the famous Porch of the Maidens which sheltered the grave of Cecrops, legendary first king of Athens, while the north porch was built over the salt well which tradition said was the gift of Poseidon. Just west of the Erechtheum was the precinct called the Pandroseum, sacred to Pandora, and within it grew the sacred olive tree of Athena.

Sculptors

Myron. The sculptors of the fifth century B.C. profited from the patient labors of their archaic predecessors. Many problems of technique had been solved by 500 B.C., with the result that new developments came swiftly after that. Myron, who flourished between 475 and 450, experimented with the portrayal of motion. His *Ladas,* a runner depicted in full career, was a daring innovation; even more famous was another study in motion, the *Discus Thrower.* People also admired Myron's bronze heifer which was so lifelike that it even fooled the cows.

Phidias. Phidias, in the middle of the fifth century B.C., was a master of technique, and famous for his portrayal of the majesty and dignity of the gods and his idealized portraits of human beings which

THE DORYPHORUS: MARBLE COPY OF A
BRONZE ORIGINAL BY POLYCLITUS,
FIRST CENTURY B.C.

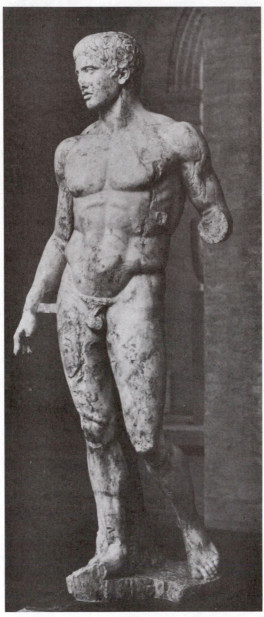

(Courtesy of the Minneapolis Institute of Arts.)

showed "men not as they were, but as they ought to be." We have spoken of his chryselephantine (gold and ivory) Athena in the Parthenon, but equally celebrated was his gold and ivory statue of the seated Zeus at Olympia. People said that Phidias had given the Greeks perfect likenesses of Zeus and Athena and that henceforth no one could imagine them as having any other appearance. Phidias also did the spectacular towering bronze statue of Athena as a war goddess (Athena Promachos) which stood in the open on the Acropolis just east of the Propylaea.

Polyclitus, Praxiteles, and Scopas.   At the end of the fifth century B.C. flourished Polyclitus, an Argive who specialized in *kouroi* and concerned himself with determining the ideal proportions of the human body; his conclusions were incorporated in the *Doryphorus* (Spear Bearer). He did a gold and ivory *Hera* for her sanctuary at Argos as well as a famous *Amazon* of which Roman copies have survived. Fully master of the techniques sought by earlier generations was the fourth-century sculptor, Praxiteles, remembered for his Cnidian *Aphrodite* as well as for the statue of Hermes with the infant Dionysus which stood at Olympia. Scopas of Paros, a contemporary of Praxiteles, was an experimenter; abandoning the custom of imparting to the faces of deities and humans a serene, untroubled expression, Scopas tried to express emotion. By parting the lips and setting the eyes deep in their sockets so that they seemed to gaze upward, he achieved an illusion of excitement or even frenzy.

Loss of Originals.   With the possible exception of the Hermes and infant Dionysus found at Olympia many years ago, we do not possess any original statue by a known sculptor. The chryselephantine Athena, Zeus, and Hera disappeared long ago, but even the stone and bronze statues have not survived, so that we must depend on Roman copies, terra-cotta statuettes, and representations on coins for our knowledge of the works of the famous artists of the fifth and fourth centuries. On the other hand, the sculptural decoration of the Parthenon, probably the work of the pupils of Phidias, the bronze *Charioteer* from Delphi, or the great bronze Poseidon (or Zeus) recovered from the sea off Artemisium are originals that suggest how much we are missing in the inferior Roman copies that remain.

Painting

Although Greek painting came to perfection in the fourth century B.C. and thus lagged a little behind sculpture, it was nevertheless one of the major arts in Greece. Unfortunately, no examples of painting survive from this period. The names of the great painters, the titles of their paintings, and commentaries on their various styles may be found in literary works of the Roman period as, for example, in the *Natural History* of Pliny the Elder. Some styles and advances in technique may be mirrored in the red-figured painted pottery of fifth-century Athens in which we can see concern with drapery, experiments in perspective, and a series of styles ending with the florid mode that came in late in the century.

The great name in fifth-century B.C. painting was that of Polygnotos, who came to Athens in the time of Cimon. It is said that Polygnotos was the first to paint women with transparent garments and varicolored headdresses and that in the faces of his figures he eschewed the traditional blankness by parting the lips and showing the teeth. Apollodoros, Zeuxis, and Parrhasius lived at the turn of the fourth century. Apollodorus may have introduced perspective, while Zeuxis was a showman who made a fortune from his talents as a painter. He painted from life with such care that at Acragas in Sicily he insisted on inspecting five girls of the city unclad in order that he might capture in his painting the special attributes of their beauty. Parrhasius of Ephesus, and Zeuxis were great rivals. In one contest of skill, Zeuxis painted a bunch of grapes with such realism that birds flew down and tried to eat them; Parrhasius countered by painting a curtain so convincing that Zeuxis called upon his rival to raise the curtain in order that he might inspect the picture it concealed.

Dramatic Poetry

Coming to the literary achievements of the classical age, we do not have to rely on later copies or commentators but can examine the originals themselves. The works of major authors in prose, poetry, tragedy, and comedy are available to us. Ideally perhaps, we might wish for greater abundance and variety, but at least there is enough on which to form some kind of judgment.

The older forms of poetry survived the archaic period, as we have seen, but, with the exception of the odes of the great Boeotian lyric poet, Pindar (*fl.* 475 B.C.), our interest is naturally drawn to the dramatic poetry of fifth-century Athens. The dramatic contests instituted by Peisistratus had given great impetus to the development of this form, which was associated with the worship of Dionysus. In the beginning it had been customary to honor the god with choral songs accompanied by simple mystery plays based on episodes in the "life" of Dionysus. The choral passages were interspersed with recitatives by the leader of the chorus; since the chorus both sang and danced, these performances were like embryonic operas. Gradually, plots and performances became more elaborate and complex with the leader taking a more important role. Mythological and legendary subjects independent of the Dionysiac myth began to be used for plots, and, as the performances began to take shape as more formal plays early in the fifth century, the playwrights entering the annual competition each submitted a group of four plays: a trilogy (a set of three plays) dealing with some myth or legend, and a satyr play which related specifically to the Dionysus story.

Aeschylus.   One complete trilogy has survived. It is the work of the first great writer of tragedy, Aeschylus, and it was performed at Athens in 458 B.C. The three plays are the *Agamemnon,* the *Libation Bearers*, and the *Eumenides*. They deal with the unhappy story of the family of Agamemnon. In the first play, Agamemnon returns from the siege of Troy to be murdered by his wife, Clytemnestra, and her lover, Aegistheus. By a series of episodes interspersed with choral passages, tension is increased until the powerful climax is reached in which the great king is assassinated and his captive, the Trojan prophetess, Cassandra, is also murdered. In the *Libation Bearers* this awful crime is avenged by Orestes and Electra, the children of Agamemnon and Clytemnestra. Orestes plots and executes the murder of his mother and Aegistheus and thus becomes guilty of the more horrible offense of matricide. In the *Eumenides* we find him pursued by the Furies, desperately seeking a way to purify himself from his own sacrilege and to end the curse which had fallen upon his family even before the time of Agamemnon. Orestes appeals to Apollo, who grants him a trial at Athens under the presidency of Athena. When the goddess absolves Orestes and ends the curse, the didactic purpose of the trilogy is revealed: Its lesson is that justice (reason) must replace and triumph over the primitive customs and superstitions typified by the Furies.

This trilogy, the *Oresteia*, shows us the point to which tragedy had developed by midcentury. The chorus had lost much of its earlier importance, the leader had been joined by other performers, and two actors usually appeared together and conducted a dialogue. The play itself had become a didactic vehicle by means of which the playwright might present an idea or dramatize a moral point for his audience. Attic tragedy is thus a valuable source for intellectual developments at Athens. By the end of the fifth century B.C., by a natural development, both comedies and tragedies were sometimes used as media for political propaganda.

Sophocles.   Aeschylus, who had fought in the Battle of Salamis and produced his first play, the *Suppliant Women,* before the Battle of Marathon, died about 456 B.C. and was succeeded by Sophocles, who lived on to the ripe old age of 90, dying in 406. A product of the Periclean Age, Sophocles endowed his plays with a dignity and majesty reminiscent of the sculpture of Phidias or the oratory of Pericles himself. Sophocles was a fine playwright and a poet of great talent. More adaptable to the modern stage than the plays of Aeschylus, those of Sophocles are frequently performed today, particularly the *Antigone, Electra,* and *Oedipus the King.* Aristotle called the *Oedipus* the perfect tragedy. It is indeed a powerful play with mounting suspense leading up to an unforgettable climax when Oedipus discovers that the plague tormenting his kingdom has been occasioned by his own unwitting sins of patricide and incest. Human futility and inadequacy are dramatized by the unsuccessful efforts of Oedipus to deny the prophecy that he will commit murder and incest just as his self-inflicted blindness and exile seem an ineffectual means of atonement for crimes of which he was not guilty by intent.

Euripides.   Euripides, the third of the great dramatists, was born about 480 B.C. and died in the same year as Sophocles. Most of his surviving plays were produced while the Peloponnesian War was in progress, and both he and his audience seem to have been affected and coarsened by that desperate conflict. A rationalist who strove for realism but often went beyond it to less admirable sensationalism, Euripides was more concerned with showing people as they were than as they ought to be. Although his plots were from mythological and legendary sources, he often used his material so that it had obvious reference to the contemporary. The *Trojan Women* dealt with the sufferings of the defeated Trojans, but few people in Athens who saw the first performance failed to understand that Euripides was criticizing the cruelty that the Athenians had just meted out to the unfortunate people of Melos. One of the best known plays of Euripides is the *Medea* in which the plot is built around the ageless perennial problem of matrimonial failure. The brilliance and talent of Euripides were admired by the ancients, and his plays were studied in the schools for centuries, but it was sometimes questioned whether he belonged in the same category with Aeschylus and Sophocles.

Aristophanes.   Since we possess the works of only one playwright, Aristophanes (446–388 B.C.), Attic comedy is harder to assess. Political, then later social, satire was the stock in trade of comedy. In broad if not vulgar humor, Aristophanes ridiculed individuals prominent in public life as well as familiar types—demagogues, jurymen, intellectuals. Socrates and Euripides were openly lampooned by him. Many situations and even whole plots of Aristophanes are clever and amusing. His plays are replete with antidemocratic sentiment as well as criticism of the

Peloponnesian War and the intellectuals of Athens. Because his comedies were topical, there are many allusions to people and events that escape us now.

Prose

In the fifth century B.C., Greek prose developed very rapidly and took its place beside poetry in the realm of literature. The rise of oratory to a position of great importance may have had much to do with the development of other prose forms. In politics and the courts it had become essential for a successful participant to be able to speak well in order to impress and persuade others. Professional teachers appeared who professed to impart or improve oratorical skill; matters of style and methods of argumentation were analyzed and systematized. From this it was only a step to the idea that other subjects could be organized and knowledge or proficiency gained through formal instruction or by means of written treatises. By the second half of the fifth century B.C. itinerant teachers, the Sophists, were traveling from city to city lecturing on a multitude of subjects—government, society, natural science, and the like—while many other persons, professionals and amateurs, became pamphleteers who wrote little essays on matters which they considered to be important. It was immediately apparent that a man could not write in the same way that he might speak. This made people conscious of the necessity for a good style in written composition just as in oratory, and they began to experiment with various modes of expression.

Herodotus.   The most enduring prose of the fifth century B.C. dealt with history and philosophy. Herodotus, the Father of History, was born just as the Persian wars ended. He came to Athens from his home in southwestern Asia Minor shortly after 450 B.C. In graceful Ionic Greek, Herodotus composed a history of the Persian wars; he was a new Homer, writing in prose the story of an epic contest between East and West. Like Homer, he never moved in a straight line but introduced many a digression from the main thread of his narrative; moreover, the presence of metrical elements in his prose indicates that he was not fully at home in the new medium. The technique of history was in its infancy, too. About a third of Herodotus' history was concerned not with the wars themselves but with a description of the known world and its people or nations. This did not bother his contemporaries: they were interested in geography and ethnology, and the word *historiai* which Herodotus used to describe his own work meant "researches" and did not have the limited meaning that "histories" would have today. In technique and method, Herodotus was only an amateur historian, but as a storyteller he was never surpassed by any of the ancients. Herodotus was a pioneer. Facilities were lacking for him to establish many facts; collections of records, formal accounts dealing with the past, and libraries which would place other materials easily within his reach were not available to him. Instead, Herodotus was forced to use traditions and legends and to gain information through personal interviews. He traveled widely throughout the Greek world and apparently visited Egypt; the whole second book of his history is an Egyptian travelogue of the kind that any curious and gullible tourist, even of the twentieth century A.D., might write after seeing the land of the pyramids. In spite of all this, Herodotus produced a great book; with all its imperfections, let it be said that it is invaluable to the historian today. Herodotus was interested in something more than mere narrative and description; his main purpose was didactic. He wanted to show that the Persians did not deserve to win the war; he felt that they had an excess of *hybris* (pride), and, like the Hebrews, all Greeks knew that "pride goeth before a fall."

Thucydides.   Reputedly the greatest of all historians, Greek or otherwise, was Thucydides, an Athenian who served as a general during part of the Peloponnesian War and spent its closing years in exile writing an account of that conflict. The compact, powerful style of Thucydides is sufficient proof that prose by his time had parted company with poetry. The influence of oratory may be seen in the inclusion of many formal speeches in his history which serve as a substitute for exposition in setting forth ideas or explaining policies. Thucydides conceived his work in the form of a tragedy; its subject was the fall of Athens from the heights of empire to the complete abasement of 404 B.C. How he might have developed this we do not know since his finished account did not go beyond the early years of the second phase of the war.

Thucydides looked upon history as a literary form and paid close attention to style and arrangement. He also tried to make history into what he would have called a science. Lacking satisfactory records for the remote past, he preferred to deal with the present so as to take advantage of his own experiences, the recollections of contemporaries, and the government documents to which he had access. In this way he hoped to get at the facts and establish truth. If the facts were known, one could analyze what happened, and men might be able to draw valuable lessons for the future from the study of the past. Like Herodotus, his basic purpose was didactic.

Whatever may be said of Thucydides' hopes for establishing history as a science, his literary aspirations led him to great heights. His history contains some of the most famous passages in all literature: the Funeral Speech of Pericles, the account of the plague, the description of the departure of the Athenian expedition to Sicily in 415 B.C., and the so-called Melian dialogue. Historians who wrote after Thucydides followed either the literary or the scientific path, but no one else was able to combine the two approaches successfully.

Xenophon.   The unfinished story of Thucydides was continued and extended down to 362 B.C. by another Athenian, Xenophon. But Xenophon was no Thucydides, and he is better remembered for his *Anabasis,* the account of an unsuccessful revolution in Persia and the part which 10,000 Greek mercenaries (and Xenophon himself) took in it. Xenophon was to write much during his lifetime. He was an inveterate pamphleteer with a good prose style although he never produced anything else as good as the *Anabasis.* Xenophon also fancied himself a philosopher. Like Plato, Alcibiades, and Critias, the leader of the Thirty Tyrants, Xenophon had been a disciple of Socrates. Like Plato, he wrote about the martyred teacher, although his recollections of Socrates are by no means the same as those of Plato.

Philosophers

No characterization of Socrates that we possess—in Xenophon, Plato, the *Clouds* of Aristophanes, or the biography by Diogenes Laertius—may be valid. It is clear, however, that Socrates was a very important figure in the history of philosophy, and a brief review of intellectual developments in the first part of the fifth century will help us to put him in proper place in the evolution of Greek thought.

The concern of the early Greek thinkers had been with mathematics, astronomy, and cosmology. In the first half of the fifth century, however, the development of the first two had reached a degree of specialization that was repellent to most people, while a welter of speculation and a dearth of solid proof brought about a decrease of interest in the third. The predominance of the city-state and concern with its affairs had focused the attention of the majority of thoughtful persons on man and society. It seemed idle in the face of immediate problems of a political and social kind to play at solving the mysteries of nature.

Early Philosophers.   The early philosophers had broken the ice of myth and superstition by speculating in a rational way about the natural world and its origins. If they had accomplished nothing else, they had at least established a method or principle for dealing with a problem by means of analysis and reason. In the absence of any tradition of strong religious authority that professed to provide a hard and fast answer to any question relating to the world, the state, or patterns of human behavior, it was quite natural for thinking people to come quickly to the conclusion that "man is the measure of all things." At the same time, the almost insuperable difficulties that stood in the way of positive proof for any theory that might be obtained through pure reasoning fostered among some extremists a skepticism that proclaimed that knowledge was relative and truth far from absolute or eternal. Since proof was hard or seemed unattainable in some cases, men cynically reasoned that persuasion was the next best thing, and they began to cultivate this art assiduously.

Sophists.   The second half of the fifth century B.C. was the Age of the Sophists. These arrogant, brilliant, and often unscrupulous, teachers were the intellectual medicine men of classical Greece. They went from town to town delivering lectures to paying audiences on a variety of subjects. The Sophists claimed to give practical instruction which would help a man to get ahead in politics or win a case in the courts. Rhetoric and argumentation were heavily stressed, but the Sophists often extended their remarks to include radical viewpoints on politics, society, religion, custom, and natural phenomena. Many of the Sophists coyly admitted to universal knowledge; this really meant that they were willing to express an opinion on any subject and, since their mental agility and dialectical skill exceeded that of most of their hearers, they were able to beat down opposing arguments and preserve the illusion of their infallibility. When Anaxagoras said that the sun was not a god but a burning stone, or when Gorgias said that man could not ascertain the truth even if it existed, conservative people felt that religion, morality, the state, and society were being undermined. They resolved to combat this subversion and adopted a violent anti-intellectualism which condemned not only the Sophists but also everyone else who dared to deviate from the norm of established belief.

Socrates.   Of all the intellectual gadflies at Athens who irritated the now tender skin of the conservatives, Socrates came to be the most hated. He did not merit the label of Sophist—he did not charge a fee for the rather indirect instruction afforded his followers, and he denied knowing anything. Instead, Socrates went about Athens questioning people regarding their beliefs about truth, justice, law, piety, and many other subjects. These were precisely the things about which most persons had strong, but usually baseless, opinions. A master of dialectic, Socrates was able to tie his victims in knots by questions that provoked a whole series of contradictory answers and left the distinct impression that the respondents were muddleheaded dunces. The so-called Socratic method is illustrated in many of the dialogues of Plato. It was an infuriating thing to be on the receiving end of Socrates' interrogations. The affair usually took place on a street corner or in the Agora with a company of bystanders to enjoy the fun along with Socrates' own coterie of bright young men—Plato, Xenophon, Alcibiades, Critias, and the rest—who often conducted interviews of their own. It was hardly surprising that in the wave of hysteria and unsettlement that accompanied Athenian defeat in the Peloponnesian War, Socrates was brought to trial for subversion in 399 B.C. and condemned to death.

If we accept the Socrates of Plato's dialogues as the real Socrates, we must see him as a great and noble person who sincerely tried to improve the Athenian character. We must also credit Socrates with having channeled philosophical speculation away from science and into ethics. In addition, his methods of logical classification and his use of inductive discourse were to benefit Greek intellectual activities of all kinds in the future.

Plato.   Whatever uncertainty exists about Socrates and his ability as a philosopher does not attach to Plato (429–347 B.C.). The literary style of Plato was to be admired for centuries, and it was a stroke of genius on his part to center his work on the dramatic figure of Socrates and also to employ the dialogue, borrowed from the theater, as his means of exposition. Ethics and politics concerned Plato most, but his approach was unlike that of the Sophists, for it was metaphysical rather than "practical." The mind, the soul, and reason were conceived as superior to matter, the body, and the senses. All aspirations must be directed toward the Good, the True, and the Beautiful; these were abstractions that enjoyed an independent existence outside the sense world. Among his most famous works are the *Republic* and the *Laws* which treat of the ideal city-state; the *Phaedo,* which describes the death of Socrates; and the *Apology* in which the trial of Socrates is related. The ideas of Plato provided the soil from which many schools of philosophy were to spring in the centuries to come.

Aristotle.   Aristotle (384–322 B.C.) began his studies as a pupil of Plato but later departed from the teachings of his master in many ways. This great philosopher came nearer than any of the Sophists to possessing universal knowledge. A large part of his life was spent in classifying and organizing various fields of knowledge. For example, he created the science of zoology, and another one of his great projects was a series of monographs on the constitutions of various Greek city-states, including that of Athens. Aristotle is called the inventor of formal logic; he also wrote an *Ethics*, a *Politics*, a *Rhetoric*, and many other important treatises. His contribution to the field of literary criticism was the famous *Poetics* which has influenced thinking about poetry and drama for centuries. The pupils and successors of Aristotle continued to employ the methods of synthesizing knowledge that he had evolved; many of them laid the foundations for new sciences in the way that Aristotle had established zoology. Unlike Plato and Socrates, Aristotle did not reject scientific speculation. His works on physics, meteorology, and related subjects were basic to all later studies in antiquity and the Middle Ages.

Hippocrates.   In at least one field, a rational approach to man's problems resulted in a practical and concrete advance. This was in medicine where the great name was that of Hippocrates of Cos, a priest who served Asclepius, the god of healing. Hippocrates came to understand disease as a natural evil that could be overcome by natural methods. The best defense against illness, he said, was to keep well by practicing hygiene and avoiding excesses. Through observation and experiment and with a knowledge of drugs obtained from Egypt, Hippocrates improved medical practice, established diagnosis and treatment on a sounder basis, and founded a school of physicians that carried on his work for centuries.

Permanence of Greek Culture

In 150 years, the Greeks had climbed from obscurity to a pinnacle of greatness and then fallen over the precipice of their own folly, never to rise again. Fortunately, more permanence attached to their cultural achievements than their political success. In art, literature, philosophy, and science, they became the teachers of the Romans and, through them, of all the future nations of the West.

Chapter Seven

One World, Many Worlds

The suicidal warfare of their city-states was not the sole cause of decline among the mainland Greeks. Trade was the key to the prosperity, and hence the power, enjoyed by these states in the period 650 to 400 B.C. Wine, olive oil, and manufactured products had been exchanged for the precious metals, foodstuffs, and raw materials from the colonies and other undeveloped areas around the Mediterranean and the Black Seas, but the nice balance of this arrangement was upset as some of the best customers of the mainland Greeks, particularly the Greeks in Italy and Sicily, began to attain self-sufficiency by producing their own oil, wine, and manufactures. A growing shortage of silver also oppressed trade, especially where it was dependent on the old triangular patterns previously described. The Carthaginians had obtained control of the silver mines of Spain, and folk movements in Central Europe may have stopped the movement of silver to the Balkan coast of the Adriatic. Commerce with the Near East, although curtailed by the establishment of the Persian empire and the support given Phoenician traders by the Persians, had not ceased, but the balance of trade was unfavorable to the Greeks since the Near East desired silver more than anything else the Greeks had to offer. The loss of markets in the West, the drying up of sources of silver, and the steady drain of silver bullion to the East seem to have brought the Greek economy into straitened circumstances during the fourth century.

For the Athenians, the shortage of silver may have been aggravated by the seizure of the Thracian mines by Philip of Macedon, the father of Alexander the Great, whose career we shall describe. Although the Thracian mines produced more gold than silver, the sources of the latter metal for the mainland Greeks were so few that even a small loss could have caused problems, and at Athens this led to feverish efforts in the Laurium area of Attica to find new veins of silver and exploit more intensively deposits mined earlier.

It is generally thought that Athens regained her prosperity after the Peloponnesian War, at least during the first half of the fourth century.

The principal source for this opinion is to be found in speeches composed for legal suits by the great Attic orators; some of these speeches were written for clients and some for cases in which the orators themselves were involved. Despite the heavy military expenses of numerous wars and the fact that there were few new building projects at Athens until late in the century, we do get the impression that there were a number of well-to-do, even rich, people in Attica who had capital to invest in various enterprises in which they themselves did not always actively participate. A person might finance the establishment of a workshop, manned by slaves and managed by freedmen or slaves, that might manufacture weapons and armor or make furniture and so on. Another investor might buy a share in a trading venture conducted by an Athenian shipowner or by a foreigner. Speculation in the grain market could be worthwhile if your greed did not result in breaking the law limiting profit in such ventures. One might also deposit money with a banker for him to invest in land or other projects at a fixed rate of interest. Many of the bankers, incidentally, were ex-slaves who had proven talents for making money. Slave owning had long been known as a means of increasing one's wealth, and, in the third quarter of the fourth century when mining flourished, owners could rent gangs of slaves to work in the silver mines for other people who had acquired leases for mining properties.

In addition to the speeches of the orators relating to the subject, there is a pamphlet attributed to Xenophon called *Ways and Means* that contains suggestions for increasing the wealth of the Athenians. It is not easy to tell whether the work as a whole is evidence for good times or just represents wishful thinking, but the strong emphasis on resuming the work in the Laurium mines dates the essay in the second half of the century.

From the prevalence of various liturgies, old and some newly imposed, it is plain that there were numerous wealthy people in Athens who were expected to contribute to the maintenance of the government and the support of the many less fortunate, poorer citizens. The rich had never liked the system, even in the days when assuming a liturgy was a mark of civic virtue. In the fourth century liturgies were a burden which some people sought to avoid.

It is an interesting commentary on the situation at Athens after the Peloponnesian War that in the "restored democracy" the poor had to be paid for attending the assembly, and they also expected to receive tokens that gave free admission to the theater. The process of the rich getting richer and the poor poorer continued into the new age, the Hellenistic. The policy of "bread and circuses," once thought to have been a Roman innovation, may be sensed in an embryonic form at Athens in the fourth century and can be seen in a well-developed stage in the great Hellenistic cities of the succeeding period.

In addition to all this, the frontiers of civilization had continued to advance. The non-Greek peoples of Italy—the Italic tribes and especially the Romans—as well as the Macedonians, situated to the north of Greece, had begun to emerge from barbarism. Newly touched by civilization, such nations became strong and dangerous. Just as the Persians in their youth had been able to overcome the older kingdoms of the Near East, so now the Romans and Macedonians would fall upon their more civilized neighbors.

Not only the Greeks but also the Persians had been subject to decline. The Persian empire had never been securely unified; it could be held together only so long as its masters could dominate the subject peoples and defend their territory from outside aggression. Divided by dynastic quarrels and weakened by court intrigue, the Persians no longer had a Cyrus or a great Darius to lead them, and the national militia that had won the victories of the earlier period had been replaced by an army consisting mostly of Greek mercenaries and subject levies that could not be depended upon to either protect or garrison the far-flung empire.

The old order was crumbling. Greeks and Persians had had their day, and a new world was in the making.

PHILIP OF MACEDON

Three years after the Battle of Mantinea, a young, able, and ambitious ruler ascended the Macedonian throne. This was Philip II, the father of Alexander, who might have gone down in history as Philip the Great if he had not sired an even greater son. A hostage in Thebes during the Theban ascendancy in the years between Leuctra and Mantinea, Philip had learned much about imperial government and finance, diplomacy, new military organization, and Greek politics. By taking advantage of the weakness and division among the Greeks, he planned to raise his country to a position of supremacy in the Balkans.

Philip's Challenges: Unify and Strengthen

Macedonia in 359 B.C. was a big country with a relatively small population. Most of its people were farmers and herdsmen, and, compared with the Greek city-states, Macedonia was backward. It had virtually no trade; manufacturing above the household level did not exist; there was no city, scarcely even a large town, in the whole area. Politically and socially, the Macedonians were still living in the Dark Ages. The principal social groups were the peasants and the nobles, and the king had little more authority than the ancient Greek *basileus*, although a person with vision and a strong personality could make something of the office. The economic development of Macedonia had been retarded because the Greeks had long ago colonized the coast and cut off the back country from direct commerce with the outside world. On the landward boundaries of Macedonia lived fierce barbarian tribes that constantly threatened the frontiers. To realize his ambitions, Philip must wrest his coastline from the Greeks and chasten the barbarians. He must unify Macedonia itself and strengthen the monarchy. The latter task would be difficult because the country was on the verge of that traditional upheaval that would replace the king with an aristocratic government, the sort of thing that had happened in Greece just before 750 B.C.

The quickest and most efficient way to strengthen the monarchy and unify the vigorous, war-loving Macedonians was to make war. Philip led his people first against the barbarians on the east, north, and west. As the campaigns proceeded, he reorganized his army in the new patterns that the Thebans had found so effective: The nobles were formed into a powerful cavalry, and the commoners were trained as hoplites and peltasts; archers, slingers, and a siege train were added to give the army even greater versatility. Philip's successful leadership made him immensely popular and consequently bolstered the position of the monarchy. Rewards and promotions for military bravery aroused enthusiasm for the army and helped the people forget class antagonisms. With the landward frontiers safely established, Philip could turn next to the coast. Cleverly playing upon the rivalries of the Greeks, he supported one town against another until he had weakened them all to the point where they could be gobbled up at leisure. Athens, Thebes, and other big states in Greece itself might have aided the north Aegean towns, but they were scarcely aware of Philip's designs before they were accomplished (353 B.C.).

Domination of Greece

The unification of Macedonia was only the first step in Philip's program. His next moves, aimed at dominating Greece itself, were aided by the follies of his intended victims. In 356 B.C. the so-called Sacred War had begun in central Greece. The Phocians, in whose territory the international shrine of Apollo at Delphi was located, were accused by the Thebans of having tampered with Apollo's treasury. When the Thebans and Thessalians attacked them, the Phocians did seize the treasury and used the proceeds to buy an army with which to defend themselves.

In 353 B.C. the Phocians carried the war into Thessaly, and the Thessalians called upon Philip for help. He repelled the invaders and later (348 B.C.) was invited by the Thebes to bring his forces into Greece and put an end to the war. After the Phocians were beaten, Philip was given their votes on the governing board of the Delphic shrine. This provided him with a sufficient excuse to enter Greece again when new fighting over Delphi broke out in 339. Too late, the Thebans and Athenians recognized their common danger and combined to oppose Philip. They were beaten decisively at Chaeronea in Boeotia in 338 B.C.

Philip's Diplomacy

The victory at Chaeronea assured Philip of a commanding position in Greek affairs, but the way for his military success had been paved by diplomacy rather than combat. The propertied classes in Greece had come to regard him as the strong man who could end intercity warfare and serve as an ally against the masses who favored "democracy." Thus, the oligarchs were willing to cooperate with him in order to protect their wealth and political prestige. In addition, about 357 B.C. Philip had taken over gold and silver mines in the area just east of Macedonia. The annual revenues from these mines were said to be about 1,000 talents (perhaps a million dollars). Not only did the Greeks hope to exchange their products for Philip's gold and silver, but also by generous bribes to Greek politicians in Athens and elsewhere Philip had acquired staunch defenders of his policies. Consequently, when a patriot like the orator Demosthenes tried to arouse the Athenians to oppose Philip, other skilled orators were not lacking to argue on the pro-Macedonian side.

Formation of the Hellenic League

In 337 B.C. Philip called a meeting of the major Greek states at Corinth. At his suggestion a Hellenic League was formed. Its members pledged themselves to end intercity warfare and to support existing governments in the various states. Deputies to the league council were empowered to enact measures binding on all member cities, and the league entered into an alliance with Philip, who was also elected commander-in-chief of the allied forces.

This was the climax of Philip's career. He was king of the now-powerful Macedonia; he was *tagos*, or warlord, of Thessaly; and he had at his disposal the forces of the Hellenic League as well as those of Epirus, an Adriatic state which he had annexed in 343 B.C.

Philip's Assassination

Philip had not invented the game, but he was a master of it. He knew that he could not rest on his laurels. He must keep moving. The way to consolidate the temporary unification of the Greeks and divert their attention from the virtual tyranny which he had imposed upon them was to launch an attack on Persia to secure the freedom of the Greeks in Asia. Therefore, in 336 B.C. Philip called upon the Hellenic League for ships and men to assist in an invasion of Ionia. An expeditionary force had already crossed the Hellespont and Philip was on the point of departure to join his forces when he was murdered. Responsibility for his assassination was never established: Members of his own family or jealous Macedonian nobles may have been at the bottom of the plot, and other likely suspects included vengeful Greeks or the crafty Persians who had been trying to stop Philip for many years. A hard-living, hard-driving, hard-drinking Macedonian "Peter the Great," Philip had made more enemies than friends, and there were Macedonians, Greeks, barbarians, and certainly Persians who did not lament his passing.

ALEXANDER THE GREAT

In spite of his mighty deeds, Philip was outshone by his son, Alexander, who ascended the throne after Philip's death.

Accession of Alexander

The murder of Philip was well timed. It stopped the invasion of Persian territory, and it threw Macedonia into confusion because of uncertainty about the succession to the throne. Under normal circumstances, Alexander, the twenty-year-old son of Philip and an Epirote princess named Olympias, would have ascended the throne without question, but Philip and his wife were estranged, and Alexander had sided with his mother against Philip. Alexander, however, had the support of the army; despite his youth he was already a military hero, who had shown his worth at Chaeronea in 338 B.C. when he led a brilliant cavalry charge that won the day against the Greeks. He now gained the throne with the backing of the troops, executed the alleged assassins of his father—perhaps to silence them—and began his short, but spectacular, reign of thirteen years (336–323 B.C.).

Defeat of the Barbarians and Thebans

The accession of Alexander was taken rather lightly by the barbarians, the Greeks, and the Persians. Outside of Macedonia, he was regarded as an untried youth who might never be the man his father had been. When the barbarians crossed the frontiers and put Alexander to the test, however, they were soon beaten and cowed by a series of campaigns during 336 and 335 B.C. In the latter year, reports circulated in Greece that Alexander had been killed while fighting in the west. On the strength of this rumor, the Thebans renounced their allegiance to Macedonia, and other Greek states prepared to follow their example. Seemingly out of nowhere, Alexander appeared before the gates of Thebes. The city was taken, the men executed, the women and children sold into slavery, and the whole town destroyed except for the temples and the house of Pindar. Terrified, the other Greeks assured Alexander of their unswerving loyalty, agreeing to revive the Hellenic League along with the scheme for the liberation of the Asiatic Greeks.

Defeat of the Persians

With a small force of 35,000, Alexander invaded northwestern Asia Minor in 334 B.C. Destroying a Persian army in a great battle at the Granicus River, he marched south along the Aegean coast of Asia to be hailed as a deliverer by Smyrna, Ephesus, and other major towns. Only Miletus and Halicarnassus, garrisoned by elements of the Persian fleet, offered opposition. By 333 B.C. Alexander was able to move through central Anatolia and follow the route of Xenophon and the 10,000 through the Cilician Gates to the plain of Tarsus. Then, as he marched around the Gulf of Alexandretta and down into Syria, a great Persian force commanded by King Darius III got behind him at Issus and cut his communications with the north. In a truly desperate situation, Alexander had to return to Issus where he won his greatest battle by daring, brilliant strategy. As Darius fled into Mesopotamia, the Macedonians resumed their southward advance. By capturing the Phoenician seaports—even mighty Tyre capitulated after a seven-month siege (332 B.C.)—Alexander was able to destroy the Persian fleet without a battle at sea simply because the fleet was manned by Phoenician sailors who deserted as their home cities went over to the Macedonian side. By the end of 332 B.C. Alexander had swept through Philistia into Egypt.

Like the Asiatic Greeks, the Egyptians welcomed Alexander as a liberator. He was recognized as the pharaoh, a god-king, the son of Amon. In 331 B.C., after completing the organization of Egypt, Alexander marched back through Palestine and Syria to begin the invasion of Mesopotamia. Darius III had offered to cede Asia Minor, Syria, Palestine, and Egypt to the conqueror and to pay in addition a handsome indemnity if Alexander would only make peace, but the offer was refused. In October 331 B.C., near Arbela in Assyria the Persians and Macedonians once again engaged in a titanic struggle, and again Alexander was victorious. As Darius took refuge in Media, Alexander marched southward through Babylonia and then eastward into Persia where he established his winter quarters in the Persian capital of Persepolis. By spring of 330 B.C. he was once more on the march, this time into Media in order to capture Darius. In the company of his eastern satraps, the Persian ruler fled toward Bactria (Turkestan) where he hoped Alexander would not follow. As Alexander pressed hard upon the retreating Persians, they murdered Darius in the area just south of the Caspian, apparently with the thought that Alexander would stop the pursuit and turn back to organize his already vast empire. On the contrary, when the Macedonian came upon the body of Darius, he announced his intention to avenge the king's murder. Wintering in Afghanistan, just south of the Hindu Kush range, the army of Alexander crossed the mountains into Bactria in the spring of 329 B.C. The next two years were spent in this remote area. Bessus, the satrap principally responsible for the murder of Darius, was captured and executed; difficult campaigns were fought against the Scythian nomads whose ancestors had killed Cyrus the Great two centuries before; and it was in Bactria that Alexander married the native princess, Roxane, said to be the most beautiful woman in Asia.

Annexation of the Upper Indus

When Alexander left Bactria in 327 B.C., he did not turn homeward but instead moved into the upper Indus country which he annexed after hard campaigning. Later, as he hoped to push on deeper into India, his troops mutinied and insisted upon turning back. Alexander was forced to consent but first he led the army down the Indus to its mouth where he divided his forces; part returned to Mesopotamia by land, but some were given the difficult assignment of building vessels and sailing back by way of the Indian Ocean and the Persian Gulf.

Death of Alexander

The last two years of Alexander's life were occupied with attempting to organize the most extensive empire the world had ever seen and in planning further exploration and conquest. Very little had been ac-

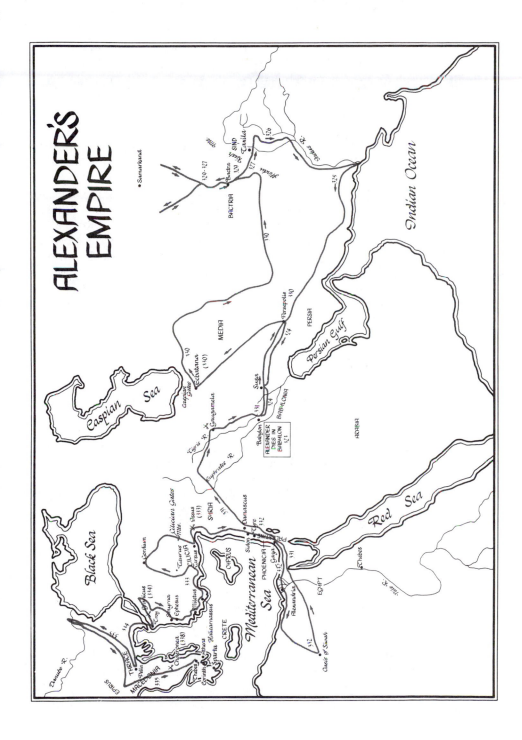

ALEXANDER'S EMPIRE

Samarkand

Indian Ocean

Caspian Sea

Black Sea

Mediterranean Sea

Red Sea

Persian Gulf

BACTRIA

MEDIA

PERSIA

ARABIA

EGYPT

SYRIA

CILICIA

CYPRUS

CRETE

THRACE

MACEDONIA

EPIRUS

PHOENICIA

BABYLONIA

SIND

Danube R.

Pella

Sparta

Corinth

Chaeronea (338)

Thebes

Athens

Byzantium

Troy

Granicus (334)

Smyrna

Ephesus

Miletus

Halicarnassus

Gordium

Ancyra

Cilician Gates

Tarsus

Issus (333)

Taurus Mts.

Damascus

Sidon

Tyre

Gaza

Alexandria

Oasis of Siwah

Thebes

Euphrates R.

Tigris R.

Gaugamela

Babylon

ALEXANDER DIES IN BABYLON 323

Susa

Persepolis

Ecbatana (340)

Caspian Gates

Bactra

Kabul

Taxila

Kunar

Hydaspes

Indus R.

335

334

333

332

331

330

329-327

328

327

326

325

324

323

340

complished by early summer in 323 B.C. when Alexander, worn out by his strenuous activities, succumbed to a fever and died at Babylon without providing for a successor. He had conquered the world and changed the whole course of history, but he was dead at age thirty-three.

THE SUCCESSORS OF ALEXANDER

Perhaps not even an Alexander could have held his empire together. There was no common denominator to use as a base to weld Macedonians, Greeks, Egyptians, Phoenicians, Babylonians, Persians, Indians, and dozens of smaller groups into a single nation. Innumerable differences in language, custom, tradition, and local aspirations all worked against unity. Alexander had a possible solution for the problem: He planned to create a ruling class of Macedonians, Greeks, and Persians to man his army, staff his imperial bureaucracy, and keep the subject masses under control. Unfortunately, this scheme called for a strong leader who could command and retain the allegiance of the governing minority; there was only one Alexander, and he had died.

Even so, the plan was not infallible. History had demonstrated that, while unity might bring prosperity to the Near East, prosperity tended to work against unity and dissolve it when good times fostered nationalist movements in Egypt, Babylonia, and other well-defined and self-conscious natural regions with memories of past glories and national independence. The Assyrian empire had been unable to cope with the problem, and the Persians had skated on thin ice for the same reasons. While it is true that there was no one big enough to take Alexander's place, and his empire did break up, it is also a fact that, as great prosperity followed on the heels of his conquest of Persia and as his empire disintegrated, the new states that emerged corresponded rather closely with the areas occupied by the four kingdoms that had formerly risen from the ruins of the Assyrian Empire.

Establishment of a Regency

When Alexander died in 323 B.C. there was no member of the Macedonian royal house capable of succeeding him. The unborn child of Roxane, even if a boy, would not be competent to rule for many years to come, and Alexander's idiot half-brother, Philip, was hardly the genius demanded by the circumstances. Alexander's great generals deliberated, argued, and compromised: When the baby, the young Alexander, was born, a regency was established to rule for him and on behalf of his half-witted Uncle Philip. This impossible arrangement was pre-

HELLENISTIC PORTRAITS: COINS

Top (left-right):   Coin of Philip with head of Zeus (possible portrait of Philip himself).

Coin of Alexander (possible portrait of Alexander).

2nd row: Two heads of Alexander intended as portraits.

3rd row: Perseus, last Antigonid king (178–168 B.C.).

Eumenes I, governor of Pergamum (263–241 B.C.).

Antiochus III, the Great, Seleucid king (222–187 B.C.).

Ptolemy I, founder of the Ptolemaic Kingdom (305–285 B.C.).

4th row: Prusias, King of Bithynia (238–183 B.C.).

Mithradates VI of Pontus (120–63 B.C.).

Mithradates I, King of Parthia (171–138 B.C.).

cariously maintained for seven years, but by 316 B.C. the fiction of the regency was abandoned, and an open contest for Alexander's empire began.

Three Great Kingdoms Emerge

Alexander had not made his conquests single-handedly but with the assistance of a number of capable, even brilliant, Macedonian generals. Eventually these came to consider themselves the rightful heirs to all, or parts, of the empire. They overthrew the regency; then they—and later, their sons—fought one another for the spoils. The ultimate winners carved three great kingdoms out of Alexander's realm, and in the end a fourth state emerged as one of the original three was split by secession. The story of the foundation of these states and their subsequent vicissitudes may be outlined as follows.

The Ptolemies.   No sooner had Alexander died in 323 B.C. than Ptolemy, one of his younger generals, took possession of Egypt and repelled all attempts of the regency to displace him. In 306 B.C. he proclaimed himself king and thus formally inaugurated a dynasty, that of the Ptolemies, which ruled Egypt until the Roman conquest of 30 B.C.

The Seleucids.   Seleucus, another general, was governor of Babylon at Alexander's death. Although temporarily driven out and forced to take refuge in Egypt, Seleucus returned to Mesopotamia in 312 B.C. to establish the second of the great Hellenistic dynasties, the Seleucid, which endured until it fell prey to the Romans in 63.

The Antigonids.   The history of the third kingdom, that of the Antigonids of Macedonia, was a little more complicated. Antigonus the One-Eyed, one of the older generals of Alexander, was determined to possess not merely a part but most of Alexander's empire. It was he who drove Seleucus out of Babylon and planned to attack Egypt and Macedonia simultaneously from his vantage point in Syria. He himself would invade Europe while his son, Demetrius, drove Ptolemy out of Egypt. The scheme failed because Demetrius was defeated by Ptolemy at Gaza in 312 B.C. Seleucus then regained Babylon, and Antigonus had to abandon his attack on Macedonia. Later on, although Antigonus and Demetrius managed to establish bases in Athens and Corinth, they lost control of the Near East and failed to regain it. Antigonus was killed fighting in Asia Minor in 301 B.C., and Demetrius was captured there by Seleucus about 285. Nevertheless, Antigonus Gonatas, the son of Demetrius, retained the family hold on Greece and finally won the throne of Macedonia in 277 B.C. where his descendants, the Antigonids, were to reign until they were overcome by the Romans in 167.

Between 277 and 200 B.C. these three major kingdoms of the Ptolemies, Seleucids, and Antigonids flourished in the Eastern Mediterranean. The Ptolemies held Egypt, Cyrene, Cyprus, and Palestine, and they fought with the Seleucids for the possession of Syria. The Antigonids had their capital in Macedonia and they tried to control Greece, although their hold on several key cities was lost after 250 B.C. The Seleucid empire at its greatest extent in the first part of the third century B.C. stretched from Asia Minor eastward to the Indus. The largest and least compact of the great kingdoms, its territorial integrity could not be maintained.

Policies and Relationships of the Three Kingdoms.   The policies of the three kingdoms and the story of their relations with one another can best be stated in terms of their needs. The heart of the Ptolemaic kingdom was Egypt. This rich prize must be protected by using Cyrene and Palestine as buffers against invasion by land, while the sea frontier needed the defense that only a navy could supply. To maintain a fleet, the Ptolemies must control access to the cedars of Lebanon and the naval stores of southern Asia Minor. This involved the Ptolemies in a series of wars with the Seleucids, who needed an outlet to the Mediterranean in Syria in order to keep up the east-west trade that was vital to the prosperity of the Seleucid kingdom. For the Ptolemies, it was a losing battle: The Seleucids got Syria, and, by the end of the third century, Palestine as well.

The Attalids.   Since relations between Seleucids and Antigonids were generally friendly from the second quarter of the third century onward, the Ptolemies tended to regard the Antigonids as potentially dangerous enemies. To keep the Antigonids off balance, the Ptolemies supported anti-Macedonian movements in Greece. In addition, to prevent the Antigonids and Seleucids from joining hands in Asia Minor, the Ptolemies encouraged the growth and independence of the Kingdom of Pergamum, which functioned like a wedge driven between Egypt's two enemies. Originally governed by Seleucid appointees, the territory of Pergamum in northwestern Asia Minor proclaimed its independence about 230 B.C. as its rulers, the Attalids, renounced their allegiance to the Seleucids.

The Parthians.   The Ptolemies were not the only foes with whom the Seleucids had to cope, and Syria was not the only territory where Seleucid control was disputed. In fact, the most serious problems of the

Seleucids arose in the east. To hold the area from Babylon to the Indus was no easy task under any circumstances, but after 250 B.C. conditions worsened when a wave of nationalism swept over Iran. Its leaders were the Parthians, originally nomadic invaders, who claimed to be the heirs of the Achaemenids, the rulers of the old Persian empire. This uprising cut the Seleucid kingdom in half: The Parthians carved out a realm in Iran, while the far-eastern provinces of the Seleucids became independent. Although a semblance of unity was restored temporarily by Antiochus III in the last quarter of the third century B.C., the eastern half was again lost in the next century, and before 150 the Parthians had captured Mesopotamia and confined the Seleucids to Syria and Palestine.

Achaean and Aetolian Leagues.   With the Ptolemies stirring up the Greeks, the Macedonians had troubles of their own which increased as the third century B.C. wore on. About 250 B.C. a league of city-states began to be formed in the Peloponnesus. This was the Achaean League with its capital at Corinth, once an Antigonid stronghold, and concentrated in the northern part of the Peloponnesus. Another combination, somewhat older in origin, was the Aetolian League which grew strong in the essentially rural areas of west-central Greece. At first the Achaean League was bitterly hostile to Macedonia, while the Aetolians were generally neutral. About 230 B.C., however, Sparta temporarily revived with Ptolemaic encouragement and aid. This alarmed the Achaeans who ultimately called upon Macedonia for help and thus brought back into the Peloponnesus the very people they had worked to expel. The Spartan revival was extinguished, but not before the Aetolians, fearing the consequences of growing Macedonian influence in Greece, went on the warpath against both Achaeans and Antigonids. Unable to get help from the Ptolemies who were under attack by the Seleucid king, Antiochus III, the Aetolians became the allies of Rome.

Roman Takeover of Eastern Mediterranean

During the last two decades of the third century B.C., the balance of power which had existed in the Eastern Mediterranean since about 275 was destroyed. For half a century, despite many wars involving the major powers, the strength of the Ptolemies, Seleucids, and Antigonids had remained about equal. By 220 B.C., however, the Antigonids under the leadership of Philip V and the Seleucids led by Antiochus III, the Great, had become vigorous and aggressive. Antiochus pushed the Ptolemies out of Asia and recaptured the eastern part of his empire as well. The Antigonids, under Philip, had repressed Sparta and reestablished some measure of control over Greece through their alliance with the

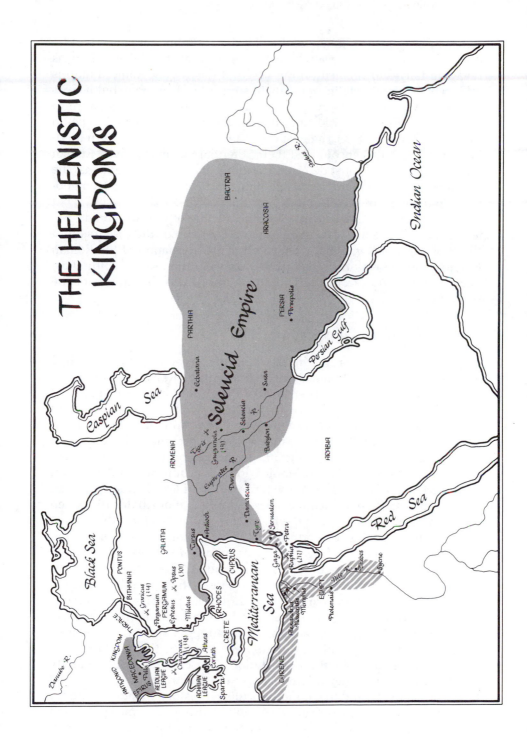

THE HELLENISTIC KINGDOMS

Indian Ocean

BACTRIA

ARACOSIA

Indus R.

Selucid Empire

PARTHIA

PERSIA
• Persepolis

• Ecbatana

• Susa

Persian Gulf

Caspian Sea

ARMENIA

Tigris R.
× Gaugamela (331)
• Seleucia R.
• Babylon

ARABIA

• *Euphrates R.*
• Dura

• Antioch

• Damascus

• Tarsus

• Tyre

• Jerusalem
• Petra

GALATIA

PONTUS

BITHINIA

Black Sea

× Granicus (334)

• Pergamum
PERGAMUM
• Ephesus × Ipsus (301)
• Miletus

THRACE

CYPRUS

RHODES

CRETE

Mediterranean Sea

• Gaza
• Raphia (217)

Red Sea

EGYPT

• Alexandria
• Naucratis
• Memphis

• Ptolemais
• Thebes
• Syene

CYRENE

ANTIGONID KINGDOM

MACEDONIA

AETOLIAN LEAGUE

× Chaeronea (338)
• Athens

EPIRUS

• Corinth

ACHAEAN LEAGUE
• Sparta

Danube R.

Achaean League. The power and ambition of Philip were such that he became the ally of the great Carthaginian general, Hannibal, who was ravaging Italy and seemed on the verge of destroying Rome. Philip is said to have planned to invade Italy in support of Hannibal, but he was pinned down in Greece by a war against the Aetolians who were in alliance with Rome. By 200 B.C. Philip and Antiochus seemed to be on the point of joining forces against the other powers in the Eastern Mediterranean, and this encouraged their potential victims to invite Roman intervention. Having just defeated Hannibal and the Carthaginians, the Romans moved eastward, humbled Philip and Antiochus, and later gobbled up the Eastern Mediterranean for themselves.

The story of Roman success and the decline of the Antigonids, Seleucids, and Ptolemies can best be treated as part of the discussion of the expansion of Rome that culminated in the formation of the Roman Empire, and we may turn instead to a consideration of the cultural aspects of the period from the Battle of Mantinea to the middle of the second century B.C.

HELLENISTIC CIVILIZATION

In 133 B.C. Attalus III, the last king of Pergamum, died. He had willed his kingdom to Rome, since he thought the Romans would probably take it anyway, and the territory of Pergamum was soon organized as the Roman province of Asia. By this time the Romans had crushed the Aetolian and Achaean Leagues, and the Antigonid kingdom in Macedonia had also been made into a Roman province with the result that the area bordering the Aegean, the homeland of the Greeks, had all become part of the Roman Empire. Rome's acquisition of Pergamum thus marked the end of an era, the termination of Greek independence.

The period from the death of Alexander to that of Attalus III is often called the Hellenistic Age. Some historians prefer 146 B.C., the year of the Roman destruction of Corinth, to 133 as a terminal date for this period, but whatever dates are used to demarcate the Hellenistic Age in this fashion, they are useful only for the study of the political and military history of Greece, and a hindrance rather than an aid in comprehending the larger story of ancient civilization. Important developments were taking place during this same period in the Western Mediterranean where Rome was rising to a position of superiority, and to separate "Greek" from "Roman" history in this age severs the thread of the principal narrative, that of cultural evolution. The civilization of antiquity had begun to enter a new phase early in the fourth century, before the time of Alexander, and this period of cultural history was to endure for several centuries after the death of Attalus. During this time civilization grew increasingly complex and spread geographically over a huge area.

The apex of development was reached in the second century A.D. rather than the second century B.C., and this was followed by a slow decline which roughly paralleled the disintegration of the Roman Empire. This last and greatest phase of ancient civilization, which began in the fourth century B.C. and lasted almost 800 years, might be subdivided into three parts: (1) the fourth through the second century B.C.; (2) the first century B.C. through the second Christian century; and (3) the third century A.D. to the end of the Roman Empire. It is the first subperiod, which might be called Hellenistic for the sake of convenience, that will be considered and defined below.

Diffusion, Borrowing, and Amalgamation

Three rather important developments occurred during the Hellenistic subperiod. First, Greek civilization was diffused to an increasing number of non-Greeks in the Near East and in the Western Mediterranean. Second, Greek civilization was gradually modified by new borrowings from the Near East; this was a consequence of Alexander's conquest of Persia which reopened the channels by which culture had flowed from the Orient westward in the period 750 to 500 B.C. Third, the amalgamation of Greek and Oriental cultural traditions slowly led to the evolution of a new culture that spread all the way from Spain to the Indus and beyond.

New Wealth and Social Changes

The conquests of Alexander not only removed the political and cultural barriers between Orient and Occident but also permitted, and even encouraged, a free flow of trade that resulted in a new era of prosperity far grander than any the world had previously experienced. Manufacturing was stimulated by the growth of trade. Great cities arose where towns had been lacking before, and the whole population of the ancient world increased to an unprecedented size. For perhaps the first time in history a real middle class appeared; the wealth of the richer bourgeoisie sometimes rivaled that of kings and nobles, and thus the middle class was able to influence governmental policies in certain states. The new wealth and the social changes which characterized the period were to have profound effects on religion, literature, and art. The new conditions of life in the Hellenistic world forced modifications of older traditions and stimulated new forms and approaches. The age resembled our own in a number of ways. Similarities may be observed in the vulgarization of the "higher" culture which took place, as well as in a decline of originality and a paucity of impressive intellectual or artistic achievement. This was partly because this civilization, like ours, owed much to a rich cultural heritage in which many forms had already been exploited rather fully.

Economic Expansion and Renewed Colonization

The conquests of Alexander did more for the ancient economy than break down trade barriers. When he took over Persia itself,, he put back into circulation vast amounts of gold and silver that had been accumulated and hoarded by the Persian kings for nearly two centuries. This had the immediate effect of relieving the shortage of coin that had been strangling the economy of the Mediterranean world; it promoted economic expansion by stimulating trade and lowering interest rates. Furthermore, as Alexander opened the doors to the Near East, he made possible a new age of Greek colonization: Thousands of Greeks left the Aegean area to settle in the Ptolemaic and Seleucid kingdoms. This relieved overpopulation in Greece and contributed to the growth of trade between East and West. As the tempo of economic life accelerated and as economic activities spread into new areas in western Europe as well as India, the development of such regions brought within them a growth of civilization and thus an expansion of the boundaries of the civilized world. Ultimately, trade contacts of importance were established with the civilized area of China.

Changes in Finance, Manufacturing, and Trade.   The brisk economy, as well as the great volume of trade and the wider area over which it ranged, brought changes in finance, manufacturing, and transportation. Large-scale banking, a tendency toward standardization of the currency, the development of big companies for trade and speculation, an increase in the size of manufacturing establishments, and a greater participation of government in business were among the new features. The great monarchies promoted and regulated trade; the Ptolemies and Pergamenes maintained government-operated factories and established state monopolies of certain products or manufactures. New roads and harbors were constructed and older ones improved; larger ships were built to carry more cargo and passengers. Sometimes aspiration exceeded the bounds of practicality: The Syracusans built one vessel too big to enter any of the harbors of Sicily, so they gave it to the Ptolemies!

Growth of Great Cities.   The great cities of the age, with their populations running into the hundreds of thousands, grew up at points best suited for trade. Alexandria in Egypt, founded by Alexander and situated where the largest channel of the Nile entered the Mediterranean, was the Ptolemaic capital and the chief port of Egypt. The surplus grain and other food products of the rich Nile Valley were brought to Alexandria for export; the perfumes and cosmetics for which Egypt was famous were manufactured in the city itself; and Alexandria was the port of entry for the wood, minerals, and other items which the country imported. Among other great metropolitan centers were Antioch in Syria, capital of the Seleucid Empire; Ephesus and Smyrna in Ionia along with the capital of the Attalids at Pergamum; Corinth, which had regained its supremacy in Greece; Syracuse, Tarentum, Carthage, and Gades, the big ports of the West. The free flow of international trade not only enriched these cities, but their very existence depended upon it. Moreover, every large city had to be fed. Egyptian agriculture could support Alexandria, and the grain fields of Tunisia could do the same for Carthage, but Corinth and many other towns had to import grain and other foodstuffs from Egypt, Sicily, or South Russia.

There were seaports, river ports, and caravan cities. Syrian Antioch on the Orontes depended upon its Mediterranean port, Seleucia, just as Rome came to depend on Ostia, but a different Seleucia, on the Tigris, or Babylon might be numbered among the great river ports. Damascus in Syria and Petra in Arabia were outstanding caravan cities, not to mention Samarkand in Bactria, a terminus for the overland trade with China.

Government

Along with other changes, new methods of governmental control were instituted.

Adaptation of the Polis.   The *polis*, the city-state of the Greeks, did not disappear in the new era, but it did have to be modified and adapted to the changed conditions. Plato and Aristotle had felt that the polis could not function in the traditional manner if its citizen body, those actively participating in government, much exceeded 5,000 in number. The important city-states of the Hellenistic Age which did retain their independence—Athens, Rhodes, and others like them—tended to be oligarchic in fact if not in theory: The assembly exercised less authority, while the wealthiest citizens generally directed governmental activity through their virtual monopoly of the council and the magistracies. In the great kingdoms, the city-state form was commonly used for municipal government with the same tendency to concentrate power in the hands of the affluent citizens. The Seleucid Empire particularly, like the Roman Empire to come, was an aggregate of city-states. In the case of the Seleucids, the cities of the Greek type had been founded as colonies within their empire to serve a number of ends: This was a means of introducing Greeks into the empire to leaven the non-Greek population; concentrated at key points for trade and defense, the colonies would serve as garrisons and to promote economic development. There was also a tendency to delegate most of the functions of government at the local or district level to the polis, while the national government began its operations at the provincial level. The city-states were allotted surrounding territories in which they were responsible for the maintenance of order, the upkeep of the roads, and the collection of taxes.

New Federations.   The Greeks of earlier times had employed the device of federation for military and religious purposes, but in the Hellenistic period it was applied more fully and directly to the field of government, as in the case of the Achaean and Aetolian Leagues. The first, composed of Peloponnesian city-states, and the second, made up of largely rural cantons in central Greece, had somewhat similar forms of organization. The chief league official was a general; other administrative posts were filled by secretaries, treasurers, and minor officials, all elected by the citizens of the league. All citizens could participate in a general assembly which had legislative and electoral powers, but government was more representative than direct since policies were usually formulated by the federal councils. The council of the Achaean League was composed of delegates from the city-states, the number of delegates for each state proportionate to its population. There was also a deliberative body called the *synod* in which each state had one vote. In the Aetolian League, each community was represented on the council in proportion to the size of its military contingent, while there was an inner council chosen from the federal one itself, and this smaller group sat as a permanent committee, together with the league officials.

New Forms of Kingship.   When the Romans came to rule the East they were to adopt the polis as the basis for local government and to modify the federal form for certain special uses in the provinces, but there was also an aspect of national government among the Hellenistic monarchies that the Romans found especially attractive. This was the Oriental type of kingship, especially in its Seleucid form. The god-king and the priest-king had been types of rulers familiar to the Near East from early times. While the Great King of Persia, however, had ruled by divine right, Alexander had seen the value of a modified theocracy in which the ruler employed the constitutional fiction of divinity. Legally, if the emperor was a god he could rule men and make the laws. His power would stem from his divinity, not from the people whom he governed. He would not only be above the law, but he would be the source of it. In addition, the formal worship of the god-king would constitute an expression of loyalty. This kind of government was already sanctified by tradition in the Near East, and the Greeks had become aware of it in the fourth century B.C. It could be an acceptable arrangement for governing Greeks and Orientals alike. No one really believed the ruler was a god, but the arrangement could function if, as in the case of most governments or most games, the participants pledged themselves to abide by the rules.

Egypt: A Special Hellenistic State

In its governmental, economic, and social organization, the kingdom of the Ptolemies in Egypt constituted an interesting and important special case among the great Hellenistic states. The king was the successor of the pharaohs and therefore a god on earth. The extreme centralization of pharaonic government was continued and refined, and a number of innovations were introduced. We know much about Ptolemaic Egypt because the subject is well documented by the hundreds of papyri surviving from this period. As in the instance of the cuneiform records of the Ur III age, when we are confronted with a wealth of material we come to realize how little we know about other periods and areas for which our evidence is infinitely less abundant. Ptolemaic Egypt is therefore deserving of a somewhat more detailed description.

Government of Ptolemaic Egypt.   At the head of the government was the reigning Ptolemy, a god-king. He appointed the great bureaucratic heads: a prime minister, a minister of finance, a chief justice, and so on. These officials served at the king's pleasure and derived their powers from him; each headed a bureau composed of a large number of lesser officials. With the exception of three Greek city-states—Alexandria, Naucratis, and Ptolemais—the rest of Egypt was the *chora*, or country, and it was divided into *nomes*, or provinces, in each of which the administration was headed by a *strategos* who had administrative, police, and judicial functions, and an *oeconomos* who controlled taxes and finance. The two-score nomes of Egypt were subdivided into *toparchies*, or districts, and these in turn into *komai*, or villages. The nome officials, *strategoi, oeconomoi,* and others, were appointed by the king, but the *strategoi* appointed the *komarchs*, or village chiefs. The government was thus highly centralized, with lines of authority extending from the king at the top right down to the lowest village functionary. It was only in the three city-states that local government was managed by the people; the citizens of these towns had an assembly, a council, and the usual complement of civic magistrates.

Native Egyptians and Foreigners.   A sharp distinction was made between the native Egyptians and the Greeks, Macedonians, and other foreigners who had special privileges not accorded the natives. No Egyptian could hold citizenship in Alexandria, Naucratis, or Ptolemais.

PAPYRUS PLANTS

(Courtesy of Aramco World.)

The natives were not encouraged to reside in the city-states but were generally confined to the towns and villages of the nomes; they could not move from place to place without special permission. Many of the foreigners, non-Egyptians, were military colonists who received plots of land in Egypt in return for service in the army or the fleet. Others became members of the huge bureaucracy that managed Egypt for the reigning Ptolemy.

Royal Ownership of Land.   All the land of Egypt belonged to the king: Some of it he kept for himself, and the rest he entrusted to others to manage for him. The royal land, retained by the king, was administered by royal officials and worked by peasants designated as royal cultivators. There were several categories of land under grant: The temples were supported by lands assigned especially to them; estates were granted to high officials for their profit and sustenance, and such lands reverted to the crown when the appointments of the office holders were terminated; soldiers were given smaller plots of land as part of their remuneration, holdings which would be repossessed by the king at the death of the recipients unless they had sons to replace them in service.

The arable land of Egypt was registered and classified; bureaucratic records showed the amount of land available for cultivation and whether individual plots were most suitable for orchards, vineyards, cereal cultivation, or the growing of other specific crops. The royal lands were carefully managed: The cultivators were instructed what to plant; a certain percentage of the yield was paid to the state, another part was retained by the cultivator for his own needs, and any surplus had to be sold to the state at a fixed price. The land under grant was taxed; most taxes on land were paid in kind, but there was a money tax on orchards and vineyards since their produce was perishable and could not be stored as easily as grain or similar products.

Taxes and Royal Monopolies.   In addition to the revenues derived by the king from land, large sums were realized from other taxes. There was a sales tax; there were taxes on houses and other property as well as slaves and animals; the native Egyptians had to pay a poll tax. Foreign commerce was subject to both import and export taxes, and there were local tolls within Egypt. Peasants were bound to work a certain number of days each year on the canals, irrigation ditches, and roads. Greeks and other foreigners living in the country might be excused from this corvée by paying a sum of money, but in the three Greek city-states citizens were subject to liturgies in the ancient Greek manner. A further source of revenue was provided by the royal monopolies: salt, products of the mines and quarries, beer, wine, olive and vegetable oil, linen, papyrus, banking, and even certain types of commerce. There were factories owned and operated by the state that bought raw products at a fixed price and sold the manufactures at a nice profit.

Under the Ptolemies, Egypt became one of the richest countries in the world. Efficiently managed and fully but not over-exploited, its yield was huge. In Ptolemaic times the amount of arable land was greatly increased by the construction of new canals, ditches, and reservoirs. Many new crops and animals were introduced. While the natives cultivated wheat, barley, sesame, flax, and the like, the Greeks tended the vineyards and olive orchards which had been virtually unknown in Egypt before the Ptolemies. Weaving, pottery making, and the manu-

PTOLEMAIC CONTRACT WRITTEN ON PAPYRUS

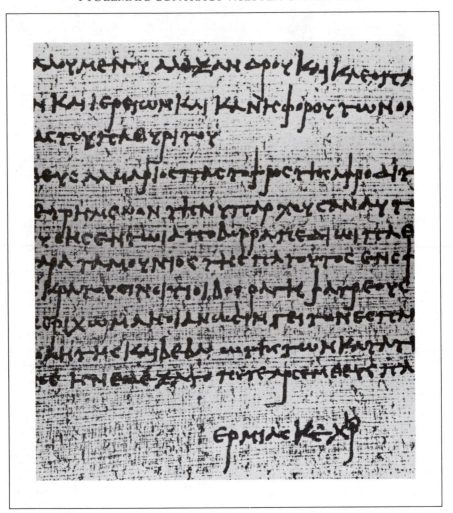

facture of glass and papyrus flourished. Wheat, linen, papyrus, and glass were significant exports, while the principal imports were timber, horses, slaves, gold, silver, wine, and olive oil.

Later Developments.   The natives of Egypt are believed to have outnumbered the foreigners about seven to one. Most natives remained in an inferior position throughout the Ptolemaic period, although mixed marriages of foreign mercenaries with Egyptian women had a slow leveling effect. In addition, a rather marked change occurred in Egypt at the end of the third century B.C. after it had become necessary for the Ptolemies to utilize the services of the *machimoi*, the native Egyptian warrior class, in order to repel the Seleucid advance. Henceforth, these nobles began to play a greater role in shaping national policies; a gradual Egyptianizing of the government set in, and the influence of the foreigners was considerably lessened. The imperialism of the earlier Ptolemaic period was abandoned for a policy of isolation and greater attention to domestic affairs.

THE NEW CULTURE

The greatest single social development in the Hellenistic Age was the rise of a middle class. This did not affect traditional Greek society as much as it did the social pattern of the Near East, where priests and nobles lost much of their former influence. Furthermore, while the middle and upper classes shared in the prosperity of the age and were able to live more comfortably than before, the lot of the poor was not improved but tended to become worse. In the great cities of the Hellenistic world, the proletariat was ill-fed and poorly housed. After the time of Alexander there had been a general rise in prices which was not accompanied by a similar change in wages. Consequently, the free laborer in the cities suffered. His position was made even more difficult by the competition of slave labor. A flourishing slave trade with barbarian lands and the numerous wars within the Hellenistic world often glutted the slave markets, thus rendering slaves abundant and relatively cheap.

Urbanization, the accumulation of wealth, and social change all affected the religious, intellectual, artistic, and literary activities of the new period. Other influences at work were the stimulating effects of the discovery by the Greeks of regions and peoples hitherto unknown to them; a growing universalism, or appreciation of the unity of the world and mankind, which arose as the limits of the civilized world were extended; and a cultural cross-fertilization which promoted a new growth of culture as East and West were brought once more into close contact.

Religion

In the Hellenistic Age, thought and belief in religious matters ranged all the way from the crudest superstition to complete atheism. As in many other phases of culture, the rural districts were less affected by change than the cities, where the impact of the new civilization was most strongly felt, but everywhere the older state cults shared in the empty formality of pomp and circumstance that was most pronounced in the new ruler worship of the great monarchies. Oriental cults were brought to the West by traders, travelers, and imported slaves. Sometimes these cults infected or were grafted on to older beliefs, but the Oriental mystery religions took root in new soil and gained many converts. As the Greeks settled in the Ptolemaic or Seleucid empires or found new homes in the Indus Valley, they often amalgamated their own beliefs with those of the natives; hybrid deities like the Egyptian Zeus-Ammon appeared. Some people were unable to reconcile the rival and conflicting claims of a multitude of religions and so became agnostics; others found all capacity for faith destroyed by the secularism of the age or by the emphasis placed on rationalism in higher education. The prevailing individualism inclined people to search for new personal religions that would bring to the individual satisfactions of one kind or another. The slaves and urban masses particularly grasped at the straws of salvation offered by the mystery religions which promised a happiness in the hereafter that was unattainable during life in this world. Universalist tendencies encouraged a drift toward monotheism.

Philosophy

In higher intellectual realms, thinkers built upon foundations provided by Plato and Aristotle. New "schools" of philosophy appeared, although Platonism and Aristotelianism survived in a more or less pure form to the very end of antiquity. In the fourth century B.C., three schools in addition to Plato's own academy continued to exploit the ideas of the master. The Cynic school, founded by Antisthenes, proclaimed that virtue was the sole good and vice the only evil; the Cynics taught that a man should pursue virtue to the exclusion of all else: He should discard convention, comfort, pleasure, and other externals and seek the inner satisfaction afforded by the attainment of spiritual virtue. A variation on this theme was composed by Aristippus of Cyrene. His school identified pleasure with virtue and accepted all forms of pleasure as sources of "the good," provided they were not accompanied by excess. The possibility of real knowledge was denied by the Skeptics, the followers of Pyrrhon. They insisted that there was a counterargument that would defeat any line of reasoning, with the result that nothing could be established or known. Their influence was to be long and persuasive; eventually, it brought a reaction which led men back to pure faith accompanied by a violent distrust of reason as a means to discover truth.

Rise of Stoicism.   None of these philosophies, including those of Plato and Aristotle, were sufficiently appealing to people in the Hellenistic Age to gain a large number of adherents. Their goals were too intellectual, or too unattainable, or simply lacking in the personal satisfaction sought by the majority. Stoicism and Epicureanism, appearing at the end of the fourth century B.C., were more "personal" and gratifying although they were derivatives of these earlier schools. Stoicism was to surpass Epicureanism in popularity, but both had many followers in the Hellenistic and Roman periods.

The Stoics, who took their name from their original meetingplace, the Stoa Poikile (Painted Porch) at Athens, were the followers of Zeno of Cyprus, who began to teach there about 314 B.C. The Stoic goal was the happiness attainable through discovery of, and adherence to, the laws of nature. Since everything in nature was conceived to be rational and good, if a man could identify and follow nature's laws, he would gain an inner satisfaction that would not be disturbed by pain, misfortune, or even death. Like Job, a man might suffer all kinds of external ills, but they would be only the means by which Providence tested and purified his soul. "Endure and accept" was the essence of Stoicism. Its practitioners so far rejected man-made law and convention that some of them came to believe in a brotherhood of Man in which there was an equality not only of races and sexes but also of slaves and free men. The Stoics accepted as part of their belief the existence of a supreme but impersonal deity who had established the laws of nature.

Epicureanism.   Epicureanism dated from 306 B.C., when Epicurus of Samos began to teach at Athens. Happiness was also the supreme good sought by the Epicurians, but they defined happiness as freedom from fear and pain. The chief fears, they felt, were generated by superstition: dread of divine anger and the perils of life beyond the grave. The Epicureans taught that the gods had no concern with human affairs; therefore, one need not fear them. They explained life and death in terms of the atoms of Democritus: Life resulted from certain combinations of atoms, and death from their separation. Death was without sensation; it was rather an eternal and painless sleep. Many Epicureans did not affect the same austerity as the Stoics; they employed their philosophic tenets to excuse the pursuit of the pleasures of the flesh and so gave Epicureanism a bad name in many circles. Partly because it was areligious, the philosophy of Epicurus never gained as many converts as Stoicism.

To become a true Stoic or Epicurean required more fortitude than most people possessed. Furthermore, there was an essentially negative attitude in both philosophies that demanded an acceptance of the world as it is. This conflicted with the basic optimism of the human animal, who has always regarded life as capable of improvement by one means or another.

Scientific Activity

The Hellenistic Age was one of progress in Greek mathematics, astronomy, mechanics, anatomy, physiology, geography, and other fields. Under the patronage of the Ptolemies, important research was done at Alexandria. Other centers of scientific activity were Pergamum in Asia Minor and Syracuse in Sicily. Stimulated by hitherto unsuspected world horizons disclosed by Alexander's conquests and enriched by a diffusion of astronomical and mathematical knowledge from Babylonia, Greek science was able to attain new heights.

The Peripatetics.   Although the followers of Aristotle, the Peripatetics, made some advances, the main scientific achievements were those of persons not connected with any school of philosophy. Aristotle's aim had been to organize and systematize knowledge. He had founded the science of zoology, and his successor as head of the Lyceum was Theophrastus, the Father of Botany, whose great work on plants has survived. Classification in the field of natural science was the forte of the Peripatetics, work that was useful if not exciting, but more spectacular accomplishments were registered elsewhere, outside of Athens and the Lyceum.

Theories of the Universe.   About 280 B.C., Aristarchus of Samos advanced his heliocentric theory of the solar system. The hypothesis was well received at first but later rejected by astronomers, who felt that a geocentric theory was more in accord with their observations. Eratosthenes at Alexandria measured the circumference of the earth and came within 200 miles of the correct figure. Eratosthenes also participated in the geographical research, stimulated by Alexander's travels and subsequent explorations by others, that promoted mapmaking and new treatises on the world and its inhabitants; the Alexandrian scientist produced a map of the world that used lines of latitude and longitude. Most educated persons of the age, incidentally, did not doubt that the earth was spherical. Moreover, about 100 B.C. the observations of Posidonius, a Stoic philosopher, led him to the belief that the moon influenced tides in the Atlantic ocean.

Euclid's Geometry.   In the early third century B.C., Euclid, the tutor of Ptolemy II, compiled the famous textbook of geometry which is still the basis for manuals in our schools. The material in Euclid's *Elements* was not original with him for the most part, although he did provide some new proofs; further solutions and proofs were adduced by Hellenistic and Roman geometers who came later. The renewed contact with Babylonia advanced algebraic, astronomical, and calendrical studies; it is particularly noteworthy that the algebraic material in the surviving Greek mathematical texts seems to be largely a restatement of the Babylonian achievement.

Archimedes. Perhaps the most brilliant, and certainly the most famous, of all Hellenistic scientists was Archimedes of Syracuse, who flourished in the second half of the third century B.C. Archimedes not only discovered the principle of specific gravity, although the "story of the crown" may be apocryphal, but he was also an astronomer, a mathematician, a master of mechanics, and the inventor of numerous machines for use in war and peace. He devised a planetarium; by a laborious process he computed the value of *pi* to a new point of exactitude; he nearly became the discoverer of the calculus. Archimedes was also given credit for having devised an irrigation machine, called the screw, and his "helix" utilized the principle of the compound pulley to move huge weights by the exertion of comparatively little force. The ingenious war machines of Archimedes became so much of a legend that it is difficult now to separate fact from fancy, but the Romans always admitted that their siege of Syracuse was prolonged for many months because Archimedes defended the town with his novel weapons.

Medicine

Medicine made great strides: Both the cause and cure of disease were studied and there were marked improvements in diagnosis, medication, and surgery. In the the third century B.C., Herophilus, the great anatomist, studied the brain and the nervous system, while his contemporary, Erasistratus, founded the science of physiology and did important work on the nervous and circulatory systems. Major centers for medical research and training were Alexandria and Pergamum.

Inventions

It is customary to stress the Hellenistic Age as one of invention, although few of the gadgets produced by mechanics and craftsmen were put to practical use. A world that had no labor shortage and thus no need for machines was amused and sometimes amazed by toys and novelties—water clocks, water organs, machines operated by pneumatic pressure, and a rudimentary steam engine. Archimedes was virtually the only scientist to promote "useful knowledge," yet it should be said that there were improvements in agricultural and pastoral activity with the use of fertilizer, rotation of crops, the introduction of new plants and trees, and the more scientific breeding of animals.

Scholarship

Egypt under the Ptolemies could boast possession of two of the Seven Wonders of the ancient world: the pyramids (not their creation) and the Pharos, the towering lighthouse at Alexandria, which they did construct. In addition, early in the third century the Ptolemies had established what might justly be termed the Eighth Wonder: the Museum and its Library.

At Alexandria, close to the palace area, the Museum, House of the Muses, became what some cynics today would term an ideal university. It housed a community of scholars of international repute, who were handsomely paid and devoted to research, and no students except for a few in the graduate category.

The jewel in the crown of the Museum was the Library, the largest of its day and probably of all antiquity. Its holdings included half a million books, or papyrus rolls, and its ultimate goal was to bring together everything ever written in Greek. A hint as to the wide-ranging nature of the collection comes from a fragmentary catalog that mentions several treatises on how to bake a cake. The Library and its development was the responsibility of a succession of the most prestigious scholars, and the post of Librarian was regarded as so distinguished and desirable that it became an object of competition among the great scholars of the Hellenistic Age. In addition to increasing the library holdings, the librarians made impressive contributions to scholarship that directed such activities into new channels still of significance today.

The process of collecting for the Library necessitated finding, selecting, collating, and editing the best manuscripts of the major Greek authors: poets, playwrights, orators, prose writers of all kinds, and the like. Zenodotus of Ephesus, the first Librarian, made a scientific edition of Homer based on the best manuscripts, and the technique of textual criticism was further developed by a number of his successors. The special scholarly interests of various librarians lay in different areas. For example, the previously mentioned geographer Eratosthenes was one, while Callimachus and Apollonius, the poets, were others. We should not neglect to mention that one of the major policy decisions at the Library was to evaluate and create lists of the outstanding authors in several categories: the ten best orators, poets, playwrights, and so on. This was in theory a good idea, but it had a most unfortunate result because it imposed the judgment of one period upon posterity. In the end these selections tended to determine what was considered deserving of preservation and doomed to oblivion the works of many authors that today might well be regarded as equal or superior to the ones chosen by the Alexandrians.

We have likened the Museum to a university, but it was more a research institute than a modern creation devoted at least in theory to teaching, but in one respect the Museum and its denizens resembled any community of scholars. The incumbents tended to be eccentric and in true scholarly fashion quarreled bitterly and feuded endlessly among themselves. This lack of harmony was notorious enough to be satirized in an epigram:

> Egypt has its mad recluses,
> Book bewildered anchorites,
> In the hencoop of the Muses
> Keeping up their endless fights.

Finally, we do not know whether the Ptolemies wished to advertise their wealth and at the same time convince the world of the superior culture they had established in Egypt. No matter how barbarous the Macedonians seemed to the Greeks, it should be remembered that some of the Macedonian kings before Philip had posed as patrons of culture and that Philip himself had chosen Aristotle to educate Alexander. Moreover, the first Ptolemy engaged Euclid to teach geometry, to which there was "no royal road" to his own son, Ptolemy II. Henceforth the tradition of royal instruction in Greek culture was continued right down to the end of the Ptolemaic regime, when the careful and extensive training received by the last Cleopatra impressed Julius Caesar who was no barbarian by any standard.

Literature

In literature, volume and variety compensated in some measure for lack of conspicuous achievement. The new affluence and urbanization enlarged educational opportunities so that literacy was more widespread than in earlier periods. With more people able to read and write, there was a larger reading public, and there were many who were anxious to express themselves in writing; thus, literary production was bound to increase in volume although older standards of excellence were not likely to be demanded by the new audience or maintained by the authors. Since so many of the older literary forms had been fully exploited or even perfected, there was bound to be a search for, and experimentation with, new literary types. This was particularly true in poetry where there was a serious effort to develop modes of expression that would be suitable for the urbanization, social changes, and new views of life that now prevailed.

Poetry.   At Alexandria, Callimachus, an inventive and capable poet, seems to have best met the challenge with his elegies, lyrics, hymns, and short epics, but he is not as well known to us as his bitter rival, Apollonius of Rhodes, who wrote a long epic entitled the *Argonautica*. This poem dealt with the legend of Jason and Medea and the quest for the Golden Fleece. Written in the style of Homer, with many passages reminiscent of the *Iliad* and *Odyssey*, the *Argonautica* was an archaizing approach to poetry, yet typical of the Hellenistic Age in its pedantry and in its romantic rather than heroic concept of the story. The *Argonautica* was not a great epic; its fundamental artificiality and the fact that Apollonius was no Homer prevented that. It was, however, extremely popular; it influenced Vergil's *Aeneid,* and its theme proved tempting to later Latin poets. Pastoral poetry was still another innovation of the Hellenistic Age, perhaps as a kind of reaction to the extreme urbanization of the period. The chief exponent of this form was Theocritus, a Sicilian poet.

Drama.   With the exception of the so-called New Comedy that reached its peak about 300 B.C. in the work of Menander at Athens, we know little about the drama in this later period. The comedy of manners had now replaced the rollicking political satire (Old Comedy) of the days of Aristophanes. The half-dozen plays of Menander known to us are what might be called tragicomedies and suggest that Euripides rather than Aristophanes was the literary ancestor of the New Comedy. The plots of Menander are not overly complex; in each play there are series of episodes that arise out of misunderstandings on the part of the characters; they are sometimes amusing but often full of pathos. The ancients felt that Menander was particularly noteworthy in his portrayal of character, but the surviving plays do not seem to bear this out. As a stylist, Menander was greatly admired. His works were immensely popular and widely known, partly because for generations he was one of the authors studied in the schools.

Prose.   The great flood of prose that characterized the Hellenistic Age has disappeared from view. We know that there were textbooks, treatises, and commentaries on oratory, rhetoric, and related fields. History and biography flourished. People wrote histories of regions and countries, universal histories, historical surveys of sculpture, painting, architecture, and many other subjects. The names of many authors are known, but most of what we know about them comes from passing references made by the authors of the Roman period.

Best known and perhaps the greatest of the Hellenistic historians was the Achaean political leader, Polybius, who lived in the second century B.C. Polybius was a well-educated man who possessed a firsthand knowledge of politics and warfare. He strove to be a scientific historian in the manner of Thucydides but was inclined to ignore the literary aspects of historical craftsmanship. Polybius made a great point of employing the most extensive and careful kind of research in attempting to establish historical facts. In this regard, he seems to protest too much— many passages in his history are devoted to discussions of method and criticisms of the shortcomings of rival historians, but recent studies have shown that Polybius was not as accurate or painstaking as he claimed to be and that he did not achieve the impartiality which he so often emphasized as desirable.

Polybius was one of a thousand hostages taken from the Achaean League by the Romans in 168 B.C. He lived in Rome for many years thereafter, became well acquainted with many prominent Romans, and decided to write a history of the rise of Rome from its victories over Carthage in the third century to its triumph over the Greeks and Macedonians in the first half of the second century B.C. Polybius wanted to explain the Romans and their success to his fellow Greeks. Not all of his long history has survived, but the extant portions are valuable today for their descriptions of certain events, his analysis of the Roman constitution, and his explanation of the workings of the Achaean and Aetolian federal constitutions. He also supplies a wealth of material about methods of warfare and the military tactics of the Hellenistic Age.

The Arts

An extensive patronage of the arts stemmed from the great accumulation of wealth by states and individuals during the Hellenistic period. At the courts of kings and in the big cities, artists had little difficulty in securing lucrative commissions. In addition to the demand for statues and paintings, all kinds of handsome new buildings were desired.

Architecture.   Hellenistic architecture differed from classical Greek architecture in several ways. The chief buildings of the earlier period had been temples and a relatively small number of government structures; in the Hellenistic Age, on the other hand, temples were still in demand, but there was an increase in the number of secular buildings: palaces, offices, meeting halls, colonnaded porches *(stoae)*, theaters, gymnasia, stadia, and the like. With so much construction, spread over a wide area, the best materials could not always be used if they were not locally available. Thus, stucco, marble veneer, and brick had to be employed in place of the solid marble characteristic of the major Periclean buildings at Athens. The arch was used more frequently, and the Corinthian and composite styles were favored over the older Doric and Ionic.

Among the famous buildings of the period were the great temple of Artemis at Ephesus, erected to replace an older structure that was

HELLENISTIC ARCHITECTURE:
VARIOUS ATTEMPTED RESTORATIONS OF THE MAUSOLEUM

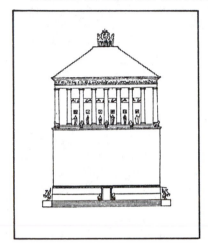 

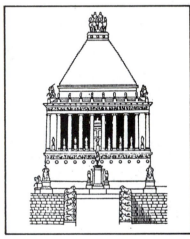 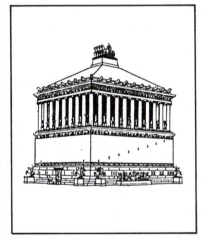

destroyed by fire the night that Alexander the Great was born; the Mausoleum, or tomb, of the Carian king, Mausolus, built in the fourth century; and the Pharos, or lighthouse, of the Ptolemies at Alexandria. Pergamum, Antioch, and Rhodes, along with Athens, were the sites of great building activity. With the foundation of so many new towns, the science of town planning, which had originated in the fifth century B.C., was now elaborated. Private houses became more pretentious as personal fortunes grew, and the whole field of domestic architecture entered upon a new era. Finally, in an age of warfare in which siege operations became more effective, the art of fortification had to advance in order to counter such changes.

Sculpture.   The Hellenistic capitals became the homes of new schools of sculpture: Alexandria, Antioch, Pergamum, and also Rhodes. In these schools there was a tendency toward eclecticism in combining elements from the styles of the major fourth-century B.C. artists: Praxiteles, Scopas, and Lysippos. The latter was the official portrait sculptor to Alexander the Great; his figures of athletes were much admired, and even today his *Apoxyomenos* is familiar to many people. The individual works of the Hellenistic period are, as a matter of fact, sometimes better known than those of the classical age: the *Dying Gaul* from Pergamum; the *Colossus* of Rhodes; the *Winged Victory* from Samothrace; and the *Laocoön* are all of Hellenistic date.

Gods and victorious athletes had been the favorite subjects of sculptors in the classical period, but in the Hellenistic Age there was more diversity. Portraiture flourished because rulers or rich and distinguished persons wished to be immortalized in bronze or stone. Moreover, types of human beings began to be portrayed: children, matrons, old people, and the like.

Painting.   In technique, painting reached what was considered perfection in the Hellenistic Age, and painting began to be used more and more for the interior decoration of palaces and private homes. We know the names of many Hellenistic painters. Many of our extant examples of Greek painting date from this period, but the proficiency of these artists seems to have exceeded their inspiration. The fourth century B.C. was the age of Apelles, the last of the great painters, whose specialty was portrait painting—a sign of the times.

ROMAN ADOPTION OF HELLENISTIC CIVILIZATION

The Hellenistic period set the stage for an even more complex epoch in which the regions of the eastern and western Mediterranean were to be joined politically as well as culturally by the conquests of Rome. The Romans would adopt Hellenistic civilization wholeheartedly. Succeeding generations would build upon the Hellenistic base until the climax of ancient civilization was reached in the second century A.D., when the greatest complexity of culture would coincide with the high point of the Roman Empire.

Chapter Eight

Rome: The City-State

Some Romans believed that after the fall of Troy the hero Aeneas led his surviving countrymen westward and settled them in Italy. Then, about the time that the Greeks were establishing their first Italian colony at Cumae in the Neopolitan area, Romulus, a descendant of Aeneas, was supposed to have founded the city of Rome in 753 B.C. It was also said that, just after the tyrant Hippias had been expelled from Athens, the Romans in 509 B.C. drove out their tyrannical last king, Tarquin the Proud, and established the Roman Republic.

Aeneas, Romulus, and even Tarquin may be dismissed as legendary, but later synchronisms of Roman with Greek history can be demonstrated as facts. While Philip of Macedon was making his country a power in the Balkans, the Romans won a place for themselves in the Italian peninsula; and, as Alexander conquered the world, the Romans proceeded slowly with the conquest of Italy. In 275 B.C. Rome defeated Pyrrhus, a distant relative of Alexander whose military prowess was thought to approach his; a century later the Romans had beaten several other Hellenistic kings whose ancestors had been Alexander's generals; and by 30 B.C. all four major Hellenistic kingdoms had been incorporated into the Roman Empire.

In an age of great kingdoms, it was something of a paradox that a city-state should emerge as the ruler of them all. Imperial Athens had been a city-state, too. Like Athens, Rome had begun with monarchy, passed through aristocracy to timocracy, and even achieved a kind of democracy. On the other hand, unlike the Athenian, the Roman democracy was quickly ruined rather than supported by imperialism; and, while the Athenian empire was maritime, that of Rome was a land empire, something the Athenians had been unable to hold. These and other parallels and dissimilarities between Rome and Athens deserve careful consideration.

THE RISE OF ROME

As in Greece, the earliest inhabitants of Italy numerous enough to be important were migrants, mainly of the Mediterranean physical type, who came well before 3000 B.C. and settled on the land as farmers and herdsmen. In the second millennium B.C., Indo-Europeans bringing the domesticated horse and an advanced knowledge of metal working invaded Greece and Italy; these migrants came in waves, and the last to arrive were iron-users. Like the Greeks in Greece, the newcomers in Italy conquered the peasant villagers and imposed upon them institutions and a culture that was of the traditional Indo-European type.

Italy Occupied by Civilized Invaders: Greeks and Etruscans

Although by the year 1000 B.C. conditions in Italy resembled those in Dark Age Greece, the histories of the two peninsulas diverged from their previously parallel courses as the first millennium wore on. On the one hand, the Greeks after 750 B.C. evolved a distinctive civilization by borrowing and adapting culture from the Near East through a process of cultural diffusion; Italy, on the other hand, was actually occupied by civilized invaders, Greeks and Etruscans, many elements of whose culture were virtually imposed upon the Italians. The Etruscans, who began to settle on the west coast just north of the Tiber River about 850 B.C., greatly influenced the Romans in the period 650 to 450 B.C., while the effects of Greek colonization, felt in south Italy as early as the seventh century B.C., were increasingly evident in Rome after 300. At a crucial stage in their development the Greeks had been able to adapt Near Eastern civilization to their needs, but the Romans had no such opportunity: Proximity forced them to accept with little change what the Etruscans and Greeks had to offer.

The character of Greek civilization has already been described, and the alphabet, literature, art, and other cultural elements which the Romans received from the Greeks can be identified easily, but the Etruscans are newcomers to these pages and merit a brief introduction.

The Etruscans

In language and culture the Etruscans were related to the Lydians, and this is one of a number of very good reasons for accepting the view of Herodotus that the Etruscans came from Asia Minor. Superior military organization and technology enabled the Etruscans to establish themselves as a ruling minority upon the native population as they settled in the Italian region that became known as Etruscanland: Etruria. A

THE ETRUSCANS

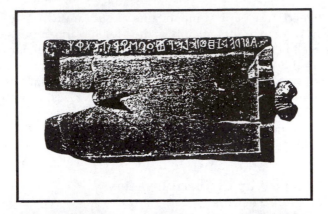

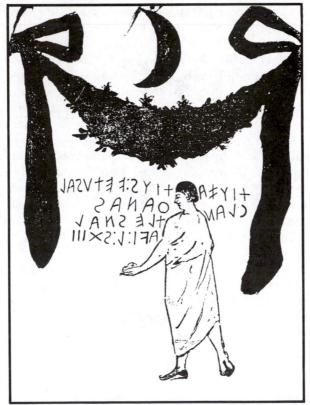

Above: Tablet containing the Etruscan alphabet (in reverse order).

Below: Etruscan tomb painting from the grave of a youth who died at the age of thirteen.

score of independent and powerful city-states, each with its capital in a strong-walled town, developed soon after the conquest: Caere, Clusium, Veii, Populonia, and Arretium were among the most famous. Eventually, Rome itself was occupied by the Etruscans about 650 B.C. and made into an *urbs* (walled city). Expanding northward toward the Po Valley and to the south almost to the Bay of Naples, the Etruscans reached the height of their power about 500 B.C. Shortly after, an invasion of the Po Valley by Gallic tribes from France and a defeat in the south administered by the Greeks forced the Etruscans to draw back into Etruria. Never politically unified, their city-states often at war with one another, the Etruscans could not work together even to save themselves from destruction at the hands of common enemies.

The Romans owed much to the Etruscans. The Etruscan occupation of Rome (650–500 B.C.) not only resulted in the formal organization of the city but also left a residue of Etruscan culture that became as "Roman" as anything else the Romans possessed in later times. This heritage was most evident in art, religion, and government. Roman temple architecture, the use of the arch, and portrait sculpture were definitely of Etruscan origin. Certain religious ceremonies, methods of divination, the notorious gladiatorial contests, and the names of several Roman deities—Juno, Minerva, Neptune, Vulcan, and Mars—came from the same source. Etruscan words were taken over into Latin; many Etruscan personal names were adapted and used by the Romans for centuries. Also borrowed were the concepts of the *pomerium*, the magical boundary of the city, and the *imperium*, the power to rule that included military command as well as administrative, religious, and embryonic judicial functions.

Roman Government

As for the Romans themselves, very little of their early history can be salvaged from tradition and legend. Descendants of the Indo-European invaders of the second millennium B.C., the inhabitants of Rome shared their language with the tribes called the Latins who had settled along with the Romans in the region of Latium on the west coast of Italy just south of the Tiber. The social and political institutions of the Latins and Romans were mostly the familiar Indo-European ones that we have already observed among the early Greeks. At Rome, the primitive Indo-European monarchy, modified by Etruscan borrowings, was the governmental form until early in the fifth century B.C.—we have already seen that the traditional date of 509 B.C. for the fall of the monarchy is no more reliable than the legendary 753 for the founding of Rome itself. The king *(rex)*, like the Greek *basileus*, was a war leader and something of a priest and judge. He was assisted by a council of the elders (Senate) like the Greek *gerousia*, and there was an assembly of the citizens, really the army, which was called the *comitia*. The latter corresponded in most respects to the Greek *ecclesia*. As in Greece, a landed nobility eventually rose to power, monopolized the council of the elders, dominated the assembly, abolished the monarchy, and set up an aristocratic government: the early Roman Republic. Even before the fall of the monarchy, the landed aristocrats, called the *patricians*, had managed to draw a sharp line between themselves and the commons, the *plebeians*. At first, many political and social privileges were monopolized by the patricians and denied to the plebeians: For example, the latter were excluded from the Senate and could not intermarry with the patricians.

The abolition of the monarchy and the expulsion of the Etruscans was a double victory for the patricians, but other and more serious battles lay ahead. Rome was ringed about by enemies who threatened her very existence, while within the state the plebeians, who outnumbered the patricians, would never rest until they had secured a full measure of political and social equality. From the founding of the Republic down to about 265 B.C., there were two major developments: The Romans gradually made themselves masters of the Italian peninsula, and the plebeians won their contest with the patricians.

Roman Defensive Aggression

One of the first acts of the Romans after driving out the Etruscans was to make an alliance with the Latin League, a group of federated tribes in Latium. Together, the Romans and Latins beat off mutual enemies, not only Etruscans but also surrounding barbarian tribes. In time it became apparent that merely to repel these foes was not enough—only the conquest of the enemy would provide security; yet, as nearby tribes were overcome, even more dangerous antagonists were discovered beyond them, and these new enemies had to be conquered in turn.

This was the process of defensive aggression rather then conscious imperialism by which Rome acquired control of Italy. It went very slowly in the beginning: At the end of the fifth century B.C. the influence of Rome was scarcely felt beyond the borders of Latium. Just after 400 B.C. the Romans felt they had scored a major victory when they captured a fortified town, Etruscan Veii just across the Tiber, but this success was offset by a major disaster about 390 when a horde of invading Gauls came down from the north, defeated the Romans in battle, captured and then sacked Rome. Destructive though it was, the Gallic invasion was a blessing in disguise: The Etruscans, too, were hard hit by the Gauls and never recovered from the invasion, while the Romans reformed their army, rebuilt their city, and emerged stronger than ever from the catastrophe.

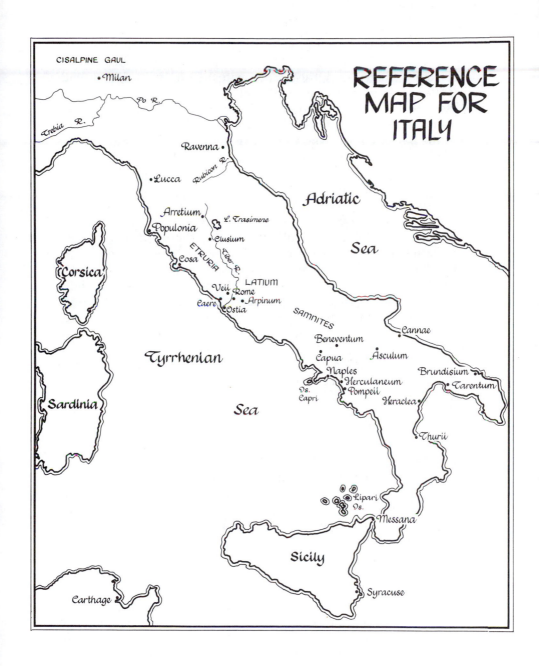

CISALPINE GAUL

• Milan

Po R.

Trebia R.

Ravenna •

Lucca •

Rubicon R.

Arretium •

Populonia •

ETRURIA

Cosa •

L. Trasimene

Clusium •

Tiber R.

LATIUM

Veii • Rome

Caere • Ostia

• Arpinum

REFERENCE
MAP FOR
ITALY

Adriatic

Sea

SAMNITES

Beneventum •

• Cannae

Capua •

• Asculum

Tyrrhenian

Naples •

Herculaneum

Is. • Pompeii

Capri

Brundisium

• Tarentum

Heraclea •

Sardinia

Sea

Thurii •

Corsica

Lipari
Is.

Messana •

Sicily

Carthage •

Syracuse •

217

During the second half of the fourth century B.C., Roman holdings in Italy began to grow. About 336 B.C., for example, the Latins, becoming fearful of Roman power, tried to abrogate their treaty of alliance with Rome; after a two-year war they were defeated, reduced to the status of subjects, and their territory brought under direct Roman control. Ten years later the Romans answered an appeal for help from the Greeks around the Bay of Naples who were being molested by the Samnites, a powerful group of native tribes in central Italy. This led to three decades of conflict between Romans and Samnites and, after several defeats, ended with a full Roman victory about 290 B.C. that left only the Greek towns of southern Italy outside the orbit of Rome. In 272 B.C., after several years of fighting against the powerful Greek city of Tarentum, the Romans gained control of the south; it was in this struggle that Pyrrhus of Epirus came to the aid of Tarentum and was beaten by Rome.

By 265 B.C. Rome dominated the peninsula of Italy. About one-seventh of the territory actually belonged to Rome, while the remainder was in the hands of states and peoples reduced to the position of inferior allies who must contribute military contingents for the Roman forces and whose foreign relations were managed by Rome. We have compared Rome and Athens on occasion, but the character of the Roman military machine in 265 B.C. invites a comparison with Sparta and the Peloponnesian League at the end of the sixth century, although the parallel is not by any means exact.

Changes in Roman Government

In this same period, between the fall of the monarchy and 265 B.C., the Roman constitution had undergone many changes. At the beginning of the Republic, the essential difference between its organization and that of the monarchy which had preceded it was that two annually elected patrician magistrates, the *consuls,* had taken the place of the king. The consuls had military, administrative, religious, and judicial functions: Possessing equal powers, they presided over the Senate; convened and presided over the *comitia curiata,* the popular assembly, composed of all adult male citizens physically and financially able to perform military service; and commanded the armies of the state, although usually one consul took the field in time of war while the other remained in Rome. The virtual monopoly of the government—offices, priesthoods, and Senate, as well as dominance in the assembly—by the patricians caused much bitterness among the plebeians, who contemplated secession from the state and early organized an informal government of their own, a kind of state within a state. Tradition had it that near the beginning of the republican period the plebeians organized an assembly and elected four officials called *tribunes* to be their leaders and representatives along with two *aediles,* minor officials who functioned as aides to the tribunes. Meeting under the presidency of the tribunes, the informal plebeian assembly passed measures called *plebiscites,* laws intended to be binding on all plebeians.

Concessions Made to Plebeians.   As the Romans battled outside enemies, their own internal class struggle jeopardized the state. The details are lacking, but it may be guessed that about 450 B.C. a military crisis forced the patricians to enlist plebeian aid. A military reorganization was followed by internal reforms that involved important concessions to the plebeians. The new Roman army in which the soldiers were grouped in centuries, or hundreds, was made the basis for a new assembly, the *comitia centuriata* (Assembly of the Centuries). This now became the principal elective and lawmaking body, and it was also given the right to act as a court of appeal in instances where citizens had been sentenced to death, exile, or the payment of a heavy fine. Citizens were assigned to census classes according to their wealth: The most affluent were placed in two categories, the knights *(equites)* and the citizens of the first class, and were given 98 votes out of a possible 193 in the assembly; in addition to a half-dozen other classes of citizens arranged in centuries also on a descending scale of wealth and given a total of 94 votes, the essentially landless citizens, called the proletarians, who had long been excluded from public life, were now admitted to this new assembly as a single century and given one vote. We are thus reminded of another parallel with Athenian history: the reforms of Solon which established a timocracy at Athens in some respects like that which had now come to Rome.

Other reforms dating from the mid-fifth century B.C. at Rome were the first codification of Roman law (Law of the Twelve Tables), the admission of plebeians to the consulate, and a concession that plebiscites, if approved by the Senate, would become laws binding on the whole Roman people, plebeians and patricians alike. The plebeian tribunes were given official status, too: Police action by the consuls could be blocked by a plebeian tribune if he chose to prohibit *(veto)* the arrest of a plebeian. Changes in the army, the creation of a new assembly, and a growth of administrative business in the government required the inauguration of additional offices of state: The consuls were given two assistants *(quaestors)* who acted as treasury officials and army quartermasters; the proper assignment of citizens to the new census classes and the determination of Senate membership was made the duty of two officials called *censors.* Every five years a new pair of censors was elected from the ranks of the ex-consuls, while the quaestors were chosen annually by the Assembly of the Centuries.

The next major constitutional changes were made about 376 B.C.

when hard times following the sack of Rome by the Gauls and general economic difficulties precipitated a new patrician-plebeian crisis. In addition to measures alleviating the condition of debtors and other bills designed to provide small plots of land for colonization by the Roman poor on newly conquered lands, it was also decreed that one consul each year must be a plebeian. Probably as a result of the rebuilding of Rome after the Gallic sack, the supervision of public works within the city, the markets, games and festivals, and the grain supply were turned over to four aediles, two plebeians and two patricians. A judicial magistrate, the *praetor,* who also took charge of Rome in the absence of both consuls, now appeared. Thus, the quaestors, aediles, and the praetor became responsible for consular functions that the consuls were now too busy to handle directly.

Reforms of 287 B.C.   The last important change in governmental organization took place in 287 B.C. when plebeian dissatisfaction, probably intensified by a depression following the end of the Samnite wars, culminated in an actual secession. In this crisis, the patricians were forced to capitulate and accord a last measure of equality to the plebeians. The plebeian tribunes, now increased to ten, were allowed to attend meetings of the Senate and exercise their veto power upon its proceedings. Furthermore, the informal assembly of the plebeians was transformed into a new body that included both patricians and plebeians. Each citizen, regardless of wealth, had one vote in this new assembly which was thus more democratic as opposed to the timocracy of the comitia centuriata where the votes were weighted in favor of the propertied classes. The tribunes called and presided over this assembly, which was the body that elected the plebeian aediles and the tribunes themselves; its legislative measures, still called plebiscites, were now binding on all citizens, whether patrician or plebeian, and no longer required senatorial approval.

The new assembly was called the *comitia tributa* (Assembly of the Tribes). It should be explained that since the late regal period, and probably before that, the Roman citizens had been arranged in tribes. At the outset of the Republic, there were four tribes: The informal plebeian assembly had met on a tribal basis, and this was the reason for the election of four tribunes, tribe leaders, one for each tribe. As the citizen body had increased in size and spread out over Italy and non-Romans had been admitted to citizenship, the number of tribes had been enlarged until there were more than thirty, although the number of tribunes had been stabilized at ten. The comitia tributa was organized on a tribal basis; that is, the citizens grouped themselves, and voted, by tribes instead of centuries in this assembly.

The comitia centuriata did not go out of existence. It continued to meet under the presidency of the consuls and to pass laws (*leges*) as it had always done. It was also the body that might decree the existence of a state of war. Still retaining its functions as a court of appeal, the Assembly of the Centuries elected the consuls, praetor, quaestors, censors, and the patrician aediles. In the future, the tribal assembly was the stronghold of the people, but the ordinary business of government continued to be transacted in the Assembly of the Centuries and the Senate.

The victory of the plebeians and the attainment of a potential democracy at Rome were soon nullified by events after 265 B.C. which turned the attention of the Romans away from their internal problems to foreign affairs that seemed more pressing. For the next century Rome was almost continually at war, and, when peace finally returned, many changes had taken place in Roman governmental procedure and in the social and economic situation of the Romans themselves. By that time it was impossible to revive the liberalization for which the plebeians had fought; the Republic itself was then in grave danger, face to face with the threat of dictatorship or some other form of autocracy.

Rome at War (265–146 B.C.)

Looking at developments in the century after 265 B.C., we should note first of all that Italy was not the only region of the Western Mediterranean that came under the domination of civilized peoples from the East. Perhaps 100 years before the Greeks arrived in large numbers as colonists in Italy and Sicily, Phoenicians had begun to settle in North Africa and Spain. Competition for markets in the West soon promoted hostility between Greeks and Phoenicians. This was intensified after Phoenicia fell to Assyria and the western Phoenician colonies were welded into a single empire by the great city-state of Carthage, the most prosperous of the North African settlements. The Carthaginians drove the Greeks out of Sardinia and most of Spain except for the extreme northeast; a Carthaginian-Etruscan alliance was made to limit Greek expansion in Italy; and in Sicily Carthage plotted a major conquest. As Xerxes invaded mainland Greece, simultaneous action by Carthage was attempted in Sicily. The embattled Greeks thwarted both antagonists, but the Carthaginians, unlike the Persians, returned to the attack. Later in the fifth century B.C. Carthage got a foothold in Sicily which was not relinquished until the Romans intervened almost 200 years later. Several times in this period, Carthage had been on the point of conquering the whole island and had been stopped only by the stout resistance of the great city of Syracuse and such help as the Syracusans could obtain from the Greeks in South Italy or mainland Greece.

Rome-Carthage Alliance.   It was ironical that once Rome and Carthage had been friends, although they would go down in history as deadly enemies. Polybius believed that there had been Roman-Carthaginian alliances on several occasions, and we do know that during the war with Tarentum (281–272 B.C.) a pact was made by the two powers: Carthage was induced to attack the Sicilian Greeks to prevent the islanders from sending aid to Tarentum. Pyrrhus and his mercenaries, hired by the Tarentines, not only fought the Romans but also crossed over into Sicily to combat the Carthaginians. In the end, although Tarentum was taken by Rome, Syracuse and some other Sicilian cities escaped the clutches of Carthage.

Rome Sides with Sicily against Carthage.   Despite the unpleasantness over Tarentum, the Italian Greeks generally regarded Rome as a friend and protector. This encouraged the Greeks in Sicily to look to Rome for aid in their struggle with Carthage, while the Romans, sensitive to the welfare of their Greek allies and subjects in Italy, ultimately chose to side with the Sicilians against Carthage. The break between the former allies was precipitated by the affair of the Mamertini, a group of Italian mercenaries who had left the employ of Syracuse and seized the town of Messana in extreme northeastern Sicily. Messana was made into a pirate nest that menaced the Greek trade passing through the narrow straits between Italy and Sicily. When the Syracusans tried to capture Messana, the Mamertini appealed to Carthage for help. Admitted to Messana, the Carthaginians drove off the Syracusans but then refused to leave the town. The Mamertini subsequently asked the Romans to expel the Carthaginians, and war with Carthage was inevitable when the Romans crossed the straits to relieve Messana.

The First Punic War.   The initial conflict between Rome and Carthage (264–241 B.C.) is known as the First Punic War. It dragged on for years because Rome was a land and Carthage a sea power; the combatants could not really come to grips with one another. As in the great Peloponnesian War, a near stalemate would result unless one side was willing to take its chances in the element in which its opponent had the advantage. After building—and losing—more than 500 ships in battle and in storms at sea, the Romans by sheer tenacity finally emerged victorious. Carthage surrendered all claim to Sicily, and the island became a Roman province; moreover, right after the war, when the Carthaginians were crippled by civil strife at home, the Romans also annexed Sardinia and Corsica.

The Second Punic War.   The results of the first Punic War were indecisive. After the war the Carthaginians were bent on revenge, while

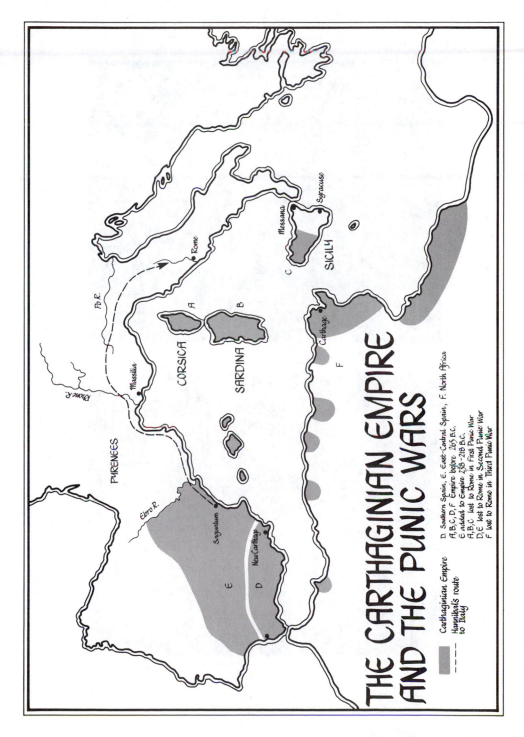

THE CARTHAGINIAN EMPIRE AND THE PUNIC WARS

PYRENEES

Ebro R.

Saguntum

New Carthage

E

D

Rhone R.

Massilia

Po R.

Rome

CORSICA

A

SARDINA

B

Carthage

F

Messana

C

Syracuse

SICILY

Carthaginian Empire

- - - - Hannibal's route to Italy

D. Southern Spain, E. East-Central Spain, F. North Africa
A,B,C,D,F Empire before 265 B.C.
E added to Empire 238-218 B.C.
A,B,C lost to Rome in First Punic War
D,E lost to Rome in Second Punic War
F lost to Rome in Third Punic War

223

OBVERSE (HEADS) AND REVERSE (TAILS)
OF A CARTHAGINIAN SILVER COIN

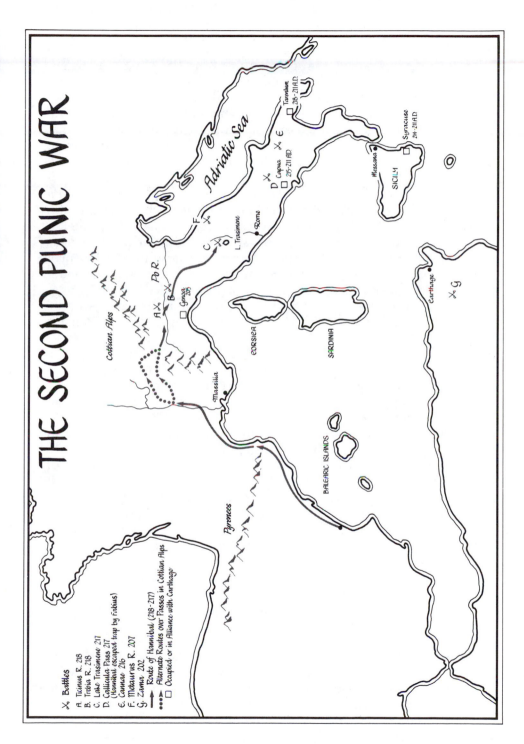

THE SECOND PUNIC WAR

Battles
- A. Ticinus R. 218
- B. Trebia R. 218
- C. Lake Trasimene 217
- D. Callicula Pass 217
  (Hannibal escaped trap by Fabius)
- E. Cannae 216
- F. Metaurus R. 207
- G. Zama 202

➤ Route of Hannibal (218-217)
➤ Alternate Routes over Passes in Cottian Alps
•••• Hannibal escaped trap by Fabius
☐ Occupied or in Alliance with Carthage

Adriatic Sea

Cottian Alps

Po R.

A
B (Genoa 205)
C (L. Trasimene)
Rome
F
D (Capua 215-211 A.D.)
E
Tarentum 213-211 A.D.
Syracuse 214-211 A.D.
Messana
SICILY

Massilia

Pyrenees

BALEARIC ISLANDS

CORSICA

SARDINIA

Carthage
G

the Romans greedily eyed the remaining empire of Carthage in Africa and Spain. Carthaginian aggression and Roman treachery finally promoted a new encounter, the Second Punic War (218–201 B.C.). In Spain, the Carthaginians had been arming the natives and expanding their holdings up the coast toward the Greek settlements in the northeast, an advance that also alarmed the Greeks in southern France. To calm Greek fears, the Romans in 226 B.C. concluded a treaty with Carthage that made the Ebro River the boundary between Roman and Carthaginian spheres of influence in Spain; the Romans pledged themselves to stay north, and the Carthaginians south, of the river. A few years later, however, when the Carthaginians attacked Saguntum, a native town *south* of the Ebro, they uncovered a secret Roman alliance with the Saguntines made in flagrant violation of the treaty of 226 B.C. Unabashed, the Romans boldly demanded the withdrawal of the Carthaginians as well as the right to try to punish Hannibal, the commander of the Carthaginian forces in Spain. When Saguntum fell and Carthage refused to surrender Hannibal to the Romans, a cause for war was provided.

The Second Punic War lasted a long time and was nearly won by Carthage because of Hannibal's brilliant generalship. Before the Romans knew what he was about, he had marched through Spain and France and invaded northern Italy, where he defeated a superior Roman force in 218 B.C. In 217 he repeated his victory in Etruria at Lake Trasimene and again at Cannae in South Italy in 216. Beaten in Spain again and again by Hannibal's brother, Hasdrubal, powerless in Italy, and faced with the defection of their Sicilian ally, Syracuse, in 213 B.C., the Romans should have lost the war, but the Carthaginian fleet failed to bring Hannibal men and supplies in Italy, Philip V of Macedon was unable to invade Italy to aid Hannibal as he had promised to do, and Hannibal himself did not attack the city of Rome when he could have captured it and probably ended the war on the spot. At last, the Romans retook Syracuse despite the machines of Archimedes; they found a general, Scipio, who could win battles in Spain; and then Scipio invaded Africa as Hannibal's army dwindled away to nothing in Italy. In a final battle at Zama in North Africa in 202 B.C., Scipio defeated Hannibal and brought the war to an end. Carthage surrendered her empire in Spain and turned over her fleet to Rome; under the terms of the peace treaty of 201 B.C., she paid a huge indemnity and promised never to make war again without Roman consent.

Rome Defends Greece.   No sooner had the Second Punic War ended than the Romans were drawn into the Eastern Mediterranean to defend the Greeks there. The Antigonid Philip V and the Seleucid Antiochus III were alleged to be planning the conquest of that region, and various Greek states, including Pergamum, wanted Roman help. Philip was beaten and confined to Macedonia (200–197 B.C.). The Romans proclaimed the freedom of the Greeks and began to support oligarchic factions everywhere. This brand of freedom displeased the Aetolians, who invited Antiochus III to come over from Asia to free them from the Romans. Antiochus in his turn was defeated (192–188 B.C.) and forced to withdraw to Syria. Macedonia and Rome fought again in a war which began in 171 B.C.; victorious in 167, the Romans abolished the Antigonid monarchy and also forced the Achaeans, suspected of pro-Macedonian sympathies, to send hostages to Rome. A new uprising in 149 B.C. saw Macedonia made into a Roman province (148) and Corinth, the Achaean capital, destroyed in 146. By this time Egypt was virtually a Roman protectorate, while the Seleucid kingdom, limited to Syria and Palestine, was living on borrowed time. In 133 B.C., as we have already seen, Attalus III willed his Pergamene kingdom to Rome; it was organized as the Roman province of Asia in 129.

The Third Punic War.   Like Corinth, Carthage had been destroyed in 146 B.C. The Romans had goaded the Carthaginians into the Third Punic War in 149 B.C. by encouraging Numidian natives to raid the territory of Carthage. When the Carthaginians begged for permission to make war on the Numidians, the Romans made war on the Carthaginians instead, and Carthage was, much to the satisfaction of chauvinistic old Cato the Elder, completely destroyed. Its territory became the Roman province of Africa.

ROMAN IMPERIALISM BREEDS NEW PROBLEMS

The changing political atmosphere inevitably led to changes in governmental structure.

Provincial Government

Between 265 and 133 B.C., the situation of the Romans had been greatly altered. Rome had acquired an empire outside of Italy: She had two provinces in Spain, the combined province of Sardinia and Corsica, and the provinces of Sicily, Africa, Macedonia, and Asia. This empire had to be administered, defended, and—most important to the Romans—taxed. Each province needed a Roman representative to govern it; he must have the power to command troops, dispense justice, and perform administrative functions. Such a governor must be a magistrate who had the same kind of imperium, or power to rule, as that possessed by the consuls and praetors in Rome. With her first provinces Rome initiated the practice of creating new praetorships, one for each province, since a praetor, though below the consuls in rank, had the imperium. For each praetor, there must also be an assistant; therefore, an equal number of new quaestorships were set up.

Praetors and Promagistrates.   By the middle of the second century B.C., when the Romans decided not to multiply the praetorships indefinitely, there were six praetors: four provincial governors and two stationed at Rome. The latter two were the city praetor and the *praetor peregrinus;* both were primarily judicial officers: The duties of the first praetor have already been described, and the second was concerned with cases involving Romans and foreigners. Because of the pressure of court business at Rome by the mid-second century B.C., it was decided to keep all the praetors in the city as judicial officers and to institute a system of "promagistracies" to supply provincial governors. The two consuls and six praetors would serve in Rome for one year; after this, they would be sent out as needed to function as provincial governors with the rank of proconsul or propraetor. There was no proquaestor; the quaestorships were simply doubled in number to provide one quaestor for each consul, praetor, and promagistrate.

Publicani: Tax Farmers.   While the Roman government set the rate of tax or tribute for each province, its collection was not in the hands of government officials. Instead, the quaestor merely received the taxes from the *publicani,* or tax farmers. These publicani were Roman citizens who organized themselves in companies and bid for the right to collect the taxes in a certain province for a period of years. They would guarantee to collect a specific amount, and whatever they managed to garner above that was their profit. In provinces where the tax was based on a fixed percentage of the yield, the publicani could make nice profits in good years and might lose money in bad ones, but the system was without effective supervision, and the state was ordinarily indifferent to moderate gouging of the provincials by the collectors.

On the whole, the imperial administration of the republican period had little to recommend it. The Romans had small concern for the welfare of their subjects; they looked upon the empire and the people in it merely as a source of revenue. Although the imperial income was such that Roman citizens were no longer required to pay direct taxes, the Romans who profited most from the empire were the officeholders, the publicani, and the contractors who leased the provincial mines, forests, and fisheries. A governor could make a fortune from his provincial command in several ways: He could accept "gifts" from grateful subjects; he could often get away with illegal exactions and special assessments; and a fruitful source of wealth was to extend the limits of the province by warfare, since the governor as commander-in-chief got a large share of the plunder from such conquests. Government officials and Roman businessmen thus had opportunities to enjoy the spoils of empire, although the rivalry of their greed often brought the two groups into conflict. Back in Rome, envy was aroused among the poorer citizens who wanted a chance at the imperial wealth, too. With the officeholders, businessmen, and the masses all striving to plunder the empire, political maneuvering harmful to the state became more prevalent as the competing factions battled for the new wealth.

New Factions Fight for Political Control

Thus, in the second century B.C., it was no longer the patricians and plebeians who fought for political control. The economic changes induced by the Punic Wars had promoted the formation of new factions at Rome.

The Senators and Proletarians. Once, Italy had been a land of small farmers whose chief produce was grain, but the small farmer had been ruined by the Hannibalic wars and by the competition with Sicily from which the state now received a million bushels of grain in annual tribute; additional Sicilian grain, produced on huge slave plantations, could be transported by ship to Rome and sold there at a lower price than the grain grown on the little farms of Italy. Many yeomen left their lands and drifted to Rome where they hoped to find employment. Their vacated farms were incorporated into the larger estates often owned by members of the senatorial, officeholding class; these big landholders had the capital to invest in slaves and to convert their estates to cattle raising or the production of cash crops: wine and olive oil. From such changes came two of the classes or factions: the senatorial class and the impoverished refugees in Rome, the proletarians. The senators, possessed of great wealth but forbidden by law to engage in trade or industry, were landholders who also tended to monopolize high offices in Rome and in the provinces; their stronghold was, of course, the Senate, and the governmental policies which they supported would naturally be those that would further their special political and economic interests. The proletarians were mainly the landless poor of Rome itself. Many were unskilled laborers who could not find steady employment, but they were citizens and their votes determined the election of officials and the passage of the laws. These voters must be courted by the politicians, who could accomplish nothing without their support at the polls.

The Equestrians. Between the senators and the proletarians was a third group, the equestrians. This was a monied class which had originally made its wealth in war contracts at the time of the Punic Wars.

From the ranks of the equestrians came the publicani who collected taxes in the provinces, the contractors who leased the mines and forests, and those who took the contracts for public works. They invested their capital in trade and industry or made nice profits from lending money to hard-pressed provincial cities and states. For their own gain, these people wished to formulate government policy; because their interests differed from those of the officeholding senators, they often opposed bitterly the policies favored by the senatorial class.

The senators, equestrians, and proletarians, then, all wanted something from the state and the empire. In the period after 133 B.C., these three factions fought for control and ruined the Republic in the process. In reality, they represented a minority in the total number of Roman citizens. Since, however, they either lived in Rome or could be present there when the assemblies met, they were able to play a more conspicuous and decisive part in politics than other citizens scattered throughout Italy or in the provinces, who could exercise their civic rights only at rare intervals when they could afford to make the journey to the capital.

Would-be Reformers: the Gracchi

Recognizing the dangerous course Roman politics was taking, various reformers attempted to return Rome to its original ideals.

Tiberius Gracchus.   Just like any one of several Greek city-states, Rome finally reached a point where *stasis*, civil war between rich and poor, oligarch and democrat, was imminent. The situation was aggravated by a post-war depression following the end of the Third Punic War and the termination of hard fighting in Spain, where the Romans had been attempting to extend their domains. Despite large currency issues, big public works programs, and other pump-priming efforts by the government, the economic situation did not improve and the city mob was ripe for trouble. At this juncture, an idealistic young noble named Tiberius Gracchus, grandson of Scipio Africanus, the conqueror of Hannibal, attempted to alleviate the condition of the proletarians by sponsoring a colonization program (133 B.C.). He proposed a distribution of unassigned public lands in Italy from which small farms would be created for the landless citizens. This would get some of the restless proletarians out of Rome, he thought, and would revive the sturdy yeomanry that had once manned the Roman legions.

There were at least two defects in the plan of Tiberius. First, the unassigned public lands were already occupied by senatorial squatters who had annexed the public domain to their own estates and had used it so long that they had created in their own minds an illusion of ownership. Such people were not going to disgorge these holdings without a fight. Second, the proletarians, while initially enthusiastic at the prospects of very nearly getting something for nothing, finally decided that the idea of leaving Rome and going to work was most unattractive. Tiberius did manage to get his land bill passed and an agricultural commission established to administer it. Then senatorial opposition crystallized, his proletarian supporters deserted, and poor Tiberius was killed in street fighting in Rome.

In fairness to the senators, it ought to be said that their objection to Tiberius lay not so much in what he wanted to do as in the way in which he went about it. Tiberius had some of the earmarks of a would-be tyrant in the old Greek sense, a renegade aristocrat leading the people against his own class. With his good military record and his family background, Tiberius had gotten off to a good start on a conventional political career that might have brought him to the consulship in a few years. As consul, he could have introduced his program of reform, but he was impatient and desirous of instant power so he sought and was elected to the office of plebeian tribune. This meant that he could call and preside over the Assembly of the Tribes and introduce his reforms directly to the people whom they were designed to benefit. When the senators got another tribune to block the legislation of Tiberius by a veto, Tiberius persuaded the assembly to depose Octavius, the offending tribune, on the grounds that Octavius had not acted in the interest of the "people" as a good tribune was pledged to do.

What disturbed the senators, then, was that Tiberius, by making something of the long-dormant post of tribune, was well on the way to revolutionizing the Roman political machine. Using the Assembly of the Tribes, an ambitious tribune could institute all kinds of changes and bypass the establishment represented by the great magistrates, the Senate, and the Assembly of the Centuries. The senatorial faction was probably therefore fighting to retain political control rather than the ill-gotten public lands.

Gaius Gracchus.   Ten years later, Gaius Gracchus, the younger brother of Tiberius, rose to political leadership in Rome (123 b.c.). Abler and less scrupulous than Tiberius, Gaius came very near to establishing a tyranny. Holding the tribuneship and thus identifying himself as a popular champion, Gaius revived and enlarged the colonization program of his brother. He also hit upon a marvelous formula for political success: He would form a coalition of proletarians and equestrians to combat the senators. The land bill and a measure to provide cheap grain for the poor won proletarian votes, while the equestrians were brought over by a public works program that promised good contracts, and they were enchanted with a bill that gave them the opportunity to collect the taxes of the rich new province of Asia. This was not all: Some years earlier noisome scandals in provincial government had led to the establishment of a special jury court to try cases of maladministration. Unfortunately, since the jurors were all senators, they seldom convicted the senatorial governors brought to trial; this was not a matter of senatorial courtesy, so to speak, but the fact was that the jurors hesitated to punish other senators for crimes which they themselves had already committed or hoped to commit when they got a chance. Gaius Gracchus proposed that equestrians rather than senators should man the juries. This would give the equestrians a real hold over the provincial governors and discourage those officials from attempting to block rapacious tax collectors and other equestrian operatives in the provinces. Just as the all-senatorial juries had tended to acquit most defendants, the new all-equestrian panels would incline toward conviction; in either case, a just verdict could not be expected.

For about two years Gaius Gracchus had things pretty much his own way until the senatorial opposition organized and began to undermine his popularity with counterprograms sponsored by a rival tribune, Marcus Livius Drusus. The bills proposed by Drusus lured away some of the proletarian adherents of Gaius, while the equestrians began to feel that he had little more to give them. Seeking to tap a new source of power, Gaius brought forward a bill to give Roman citizenship to the Italian allies; this would yield thousands of votes from grateful new citizens. However, the senators, equestrians, and proletarians had one common area of agreement: They did not want to share their citizen rights with anyone else. Large numbers of all classes turned against Gaius; he was hunted through the streets of Rome and finally committed suicide in order to deprive his pursuers of the pleasure of killing him.

Tiberius and Gaius had failed to achieve democracy, to better the lot of the proletarians, or to create a strong tribunate to counter the senatorial monopoly of power. The senators had weathered the first real challenge to their authority, but other leaders would come after the Gracchi, copy their strategy, revive the equestrian-proletarian coalition, and plot to enfranchise the allies. In the political chess game introduced by Gaius, there were set moves: One began by proposing land for the landless, then cheap or even free grain, advantages for the equestrians, restrictions on the senators, and so on. The power struggle initiated in 133 B.C. would continue until the warring factions had destroyed themselves and the Republic as well.

Gaius Marius: Equestrian Triumph

About ten years after the death of Gaius Gracchus, repeated blunders in the conduct of a North African war jeopardized the position of the senate in politics at Rome. A Numidian king named Jugurtha had murdered his way to the throne and, in the process, killed some people supposedly under Roman protection; he also molested the Roman province of Africa. Attempts to punish Jugurtha failed; he beat senatorial commanders in the field, bribed them to accede to disgraceful peace terms, and then even came to Rome to testify against his accomplices in a senatorial investigation. At last, Gaius Marius, an equestrian with a good military record, was elected to the consulship and sent to Africa against Jugurtha. Marius defeated the Numidians in a two-year campaign which ended when Jugurtha was captured in a cloak-and-dagger operation by Sulla, the quaestor of Marius. The Numidian king was brought to Rome, tried, tortured, and executed (105 B.C.).

Marius was the man of the hour. His victory was hailed as an equestrian triumph, and senatorial prestige sank to a new low. No sooner was he back in Italy than Marius was called upon to save Italy from a barbarian invasion threatened by two Germanic tribes, the Cimbri and Teutones, who had ravaged southern Gaul, defeated senatorial commanders, and seemed about to penetrate the Po Valley. Marius was more than equal to the occasion. He beat the Teutones, then the Cimbri, and returned to Rome more popular than ever.

In the year 100 B.C., with peace and security restored, Marius entered upon his sixth consulship. His fighting days were not over since now he must contend in the arena of politics, a battlefield on which his military skill would avail him nothing. In Rome, the war hero was a figurehead, the standard-bearer in name only of a coalition of equestrians and proletarians that had been put together by two unscrupulous demagogues, Saturninus and Glaucia. Marius had no control over these ruffians, whose political tactics covered a broad range of atrocities from bribery to assassination, nor could the great general cope with the experienced strategists in the Senate who were on the opposing side. The Senate maneuvered Marius into a position where he had to declare martial law in Rome and lead a senatorial posse against his own followers, whose excesses had precipitated the crisis. Saturninus and Glaucia were killed, Marius was discredited, and the Senate regained its control of the government (99 B.C.).

Marius, once hailed as the saviour of his country because of his victories over Jugurtha and the barbarian invaders, had done Rome more harm then good. He had popularized the idea of combining military glory with political leadership; some of his more versatile successors would make efficient use of this combination. He had reorganized the Roman army; he had not only improved its military capabilities, but by inaugurating a policy of accepting enlistments instead of relying on conscription, he had also created a professional army that might become a tool of politicians since the soldiers were more devoted to their commanders than to the interests of the state. Because of the succession of crises which faced the Romans between 107 and 100 B.C., Marius, who appeared to be the only man capable of dealing with Jugurtha and the barbarians, had been chosen consul six times in defiance of the law that required an interval of ten years between successive consulships. This set a dangerous precedent, contributing to the disintegration of the Roman constitution which had already set in.

New Problems

The Romans were very human in that they were beset by certain shortcomings that have caused trouble for mankind from prehistoric times to the present. Frequently the Romans, when faced with a problem, either tried to pretend that it did not exist or adopted some temporary, makeshift solution that was only a palliative and not a cure. Consequently, in the early part of the first century B.C., they paid the penalty for their failure to face up to the problems of citizenship for the Italian allies, maladministration in the provinces, and the decline of the navy. By the year 90 B.C. the allies were determined to have Roman citizenship or complete independence; the provincials in Greece and Asia were on the verge of revolt because of the ruthless exploitation to which they had been subjected; and the neglect of the Roman fleet had brought a decay that encouraged widespread piracy, something completely out of hand by this time.

Citizenship for Italian Allies

On several occasions after the death of Gaius Gracchus, ambitious politicians had attempted to gain citizenship for the Italian allies. The Romans as a whole were more than cool to this idea, and any political schemer with his eye on the potential allied vote would find himself bitterly opposed by other demagogues who wanted to turn the trick themselves.

The allies finally tired of waiting for action in Rome and rose in revolt. The so-called Social War (90–88 B.C.), the struggle between Rome and her allies, caught the Romans off guard. The revolt began with the allies located in central Italy, but the Romans managed to contain it by promptly granting citizenship to all allies who had not yet taken up arms or who would stop fighting at once. After initial defeats, the Romans won the war by hard fighting; on the other hand, the allies got what they wanted since all were made citizens. The Roman citizen body was thus greatly increased, and it was important that many new persons were now enrolled in the senatorial and equestrian classes, as well as in the lower census ranks.

Chapter Nine

The Decline and Fall
of the Roman Republic

PROBLEMS AND SOLUTIONS

In the sixty years from the end of the Social War to the demise of the Republic and the founding of the Principate (27 B.C.), Roman affairs were in turmoil. Riots in Rome, political assassinations, civil wars spreading from Italy to the provinces, bloody reprisals and the general collapse of constitutional government sullied a period that might have been remembered as one graced by some of the most brilliant and talented individuals in all of Roman history: Caesar, Cicero, Catullus, Lucretius, Vergil, and Sallust.

The desperate illness of the Republic was plain to see, and various remedies were proposed to restore it to health. One of these stressed reaction, a retreat to a legendary past that was dead and gone; another sought to reconcile the realities of the present through an unrealistic compromise that would unite two potentially strong but traditionally hostile groups into a single ruling class; in still another the past and present were to be discarded for a future that most Romans were not yet prepared to accept: Scrap the Republic and install an autocracy.

These suggested panaceas had one thing in common: they were impractical. It was either too early or too late to persuade or force the Romans to unite for their common good, and if anything of a positive nature could be said about the last six decades of the Republic it would be that there were few dull moments in politics.

SULLA: A NEW VARIETY OF DICTATORSHIP

As the Social War ended, the senatorial faction seemed to be in the saddle at Rome. Its leader was the former quaestor of Marius, Lucius Cornelius Sulla, the man who had captured Jugurtha and had just shown himself to be the best general in the Social War. Faced with both foreign and domestic problems, Sulla judged the first to be more serious and immediate and demanding of his personal attention.

On the Black Sea coast of Asia Minor was the semicivilized kingdom of Pontus that adjoined the Roman client kingdom of Bithynia and was within striking distance of the Roman province of Asia. Unimportant before about 120 B.C., Pontus had been increased in size and strength over a period of three decades by a crafty and energetic king, Mithridates VI. Generally careful not to have trouble with Rome, Mithridates was determined to get control of Bithynia and had already had a brush or two with the Romans. Then, while the Social War was in progress and it appeared to some foreigners that the Romans might be defeated by the Italian allies, Mithridates hatched a plot with the dissatisfied subjects of Rome in the province of Asia. In 88 there was a general uprising of these provincials in which, it was said, 80,000 Romans were massacred in a single day. Mithridates moved in and, when the revolt spread from Asia Minor to Greece, where Athens and other towns proclaimed their independence from Rome, the Greeks invited Mithridates to help them. The situation was indeed serious, and, given Sulla's reputation as a general and the fact that he had already opposed Mithridates in Asia on a previous occasion, it seemed appropriate to send him out again.

However, before we can follow that story we have to see what was happening in Rome in the domestic crisis that Sulla thought was unimportant.

The Social War had ended with a victory for the Romans in which diplomacy and concessions overshadowed their few triumphs on the battlefield. The allies had won citizenship but only in name. They could not exercise their political rights as voters and officeholders until they were formally enrolled in the Roman tribes, and it would be many years before this was accomplished. Some Romans wanted to enroll the thousands of new citizens in only eight of the thirty-five tribes in order to minimize their potential voting power since they would outnumber the Romans about three or four to one! Other politicians, like Gaius Gracchus years earlier, were anxious to capitalize on the voting strength of the allies.

Another domestic matter demanding attention was the plight of many debtors of senatorial rank who had found the race for office increasingly expensive or were the victims of their own extravagance. Facing possible expulsion from the senatorial class, they hoped for a moratorium on their debts or would accept a scaling down of the rate of interest. Feelings ran high, for in some quarters little sympathy was felt for the debtors. In 89 B.C., when the urban praetor tried to impose a moratorium on the basis of an old law, he was lynched in the forum by a mob of creditors.

In 88 B.C. an activist tribune in the style of the Gracchi and the second Marcus Livius Drusus proposed legislation that would expel the debtors from the Senate, enroll the new citizens equally in each of the tribes, and substitute Marius for Sulla in the command against Mithridates. Riots broke out. Sulla narrowly escaped assassination and left Rome to join the troops in the south that were mustering for the campaign against Mithridates. The legislation of the tribune, Sulpicius Rufus, was adopted in Rome, but Sulla led his army northward, captured the city, outlawed Marius and Sulpicius, and rescinded the radical laws of the latter. Marius fled to Africa, but Sulpicius was caught and killed, and having settled these matters (or so he thought), Sulla set off for Greece in 87.

It took Sulla more than four years to drive Mithridates out of Greece and Asia back into his own kingdom of Pontus. Ravaging Greece and imposing ruinous penalties of tribute upon the reconquered provincials in Asia, Sulla could have toppled Mithridates from the throne and annexed Pontus, but he did not. Instead, the victorious Roman dealt rather leniently with Mithridates because he was extremely anxious to get back to Rome where a new civil war had unseated the senatorial faction and installed the partisans of Marius in power. As a matter of fact, the revolution had occurred almost as soon as Sulla had departed from Italy. Marius had captured Rome, set up a government that disavowed Sulla, and instituted a general massacre of Sulla's senatorial supporters. Although Marius died in 86 B.C., the revolutionists had retained their hold upon the state so that, when Sulla came back with his army in 83, he had to capture Rome and reestablish his faction in authority.

Sulla found governmental affairs a complete shambles. Even if his own proconsular authority had not been revoked by the Marians, it would have long since expired. There was, in fact, no legitimate government, yet somehow a new regime must be established in a constitutional manner. This was accomplished by appointing Sulla *dictator* "for the purpose of reconstituting the Republic."

The dictatorship was an "extraordinary" magistracy which had fallen into disuse over a century earlier. Before that the device of dictatorship had been employed several times in the period 450 to 200 B.C. when the ordinary magistrates seemed unable to cope with some military, political, or economic crisis. On such occasions the constitution would be suspended and a supreme official, the dictator, appointed with power to enact laws and to take the necessary steps to end the crisis.

As soon as the danger passed, the dictator was supposed to resign his office and restore normal government; in any event, his term could not exceed six months. The plebeian secession of 287 B.C. had brought the appointment of a dictator, Hortensius, whose "Hortensian Laws" had established the tribal assembly. Still another famous dictator was Fabius who had served his country well in a military crisis when Rome had nearly collapsed after being defeated by Hannibal at Lake Trasimene and again at Cannae.

Now, in the new crisis of 82 B.C., the dictatorship was revived, but it took a new form: Instead of serving for six months, Sulla remained in office until his voluntary retirement in 79. During his three years as dictator he tried to reform the government in such a way that it would attain a new stability and an immunity to civil strife. Sulla was a senator and a reactionary. He wanted to bring back the senatorial oligarchy of the mid-fifth century B.C. To this end he increased the size of the Senate, reestablished its veto over legislation, removed the equestrians and restored senators to the jury courts, and curtailed the power of the tribunes. He even tried to exterminate the equestrians by confiscating their property and killing as many of them as he could catch.

It is interesting to note that, when Sulla landed in southern Italy in 83 and prepared to overthrow the Marian government, he was joined by a number of his old supporters and some new ones as well. Among them were individuals who were destined to play major roles in the years to come. Gnaeus Pompey, later known as Pompey the Great but at that time scarcely more than a teenager, raised an army on his own initiative and came to Sulla's aid. Marcus Licinius Crassus, just back from exile in Spain, also joined up, and another partisan was Lucius Sergius Catilina (Catiline), soon to add to his already unsavory reputation by savage cruelties that would repel even Sulla. An additional prize acquisition was Caius Verres, the later target of Cicero's orations, who deserted to Sulla from the Marian side, bringing along the war chest of the general he had been serving as quaestor.

Sulla's bloodletting and reactionary reforms failed to accomplish their purpose. The enlargement of the Senate membership would stand the test of time, but the only permanent and useful change made by Sulla lay in the field of criminal law in which he increased the numbers and functions of the *quaestiones* (jury courts). The original *quaestic* created in 149 B.C. dealt only with cases of extortion in the provinces involving provincial governors and lesser officials. Sulla added six new types of cases to be tried in the jury courts: treason, murder, assault and battery, forgery, bribery in elections, and embezzlement of public funds. This not only extended the judicial functions of senators but also created opportunities for political visibility and advancement for skilled orators appearing as advocates (trial lawyers) who acted as prosecutors or argued the case for the defense. As we shall see, Cicero among others was able to exploit this new opportunity to advantage.

After Sulla (78–60 B.C.)

Sulla, like most reactionaries, had cherished the belief that he could turn back the clock, go upstream against the current of time and change. Few of his close associates were in complete sympathy with him, and many who had joined his faction in the civil war against the Marians began to work for the destruction of his legislation as soon as the iron-willed old dictator died in 78 B.C. His opponents, moreover, had not been exterminated; great numbers had taken refuge in Spain, where they formed a government in exile and allied themselves with Mithridates and the pirates to wage war against Sulla's forces all around the Mediterranean. This forced the government at Rome to fight on several fronts simultaneously after Sulla died. A special commander was sent against the pirates; Lucius Lucullus, Sulla's quaestor in the earlier war with Mithridates, was dispatched to oppose the Pontic king; and Gnaeus Pompey, a young favorite of Sulla's, was ordered to combat the Marians in Spain.

Although he was to receive more credit then he deserved for the final victory in Spain, the truth of the matter was that Pompey was no match for the Marian general, Sertorius, who had been sent to Spain in 83 or early in 82 B.C. Sertorius had served with distinction under Marius in the war with the Cimbri and Teutones but had become estranged from his leader by the massacres of 87 that accompanied the recapture of Rome by Marius after Sulla had gone to Greece. At first the Marian exiles in Spain did not welcome the arrival of Sertorius and their treachery forced him to flee to Africa, but he returned to the Iberian peninsula in 80 and thereafter defeated a series of Roman armies sent from Italy against him. When Pompey came out in 76, he fared no better than his predecessors until Sertorius was assassinated in 72 by a jealous subordinate whose inferior talents even Pompey could excel. Brave, but not fortunate; it was too bad about Sertorius. He alone of the Marian generals might have overcome Sulla in 82; in the 70s, at one point the government in Rome might have been willing to compromise and invite him back to Italy. Later, that opportunity was lost. To keep going in Spain, Sertorius felt obliged to ally himself with Mithridates and the pirates. This antagonized the Romans in Italy as well as his own Roman troops in Spain. In addition, the Spanish natives whom he had trained and made into excellent soldiers idolized him and thought of him as a second Hannibal who might free them from Rome, but in Roman eyes Sertorius was a renegade deserving of extermination.

As these commanders struggled with indifferent success on the far-flung borders of the empire, a violent rebellion broke out in Italy in 73 B.C. This was the Revolt of the Gladiators; it was led by the famous Spartacus who defeated several Roman armies sent against him in his stronghold on Mt. Vesuvius. The end finally came in 71 B.C. when the revolutionists split into two groups in an attempt to escape from Italy; one of them was defeated in the south by the praetor Marcus Licinius Crassus, a former adherent of Sulla, and the other was destroyed in the north by Pompey as he came back victorious from Spain.

The triumphant generals, Pompey and Crassus, were heroes of the day. Though neither was eligible for the consulship, they both ran for the office, won the election partly by refusing to disband their armies, and became the chief magistrates of Rome for the year 70 B.C. During that twelve months their chief accomplishment was to wipe out the last vestiges of the reforms of their onetime leader, Sulla. The tide of political sentiment had turned, and neither Pompey nor Crassus wished to sacrifice political popularity merely to honor the memory and last wishes of their deceased patron.

A New Political Game

From the year 70 B.C. to the end of the Republic four decades later, the senatorial, equestrian, and proletarian factions continued their quarrels but they, like the army, were only gaming pieces in a gigantic political chess match in which the players were a succession of ambitious and unscrupulous individuals who sought power for themselves: Pompey, Crassus, Caesar, Catiline, Mark Antony, and several others. In 70 B.C. Crassus was the champion of the Senate, while Pompey was identified with the "popular" faction; within a few years they had changed sides, with Crassus a popular leader and Pompey the darling of the Senate. Marcus Tullius Cicero, of whom we shall presently hear more, began life as an equestrian and became the most senatorian of senators. Julius Caesar, a senator of ancient and distinguished lineage who later constituted almost a one-man faction, was in his youth a faithful and stubborn supporter of Marius.

Pompey

After rebellion in Italy and Spain had been crushed, it still remained to deal with Mithridates and the pirates. Lucullus had initial successes on the eastern front; he drove Mithridates from Asia and even out of Pontus to a refuge in Armenia. The pirates, however, were bolder than ever; not content with preying on Mediterranean commerce, they had begun to raid the Italian coast. In 67 B.C. a tribune named Gabinius proposed a special command against the pirates which would place in Pompey's hands a great army and fleet as well as authority over all Roman governors around the Mediterranean. The bill envisioned a three-year campaign, but Pompey in a whirlwind attack destroyed the pirates in three months. This left Pompey with a huge military force, a command that had more than two and one-half years to run, and nothing much to do. At this juncture, however, the army of Lucullus mutinied, his campaign against Mithridates came to an abrupt halt, and Mithridates slipped back into Pontus to start hostilities all over again. In 66 B.C. a tribune named Manilius, supported vigorously by Cicero, proposed the transfer of the command against Mithridates from Lucullus to Pompey. The bill passed; Pompey drove Mithridates out of Pontus and into a Crimean exile where he died in 63 B.C. Pompey meanwhile annexed several chunks of territory in the Near East, including the Seleucid kingdom in Syria, and then returned victorious to Rome in 62 B.C.

Crassus

During Pompey's absence Rome had been anything but quiet. Crassus, bitterly jealous of Pompey and now allied with the Populares, the equestrian-proletarian faction, had plotted and schemed continuously to destroy his rival and gain power for himself. One of the richest men in Rome, Crassus spent a fortune buying votes and promoting the election to high office of his henchmen, among whom were Julius Caesar and the infamous Catiline. The latter, an impecunious noble, had a long record of immorality and crime: He had been one of the most blood-thirsty partisans of Sulla during the reign of terror (83–79 B.C.); it was said that he had killed his own brother and seduced one of the Vestal Virgins; all sorts of rumors were rife concerning Catiline's misconduct in the praetorship and as a provincial governor. Crassus backed Catiline several times for the consulship, but even bribery and intimidation of the voters could not secure his election. In the counsular elections of 64 B.C., Catiline failed again; instead, the voters chose Cicero, the candidate of the Optimates, the senatorial party, while the other consular post was won by Antonius, backed by Crassus.

This meant that the consuls for 63 B.C. were Cicero and Antonius. Cicero, well-known as a fine orator and a brilliant trial lawyer, had already been a quaestor in Sicily and a praetor in Rome. In the year 70 B.C. his conviction of the dishonest Sicilian governor, Verres, in the face of an almost certain acquittal at the hands of a senatorial jury, had ensured the political success of Cicero. Now he had attained the highest office in the Republic, a feat regarded as almost impossible of achievement by a person of such obscure origin, and his consulate was to be remembered forever as the year of the Catilinarian conspiracy—Cicero personally saw to that!

In the consular race of 63 B.C., Catiline had tried and failed once more. He then plotted revolution. Supported, it was alleged, by impoverished senators and dissatisfied proletarians, his plan was to assassinate the high-ranking government officials and take over the city of Rome. This scheme was detected and foiled, but Catiline boldly remained in Rome instead of joining his army, which was mustering in Etruria. He continued to attend meetings of the Senate until challenged by Cicero in the immortal *First Oration against Catiline*. Some of the conspirators, including Catiline, then went to Etruria from whence they continued to communicate with their partisans still in Rome. Late in the year Cicero was able to produce positive evidence against the conspirators; those in Rome were rounded up and executed, while early in 62 B.C. Catiline was killed and his army destroyed in a great battle in the north.

Political Stalemate in Rome

The next two years saw a political stalemate in Rome. Crassus and his followers continued their feud with the Senate and Pompey. The friends of Lucullus, the man whom Pompey had replaced in the war against Mithridates, along with most of the senators, were hostile to Pompey. A smaller faction, composed of Pompey, Cicero, and their supporters, struggled to no avail against Crassus and the partisans of Lucullus; it was fortunate that Crassus and Lucullus were irreconcilable enemies since an alliance of these two would have finished Pompey in short order. The deadlock was finally broken in 60 B.C. when Julius Caesar returned from his propraetorian command in Spain in order to run for the consulship.

Julius Caesar and the First Triumvirate

Julius Caesar was a brilliant and versatile man who possessed the combined attributes of an Alexander, a Peisistratus, and an Alcibiades. Once a staunch Marian and more recently the chief political strategist of Crassus, Caesar now wanted the consulship and saw clearly that the support of Crassus would be insufficient for his purpose. He therefore proposed a coalition of the forces of Crassus and Pompey. This would end the deadlock, produce enough voting strength to overpower the senatorial faction, and get Caesar the office he desired. Once consul, he would then repay both Pompey and Crassus by initiating the legislation they had been unable to secure: a ratification of Pompey's diplomatic settlements in the Near East, land as a bonus for Pompey's veterans, and measures that would profit the equestrian friends of Crassus. Thus in 60 B.C. the famous First Triumvirate was formed; this was an unofficial coalition of Pompey, Crassus, and Caesar for the purpose of controlling politics at Rome. Cicero, incidentally, was invited to join the

combination, but he thought himself too important to need such an alliance; at the moment he was committed to his impossible dream of the
"Concord of the Orders" designed to bring the senators and equestrians
together and harness them to the same chariot that he, Cicero, would
drive.

The First Triumvirate dominated the political scene at Rome for the
next seven years. Caesar got his consulship for 59 B.C. and followed it
up with two five-year commands of an extraordinary nature in Gaul, in
the course of which he added all of what is now France to the Roman
Empire, invaded both Germany and Britain, and made a fortune in
plunder that enabled him to repay all that he had borrowed from Crassus and remain a rich man besides. Nevertheless, the wars in Gaul were
more important for other reasons. Long years of difficult campaigning
in a foreign land gave Caesar an opportunity to combine his great natural talents with actual experience in the field so that he emerged as a
leader and strategist almost beyond compare. It was no wonder that
Plutarch in his *Parallel Lives* chose to link Caesar with Alexander the
Great. Caesar's *Commentary on the Gallic War* became a textbook studied
by future generals of all periods. Of more immediate significance was
the fact that a number of Caesar's officers in Gaul gained experience
qualifying them for major commands in the civil wars still to come: Mark
Antony, Caesar's successor; Labienus and Quintus Cicero who sided
with Pompey against Caesar; Decimus Brutus, one of Caesar's assassins
and an enemy of Mark Antony; and the elder son of Crassus who perished with his father in the disastrous campaign against the Parthians
in 53 B.C. Needless to say, it was vital to Caesar's victory in the civil war
of 49 to 45 that campaigns in Gaul had provided him with a loyal army
of experienced and well-trained veterans more devoted to him than to
the Roman Republic.

The multifaceted genius of Caesar was manifested not only by his
military exploits or the administrative skill he displayed as dictator, but
even before the creation of the First Triumvirate Caesar was known and
admired as an orator rated by some as superior to Cicero. We do not
have any of his orations, yet the Gallic commentaries are more than
sufficient testimony that he was a master of prose. Lucid, packed with
memorable descriptions and exciting narratives, eagerly read by Caesar's contemporaries for the information about Gaul, Britain, and Germany available for the first time, the work was a literary triumph even
though its purpose was recognized as propaganda intended to publicize
its author.

Caesar's *Commentaries* should be read, not summarized. Like many
other great books that have come down to us from classical antiquity,
the principal value of the work is not lost or sacrificed in translation.
Caesar wrote for adults, not children, and it has been unfortunate in

modern times that "Caesar" was used as an introductory textbook for what we now call "ninth-graders" just beginning their study of Latin. For most of them the importance and excitement of the book were obscured in the struggle to learn a foreign language, and not many were sufficiently able to overcome their dislike for the experience to want to return to the *Commentaries* later in life.

Friction in the Triumvirate

Despite its strength and initial successes, the First Triumvirate did not operate without friction. The three men were rivals, not friends, and although Pompey's marriage to Julia, Caesar's beloved daughter, kept her father and her husband from each others' throats until her death in 54 B.C., there could be no real truce between Pompey and Crassus, who had been enemies since the death of Sulla. Trouble began even before Caesar left for Gaul. As consul in 59 he was the only member of the triumvirate with any official standing, so it was his responsibility to find a way to control or eliminate the most dangerous opponents of the triumvirs, who would certainly become active in 58 when his consulship had ended. This made Cicero and Cato the Younger his prime targets.

Cicero had virtually made a business of thwarting the schemes of Crassus since 66 B.C., and because he had refused to join the unholy trinity in 60 he must be defused in some other way. Equally dangerous was Cato the Younger, the great-grandson of Cato the Censor, who was so cantankerous that he seemed to be the reincarnation of his redoubtable ancestor. A man of ostentatious probity who always had a "good" reason, if not the real one, for his long-standing opposition to Crassus, Pompey, and Caesar, Cato was much admired though not loved by many Romans of all classes; he was also the friend of Lucullus and the most belligerent of that faction in the Senate. Catos's major fault, other than that he was uncompromisingly stiff-necked, was that he always managed to do the right thing at the wrong time!

Caesar was equal to the occasion. In 59 B.C. he managed to secure election to the tribunate for Clodius, a useful tool of Crassus who had already proved his worth by fomenting the mutiny of Lucullus' army in the Mithridatic war. Because Clodius was a patrician, a member of the ancient and prominent Claudian clan, he was not eligible to be a tribune, but Caesar got around that obstacle by having Clodius adopted into a plebeian family. In 58 Clodius won popular support by sponsoring several measures that pleased the proletarians and the equestrians. Then he proposed a measure that would outlaw any person who had put a Roman citizen to death without trial. Cicero was not named but no one doubted that he was the target of the bill since he had advocated the execution of the Catilinarian conspirators arrested in Rome in 63.

While the proposal of Clodius was being debated in the tribal assembly, Cicero blustered that he was so important he could not be touched and that Pompey would protect him, but as the days went by and Pompey was never at home when Cicero called and did not reply to pleading letters sent by Cicero, the embattled orator got the point. Since the passage of the bill was certain, Cicero left Rome and went into voluntary exile outside of Italy. So much for Cicero, and Cato proved less of a problem. He was appointed to organize and administer the new province of Cyprus. Although Cato knew the real purpose of the appointment, his personal code of ethics made it imperative that he accept since it was an official order from the government.

This victory for the triumvirs was short-lived. Clodius, at the urging of Crassus, began a series of thinly disguised attacks on Pompey, who felt impelled to get a tame tribune of his own who would oppose Clodius. This was Milo, who engineered the recall of Cicero from exile in 57 and then launched a series of counterattacks on Clodius. In the end, both Clodius and Milo organized gangs of supporters that clashed in the streets and disrupted the conduct of government business.

The growing feud between Crassus and Pompey and the impending danger that his first five-year command in Gaul would not be renewed made it essential for Caesar to try to prolong the First Triumvirate. To that end he called a conference of his colleagues to meet at Luca on the border of Cisalpine Gaul in 56. There it was agreed that Caesar would receive another five-year command in Gaul when his present grant expired in 54 and that Pompey and Crassus would share the consulship in Rome for 55 and after that each of the pair would be given a five-year command: Crassus in Syria and Pompey in the two Spanish provinces. This should remind us that the name of the game was power derived from the military command, involving an extraordinary imperium and the immunity from prosecution that would last until the grant expired.

Artificial respiration would not prolong the life of the triumvirate. Julia died in 54 B.C., and in 53 Crassus was killed in Syria after provoking a war with the Parthians. Open rivalry developed between Pompey and Caesar, and the gang warfare of Clodius and Milo continued until Clodius was murdered and Milo fled to Gaul to escape prosecution.

As Pompey was drawn into an alliance with the senatorial faction, a scheme was hatched to accomplish Caesar's downfall. The aim of Caesar's enemies was simple enough: They wanted to deprive him of any command or office so that as a private citizen he would be vulnerable to such legal prosecution as they might choose to bring against him. Caesar had hoped to follow his second five-year command in Gaul with the consulship and then another provincial assignment, while his opponents planned to break this chain either before or after the consulship.

As Caesar neared the end of his Gallic command, he realized that it would not be possible to come to terms with Pompey and the Senate; he was going to have to fight for his life in the most literal sense.

Caesar Begins Civil War.   In 49 B.C., refusing to give up his command, Caesar began the civil war by crossing the Rubicon, a river marking the boundary between his province and peninsular Italy. He captured Rome, drove Pompey out of Italy, defeated Pompey's supporters in Spain, and then routed Pompey himself in a showdown battle at Pharsalus in Thessaly in 48. When Pompey fled to Egypt, he was assassinated there by Ptolemy XII. Far from showing any gratitude to Ptolemy, Caesar came to Egypt and punished the king for the offense of having killed a Roman citizen by elevating Cleopatra, Ptolemy's sister, queen—and enemy—to the rulership of Egypt.

After a rather close call with the Egyptian partisans of the deposed Ptolemy (who soon obliged Caesar by getting himself drowned in the Nile), Caesar gave Cleopatra her younger brother as a consort and then settled down for a nice winter holiday with the Egyptian queen. The romance of Cleopatra and Caesar—if that is what it was—has inspired historians, novelists, and playwrights for centuries. The myth of her beauty grew with the passing years, but if we look at the contemporary sculptured portraits and those on coins she seems to have been attractive, though not breathtaking, as a girl but definitely an old hag at thirty-five. For all practical purposes captured, but not necessarily captivated, by Caesar and in view of her later success in managing and then in desperation betraying Mark Antony, we might see Cleopatra as a patriot determined to make whatever personal sacrifice was required to preserve the independence of her country. But what about Caesar? With all his previous experience with several marriages and numerous uncounted conquests outside the bonds of matrimony, would he succumb to the charms of a mere girl thirty years his junior? Or was he still vulnerable? Yet Cleopatra was probably the best-educated and most intellectual woman Caesar had ever encountered, definitely his equal on that level. And then there was the mystery, even for Caesar, of association with the Egyptian goddess who knew dark mysteries inaccessible to him. Or was Caesar just as practical and tough-minded as our hypothetical Cleopatra? If so, they were a well-matched pair!

At any rate, by spring the realities of life in this world forced Caesar to action. After restoring order to the Near East—Veni, Vidi, Vici—he returned to Rome, settled the unrest there, then quickly disposed of the Pompeians still at large in Africa (46 B.C.) and Spain (45 B.C.).

Caesar Becomes Dictator.   Despite rumors that he intended to marry Cleopatra and establish a monarchy of the Hellenistic type, Caesar probably planned an autocracy in which he would be the supreme magistrate. Like Sulla, he held the dictatorship; a clue to his intentions may perhaps be found in the fact that within less than five years (49–44 B.C.) his term as dictator, at first indefinite, was extended to one of ten years, and then for life. In addition to the dictatorship, Caesar assumed other offices and acquired special powers that concentrated all authority in his hands: Each year he held the consulship; as *pontifex maximus*, a lifetime post which he had held since 63 B.C., he was the principal religious official; although he did not hold the tribuneship, he took the power of that office, and this allowed him to convene the Assembly of the Tribes and provided a power of veto over the acts of magistrates and proceedings of the Senate and assemblies; special grants made him commander-in-chief of all Roman forces, director of foreign policy, perpetual censor without a colleague, and gave him the right to nominate and even appoint officials and magistrates, supervise the coinage, and legislate at his pleasure.

Caesar's Reforms.   It cannot be said that Caesar abused his power. He apparently felt that only dictatorship could restore peace, stability, and efficient government. As dictator, he instituted many reforms of a beneficial and lasting character. He reduced provincial taxes and began a comprehensive program of colonization by Roman citizens in the provinces, which provided lands for veterans and removed thousands of the troublesome proletarians from Rome. He began the much-needed codification of Roman law; he introduced a new and better calendar which ever afterward bore his name and was used in western Europe for over sixteen centuries. Local government in Italy was reorganized; a pattern of municipal administration based on the reformed city government of Rome itself was evolved and later extended to towns in the western provinces.

Unfortunately for Caesar himself, Rome was not ready for autocracy, and Caesar made the mistake of trying to become reconciled with his enemies instead of liquidating them. Humanity and dictatorship proved incompatible: In March of 44 B.C. Julius Caesar was assassinated by senatorial conspirators and breathed his last at the foot of Pompey's statue.

The Second Triumvirate: Antony, Lepidus, Octavian

Caesar's assassins proved too inept to establish the normal government which they imagined would restore itself following the death of the dictator. Moreover, Caesar was survived by ambitious subordinates who were determined not to let their power slip away. Mark Antony and Lepidus, his principal henchmen, arrayed themselves against the

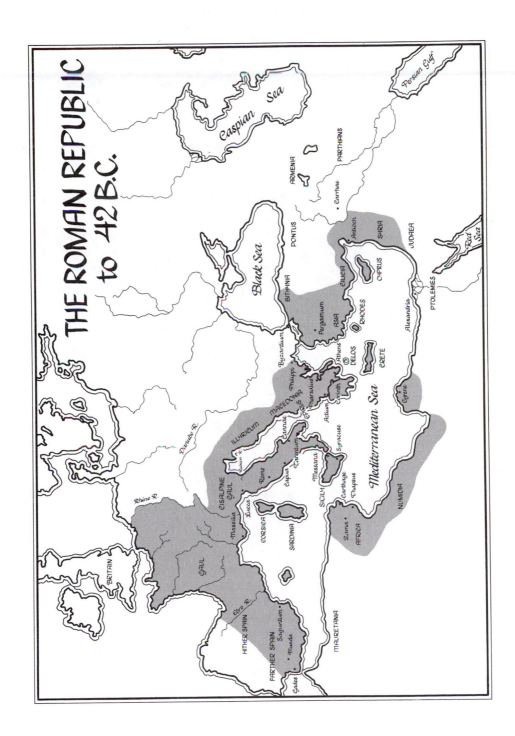

THE ROMAN REPUBLIC to 42 B.C.

Persian Gulf

Caspian Sea

Red Sea

PARTHIANS

ARMENIA
• Carrhae

PONTUS

Black Sea

BITHYNIA

Byzantium

Antioch
CILICIA
SYRIA
JUDAEA
CYPRUS
Alexandria
PTOLEMIES

Pergamum
ASIA
◊ RHODES

◉ Athens
DELOS
Corinth
CRETE
Cyrene

MACEDONIA
Philippi
EPIRUS
Pharsalus
Actium

ILLYRICUM
Rubicon R.
Ravenna
Tarentum
Syracuse

Danube R.

CISALPINE GAUL
Rome
Capua
Messana
SICILY
Carthage
Zama •
Thapsus
AFRICA
NUMIDIA

Mediterranean Sea

Rhine R.
Massilia
Lucca
CORSICA
SARDINIA

BRITAIN

GAUL

Ebro R.
HITHER SPAIN
Saguntum •
FARTHER SPAIN
• Munda
Gades •
MAURETANIA

249

COINS FROM THE END OF THE ROMAN REPUBLIC

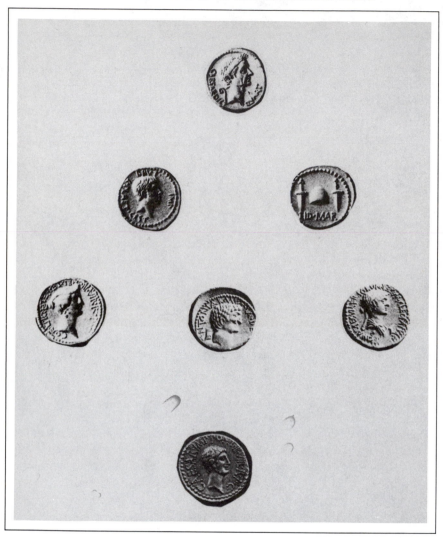

Top: Julius Caesar.
2nd row: Brutus and daggers and liberty cap commemorating Ides of March.
3rd row: Antony (center) and two of his wives: Octavia (left) and Cleopatra (right).
Bottom: Octavian.

Senate, and a new civil war ensued. Young Octavian, Caesar's grand-nephew who had been named son and heir of the dictator in his will, eventually joined Antony and Lepidus. Victors in Italy by 43 B.C., these three men assumed what amounted to a triple dictatorship. They were constituted by law a board of three for the purpose of reorganizing the Republic. This was the Second Triumvirate; it differed from the earlier combination of Crassus, Pompey, and Caesar in that it was not an informal coalition but rather a formal, constitutionally recognized committee. The new triumvirs had virtually destroyed their opposition by the Battle of Philippi in 42 B.C. Cicero, who had bravely stood up to Antony, had already been put to the sword in 43.

End of the Republic

Like the members of the First Triumvirate, there was no love lost among those of the Second. As Lepidus, the weakest of the three, was pushed into the background, a bitter contest for supreme control developed between Antony and Octavian. Even a compromise arrangement by which Octavian took the western half of the empire and Antony the East proved a failure. Antony divorced Octavian's sister, whom he had married in 43 B.C. as a token of alliance with Octavian, and married the Egyptian queen, Cleopatra. Later, he outraged public opinion by giving away eastern Roman provinces as kingdoms to Cleopatra and the children which she had borne to him and Julius Caesar. Rome declared war on Cleopatra—Antony was not mentioned. When Antony and Cleopatra moved to invade Italy, they were defeated by Octavian in the Battle of Actium, just off the west coast of Greece (31 B.C.). Octavian pursued the pair to Egypt, besieged them in Alexandria where both Antony and Cleopatra committed suicide, and the long period of civil war was ended at last. Octavian returned to Rome in 30 B.C. to commence a new, and this time, effective reorganization that was to end the Republic and replace it with another kind of government called the Principate.

GREECE CAPTURES HER CAPTOR, ROME

The expansion of Rome in Italy and the subsequent acquisition of an empire outside the peninsula brought many changes in Roman life and culture. We have already seen something of the social and economic changes that occurred; reference has been made to the appearance of the senatorial class, the equestrians, and the unfortunate proletarians, and it should be noted also that there was a rapid development of a big rural and urban slave population in the last two centuries B.C. Long before the Italian allies were admitted to Roman citizenship, the Romans had ceased to be Roman in the original sense because many emancipated slaves of Greek and Oriental origin were becoming citizens and "Romans," too.

The Wealth of Empire

Accumulation of wealth from a growing empire did more than spawn the equestrian class. It brought a shift in the economic center of the Mediterranean world, for Rome became the financial capital of this whole region in the first century B.C. The new wealth, moreover, permitted many Romans to live in a luxury that would have horrified their ancestors. Gone was the old Roman frugality and with it the dignity and austerity that had once typified the national character. The wealth of empire, said many Romans, had debauched the morality of the people. Although we cannot say whether the public and private scandals that tainted the reputation of the upper class infected the commons as well, it would be difficult to write a candid biography of virtually any prominent Roman of the first century B.C. without reference to his financial or political dishonesty, cruelty, multiple marriages and divorces, and his addiction to adultery, gambling, and drinking; some even added incest and homosexuality to their other aberrations.

Social Disintegration

In this case, however, wealth was not the root of all evil, for the experience of the Romans was anything but unique. History—and the present—provide many other examples of the confusion and dislocation that occur when a relatively simple culture is completely overwhelmed by contact with a complex civilization. While cultural interaction in such instances may have a beneficial and even stimulating effect on some phases of activity—intellectual, literary, artistic, or the like—social disintegration almost always takes place. On the field of battle the Romans had overcome the Greeks, but Greek civilization turned the tables on the Romans.

Rome Culturally Assimilated into Hellenistic World

It was perhaps inevitable that contact with the Greeks should influence the culture of Rome.

Language, Religion, and Art.   Between the third century B.C. and the beginning of the Christian era, Rome was culturally assimilated into the Hellenistic world. The process began when the Romans came into close contact with the Greeks of South Italy and Sicily, and it was accelerated as the Romans moved into the Eastern Mediterranean. The Greek language began to influence Latin; many Greek words were added to the Latin vocabulary, and even the grammar of Latin was not immune to Greek influence. Romans learned Greek. Eventually the educated people were bilingual; they read Greek and wrote in Greek and spoke Greek with the same facility with which they used their native tongue. Roman oratory was modified and finally dominated by Greek style and theory. Greek philosophy began to interest some Romans in the second century B.C.; by the first century every educated person studied Plato, while many had become devotees of Stoicism or Epicureanism. Greek and Oriental religious ideas penetrated the religion even of the common people, while the old Roman and Italian cults lost their authority; as early as 186 B.C. the Dionysiac mystery cult was so widely diffused that the Senate tried to suppress it. Buildings in the Greek architectural style began to be erected in Rome. In the second century B.C. works of Greek sculptors and painting were brought from Greece to Italy by the victorious Romans; when the supply of original works of art began to run out, Greek sculptors and painters were hired to produce copies and new "masterpieces."

Literature.   The Greek conquest was most pronounced in literature. It is customary to date the beginnings of a formal Latin literature about the middle of the third century B.C. when a Greek slave named Livius Andronicus brought from Tarentum to Rome began to produce plays and poems in Latin; his tragedies and comedies were translations or adaptions from Greek plays, and his major poetical venture was a translation of the *Odyssey*. Livius Andronicus was followed by others, mostly non-Romans, who produced plays and epic poems in Latin. Ennius, coming from South Italy at the time of the Second Punic War, wrote an epic on the First Punic War. Naevius of Capua wrote comedies so full of political invective that he might be called a Roman Aristophanes, and he also wrote an epic poem on the Second Punic War. Plautus from North Italy and an African slave named Terence brought Latin comedy to its highest point early in the second century B.C. Also in the second century, a distinctly Roman contribution to poetry was made by the creator of satire, Lucilius. Called the "originator of the art of critical sniffing," he was the undisputed father of a new form later brought to perfection in the imperial age by Horace, Persius, and Juvenal. As for prose, with the exception of oratory, developments lagged behind those in poetry. Crusty old Cato the Censor, the enemy of Carthage, the Scipios, the Greeks, and practically everyone else, was the best of the early prose writers. A contemporary of Plautus and Terence, he was hostile to the growing Greek influence; in defiance of it he wrote in Latin a most interesting work on agriculture and a prose history of Rome in seven books.

Latin Literature

Latin literature finally came of age in the first century B.C. Two of the finest Latin poets, Lucretius and Catullus, flourished in the days of the First Triumvirate. The former is known for a single long poem, *De Rerum Natura,* which expounded the philosophy of Epicurus and constitutes a major source of our information about Epicureanism. Catullus was influenced by the early Greek lyric poets and also by the Alexandrian Callimachus of the Hellenistic period. Like Callimachus, he experimented with the short epic, but he is best known for his poems addressed to Lesbia—in real life a dissolute Roman noblewoman, the sister of Clodius, with whom Catullus had an unfortunate love affair. Although the *Aeneid* belongs to the early Principate, Vergil had already established his reputation as a poet before the Republic had ended.

Prose.   Oratory continued to be the brightest jewel in the crown of Latin prose in the first century B.C., but its position did not go unchallenged. Caesar's *Commentaries* was a major contribution to Latin letters; his account of the conquest of Gaul might be regarded as a companion piece to Xenophon's *Anabasis:* Both authors were eyewitnesses of the events they recorded, and both were influential as prose stylists. Sallust, a contemporary and partisan of Caesar, produced the first mature historical works in Latin. Sallust wrote about the conspiracy of Catiline and the period just after the death of Sulla, but his major effort was a history of the Jugurthine War. Although the ancients called him a Roman Thucydides, Sallust fell somewhat short of the master in impartiality and eagerness to discover the truth; he was basically a political pamphleteer with a good prose style, yet he ranks with Livy and Tacitus as one of the three greatest Roman historians.

Ciceronian Age

We often call the period from 70 to 43 B.C. the Ciceronian Age. And with good reason, for Cicero, the greatest of Latin prose writers, dominated the field. The influence of his magnificent style was to be felt as long as Latin was written or spoken, and it became a model for those who wrote in other languages. Supreme as an orator, Cicero was also a literary critic and a popularizer of Greek philosophy. Not the least of his accomplishments was the establishment of the letter as a literary form;

among his literary descendants in the epistolary field were Pliny the Younger, St. Basil, Madame de Sévigné, and Lord Chesterfield.

Verrine Orations.   Born in 106 B.C. at Arpinum in Latium, also the birthplace of Marius, Cicero was educated at Rome where he studied literature, philosophy, and Roman law. In his twenties he first began to make his reputation as an orator and an advocate (trial lawyer), but during the later years of the dictatorship of Sulla he found it prudent to undertake the study of oratory in Greece and Asia. As more settled conditions prevailed, he came home to Italy to enter politics. His quaestorship in Sicily (75 B.C.) was so successful that the Sicilians looked upon him as a friend and begged him to take charge of the prosecution of the rapacious Verres in the year 70. His victory in this case, as we have seen, won him election to the praetorship and later the consulate. The trial of Verres displays Cicero at his very best as a courtroom performer; the four Verrine Orations are exciting to read and show us how Cicero planned his case.

Philippics.   Nearly eighty Ciceronian orations have survived. In addition to those against Verres, perhaps the best known are the four against Catiline, the oration supporting the Manilian Law that conferred on Pompey the command against Mithridates, the speech on behalf of the poet Archias who claimed the right of Roman citizenship, and the dozen or more *Philippics* attacking Mark Antony. These last, modeled on the orations of Demosthenes against Philip of Macedon, won Cicero the hatred of Mark Antony and sealed the death warrant of the great orator. Cicero was not always as brave and steadfast in his political warfare as he appeared in the orations against Catiline and Antony; on occasion he groveled before Caesar, welshed on his defense of the tribune Milo, and stayed away from the Senate on the day of Caesar's assassination even though he knew and approved of the plot, but he redeemed himself in the *Philippics* by instigating and carrying on the fight against Antony even though it was a hopeless cause.

Philosophical Works.   Cicero was a commentator on philosophy rather than a philosopher himself. He imitated Plato in his *Republic* and the *Laws.* Both Platonism and Stoicism are represented in other works: *De Officiis,* on duties; *De Natura Deorum,* on the nature of the gods; the *Tusculan Disputations;* his essays on old age and friendship, and many others. Cicero also wrote on the theory of oratory and the training necessary for an orator as in *De Oratore, Orator,* and the *Brutus.* He often employed the dialogue form popularized long before by Plato.

Cicero's Letters.   More than 700 letters written by Cicero have survived. Some of these are private and personal, while others were composed with a view to publication. In the private letters, especially those addressed to Atticus—his friend, banker, publisher, and investment counselor—Cicero discloses much about his own character, business deals, and political intrigues, matters which he certainly would not have cared to expose to public view. Among the other letters are communications addressed to men in public life, dispatches sent to the Senate when Cicero was governor of Cilicia, and letters on literary and philosophical subjects. One epistle to Quintus, Cicero's brother, discussing the proper administration of a province must have been composed as a treatise for general circulation.

By the first century A.D. ancient civilization had begun the last stage of its ascent to the apex of its development reached in the second century A.D. The Hellenistic phase proper had ended with the Roman assimilation of Greek culture, and the Romans were beginning to make contributions of their own. Soon, moreover, the Roman Empire would give a political unity to a large area already unified in the economic and cultural sense.

Chapter Ten

Rome: The Early Empire

While adequate for a city-state of limited size, the governmental system of the Roman Republic was not suited to the needs of an empire. This fact had been driven home in the most painful way as the Romans writhed through the agony of a half-century of civil war, beginning with the quarrels of Marius and Sulla and ending with the triumph of Octavian over Mark Antony. The Republic had never pretended to serve the governed—the subjects of Rome—but now it had failed the masters, its own citizens. Somehow, a stable, responsible government must be established; if such a miracle could be accomplished, ways might be found to control the army, to put imperial finance on a sound basis, to remedy the economic dislocation resulting from prolonged civil war, to improve provincial administration, and to discover the logical, defensible boundaries of an empire that had been built more by accident than design. Stability was the first order of business; its priority was such in the minds of most people that another major problem seems to have received no consideration: The citizens of Rome were too numerous and too widely dispersed to participate directly in government as they had in the earliest period of their independence, and representative must replace direct government if the republican form was to be retained. Unfortunately, the Romans were too weary, confused, and divided to consult with one another in order to work out their common salvation. Virtually at their wits' end, they wanted to be led, instructed, and protected. Like tired children, they wanted the guidance of a parent. Thus, Octavian, virtually the only major survivor of the civil wars, became the Father of his Country *(Pater Patriae)*—and its ruler.

FOUNDING THE PRINCIPATE

After his annexation of Egypt following the death of Antony and Cleopatra, Octavian returned to Rome and gradually mustered out his soldiers. Holding the consulship year after year, Octavian also possessed some special powers, perhaps a residue from his triumvirate or some authority provided for the war against Antony. Later, when something like normalcy seemed to have been regained, Octavian in 27 B.C. offered to relinquish to the Senate and people all his extraordinary powers. We shall never know whether this offer was genuine or merely a trial balloon, but it was firmly refused; instead, Octavian was implored to continue his leadership. Retaining the consulate, he received a special ten-year proconsular command which gave him control of Egypt and most other provinces in which troops were stationed; he was also honored by a special title, Augustus (the Revered). Although in his own time he was known variously as Octavian, Caesar, Octavian Caesar, or Caesar Augustus, we shall henceforth refer to this first Roman emperor as Augustus. This is in accordance with a usage that began shortly after his death and has been continued to the present day.

Increase in Augustus' Power

As time passed, Augustus apparently found the consulship poorly suited to his needs. He gave up his annual tenure of this office after 23 B.C. and instead based his power on the proconsular imperium, subsequently renewed for ten- or five-year periods, and on the tribunician power which was annually renewed; like Julius Caesar before him, he had the power but not the office of a tribune. The proconsular imperium gave Augustus control of the key provinces as well as command of the army, while the tribunician power provided authority in Rome. In addition, in order that he might deal with a series of crises that subsequently arose, Augustus was given by law various extraordinary powers that were gradually added to his proconsular and tribunician authority so that his position became stronger and stronger as the years passed. In 23 B.C., for example, in order to conduct negotiations with the Parthians, he received the right to make war and peace in the name of Rome. During a famine in 22 B.C. he was entrusted with control of the grain supply of the city. As *princeps senatus*, he had the privilege of speaking first on any matter under discussion in the Senate; as *pontifex maximus*, he was the most important religious official in the state; he was also given the right to examine the qualifications of candidates for high office and to confirm or deny their candidature.

Augustus Founds the Principate

Augustus was the founder of the Principate, the new governmental form that replaced the Republic and lasted for three centuries until Diocletian introduced the autocracy of the late empire. The term "Principate" derives from the title of *princeps* (first citizen) which Augustus

AUGUSTUS (27 B.C.–A.D. 14)

Coin portraits of the Roman emperors are generally good, reliable likenesses and often reveal something of the imperial temperament, as will be seen from other examples in the following pages.

himself felt best described his position. A chief magistrate, or president, with permanent tenure, he scrupulously avoided any pretense of autocracy by refusing to accept the dictatorship or the office of Prefect of Morals, the perpetual censorship assumed by Julius Caesar. It must not be imagined that Augustus constructed the Principate in accordance with some preconceived master plan. The Principate just grew. If Augustus had died of the serious illness that nearly carried him off in 22 B.C., the Principate probably would have died with him. As it turned out, Augustus lived on until A.D. 14; by then people had become accustomed to the new arrangement—few, indeed, then living could remember any other, and only a handful of dreamers or idealists considered the possibility of restoring the Republic.

Differences between Principate and Republic. How did the Principate differ from the Republic? The machinery of republican government continued to operate but on a limited scale. The assemblies, for example, gradually withered away, while the Senate gained in importance as a lawmaking body, and even the election of officials was transferred to the Senate by Tiberius, Augustus' successor. There were still consuls, praetors, quaestors, aediles, and tribunes, but the term of the consuls was progressively shortened until it became customary to have six pairs of consuls a year; proconsuls and propraetors continued to govern the limited number of provinces not under the direct supervision of the princeps; the four aediles and ten tribunes lost their original functions and instead were assigned to administer the fourteen regions into which Augustus divided the city of Rome. The Senate, with a membership of 600, was a deliberative body that advised the princeps; and in addition to its legislative and elective functions, it also functioned as a high court before which senators might be tried.

Function of the Princeps.   The princeps was a long-term chief executive who had acquired several of the functions of the republican magistrates and received some new ones in addition. He commanded the army and controlled the foreign relations of Rome; he was responsible for the care of the city, including its grain supply; and he governed the most important provinces. In time, the princeps became a combined chief justice and attorney-general as well as a source of law through his decrees and judicial decisions. By virtue of his tribunician power, he possessed a veto that no magistrate or assembly could override.

Equestrian Participation in Principate.   Although the trend was in the direction of autocracy, the early Principate was more of an oligarchy than anything else. Theoretically, the princeps and the Senate conducted the administration of the state, but the equestrians came to share in the government almost as fully as the senators. Equestrian participation arose from the fact that the princeps could not personally perform all the duties that had been assigned to him; he needed assistants and subordinates to work under his direction. Some positions were too menial and others too confidential to be entrusted to the senators. Thus, the princeps turned to the equestrians, for they had something to gain by cooperating with him since they were his potential allies, just as the senators were potential enemies. As an imperial bureaucracy developed, its highest posts, known as prefectures, were filled by equestrians appointed by the princeps and serving at his pleasure. The emperor's bodyguard, the praetorian guard as it was called, was commanded by the praetorian prefect, an officer of equestrian rank. Other high equestrian officials were the Prefect of Egypt, who governed that country as an imperial viceroy; the Prefect of the Grain Supply; the Prefect of the Watch, who was in charge of the combined police and fire department introduced by Augustus for the city of Rome; and the Prefect of the City, who administered Rome when the emperor was out of town. Either senators or equestrians might be appointed as "imperial legates with propraetorian power" to govern the provinces for which the emperor was responsible. A large number of subordinate imperial posts were also filled by equestrians; a common title for the incumbent of such a position was procurator.

Augustus Controls the Military; Imperial Boundaries Established. Augustus exercised a firm control over the army, established a military treasury out of which veterans' pensions might be paid, and improved the administration of the provinces. Provincial taxes were reduced, while the provinces were better governed than before; this was especially true of the imperial provinces in which the governors served longer terms and had a chance to become familiar with the problems and needs of the territories they administered. Augustus completed the conquest of Spain and also acquired new territory along a line south of the Danube in continental Europe. The North Sea, the Atlantic Ocean, the Rhine, and the Danube were ultimately established as the northern and western boundaries of the empire. The Rhine-Danube frontier, though clearly defined, was a long one; at one time during the reign of Augustus the Romans did advance into Germany as far as the Elbe, and an Elbe-Danube frontier would have made the line in the north much shorter and more economical to defend, but a series of disturbances and a crushing defeat of Roman forces in Germany in A.D. 9 forced a withdrawal to the Rhine. The Sahara and Arabian Deserts made good boundaries in Africa and the Near East, although there still remained the task of finding a satisfactory line in Asia Minor and in northwestern Mesopotamia where Rome faced the dangerous Parthians. In Asia Minor the problem was solved temporarily by using a number of vassal kingdoms as buffer states, but the Euphrates, which separated Syria and Mesopotamia, was less satisfactory because it was a line that could be maintained only by keeping a big force in Syria to discourage Parthian attacks.

Provision for a Successor

The greatest single achievement of Augustus had been to provide the Romans with a stable government undisturbed by internal discord. But what would happen when he died? Would the army get out of hand and its generals fight for power? Would some powerful senator seize control and establish an autocracy? Or would the factions engage in ruinous civil war? Somehow the regime of peace must be continued, and gradually Augustus evolved what he believed to be a solution for this problem. He must provide for a successor; this man must be identified publicly, and he must possess powers that would enable him to carry on without a break when Augustus died. Augustus himself had come to power largely because he was the adopted son of Julius Caesar; furthermore, Caesar had been deified after death so that the position of

Augustus was analogous to that of a Hellenistic king, especially like that of a Seleucid ruler since the Seleucids had practiced the apotheosis of deceased kings. There was every indication that Augustus himself would be deified; already there were temples dedicated to Roma and the Genius (guardian spirit) of Augustus. Therefore, the successor of Augustus ought to be a blood relative, preferably a descendant of Augustus and a member of the Julian clan.

The problem was to find a successor with these qualifications. Augustus had only one child, his daughter Julia. She must provide him with grandsons. In 25 B.C. Julia was married to Marcellus, a cousin who was the son of Octavia, the sister of Augustus. But Marcellus died in 23 B.C. When Augustus became very ill a few months later and thought himself to be at death's door, he gave his signet ring to his friend Agrippa, the outstanding general of the period. After Augustus regained his health, he caused Julia to be married to Agrippa. Moreover, Agrippa was given the proconsular imperium and tribunician authority so that he became virtually the colleague of Augustus. Agrippa and Julia soon had two sons, Gaius and Lucius, who were adopted by Augustus as his own sons in 17 B.C. Five years later, when Agrippa died, Gaius and Lucius were still too young to enter public life so that Augustus was forced to turn to his stepson, Tiberius, the eldest child of his second wife and now empress, Livia. Almost as a matter of course, Tiberius was promptly married to Julia, but when Gaius and Lucius reached adolescence, Tiberius was pushed into the background while the two boys were advanced to honors and offices inappropriate to their tender years. By A.D. 4, however, both Gaius and Lucius were dead. Their younger brother, Agrippa Junior, a fifteen-year-old said to be degenerate in a number of ways, was passed over as distinctly unsuitable for the succession, although the real reason for the decision may have been that his mother, Julia, had disgraced the family and was in banishment for adultery. At any rate, Augustus turned back to Tiberius as a last forlorn hope. Tiberius was adopted by the emperor and given the proconsular imperium and the tribunician power. So it was that when Augustus died in A.D. 14, a successor had been identified and already invested with the power to rule.

EMPERORS: GOOD, BAD, AND INDIFFERENT

For nearly 200 years after the death of Augustus, the Principate which he had founded was to function reasonably well. Compared with the Republic, the Principate seemed better than it really was, but the new system had serious defects for which remedies were not found. First, it was an ineffectual compromise between old and new, between a republic and an autocracy. Second, the senators were never reconciled to their loss of power; on occasion, they were openly hostile to the princeps, while at other times they failed to assume the responsibilities of partnership with him when offered the opportunity. Third, the principle of dynastic succession established by Augustus seldom brought competent rulers to the throne. The Principate needed an Augustus to make it work. The chief executive must be strong, able, experienced, and devoted to his job of ruling the empire, yet the selection process instituted by Augustus and sanctified, as a matter of fact, by traditional Roman practice did not take any of these things into account. "Family," especially aristocratic lineage and therefore "good" breeding, was very important to the Romans. The idea was fallacious. Despite the fact that membership in a "fine" family usually meant that an individual had more advantages than most people, the Romans made the painful discovery that a barrel might contain more than one rotten apple. The succession worked best in the second century A.D. when, by a historical accident, there was a series of emperors without sons or other close male relatives to succeed them. The rulers from Trajan to Marcus Aurelius were mature, able, and experienced, and they were chosen because they possessed those qualities.

Chronological Periods for Roman Emperors

In the period A.D. 14 to 192 the Roman emperors fall chronologically into three main groups: the Julio-Claudians, 14–68; the Flavians, 69–96; and the so-called Good Emperors, 96–192. Actually, Commodus (180–192), the last in the string, was a very bad emperor, but his immediate successors were even worse, so that A.D. 192 as a dividing point has the advantage of being convenient and not entirely misleading. The Julio-Claudians were relatives or descendants of Augustus: Tiberius (A.D. 14–37), his stepson; Caligula (37–41), a grand-nephew; Claudius (41–54), a nephew of Tiberius; and Nero (54–68), stepson of Claudius and great-great-grandson of Augustus. The Flavians were a new dynasty consisting of Vespasian (A.D. 69–79) and his two sons: Titus (79–81) and Domitian (81–96). With the exception of Commodus, the son of Marcus Aurelius, the Good Emperors were not closely related to one another.

The Julio-Claudians

The Julio-Claudians are probably the best known of the emperors.

Tiberius.   Although hated and maligned by later historians and biographers, the Julio-Claudians—with the exception of poor, disturbed Caligula—were not entirely without merit as rulers. Tiberius tried hard to follow to the letter the policies already established by Augustus, but

ROMAN MATRON (A.D. 50–60)

(Courtesy of the Minneapolis
Institute of Arts.)

he received little credit for his efforts. Caught in the backlash of resentment against the Principate, Tiberius could not establish good relations with the Senate, while the people blamed him for a nearly empty treasury that necessitated a cut in expenditures for their entertainment; actually, the alleged parsimony of Tiberius was forced upon him by the overspending of Augustus. Over fifty years old at his accession, the emperor did not improve with age. Withdrawn and bitter, hating a position he had taken only as a matter of self-defense—or at best, because he felt duty-bound to take it—Tiberius became suspicious and fearful of treason. He put a number of senators to death for real or fancied conspiracies but he did not detect until almost too late the most dangerous plot of all hatched by his trusted praetorian prefect, Sejanus (A.D. 31).

By that time, Tiberius had already withdrawn from Rome to the island of Capri where he finally died in A.D. 37.

Caligula.   Gaius, usually known by his nickname of Caligula, was the grandson of Tiberius' deceased brother, Drusus. Young, lively, and open-handed, he seemed infinitely preferable to dour old Tiberius, but the index of his popularity dropped sharply after he became insane. If we are to believe the later biographer, Suetonius, some of Caligula's merry pranks—shoveling gold dust off the roof of the Capitol or giving the consulship to his favorite horse—were harmless enough, but his many cruelties and his fondness for testing new poisons on human subjects—preferably of senatorial rank—soon brought his reign to an end: he was the victim of a senatorial conspiracy in A.D. 41.

Claudius.   With Claudius, the uncle of Caligula, the story of the Julio-Claudians lost none of its comic opera flavor. Physically defective and not always mentally in focus, poor Claudius had been deliberately excluded from public life since early childhood. The assassination of Caligula, however, made Claudius almost the last of the Julio-Claudians and therefore an obvious candidate for the throne. While the exultant senatorial assassins debated the restoration of the Republic, the praetorian guard found Claudius cowering in the palace and proclaimed him emperor; fearful of the praetorians, the Senate quickly confirmed the nomination of this nearly forgotten man.

CLAUDIUS (A.D. 41–54)

Contrary to almost universal expectation, Claudius served the empire well. He organized the imperial bureaucracy in a more efficient way by establishing governmental departments for the treasury, royal correspondence, petitions, records, and the like. Claudius also gained a measure of popularity by promoting a Roman invasion and conquest of Britain, a step which Augustus and Tiberius had refused to take. A very learned man with antiquarian interests, said to be the last person in Rome to know Etruscan, Claudius could learn from books but not from experience: After executing his empress, Messalina, who had conspired with her lover to seize the throne, Claudius made the mistake of marrying his widowed niece, Agrippina, sister of Caligula, and adopting Nero, her young son. With that much accomplished, it did not take long for Agrippina to poison Claudius and put Nero in his place as emperor (A.D. 54).

Nero. Few senators regretted the passing of Claudius. They had despised him for his physical infirmities, his absentmindedness, and his fondness for wine which often made him more disorganized than usual. Nero, on the other hand, was very popular during the first five years of his reign when he was not allowed to rule and the government was run by his mother; the philosopher, Seneca; and the praetorian prefect, Burrus. But Nero came of age, eliminated by violent means Burrus, Seneca, and his own mother, and then abandoned affairs of state to a praetorian prefect of his own choosing, the notorious Tigellinus. It is well known that Nero's subsequent activities fostered an impression that he was

NERO (A.D. 54–68)

rather more interested in music and the theater than in government. In addition to his concerts, the Romans suffered another catastrophe: a great fire in Rome in A.D. 64 that caused vast destruction of property and considerable loss of life. In the hysteria following the disaster, a rumor was circulated that Nero had deliberately burned the city, but he diverted this resentment by blaming the Christians for the fire and instituting the first great persecution. A nearly empty treasury and military discontent finally led to Nero's downfall in A.D. 68. An army uprising began in Gaul and spread to Spain where Galba, a senatorial governor, was proclaimed emperor. In a panic, Nero committed suicide, lamenting, "What a great artist the world is losing!"

The Flavians

During A.D. 68 and 69, Rome had four emperors in rapid succession: Galba, Otho, Vitellius, and Vespasian. With the exception of Otho, these men were the nominees of the Roman legions situated in various regions of the empire: Those along the lower Rhine supported Vitellius; those in the Near East, Vespasian; and Otho was placed on the throne by the praetorian guard. As the historian Tacitus was to remark later, the fatal secret of the empire had been discovered: An emperor could be made elsewhere than at Rome.

Variously known as the Year of the Four Emperors or the First War of the Legions, this year (A.D. 68/69) came to an end in virtual anarchy. Galba, brought from Spain by the invitation of the Senate and the praetorian guard, soon lost support when he refused to pay the guard the sum promised by his partisans and then failed to choose an acceptable person as his potential successor. In January 69 he was assassinated and replaced by Otho, another senator and once a favorite of Nero, but he in turn could not halt the invasion of Italy by Vitellius and the legions from the Rhine. After Otho's suicide (April 69), matters did not improve. The incompetent Vitellius was overwhelmed by the coming of the Danubian legions who had professed to avenge Otho and then declared for Vespasian. Vitellius offered to abdicate but was prevented by his own soldiers and finally killed when the Danubian legions captured Rome. The ensuing period of confusion and disorder ended with the arrival of Syrian troops under the command of Mucianus, the Syrian governor and adherent of Vespasian, who brought about the formal election of Vespasian at the end of 69. The new emperor made his way to Rome in January 70 to inaugurate the Flavian regime that would endure until A.D. 96.

Titus Flavius Vespasianus had been sent by Nero to Judaea to quell the revolt that had broken out there in 66. He was fully occupied with that task when the legions in Egypt rose in revolt (July 69) and proclaimed him *imperator,* their imperial candidate. It is uncertain whether Vespasian had already considered bidding for the throne, but when other eastern legions joined with those in Egypt he had little choice but to accept the acclamation.

Vespasian came from a family that had struggled up from obscurity to equestrian rank. One of his ancestors had been an auctioneer and another a publican tax collector, but the new emperor had himself attained senatorial status through a long record of government service and military successes. Nevertheless, his equestrian background and personal lack of refinement did not endear him to the senatorial nobility. Obviously unappreciative of the arts, he had fallen asleep on one occasion when Nero was singing, and his Lincolnesque brand of humor was offensive to those who possessed more delicate sensibilities. Nor did it help that he knew enough Greek to voice certain obscenities in that language.

At this point, however, Vespasian was definitely what the empire needed. He was respected by the soldiers, but in addition he was a businessman and something of a financial expert as well as a good administrator, all of which placed in a position to make some significant changes. In the beginning he instituted wide-ranging economies and higher taxes that soon wiped out the huge deficit accumulated during Nero's reign and its subsequent disorders; further recovery was aided by a windfall disclosed in a survey of the provinces, establishing that some of the wealthiest areas were not paying their fair share of the taxes. By no means unimportant in economic stabilization was the great treasure that accrued from the capture and sack of Jerusalem by Vespasian's son Titus in the year A.D. 70. This was especially helpful when Vespasian adopted the time-honored Roman cures for depression that included a big building program and an increase of money in circulation.

During the decade that Vespasian ruled, other reforms were either completed or set in motion. These included the ending of revolts in the provinces, the rebuilding of Rome necessitated by the great fire of 64, the shortening of the Rhine-Danube frontier, the northward advance of the frontier in Britain, and appropriate chastening of the praetorian guard by reducing its size. Finally, about the middle of his reign Vespasian assumed the censorship and revised the rolls of the Senate by removing those he considered undesirable and appointing new members from the ranks of the equestrians and qualified citizens in the provinces.

To ensure peaceful succession to the throne, some years before his death the emperor associated his elder son Titus with himself by grants of the proconsular imperium and the tribunician power. Thus there was no hiatus or confusion as Titus assumed the throne in 79. A good soldier, and popular because of his comparative youth and liberal spending

VESPASIAN (A.D. 69–79)

habits, there were some things about Titus that a few people found disturbing. Handsome, strong, possessed of a remarkable memory, he had also mastered what was regarded as the black art of stenography, known only to scribes. Added to that he wrote poetry and sang, and there was some reason to fear that he might become a second Nero. Still another cause for concern was his notorious affair with the Jewish princess Berenice. Public indignation was aroused when he brought her to Rome; there was so much talk about a second Cleopatra that he had to send her back home. We shall never know whether Titus would have been one of the great emperors or one of the worst. He died in A.D. 81, and his reign is remembered chiefly for the eruption of Vesuvius in 79, a great fire in Rome in the following year, and the dedication of the Colosseum which would finally be completed a few years later. Something of a Boy Scout who counted the day lost in which he failed to do a good deed, Titus may indeed have merited a longer and happier reign.

The rule of Domitian (A.D. 81–96) seemed longer than it actually was, or so it was said by his numerous enemies. Jews, Christians, philosophers, and astrologers were not among his favorites. As the years passed his relations with the Senate deteriorated, and the failure of the army to deal with the Dacians who crossed the Danube at will to raid Roman territory caused great dissatisfaction, particularly when the only way Domitian could stop Dacian attacks was to pay them protection money. The target of several conspiracies, some real and some fancied, the emperor became suspicious of all except his closest associates, and his fears goaded him to take extreme measures. Then when he proclaimed himself *Dominus et Deus* (Lord and God), a title used on his coinage and official inscriptions, it was a little too much for the Romans; 200 years would elapse before they would accept this fiction of autocracy. In the end, a palace conspiracy aided and abetted by some of the praetorian guard brought down the last of the Flavians.

The Good Emperors

The murder of Domitian was an event more desired than anticipated, so the army was caught by surprise and for once the praetorian guard did not have a candidate for the throne. As a result the traditional but unaccustomed task of nominating the next princeps fell upon the Senate, which proved to be woefully unprepared and out of practice in making decisions. In the end the senators took the easy way out by choosing the person judged to be its senior member. This was Nerva, a distinguished jurist, close to seventy years old, who soon showed himself unequal to the task confronting him. As his principal advisors, Nerva put together a "cabinet" of once-prominent oldsters, several of whom were over eighty years of age. The new emperor did win initial approval by bringing back some of those exiled by Domitian and embarking upon a program aimed at improving the Italian economy, but he did not take action against certain of his friends who had been notorious supporters of Domitian. Before long, criticism began to surface that Nerva was another Galba who in the words of Tacitus "might have been thought capable of ruling if he had not ruled," and like Galba he lacked a son to succeed him. Faced with the growing animosity of the army and the praetorians, Nerva saved himself and the empire in A.D. 97 by adopting as his son and colleague Marcus Ulpius Traianus (Trajan), already a noted and successful general who had the support of the army. The crisis passed and, equipped with the tribunician power and the proconsular imperium, Trajan became princeps when Nerva died in 98.

Trajan (A.D. 98–117) was one of the best-loved and considered the most successful of all the Roman emperors. Like his father, who had a good military record and proved his worth as a provincial governor, Trajan was a native of the old Roman colony of Italica in Spain and was thus the first emperor to be born outside Italy. In his middle forties at the time of his accession, he had won the endorsement of the army by victories over the Germans on the Rhine frontier. It was therefore not surprising that Trajan was expected to deal with the Dacians, who had resumed their depredations across the Danube into Roman territory. In two campaigns, 101–102 and 105–107, Trajan first chastised the Dacians and made their ruler, Decebalus, a client king of Rome; but Decebalus soon resumed hostilities and left the Romans little choice but to annex his kingdom. This time Trajan carefully prepared for the conquest by

TRAJAN (98–117)

assembling a big army and building his famous bridge across the Danube. Decebalus committed suicide; his country (modern Romania) was made a Roman province and opened up to Roman colonization. With the plunder from the second campaign, Trajan was able to stabilize Roman currency and had sufficient funds to support a big building program. In the six years following the Dacian victory the emperor turned his attention to Italian affairs. He built a new forum in Rome—where his famous column decorated with reliefs illustrating the Dacian wars still stands—and he constructed new roads and harbors and provided Rome with a new aqueduct. Coins bearing the legend *Restitutor Italiae* called attention to his concern for the Italian economy. He enlarged the scope of the *alimenta* introduced by Nerva, which provided low-cost loans for hard-pressed Italian farmers and devoted the interest paid to the support and education of orphans.

Trajan was also concerned with the problem of trade with the Far East, where the balance was unfavorable to Rome due to high transportation costs. As early as A.D. 106 his general Palma had overrun and annexed the kingdom of the Nabataean Arabs across the Dead Sea from Judaea. This gave the Romans control of the great caravan city of Petra and access to a harbor on the Gulf of Aqaba, in turn leading to the Red Sea. Soon an Egyptian canal was constructed from the Nile to the Red Sea, and a Roman fleet was created to patrol this important body of water that led to the Indian Ocean where the monsoon winds would enable traders to sail to India as well as southward to the spice land of Zanzibar.

In A.D.113 Trajan left Rome, never to return. His objective originally was to bolster the eastern frontier against the Parthians. This involved gaining control of Armenia, then governed by a Parthian nominee, and getting a foothold in northwestern Mesopotamia on the eastern side of the Euphrates. Early successes led, in 116, to an invasion of the heart of Parthian territory and the capture of Babylon as well as Ctesiphon on the Tigris, the Parthian capital. Two new provinces were created, Armenia and Mesopotamia, and Trajan penetrated as far as the head of the Persian Gulf where he dreamed momentarily of opening another all-water route to India, thus eliminating the profitable Parthian role as middlemen in the trade with the Far East. But this was not to be as widespread Jewish revolts erupted in the Middle East and Trajan was forced to withdraw from Mesopotamia to cope with these disorders. Seriously ill, he felt obliged to return to Rome, but he died, probably of a stroke, at Selinus in Cilicia in the early autumn of 117.

The next emperor, Hadrian (A.D. 117–138), was a talented and conscientious administrator who, in the course of his reign, inspected almost every province of the empire as he made a series of unprecedented tours. He also made a number of changes in the central government that raised the whole operation to a more professional level. The son of Trajan's cousin, Hadrian had become Trajan's ward at an early age and was subsequently married to Sabina, granddaughter of Trajan's sister, Marciana. Carefully educated and with two decades of experience in the government and the army, Hadrian was governor of Syria when Trajan died, and one would think that his succession to the throne would be virtually automatic. The actual circumstances of the accession, however, were somewhat clouded due to certain rumors circulated by his enemies. The truth is hidden from us now, but it was later alleged that a will, purporting to be that of Trajan naming Hadrian as his successor, was really a forgery manufactured by Plotina, Trajan's empress, who was very fond of Hadrian. At any rate, Hadrian was acclaimed emperor by his own soldiers in Syria and by Trajan's troops in Selinus so that the Senate in Rome quickly ratified Hadrian's appointment, and soon thereafter found an excuse to execute for treason four of Trajan's greatest marshals who were known to be hostile to Hadrian.

It was at best a messy business, even though Hadrian denied any knowledge or approval of the purge. It seems that the grudges of the victims ran deep; some went back many years. Palma, for example, was the governor of Syria in A.D. 106 who had annexed the Nabataean kingdom, apparently on his own initiative. He was promptly relieved of his governorship, replaced as the commander in Arabia Petraea, brought back to Rome, given a consulship and partial triumphal honors, and never used again. This might suggest that he had offended Trajan by acting without official approval and tarnishing somewhat the glory of

HADRIAN (117–138)

the conquest of Dacia then in progress. The case of the fiery and ruthless Moor, Lucius Quietus, was more recent as well as understandable. Quietus had served Trajan well in the Dacian and Parthian wars and had been assigned to deal with the uprising in Judaea in 116, a task that was congenial to his temperament and possible hatred of the Jews. His measures were so extreme that Hadrian dismissed him and appointed a more moderate successor.

Arriving in Rome in A.D. 118, Hadrian renewed the oath already taken by Nerva and Trajan never to put a senator to death. His subsequent relations with the Senate were good, but he was forever the target of critics who complained that he spent too little time in Rome, was a compulsive reformer who was always making changes whether they were needed or not, and was so enamored with Greek culture that he tended to ignore his Roman heritage; they called him Graeculus, a little Greek. He did indeed spend quite a bit on the embellishment of Athens, among other things building a fine library and completing the huge temple of Olympian Zeus begun by Peisistratus seven centuries earlier; one whole subdivision of southeast Athens became known as the "Athens of Hadrian." On the other hand, Hadrian spent liberally on Rome and the provinces; his great mausoleum in Rome still stands as does the reconstruction of the Pantheon of Agrippa damaged in the fire of A.D. 80 and magnificently altered by Hadrian's architect, Apollodorus, who had previously designed Trajan's epoch-making bridge across the Danube. Another well-known monument of Hadrian's reign is the wall in Britain, still visible in part, that spanned the island from the mouth of the Tyne to the Firth of Solway and in that age marked the northern boundary of Roman territory.

Hadrian's Wall was symbolic of his frontier policy, which aimed at establishing practical defensible limits for the empire. Trajan's provinces of Mesopotamia and Armenia were abandoned, and the shortened Rhine-Danube line was fortified. Hadrian even considered giving up Dacia but was dissuaded by his advisors. He did, however, pay special attention to the army by reforms and frequent inspections of the troops during his travels.

At home Hadrian took the first meaningful steps in the codification of Roman law, planned long before Julius Caesar and not completed until the reign of Justinian in the sixth century A.D. Another important move of Hadrian's was the remission of back taxes in Italy (the so-called Burning of the Bonds) and later in the provinces. Imperial support of students and teachers in Rome and elsewhere, coupled with private philanthropy, aided the spread of literacy. In this respect, at least, the time of the Good Emperors was one of enlightenment.

In the imperial government we find that there were now two praetorian prefects, one a military man and the other a legal specialist, a noted jurist. Another radical and essential change instituted by Hadrian was the elevation of the post of *praepositus* to equestrian status. Under Claudius the imperial secretaries had been his personal freedmen who were in charge of imperial correspondence, funds, judicial matters, and speech writing. The scope of these activities had become so large that their direction required persons of social and political stature and experience; the influence of the freedmen had always been resented and justly so as it turned out. Henceforth a praepositus was an equestrian who had advanced up the ladder of officeholding above that of procurator and might rise higher to become an imperial curator or even a prefect. Incidentally, it should be noted that under the Good Emperors we see traces of a selection process in which the capabilities of young people who entered the imperial service were screened as they performed military and governmental functions so that some were earmarked for the armed forces and others with different talents were diverted to the civil service. There were exceptions, of course, but often ability won out over favoritism.

The good sense of Hadrian rather failed him on his last great eastern tour of A.D. 129 to 132. Jerusalem had been little more than a Roman legionary camp since its capture by Titus in A.D. 70, but Hadrian about 130 made it a Roman colony called Aelia Capitolina and erected a shrine of Jupiter Capitolinus on the site of the last Temple. This fanned the still-glowing embers of the revolt of 116 and precipitated the bloody Bar Kochba war of 132 to 135 in which the Romans temporarily lost control of Judaea.

Hadrian had returned to Rome in A.D. 132. It is far from certain that he made another trip to the East, but we do know that other problems soon claimed his attention. He was ailing and had to face the question of the succession. In 136 he adopted as his son and heir a friend called Lucius Ceionius Commodus Verus whose name was altered to Lucius Aelius Caesar; at this point the cognomen Caesar did not indicate a family name but rather a title denoting a junior emperor as opposed to Augustus, the title of the senior princeps. Aelius was not a distinguished or popular choice and may have done everyone a favor by dying in 137. The following year Hadrian adopted Titus Aurelius Antoninus who became emperor when his sponsor died in July.

Antoninus, later known as Antoninus Pius, reigned from A.D. 138 to 161. He was only ten years younger than Hadrian and had already had a long and creditable career in public service from which he had planned to retire. He may have been a distant relative of Trajan's empress Plotina, but it was more relevant that he was married to Faustina, the great-granddaughter of Trajan's sister Marciana. The reign of Antoninus was relatively peaceful. His foreign policy was anything but aggressive, and at home his relationship with the Senate and his subjects was generally good. A glowing tribute to his character may be read in the first portion of the *Meditations* of Marcus Aurelius. The title Pius awarded to Antoninus originated in part from his successful battle to win deification for the deceased Hadrian against the wishes of some in the Senate determined to condemn the memory of the late emperor and nullify his acts. Antoninus was also honored as *Pater Patriae* and re-

ANTONIUS PIUS (138–161)

ceived the additional title of *Felix* (fortunate). Both Pius and Felix were added to the titulature of future emperors, many of whom were neither pious nor blessed with good fortune. Very little is known about events in the reign of Antoninus. It was said that, unlike Hadrian, he never traveled, but this question and others relating to the period might be settled by a new and in-depth study of now-available evidence.

Childless except for a daughter, Faustina, named for his wife, Antoninus did not lack for successors because Hadrian had insisted that he adopt Lucius Verus, the son of Aelius, and Marcus (later Marcus Aurelius), the son of Annius Verus, his wife's cousin. This led to a rather interesting complication when Marcus Aurelius married Faustina the Younger, Antoninus' daughter, so the elder Faustina, the aunt of Marcus and his mother by adoption, became his mother-in-law! It is true and of some consequence, though seldom stated, that all of the Good Emperors, with the exception of Nerva, were connected with the family tree of Ulpius, the grandfather of Trajan.

At any rate, Antoninus was succeeded on the throne by his two adopted sons who reigned together as co-Augusti from 161 to 169 when Lucius Verus died. Thereafter Marcus ruled alone until the last three years of his life during which his colleague as Augustus was his own son, Commodus, the next emperor. Nevertheless, the main story of the period 161 to 180 is that of Marcus Aurelius himself, to which we shall now turn.

As a person Marcus was the best of the Good Emperors, even Antoninus. At the very least he excelled them all in good intentions. A philosopher-emperor, he needed all the help his philosophy could give him, beset as he was by multiple trials and tribulations. By all accounts he was modest, sincere, hardworking, and conscientious, almost a saintly ruler who did not deserve the hard luck that fortune dealt him: famine, floods, earthquakes, plagues, barbarian invasions, near imperial bankruptcy, family problems, and personal illness. He was born in A.D. 121 and was remembered as a solemn child who received advanced instruction in literature, drama, music, geometry, grammar, and rhetoric. He had two famous tutors in oratory: Fronto in Latin and the Athenian senator Herodes Atticus in Greek. To the bitter disappointment of Fronto, Marcus virtually abandoned oratory for philosophy, assuming the dress of a philosopher at the age of twelve, even before he could grow the beard that was an essential part of the uniform of a philosopher. He became what usually passed for a Stoic in those days, but the *Meditations* show him to have been more of an eclectic. Far from an introvert, Marcus Aurelius was fond of boxing, wrestling, and hunting. He was recognized as a good soldier who also had experience in government as the Caesar of Antoninus for over twenty years and a term as the governor of Asia.

MARCUS AURELIUS (161–180)

He and Faustina II were the parents of thirteen children, most of whom died in infancy or early childhood—a sad commentary on the state of medical knowledge in the days of Galen, who was the personal physician of Marcus Aurelius. Among their children the imperial couple had two sets of twins, but of these four only Commodus, the future emperor, survived although his older sister, Lucilla, who married Lucius Verus, may also have been a twin.

The reign of Marcus Aurelius was punctuated by wars, a revolt in Egypt, and a serious uprising led by a trusted general. The Parthian wars (A.D. 163–166) were the responsibility of Lucius Verus, who failed to prosecute the campaigns vigorously, but victory was achieved by Avidius Cassius, the best general of the period. The returning troops from the East brought back with them a serious plague believed by some to have been devastating to the Romans, although hard evidence is lacking. Between 170 and 175 Marcus campaigned along the middle and upper Danube against the Quadi and Marcomanni; scenes from this war (as in the case of Trajan's Dacian war) are illustrated on a column set up in Rome by Marcus. In 175 a rumor spread that Marcus had been killed in the fighting, and, out in the East, Avidius Cassius proclaimed himself emperor. Potentially serious, the revolt was soon brought to an end when Cassius was killed by his own soldiers and his head sent to the emperor. Within three years, new fighting broke out along the Danube. Marcus went to the front in 179, taking Commodus with him, but he died there in the midst of the campaign in the spring of A.D. 180.

It would be nice to think that the character of Marcus Aurelius is best revealed in the *Meditations* and his letters to his teacher and friend, Fronto. In the opinion of his contemporaries, his worst fault was his blind devotion to his family. He was accused of nepotism; people also thought that Faustina was an unfaithful wife and a conspirator in the revolt of Cassius; worst of all, they said, he did not see or would not recognize the faults of Commodus.

In the best Stoic tradition, Marcus accepted the good and the bad things in his life as decreed by fate or some power that ruled the universe. At the end of the *Meditations* we find him repeating one of his similes that life resembles a drama, the length of which is controlled by the praetor who dismisses an actor after three acts instead of five, "but in life the three acts are the whole play; for what shall be a complete drama is determined by the one who was the cause of its composition and now of its dissolution. But you are the cause of neither. So depart satisfied, for the one who releases you also is satisfied."

Commodus (A.D. 180–192) was definitely not a good emperor. Only nineteen when his father died, he was ill-prepared for the task he had inherited. Growing pressure on the frontiers, an economic decline accelerating over several generations, and senatorial resentment that had been growing since the reign of Hadrian were problems that would have taxed the skill and wisdom of a better man than Commodus. He soon antagonized the Senate, failed to control the army, and finally became insane. Some people noted that he had the same birthday as Caligula, whose merry and not so merry antics he soon repeated and even surpassed.

We do not have to accept all the details that Dio Cassius, the historian and member of the Senate at this time, records about the reign of Commodus, but some are verified by inscriptions and coins and by the accounts of other contemporaries. Army revolts, conspiracies, and riots in Rome were climaxed by the assassination of Commodus, orchestrated by his closest associates in the palace on New Years' Eve 192.

Mad as a hatter toward the end, Commodus renamed Rome the "Colony of Commodus" and portrayed himself as Hercules, appearing in public wearing a costume that included the lion skin and club of that hero. He renamed the Roman months so that the revised list contained his own name as well as his many titles: Amazonius, Invictus, Pius, Felix, Lucius, Aelius, Aurelius, Commodus, Augustus, Herculeus, Romanus, Exsuperatorius (Most Surpassing). His crowning achievement (no pun intended) came when he replaced the head of the famous colossal statue of Nero with his own likeness!

SIC TRANSIT GLORIA MUNDI

POLITICAL, SOCIAL, AND ECONOMIC ASPECTS OF THE EARLY EMPIRE

With the change from Republic to Empire, other elements in Roman life changed as well.

Political Aspects

Between the reign of Augustus and that of Hadrian, government under the Principate expanded and matured from a purely household affair to a well-organized and smoothly functioning bureaucracy in which much of the ordinary business could be carried on without close supervision by the emperor. As a matter of fact, the newer machinery operated better than the old because even in the senatorial provinces the emperor provided more direction and leadership than it had been possible for the Senate to supply under the Republic.

Participation of Upper Classes.   By the second century A.D., to judge by the famous letters of the younger Pliny to Trajan, governors in the senatorial provinces made few decisions and preferred to consult the emperor about the smallest details of administration. A remarkable change was the increased participation of non-Italians in the army and in the government as a whole. This development mirrored the Romanization of the western provinces, as well as the determination of the emperors to bring the Greeks of the East into their service. By the late first century A.D. there were many western provincials of senatorial and equestrian rank who had risen to high posts; the emperors, Trajan and Hadrian, had been born in Spain, while the family of Antoninus had come from Gaul. In the second century, numerous Greeks, especially from the cities of Ionia and Greece itself, were elevated to senatorial status and used as provincial governors. In this way the upper classes throughout the empire came to participate to some degree in public affairs.

Central Authority Intervenes in Local Affairs.   The Roman Empire, like many of the empires that had preceded it, was an aggregate of communities; these communities carried on local self-government and were saddled with the responsibility of raising and collecting the monies required by Rome as taxes. At the provincial level, government was in the hands of imperial representatives whose concern was defense, maintenance of internal order, and the overall welfare of the province, although by the second century the emperor was having to intervene frequently in municipal affairs. In the West, local problems were largely financial, but in the East, especially in Asia Minor, there were in addition intercity rivalries that might involve physical violence and must be calmed by the intervention of the governor or even the emperor himself.

The final results of the two trends—the empirewide participation of the upper classes in the government, and the necessity for the central authority to intervene in local affairs—were important for the future. The first did not promote imperial unification but rather a dangerous regionalism that almost destroyed the empire, while the second paved the way for the autocracy and extreme centralization that pulled the empire together again in the late third and early fourth centuries A.D. It was within the power of the Romans to have developed a representative, parliamentary type of government which might have avoided both regionalism and autocracy. The situation was most propitious for such an innovation during the reigns of Hadrian and Antoninus Pius, but no one seems to have thought to seize the opportunity thus offered.

Growth of Provinces.   During the first century and a half of the Principate, the empire grew in size. Mauretania in Africa, Britain, Thrace, Dacia, new provinces in Asia Minor, Arabia Petraea, and territory in northern Mesopotamia were added to the regions possessed by Rome at the beginning of the first century A.D. At the death of Augustus there were twenty-eight provinces, but the acquisition of new lands and the subdivision of the older provinces raised the number to forty-five in the time of Hadrian. Romanization made great strides in the West with the establishment of Roman colonies in Africa, Spain, Gaul, and Britain and the founding of many municipalities. Latin was the official, even the prevailing, language in some of these areas, and municipal government was modeled on that of Rome. Roman colonies were not so numerous in the East; in the many new towns that grew up in Asia Minor, especially in Pisidia and Phrygia, the Greek city-state was the model taken for municipal administration, and Greek was the language most commonly spoken. Egypt remained a special case: The Romans modified the Ptolemaic form of administration only slightly as far as political organization was concerned; although Roman veterans were settled in the country, native Egyptians and Greeks continued to form the bulk of the population.

Economic Aspects

The increasing size of the far-flung Empire resulted in changes in the Roman economy.

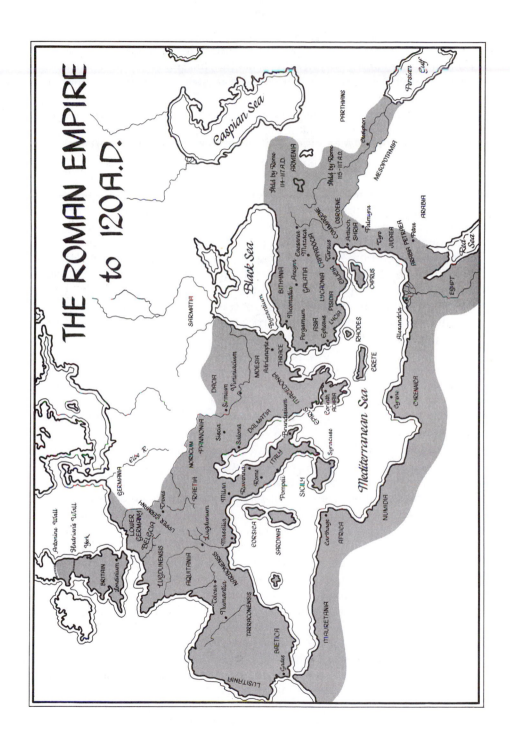

THE ROMAN EMPIRE to 120 A.D.

Antonine Wall
Hadrian's Wall
York
BRITAIN
Londinium

GERMANIA
Elbe R.
LOWER GERMANIA
BELGICA
UPPER GERMANIA
Treves
Lugdunum
Massilia
LUGDUNENSIS
AQUITANIA
NARBONENSIS
Toleso
Numantia
TARRACONENSIS
LUSITANIA
Gades
BAETICA

RAETIA
NORICUM
PANNONIA
Siscia
Milan
Ravenna
Rome
ITALY
Pompeii
CORSICA
SARDINIA
SICILY
Syracuse

SARMATIA

DACIA
Sirmium
Viminacium
MOESIA
Adrianople
Byzantium
THRACE
MACEDONIA
DALMATIA
Salona
Brundisium
EPIRUS
Corinth
ACHAIA

Black Sea

BITHYNIA
Nicomedia
Pergamum
Ephesus
ASIA
Aneyra
GALATIA
LYCAONIA
CAPPADOCIA
PISIDIA
LYCIA
PAMPHYLIA
Caesarea
Mazaca
Tarsus
CILICIA
RHODES
CRETE
CYPRUS
Antioch
SYRIA

Caspian Sea

Held by Rome
114-117 A.D.
ARMENIA

COMMAGENE
OSROENE
Palmyra
Tyre
JUDEA
ARABIA PETRAEA
Petra

Held by Rome
115-117 A.D.
MESOPOTAMIA
Ctesiphon
PARTHIANS
ARABIA

Persian Gulf

EGYPT
Alexandria

Cyrene
CYRENAICA

Mediterranean Sea

Carthage
AFRICA
NUMIDIA
MAURETANIA

Red Sea

281

Growth of Trade and Increased Population.   The great size of the Roman Empire and the generally peaceful conditions within it encouraged a growth of trade that stimulated industry and brought economic activity to a high pitch. This was accompanied by an increase in population, possibly to a total of 50 million within the empire itself. Africa, Spain, and Gaul were the most prosperous regions of the West, largely because the latter two had begun to provide for themselves agricultural and manufactured products once purchased from Italy. This self-sufficiency, incidentally, was the reason for the decline of the Italian economy that necessitated the steps taken by Nerva, Trajan, and other second-century emperors to save Italy from economic collapse. Depressed areas were also to be found in the East; Greece and Egypt fell into this category, but Asia Minor, Syria, and Palestine prospered. Greece had never recovered from Sulla's campaign against Mithridates, while Egypt was ruined by Roman absentee ownership within a century and a half after annexation. For a time, the newer provinces on the periphery of the empire were able to carry the burden of a decaying center, and thus the illusion of prosperity was perpetuated for years after the actual recession had set in.

Silver Shortage.   Outside the empire, trade was brisk with central Europe, Mesopotamia, Arabia, India, China, and even Indo-China. From Oriental lands the Romans imported silk, cotton, spices, ivory, precious stones, furs, sugar, and aromatic woods and herbs. In return they sent their glass, textiles, wine, oil, and precious metals. Whether to the North or the East, the balance of external trade did not favor Rome. Vast amounts of silver and no small sums in gold left the empire year after year, never to return. As the second century wore on, the steady drain of silver from the empire and a drop in silver production began to cause serious monetary problems. This was the start of a silver shortage that plagued the Mediterranean for centuries to come.

Problems of Land Transportation.   Even more than in the Hellenistic Age, the Roman imperial period saw great improvements in transportation with the building of roads and the construction of harbor facilities, but the Romans found the high cost of land transportation an obstacle that could not be overcome; this was one reason why Italian products could not compete in Gaul and Spain with the local imitations, and it was also the reason why Rome was at a disadvantage in its trade with Germany and the Orient. In the latter case, goods of light weight and small bulk were imported into the empire, while the Roman exports tended to be both heavy and bulky; the cost of a journey of a few hundred miles by land could increase the price of a product to a point where it was difficult to sell it at all. An all-water route by the Red Sea and the Indian Ocean gave a fair chance of profit in the commerce with India, but the caravan routes to China allowed no such opportunity. In Gaul and Germany, the Romans used the inland waterways as best they could; all over the empire, wherever it seemed feasible, people dreamed of canals. The difficulty and slowness of land transport also posed problems that were not economic; the Romans, like the Athenians, were to find that a land empire was more difficult to maintain than a maritime one.

Social Aspects: Classes

With the expansion of the empire, the colonization of Romans in the provinces and their inevitable intermarriage with the provincials, and liberal grants of Roman citizenship to individuals and communities, the Romans of the early empire were more non-Roman than ever. St. Paul, for example, was a Roman citizen, but his enthusiasm for Rome could hardly be called fanatical. It was at first most important to him that he was a Jew and a citizen of Tarsus; later, his principal allegiance was to the new faith to which he had been converted. Even among those of more pronounced Roman ancestry, patriotism lost its ancient meaning; much too often, a man was a senator or an equestrian before he was a Roman.

The senators under the empire tended to give up the interests in trade and finance which they had acquired in the late Republic and to revert to their older position as a landholding aristocracy. As in the Hellenistic Age, the middle class was large and continued to grow. The proletarian elements also increased in numbers with the continued growth of cities. Slavery, on the other hand, began to decline. With the advent of the Pax Romana, the Roman Peace, characteristic of the late first and early second centuries A.D., and with the great expansion of the empire, neither war nor trade provided the vast numbers of slaves known to the pre-Christian centuries. The price of slaves rose so that it became more economical to employ free laborers. The decline of slavery, moreover, led to an increase in the size of a distinct class of persons, the freedmen. These were emancipated slaves and their descendants. Attached to their former owners as clients, the freedmen were not wholly free nor were they accepted as equals by those who had never known the taint of slavery. While most freedmen remained in a lowly situation as servants and retainers, some acquired great wealth, and others attained powerful influence in the imperial bureaucracy. Members of this class existed in social limbo, hated by the slaves and often mistrusted by free men who resented particularly the freedmen who were successful in business or government.

Chapter Eleven

The Climax of Ancient Civilization

Just over two centuries ago, Edward Gibbon, in his famous *Decline and Fall of the Roman Empire*, wrote:

> If a man were called upon to fix the period in the history of the world, during which the condition of the human race was most happy and prosperous, he would, without hesitation, name that which elapsed from the death of Domitian to the accession of Commodus.

The years A.D. 96 to 180 that received this somewhat extravagant praise from Gibbon constitute an epoch often called the Pax Romana (Roman Peace). In reality it was not as peaceful as Gibbon suggested, nor as happy. Today some scholars would see it as the lull before the storm in which trends can be detected that presaged the coming disintegration of the Roman empire and of ancient civilization as well.

Therefore if we are to extend our discussion to begin with the establishment of the Principate and end with Marcus Aurelius, it must be explained that "climax" here does not necessarily mean the apogee of civilization spelled with a capital C. True, although ancient civilization was most complex and geographically widespread and urbanization had reached its maximum in the early empire, many peaks of cultural achievement had been attained earlier, so that the adjective "great" must be used sparingly in reference to certain features of the age under consideration in this chapter.

Nevertheless, it is an epoch about which we have an abundance of information, thanks to the enormous residue of its literary production that we still possess, no matter how much may be lost, and in addition its visible material remains of every kind are to be found widely distributed within the boundaries of what had once been the Roman empire. Great or not so great, if we take the trouble to read what was written then or to study the monuments still to be seen, the net impression of the whole will reveal to us vistas of a moment in the past unparalleled in such detail for other periods of antiquity.

EDUCATION

In the period of the Early Empire, literacy was even more wide-spread than in the Hellenistic Age. In addition, more people than ever before received a formal and extensive education that began in early childhood and continued into late adolescence. In almost every town and city of the empire there were schools supported either by public funds or by private philanthropy. Few girls went to school, but many boys received elementary training in reading, writing, and arithmetic. This beginning phase of schooling was called grammatistic; it was usually a four-year curriculum begun at the age of seven. In the West the instruction was in both Greek and Latin, while in the East Latin was often omitted. Twelve-year-olds went to the school of grammar where the stress was on correct expression, grammar, geometry, music, and especially literature. The best of the ancient authors and some contemporary ones were carefully read and studied for content and style. The main "school authors" were Homer, Hesiod, Euripides, Menander, Thucydides, Demosthenes, Plato, and Pindar on the Greek side; in Latin, Ennius, Naevius, Plautus, Terence, Cicero, Sallust, Vergil, Horace, and Livy were most commonly read. Literature was also a major subject in the schools of rhetoric, the next higher level in which students ranged in age from fifteen to eighteen or even twenty. Commonly read at this stage were Xenophon and Aristotle, Sophocles and Aeschylus, Aristophanes, the older lyric and elegiac poets, and the Attic orators. In the schools of rhetoric, however, the main emphasis was on oratory and style. *Rhetoric* was defined as the art of speaking well; in addition to studying the great orators of the past and learning the techniques of oratory, the students had continuous practice in declamation.

This essentially uniform system of education not only gave everyone the same kind of training, but it also provided a common frame of reference so that educated people could communicate intelligibly with one another. On the literary side, a liberal education in the best sense was acquired, but the curriculum was narrowly circumscribed; it lacked a diversity that might have been stimulating, and it slighted natural as well as social science. An even more serious defect was that the curriculum had crystallized, even ossified, in the late Hellenistic Age. It looked to the past and ignored the present. In the Roman imperial period, when a host of new problems needed fresh viewpoints for their solution, the educational system deadened people's minds with its uniformity, narrow horizons, and exaltation of the authority of antiquity.

After the school of rhetoric, some people went on to professional training in law or medicine or pursued the formal study of philosophy. Into each of these fields they tended to bring the methods and attitudes acquired in their earlier schooling. Creativity and originality were anything but encouraged by this: In science or in medicine, much of the "research" involved a sampling of the opinions of the ancient authors rather than a careful program of observation and experiment. Ransacking obscure authors of the past to discover a forgotten novelty meant that people were picking the brains of the dead instead of using their own.

SCHOOLS OF PHILOSOPHY

Of the "postgraduate" studies, philosophy was the one most generally undertaken. Some got only a smattering of it, while others spent years in the pursuit of "wisdom and virtue." There were many "schools" of philosophy: Platonic, Peripatetic (Aristotelian), Stoic, Epicurean, Neo-Pythagorean, Cynic, and so on. Some people attached themselves to one particular philosophy and adhered to it, but many others sampled several brands and evolved an eclectic philosophy of their own. As a matter of fact, the professional philosophers and teachers of philosophy more often than not were eclectics themselves, and it was rare to find a school represented in its purest form.

Stoicism

Characteristic of philosophy in the Roman imperial period was the strong emphasis placed on ethics, almost to the exclusion of the science and dialectic on which the philosophic systems were based. Stoicism, the most popular brand of philosophy, was one in which the stress on morality, the attainment of virtue, outweighed everything else. Those who gave instruction in Stoicism were more often preachers than teachers. Their powers of evangelism were such that people were actually *converted* to Stoicism and underwent an emotional experience that corresponded to a religious conversion.

While it was fashionable for authors who surveyed the contemporary scene to bewail the decline in Roman morality, and the later Christians were convinced that the pagans were sunk in moral degradation, it was a fact that in the first and second centuries A.D. people strove eagerly for goodness and virtue. Not for a long time, perhaps never before, had morality been so popular and seemed so desirable. The *Meditations* of Marcus Aurelius or the moral essays of Seneca were typical rather than isolated examples of the trend of the times. Stoicism had much in common with Christianity, and many persons who moved over from philosophy into the new religion found the transition an easy one to make.

Rulers as well as their subjects were affected by the moral aspirations of the age. The emperors of the second century A.D., especially

PORTRAIT OF A YOUNG ROMAN NOBLEMAN,
SECOND CENTURY A.D.

(Courtesy of the Minneapolis Institute of Arts.)

Marcus Aurelius and Antoninus Pius, had the highest concepts of duty and tried hard to fulfill the responsibilities of the throne. The government itself was conducted on a humanitarian basis; not only was an effort made to expand the educational system, but also there were programs for the improvement of public health, of assistance to orphaned children, and efforts to revive the economy of depressed areas. The social services to which the government committed itself involved expenditures that could be borne in prosperous times, but they helped to unbalance the budget when revenues fell off.

RELIGIONS AND BELIEFS

Philosophy was not for everyone. To many people it seemed aus-
tere and barren when compared with certain religions of the age that
provided all the consolations of philosophy and promised other things
besides. The imperial cult and a number of the ancient religions that
had degenerated into pure formalism were not in this category, but the
mystery religions of the Near East did provide a satisfaction and comfort
that could not be found elsewhere. The cult of Dionysus from Greece,
that of the Great Mother from Asia Minor, that of Isis and Serapis from
Egypt, and Mithraism from Iran were most prominent among those
spreading over the empire. Mithraism was especially attractive to the
soldiers of Rome who carried the cult with them to Rome, Africa, Britain, and the camps along the Rhine and the Danube. Judaism had acquired many converts during the Hellenistic Age, and it still attracted a
few in the early Roman imperial period. In Alexandria and Antioch the
synagogues had many members; almost every major city in Asia Minor
and Greece had a sizeable Jewish community, and this was also true of
Rome and some of the towns in the West. The refusal of the Jews to
"worship" the emperor, and the uprisings in Judaea in both the Flavian
and Hadrianic periods made the government suspicious of the Jews, but
it was the competition afforded by Christianity rather than imperial dis-
approval that turned potential converts away from Judaism.

Christianity

Out of this period came the world religion Christianity.

Origin and Rise of Christianity.   The period of the Principate coincided with that of the origin and rise of Christianity, the cult that
would destroy paganism and become the state religion of the Later Roman Empire. Jesus was born during the reign of Augustus and crucified
late in the reign of Tiberius. At this time Judaism was fragmented into
many sects, ranging all the way from the rigid formalism of the official
religion maintained by the priests in Jerusalem to small messianic
groups whose beliefs were amorphous, chaotic, and anything but orthodox; the famous Dead Sea Scrolls have revealed much about one of
these peripheral sects. Some Jews had been influenced to a considerable
degree by Greek philosophy; others, by the Oriental mystery religions.
Disputes over doctrine were acrimonious in Judaea and often culminated in physical violence; the major sects formed into political parties
that made war on one another and tried to win the support of the Roman authorities against their rivals.

Christianity began as a reform movement within Judaism itself, a protest against the empty and meaningless formalities of cult practice that passed for worship in Jerusalem among those of the priestly class. This was more than enough to arouse priestly opposition; the priests also found allies among the rich who were convinced that Jesus was inciting class warfare. As the following of Jesus increased, the opposition felt obliged to halt the movement by the strongest possible measures.

After the crucifixion, there was a period of confusion and doubt among the disciples until it was realized that there was no place within Judaism for Christianity. Missionaries discovered that Hellenized Jews outside of Palestine were often receptive to the new religion and that many converts could be found among former Gentiles who had adopted Judaism; from this it was only a step to the inauguration of missionary efforts among the pagans. With the conversion of Paul, a Hellenized Jew of Tarsus, Christianity won a valuable leader, for not only was Paul a man learned in Jewish theology, who could debate with scholars in the synagogues, but also his mastery of the Greek language and familiarity with Greek culture enabled him to meet educated Gentiles on equal terms. The boundless energy and versatility of Paul served him well on the long journeys and in the difficult situations of his subsequent missionary career. He was able to form, organize, and hold together the Christian communities in Syria, Asia Minor, Greece, and Rome. His success was an inspiration to other missionaries, and the faith spread.

The earliest Christians expected Jesus to return momentarily; for some time they made no attempt to evolve an organization that would be self-perpetuating. As the years passed, however, and the congregations grew in size, problems arising from administrative and financial affairs gradually forced the Christians to choose officials to perform functions of various kinds. Within the churches there came to be a division of religious and secular responsibilities; the elders, who at first had administered the affairs of the local Christian communities, became priests and set apart from laymen by the ceremony of ordination. Overseers (bishops) became the chief officials of those churches located in the major towns: Rome, Antioch, Alexandria, Corinth, and so on.

Complex Rituals and Theology.   In time also, ritual and theology became more complex. The early Christians had been accustomed to gather for prayers, hymns, readings from the Old Testament, and a few remarks by some member of the congregation—or perhaps a letter from Paul or another missionary might be read. To become a Christian, the convert only needed "to confess Christ" and be baptized. But all this changed: Baptism and the Eucharist became sacraments administered by the priests, a catechism and a creed were introduced, and the ritual was progressively elaborated.

Rise of Christian Literature.   While the Apostles still lived, the new faith was propagated and transmitted orally. The memory of Jesus was preserved in the recollections of his associates and in the *Logia,* or Sayings of Jesus, and much of the preaching consisted of exhortations to morality or elucidations of the prophetic message of the Old Testament in support of the view that Jesus was the Messiah. Then, a Christian literature began to evolve: The Synoptic Gospels were written to immortalize and consolidate the oral tradition, and the apostolic letters were preserved, read, reread, and copied. By the beginning of the second century A.D., other letters by churchmen as well as didactic compositions were added to this literary store. Next came "apologies" that defended Christianity against pagan slanders and sought to present the Christian point of view; some of these tracts were conciliatory in their attempts to harmonize pagan and Christian ideas, but others were devoted to attacks on paganism and Greek philosophy. "Acts," moralizing stories, and didactic works continued to be produced; by the end of the second century A.D., theological questions that had never occurred to the early Christians began to be discussed and debated in major works by prominent churchmen.

Theological Disputes.   Differences of opinion with regard to Christian doctrine had begun to arise before the first century A.D. ended. The tenets of the faith had never been sharply defined, and many converts brought ideas of their own with them into Christianity. In the course of the second century, violent theological disputes occurred. Various sects of Christians developed; these were founded and led by strong-willed and often brilliant men who insisted that only they had the true faith; such leaders were frequently former pagans who were fairly recent converts. In the resultant contests and secessions, the losers were branded as heretics. Before A.D. 200, Bishop Irenaeus was able to list about twenty-five major heresies, while a half-century later Hippolytus knew twice as many. Tradition and authority were invoked by orthodox churchmen in combating heresy. The teaching of the Church, they said, was everywhere and always the same; it was based on the witness of the prophets, the apostles, and all the disciples. The yardstick was the rule of faith as expressed in the Creed; such a rule encouraged questions only among heretics.

Greek Philosophy and Christianity.   While Western prelates strove to hold the line by emphasizing faith and discipline, those in the East frequently held different views. Many educated Greeks who became Christians felt that there were truths in Greek philosophy applicable to the study and understanding of Christianity. Furthermore, they rejected the idea that the entire Old Testament could be literally interpreted; on the contrary, they felt that allegory was the key to understanding. This point of view was especially popular among the Christians in Egyptian Alexandria, long a center of scholarship and the place where a learned Jew named Philo had introduced the allegorical method in Jewish theology. While Clement of Alexandria and his successor, Origen (ca. A.D. 230), advocated this approach and just managed to stay within the pale of orthodoxy, others strayed farther afield: Some of these were the so-called Gnostics.

Doctrinal disputes continued on into the fourth century A.D. and became increasingly virulent. In the end, the alliance of church and state, the formulation of the Nicene Creed, and the establishment of the canon of the New Testament helped the Christians to close up their ranks. Heresies still cropped up, but they were less devastating in their consequences than those of the second or third centuries A.D., when Christian unity was threatened at a most crucial period.

Periodic Persecution of Christians.   From the time of Nero until the opening years of the fourth century A.D., the Christians were subjected to periodic persecution conducted under the auspices of the Roman government. This was in part due to misunderstandings of one kind or another: The Christians were confused with the Jews by many pagans who were anti-Semitic; the Roman government took a dim view of secret societies, a category in which the Christian congregations seemed to belong; it was also said that the Christians were cannibals—clearly a misunderstanding about the Eucharist. Furthermore, various sayings of Jesus taken out of context might be interpreted as subversive and anarchistic. Many Christians were conscientious objectors who refused to serve in the army; all devout Christians refused to perform the customary pagan rite of worshipping the emperor's statue—regarded as a test of loyalty by the government. For these and other reasons, the Christians were considered dangerous to the state and society; they were subversives who must change their ways or suffer the consequences. Most of the early persecutions were conducted on a local basis, but in time attempted purges were empirewide in scope. Some Christians apostasized but the majority stood firm; many eagerly sought a martyr's crown. Persecution, in fact, may be said to have strengthened the faith and held the Christians together.

Christian Art and Pagan Temples.   Christianity, like Judaism, was a complex cultural affair composed of many items borrowed from diverse cultures of the past. Rooted in Judaism, it borrowed much from Greek philosophy and adopted concepts familiar to many people from their experience with the Oriental mystery religions. As Christian art developed, it employed symbols of well-established meaning among

Jews and pagans. Eventually, pagan temples—as, for example, the Parthenon and the "Theseum" at Athens—became Christian churches, while pagan shrines in the countryside were devoted to the adoration of Christian saints.

LITERATURE, ART, AND ARCHITECTURE

Along with the expansion of the Empire, and its exposure to other cultures, came an outpouring of the arts.

Literature

In volume and variety, the literary remains from the first two centuries of the Principate exceed those surviving from any other period of antiquity. In quality, these works generally fall short of the standards set in the fifth and fourth centuries B.C. or in the Ciceronian period, but most can be read with interest, and a few are truly outstanding. Although increasing in direct proportion to the growth of the three familiar elements—literacy, wealth, and patronage—the massive literary production of the early imperial period may not have exceeded that of the Hellenistic Age as far as works in Greek were concerned. Much of Hellenistic literature failed to survive because it was adapted, translated, or plagiarized by writers of the Roman Empire. On the other hand, more was written in Latin than ever before, and it is evident that after the time of the Good Emperors the glacier of literary production began to recede and left the works of the first two centuries as a sort of terminal moraine.

Common Characteristics.   The literature of the period under discussion had certain marked characteristics. First, it was bilingual: The same literary forms were employed by both Latin and Greek writers, and some authors wrote in both Greek and Latin. Second, while there was some experimentation with new forms or styles, the so-called "doctrine of classicism" had been widely accepted so that writers took as their models in Greek the poets of the Archaic Period, the Athenian dramatists and orators, and Herodotus, Thucydides, and Plato; or in Latin, Cicero and his contemporaries along with selected authors of the Augustan Age were held up as the standard. Third, there was little inspiration derived from the area of politics; where in the first century B.C. the political struggles in Rome had made oratory great, under the Principate politics was hardly a safe topic for public discussion, and furthermore most writers were not participants in Roman political life.

Vergil's Poetry.   The reign of Augustus coincided with a major period in Latin literature; moreover, a number of prominent Greek authors—the geographer Strabo, the historian Diodorus, and the great literary critic and antiquarian Dionysius of Halicarnassus—flourished at that time. Vergil (70–19 B.C.), the poet laureate of the early years of Augustus' reign, was best known for his great epic, the *Aeneid*, which celebrated the founding of Rome. The literary ancestors of the *Aeneid* were Homer, Apollonius of Rhodes, and the early Latin poets, Ennius and Naevius, but Vergil's work was not the product of imitation or scholarly archaizing; rather, it was inspired by a fervent patriotism and an optimism for the future engendered by the reforms of Augustus. To recount the story of Aeneas was to compliment the family of Caesar and Augustus; Vergil also made reference to his own age and prophesied that it would be golden. The *Aeneid* well served the program of Augustus to revive the Roman national spirit, and a certain element of propaganda was also to be found in Vergil's earlier didactic poem, the *Georgics*, written in imitation of Hesiod's *Works and Days* and intended to encourage agriculture and glorify Italy. The still earlier *Eclogues*, composed during the period of the Second Triumvirate and inspired by the bucolic poetry of Theocritus, contained, like the later poems, references complimentary to Vergil's contemporaries. The works of Vergil soon attained in Latin poetry a position comparable to that of Homer in Greek; his poems were read and studied in the schools and imitated by his successors.

Horace.   After the death of Vergil, Horace (65–8 B.C.) became the principal court poet. He was given the task of composing a hymn to be sung at the Secular Games of 17 B.C. when the Romans celebrated the beginning of a new era, or *saeculum*, which had been heralded by the appearance of a comet. This ceremony was another part of the program of Augustus to achieve national regeneration, and we have the *Carmen Saeculare* which Horace produced for the occasion. Fortunately, the fame of Horace does not have to rest on this single effort, not one of his best, but we have in addition his *Satires*, *Odes*, *Epistles*, and *Epodes*. One of the most interesting of the *Epistles* is the witty and penetrating *Ars Poetica* (Art of Poetry) which shows an indebtedness to Aristotle's *Poetics*, although its concern is with both Latin and Greek poetry and the problems of the poet himself.

Livy.   Livy (59 B.C.–A.D. 17) was the most eminent prose writer of the Augustan Age. For many decades he labored over his great history of Rome; its 142 books carried the story from the founding of the city by Romulus down to 9 B.C. Livy's history, like Vergil's *Aeneid*, was intended to glorify Rome. A literary rather than a scientific historian, Livy was most proficient at narrative and somewhat indifferent to the techniques of research. Only about one-fourth of his history has survived: the first ten books which deal with the period 753 to 293 B.C. and a later section covering events from the Second Punic War through the defeat of Macedonia in 168. Ranked with Sallust as a great Roman historian, Livy became a "school author" along with Vergil and Horace.

Josephus, Arrian, and Appian.   Perhaps only a few among the great crowd of writers who flourished during the next century and a half are deserving of high praise, but their works tell us much about the age in which they lived. Among the historians who wrote in Greek were Josephus, Arrian, and Appian. Josephus, a Jew who became the intimate of the Flavian emperors after the Jewish War of A.D. 66 to 70, wrote valuable accounts of the history and antiquities of his people. Arrian was the author of one of the best accounts of the campaigns of Alexander the Great, and before his death about A.D. 175 Arrian also published his notes on the lectures of the Stoic teacher, Epictetus. Appian of Alexandria, another second-century writer, dealt with the foreign and civil wars of the Romans during the period of the Republic.

Plutarch and Suetonius.   Biography vied with history in popularity under the Roman Empire. Two famous biographers flourished at the beginning of the second century A.D.: Plutarch and Suetonius. The latter is best remembered for his *Lives of the Twelve Caesars* (Julius Caesar to Domitian), a lively and amusing work written without much concern for accuracy or impartiality. Plutarch of Chaeronea in Boeotia was a Platonist who wrote in Greek the parallel lives of famous Greeks and Romans: Cicero and Demosthenes, Caesar and Alexander, and many more. Plutarch was also the author of a great number of predominantly philosophical essays which were uplifting and entertaining rather than profound; these were gathered together in a huge collection known as the *Moralia*.

Tacitus.   Tacitus, a contemporary of Plutarch and Suetonius and a high-ranking Roman senator, wrote a semibiography, really a panegyric, on his father-in-law Agricola, who was a famous Roman general. Tacitus was also the author of a brief work on the history and people of Germany, as well as a dialogue on oratory which was a rather significant piece of literary criticism, but his fame rests mainly on his *Histories* and *Annals* which together carried the history of the Principate from the death of Augustus to that of Domitian. It was the purpose of Tacitus to blacken the reputations of the Julio-Claudian and Flavian emperors, and he was so successful in this that it has taken the work of several generations of modern scholars to show that these rulers were not all villains and incompetents, as Tacitus had maintained. The talent of Tacitus might be said to be entirely literary, but prodigious; he had great skill in narration and description, but he was biased, inaccurate, and inconsistent. It may be significant that the ancient critics did not concur with modern ones in ranking Tacitus with Livy and Sallust as one of the greater Roman historians.

Pliny the Younger.   Pliny the Younger was a senatorial contemporary and admirer of Tacitus. A prominent advocate and orator, Pliny is most famous for his letters, of which more than a hundred have survived—mainly due to the fact that he carefully selected these for publication. Epistolography (letter writing) had become a literary genre, an art about which a number of treatises in Greek and Latin had been written, and Pliny wanted to put his best foot forward; he had no desire to suffer the fate of poor Cicero, whose letters had been posthumously chosen and published, some with malice aforethought. Pliny's letters were addressed to relatives, friends, and prominent persons in Rome. Most categories then distinguished by the authorities on epistolography were represented in Pliny's collections: personal; those dealing with literary matters; and letters of recommendation, congratulation, consolation, and the like. The letters are illuminating and valuable because they tell us about so many aspects of the life of a Roman senator in Flavian times and the early era of the Good Emperors; in addition they provide a portrait of Pliny himself, a real human being, well intentioned, not overly complex, justly pleased with modest triumphs. His legal practice was extensive; also he was acquainted with the literary lights of his age and had some aspirations of his own as an author and critic; a philanthropist who benefited his neighbors in the Lake Como area in the Po Valley where he was born and had property, he was wealthy enough to have two country homes in the vicinity of Rome and never suffered from a shortage of the material comforts of this life.

One whole book of Pliny's epistles, the tenth, was devoted to his correspondence with the emperor Trajan after being appointed governor of Bithynia with the special mission to straighten out the tangled finances of the big cities of that area. As a recognized treasury expert, we find him dealing sensibly with these problems. Best remembered in this book is the letter in which Pliny describes what he has learned about the Christians there and requests the emperor's advice on how to deal with them. Equally memorable is Trajan's reply (X.97) which instructs Pliny to ignore anonymous communications accusing certain individuals of being Christians since these "create the worst sort of precedent and are quite out of keeping with the spirit of our age." Just as famous are the two letters (VI.16 and VI.20) that Pliny wrote to Tacitus describing the eruption of Vesuvius in A.D. 79 and the death of Pliny's uncle in that catastrophe.

Pliny the Elder.   Pliny's uncle was Pliny the Elder, prominent in public life under Nero and Vespasian; he was serving as an admiral of the Roman navy when he perished near Pompeii in the eruption of Vesuvius. The elder Pliny was a prolific writer and had a reputation as a great scholar. His surviving work, the *Natural History*, is an encyclopedia that covers natural and physical science as well as geography, medicine, and art history. Most of Pliny's information, and misinformation, was derived from his extensive reading of a host of Greek and Latin authors; he collected in 36 books, "20,000 noteworthy facts obtained from one hundred authors" and some 2,000 volumes. Credulous and lacking discrimination, Pliny enjoyed a reputation as an authority that was not entirely deserved.

Seneca.   The elder Pliny must have known both Seneca and Petronius, who were luminaries at court in the early years of Nero's reign. We have already referred to Seneca as a Stoic essayist, but he also wrote the *Natural Questions*, which dealt with earthquakes, comets, and other phenomena, and he composed tragedies based on the plays of Euripides. Seneca was a stylist whose literary experiments enjoyed a considerable vogue but were later rejected in favor of "classicism."

Petronius and Apuleius.   Petronius was an elegant and witty senator believed to have been the author of the *Satyricon*, a clever and salacious novel that contemporaries identified as a satire lampooning Nero and his associates. Another famous novel was the *Metamorphoses*, or *Golden Ass*, written by Lucius Apuleius, a rhetorician from North Africa who lived in the second century A.D. Combining mysticism and satire, the story recounts the adventures of a magician who intended to change himself into a bird but became a donkey instead.

The "Second Sophistic."   The second century A.D., many people believed, was a new Age of Sophists, but the incorrigible exhibitionists who paraded their rhetorical pyrotechnics through city after city of the empire were fortunate that none of the old masters of the fifth century B.C. could appear to challenge them. Pretenders to encyclopedic knowledge, the new sophists were mostly oratorical entertainers who lectured, with or without preparation, on a variety of subjects: science, philosophy, literature, art, and many others. Some were teachers; others were merely performers. Highly paid and greatly admired, they were arrogant and overbearing; they rebuked emperors, sneered at lesser folk, and fought bitterly among themselves. One sophist of

Smyrna named Polemo arrived home one night to find the Roman governor of Asia occupying his house. With scant courtesy, Polemo told the official to find lodgings elsewhere. This particular governor just happened to be Antoninus Pius, the future emperor. A Nero or a Domitian would have had Polemo's head, but Antoninus often joked with Polemo about the incident later on. When Adrian of Tyre was appointed professor of rhetoric at Athens, he began his inaugural lecture with the words, "Once again letters have come from Phoenicia!" More honest than most, Philagrus of Cilicia admitted that his disposition was so bad he could not even enjoy himself.

Dio of Prusa.   Dio of Prusa, one of the best Greek orators of the age, was a cut above most sophists. He was a friend of Trajan and played a significant part in the civic politics of western Asia. Dio was "converted" to philosophy and boasted that he had advanced to the exalted position of a philosopher. Most professional orators, on the other hand, denied the preeminence of philosophers in a scholarly *cursus honorum* that Dio and the philosophers would insist ran the gamut from grammarian, rhetorician, orator, and finally philosopher. Whatever the true pecking order may have been, it demonstrates a certain dreariness of aspiration in this age.

Lucian of Samosata.   Lucian of Samosata, who flourished in the second half of the second century, was a popular lecturer who traveled widely to entertain audiences all over the empire. A Greek, with considerable literary talent and a fine feeling for literature, Lucian was a satirist who poked fun at the sophists, philosophers, rhetoricians, and other popular idols of his day. Dozens of his essays and dialogues have survived, and almost all are extremely amusing. Lucian knew the story of Jonah and the whale; he elaborated on it in his untrue *True History* in which a whale swallowed a whole ship, crew and all. The interior of the whale was so capacious that it contained islands and continents, and many nations of people. The mariners, after sailing around for a bit, finally forced the whale to disgorge them by starting a forest fire in his stomach.

In Addition.   The foregoing list is by no means an exhaustive catalog of the Greek and Latin authors of the early imperial period nor has it included some works that are of great interest to the specialist and the general reader as well. Vitruvius, a Roman military engineer who served Augustus, was the author of the fascinating and informative *De Architectura* that in ten books dealt with Greek and Roman architecture and related matters including building materials, types of public and domestic structures, surveying, aqueducts, elementary astronomy, machines using water power, and engines of war (catapults, scorpions, etc.). Among the most memorable sections are those on the acoustics of a theater and the means of amplifying sound, making Roman cement for underwater foundations, planning a farmhouse, sundials and water clocks, machines for raising heavy weights, how to find water and dig a well, and the construction of hodometers for measuring distances traveled by land or sea.

Celsus, an encyclopedist, flourished under Tiberius. His extensive work on medicine, most of which has survived, is a mine of information about medical practice in the first century A.D. Under the Julio-Claudians, many authors from Roman Spain came to Rome. One of these, along with the philosopher Seneca and the epic poet Lucan, was Columella, who produced a comprehensive work on agriculture which also included animal husbandry, rural architecture, and gardening, a subject dear to the hearts of Italians in the classical period. In Flavian times Pliny the Younger knew and admired another Spaniard, Martial, famous for his epigrams and a contemporary of the last great satirist, Juvenal, an Italian born and bred. Pliny also attended the lectures of Quintilian, a Spanish rhetorician and teacher of oratory who became an imperial tutor under Domitian. Quintilian's impressive *Institutes of Oratory* is well worth reading for its description of Roman education from childhood to maturity. Pliny's letters also tell of his respect for Julius Frontinus, general, strategist, and engineer who wrote an engrossing and detailed book on the aqueducts of Rome.

In the second century the outstanding names are those of Galen and Claudius Ptolemy. Galen of Pergamum wrote on both medicine and philosophy and for several years served as the personal physician of Marcus Aurelius. A prolific author, so much of Galen's work in Greek is still available to us that some of it has yet to be translated into English. In the history of classical medicine, the two most prominent names are those of Hippocrates and Galen, the one at the beginning of the story and the other very near the end. Claudius Ptolemy of Alexandria was interested in astronomy, mathematics, geography, and optics. Both his *Almagest* and *Geography* continued to be read and studied for centuries after his death. The *Almagest* in particular is not in the category of light reading, and anyone inclined to discount the intellect of the ancient scientists ought to be required to study through it. Still, like most of the ancients, Ptolemy believed in *astrology;* it is not easy to reconcile the fact that the author of the *Almagest* also wrote the *Tetrabiblos!*

It is quite possible that we shall never know the full extent of the Greco-Roman achievement in science and medicine. When we read the extant works of Archimedes (second century B.C.) and those of Claudius Ptolemy (second century A.D.) the enormous gap between their knowledge and ability and that of most other writers on science whose works have survived is not easy to comprehend, although there are several possible explanations. For one thing, science may well have become too difficult for anyone except the specialists to comprehend, particularly since there were insufficient opportunities for science education except through a kind of apprenticeship with a master while the ordinary educational facilities beyond an elementary level mainly stressed oratory and philosophy. Moreover, the authors of the huge encyclopedias that we still possess (for example, Celsus, Vitruvius, Pliny the Elder) do not seem to have been truly expert; in the imperial period condensations and distillations were so popular in every field, not just science, that big works like Livy's Roman history failed to overcome the trouble of perpetuating the manuscripts. More specialized writings in Greek by Heron, Diophantus, and Pappas dealing with mathematics and science were perpetuated or sometimes later translated into Arabic. This does not necessarily mean that once there was nothing comparable in Latin. It was rather that with the breakup of the unity of the civilized world and the development of other interests or priorities in the West, certain parts of the classical heritage had a better chance of longer life in the Greek-Byzantine East where Greek remained a living language and Latin had never really caught on.

Still another explanation deserves consideration. The overwhelming prestige of philosophy was not conducive to stimulating scientific advances. The "science" that was basic to the various philosophies was out of date by the beginning of the first century B.C., but the tendency to explain the mysteries of medicine or the phenomena of science in terms of the "science" on which the philosophies had been constructed stood in the way of the acceptance or even the consideration of opposing hypotheses. Seneca, the author of the *Natural Questions,* is a case in point; if an alternative explanation was at variance with what he had learned from Stoicism he refused to consider it. In medicine we find that there were several "schools": the Empirics, who where Skeptics, stressed cures; the Dogmatists, who concentrated on causes, went back to Hippocrates and the Aristotelian Peripatetics; the Pneumatists were Stoics and the Methodists Epicureans. Only the Eclectics, like Galen, felt free to pick and choose what seemed to fit the circumstances.

Architecture and Art

Turning from literature to the arts, we may note that architects, sculptors, and painters seldom lacked for employment during the first two centuries of the empire. Public and private building went forward at an unprecedented rate. Not only Rome but also every other city was building temples, porticos, libraries, theatres, amphitheatres, and baths. The emperors had large and complex palaces in and out of Rome;

ARCH OF HADRIAN IN ATHENS

(Courtesy of J. M. F.)

many private persons of wealth had big town houses and extensive country villas. Imperial monies, municipal funds, and private donations financed many a new public structure in Athens, Ephesus, Antioch, and numerous other towns in the East, Africa, and the West.

Arches, Barrel Vault, and Dome.   Because there was so much building and because of transportation costs, the best materials were seldom used; therefore brick, stucco, and marble veneer were more commonly employed in construction than marble itself. The orders of Greek architecture and the composite orders were still used for facades

A STREET IN JERASH

(Courtesy of Aramco World.)

and exterior ornamentation, but the great size of many types of buildings and the need for interior space encouraged the development of the
arch, barrel vault, and dome, thus doing away with the necessity, as in
Greek buildings, for a forest of columns within the structure.

Covered Theatres, Amphitheatres, and Public Baths.   Among new
types of buildings were the covered theatre and the amphitheatre, along
with the great public baths with their many rooms for special purposes
and arrangements for both hot and cold water. Still another innovation
was the *basilica,* or law court, a colonnaded hall with a central vault.
Moreover, the ornamental gateway to many a civic center, or forum, was
provided by a Roman triumphal arch decorated with sculptured reliefs
and panels.

Paintings, Mosaics, and Relief Sculpture.   Not only relief sculpture but also paintings and mosaics were used in architectural decora-

ROMAN MOSAIC

(Courtesy of the Minneapolis Institute of Arts.)

Late Roman/Byzantine multicolored mosaic illustrating the use of *tesserae* (tiles) in creating a composition.

tion. Mosaics with bright colors and complex motifs adorned both public and private buildings all over the empire, while wall paintings, as at Pompeii and Herculaneum, were also common. Relief sculpture might be purely ornamental, or it might be packed with symbolism, or again it might serve a narrative purpose. On the famous *Ara Pacis* (Altar of Peace) erected by Augustus, both symbolism and narrative were employed, while on the triumphal columns of Trajan and Marcus Aurelius, the principal events of military campaigns were narrated in spiral bands of relief.

Portraiture.   In both painting and sculpture in the round, the use of the monumental, even the colossal, was common. We hear of gigantic statues of the emperors and huge canvasses. The major contribution of the Romans to sculpture was the use of portraiture: In the portrait busts and statues that survive, we can see the emperors as they appeared to contemporaries, not idealized as rulers had been in earlier periods. There was no single Roman style or technique of sculpture: Alexandrian, classical Greek, and Etruscan influences can be discerned. Like the triumphal arch in architecture, a Roman innovation in sculpture was the equestrian statue.

This was ancient civilization at the full: far-flung, complex, yet dangerously uniform and choked with the banal and mediocre. Quantity, not quality, activity, but not creativity, were distinguishing characteristics that boded ill for the future. Secure in its complacency, the comfortable little world of the second century A.D. scarcely sensed the cultural, political, and economic bankruptcy that was spreading under the skin of civilization and would soon attack its vitals.

Chapter Twelve

The Road to Autocracy

The Roman world had survived many changes throughout its varied history. In its last stages, Rome looked to autocracy to restore it to its former position.

SEVERAN DYNASTY

The assassination of Commodus on the last day of A.D. 192 set off a chain reaction resembling that which had followed the suicide of Nero. Pertinax, the first nominee of the factions at Rome, offended the praetorian guard and was soon deposed in favor of a wealthy senator named Julianus who bought the imperial nomination by offering the guardsmen well over $1,000 apiece for their support. Then, the army had its say: The legions in Britain nominated their commander, Albinus; those in the East, their general, Niger; and the troops along the Danube supported their own leader, Septimius Severus. Septimius easily won the race to Rome. Julianus was executed, and Albinus was bought off by appointment to the post of Caesar, or junior Augustus. After defeating Niger in the East, however, Septimius turned on Albinus and destroyed him in A.D. 196. In this manner the new dynasty of the Severi came to power; they were to hold the throne until A.D. 235.

Septimius Severus (A.D. 193–211) was primarily a military man, and he began the militarization of the Principate. Septimius also represented certain regional elements in the empire; born in Africa himself and married to the daughter of a Syrian priest, his sympathies were not with Italy and the Italians. In fact, he disapproved of the special favor with which Italy had always been treated at the expense of the rest of the empire, and many of his reforms were intended to reduce Italy to the level of the other provinces. To achieve this end and to punish the praetorians for their assassination of Pertinax, more provincials were admitted to the praetorian guard as well as to the post of centurion in the legions. Moreover, since upon retirement centurions and their descen-

SEPTIMUS SEVERUS (193–211)

dants were eligible for membership in the equestrian class, this made it possible for commoners to attain higher social status through military service. Septimius was no friend of the senatorial class, either: He began to use equestrians in high military posts and provincial governorships that had once been monopolized by senators. In addition, judicial authority in Italy was taken from the Senate and given to the city and praetorian prefects.

One of the concerns of Septimius was to justify his usurpation and to legitimize his position as emperor. First posing as the avenger of Pertinax, he later promoted the fiction of a connection with the family of Marcus Aurelius. Better known by his nickname of Caracalla, the eldest son of Septimius was officially called Marcus Aurelius Antoninus; thus, for propaganda purposes the name of Marcus Aurelius was as useful to the Severi as the name of Caesar had been to the Julio-Claudians.

Caracalla

After he had campaigned successfully against the Parthians and fortified certain of the northern frontiers, Septimius Severus died at York in Britain while he was attempting to stabilize the boundary there. The throne was left to both sons of Septimius, but Caracalla soon assassinated his younger brother, Geta, and ruled alone (A.D. 211–217). His reign was notable for a financial crisis which he tried unsuccessfully to solve by a major currency reform and for his promulgation of the so-called Antonine Constitution (decree) of A.D. 212. This decree extended

CARACALLA (211–217)

Roman citizenship to virtually all of the subjects of Rome; the apparent object of this measure was to simplify judicial administration and to increase the number of people liable for certain taxes and municipal services. In a sense, it was Romanization by decree.

Near the end of his reign, the behavior of Caracalla became rather peculiar. It was said that he fancied himself a second Alexander the Great and that he not only adopted the old Macedonian dress but also organized a whole legion to fight as a Macedonian phalanx. In A.D. 216 he precipitated a war with the Parthians on the pretext that their king had refused to give his daughter in marriage to Caracalla. Shortly thereafter (217) Caracalla was murdered by his praetorian prefect, Macrinus, who had learned that the emperor had targeted *him* for execution. Macrinus was then proclaimed emperor by the troops, but within a year he fell victim to a counterrevolution (218).

Elagabalus

The fall of Macrinus ushered in one of the most bizarre episodes in Roman history. Julia Domna, the empress of Septimius and the mother of Caracalla and Geta, had committed suicide when Caracalla was assassinated, but she had a sister, Julia Maesa, who had returned to the family home in Emesa in Syria where their father had been the high priest of Elagabalus, a sun god worshipped in the form of a black stone. Julia Maesa had two daughters, Julia Soemias and Julia Mammaea, each of whom had a young son. The child of Soemias was named Bassianus and Mammaea's boy was called Alexianus.

RUINS OF BAALBEK IN SYRIA

(Courtesy of Aramco World.)

Grandmother Maesa was determined to regain the throne of the Severi. Following an eclipse of the sun in A.D. 218 she capitalized on the superstitions of nearby soldiers by announcing that Bassianus was really the son of Caracalla and that the eclipse indicated the will of the sun god that the dynasty should be reinstated. This successfully instigated a revolt that spread rapidly. Macrinus was overthrown. Bassianus, who actually did resemble Caracalla, was renamed Marcus Aurelius Antoninus and became the new emperor.

At the age of fifteen this third "Marcus Aurelius" was a confused child at best. As the high priest of Elagabalus he took that position so seriously that he believed himself to be the earthly manifestation of his god and preferred to be called Elagabalus. Before his brief reign ended in A.D. 222, some people referred to him as the "false Antoninus," or Sardanapalus. Apparently a monotheist of sorts, he built a temple to his god, the *Deus Solus*, in Rome. He also seemed to be confused about his sex. Arrayed in silk garments and heavy cosmetics, he sometimes appeared as the priestess of his god. He contracted marriages with six women in rapid succession, one a Vestal Virgin, but also married his charioteer and so briefly became an empress. The ancient authors credited him with endless merry pranks, outdoing even Caligula; but we must expect some exaggeration, since his life was too short to have included all of them.

Elagabalus at last exhausted the patience of his grandmother, who persuaded him in A.D. 221 to adopt and name as Caesar his even younger cousin, Alexianus, later known as Severus Alexander. Having thus ensured the continuation of the dynasty, it did not take Maesa long to dispose of Elagabalus and replace him with Alexianus.

Severus Alexander

Severus Alexander A.D. 222–235 was the last ruler of the Severan dynasty. The real power during his reign was exercised by his mother, who allied herself with the Senate, but against the opposition of the army and the equestrians the arrangement was difficult to maintain. The army finally got out of hand and superseded Severus Alexander with one of its generals, Maximinus, a Thracian said to be the first of the Roman emperors who was not a Roman citizen by birth.

A CONFUSED HALF-CENTURY

In the confused half-century that followed, the three-year reign of Maximinus would be counted as a long one, for the empire was to have at least twenty-six emperors between A.D. 235 and 285. Since only one

MAXIMINUS (235–238)   PHILIP THE ARAB (244–249)

Two of the numerous emperors who reigned briefly during the half-century of anarchy in the third century A.D.

of these rulers died a natural death, a statistician might conclude that the chances were twenty-five to one that an emperor of this age would die either by assassination or on the battlefield. The army made and unmade emperors almost at will; barbarian pressure increased on the frontiers; and in the East the Parthians were replaced by a new and vigorous group of Iranian nationalists, the Sassanians, whose attacks the Romans found hard to fend off. Famine, plague, earthquake, and other disasters racked the empire. The treasury was often empty, the silver shortage worsened, and trade declined.

Military Disaster

By the middle of the third century, the empire seemed on the verge of dissolution. The emperor Valerian (A.D. 253–258) was captured by the Sassanians after a military disaster comparable to that suffered by Crassus at Carrhae in 53 B.C. Gallienus (A.D. 253–268), the son and colleague of Valerian, managed to hold on to the center of the empire, but the Near East split off into an independent kingdom with its capital in the caravan city of Palmyra, and in Gaul and Britain there was another independent state. The Goths, a barbarian group who had come from the Baltic into South Russia, now ravaged the Balkans and Asia Minor in a series of raids by land and sea.

CAPTURE OF VALERIAN BY SHAPUR I

(Courtesy of the Oriental Institute, Chicago)

The Soldier Emperors

After the death of Gallienus, a succession of soldier emperors, including the great Aurelian (A.D. 270–275), beat back the Goths, overcame the Gauls and Palmyrenes, and chastised the Sassanians so that the frontiers of the empire were reestablished and its internal unity restored. To build on these temporary successes, however, sweeping reforms had to be made to solve the numerous problems that the disorder of the third century had brought into sharp focus. These problems may be enumerated as follows.

First, the army needed reorganization in order to resist more effectively the barbarian and Persian attacks, but the soldiers must also be made to serve the state instead of individual generals; discipline and loyalty had somehow to be restored. Second, the Principate, like the Republic before it, had been irreparably damaged by the disintegration of constitutional practice. It would be best to find some new basis for the imperial power and the succession to the throne. Third, one way or another, regionalism or separatism must be ended and the empire truly unified. Fourth, the individual must be subordinated to the state, class conflict eliminated, and subversive minorities eliminated or controlled. Fifth, economic reforms deserved a high priority: Currency problems needed solution; the cost of government must be cut and the taxation system reorganized; economic activity had to be revived. Sixth, there was a manpower shortage; this did not mean that there had been a serious population decline, but rather that a more efficient use or direction of activity was necessary. Finally, there was the problem of "barbarization." Not only were larger and larger contingents of barbarians being used as auxiliary troops, but also the legions themselves were composed of an increasing number of men of barbarian origin; this was true not merely of the men in the ranks, but of their officers as well—and from the army, the officers were moving into government positions. In addition, whole tribes of barbarians had been allowed to settle in the frontier provinces along the Danube; often these people had been pushed over into Roman territory by other barbarians behind them. In theory, those who had been given lands within the empire would be just as anxious as the Romans to keep out other barbarians, but the effectiveness of such people and the degree of their cooperation was frequently overestimated.

At the end of the third century and in the early years of the fourth century A.D., a determined effort was made to save the empire. Sweeping reforms created the illusion if not the reality of a complete break with the past. To say that the Principate was replaced by the Autocracy suggests only a political change, but the alterations made after A.D. 285 were much more comprehensive than that.

THE AUTOCRACY

In A.D. 283, the Emperor Carus left his elder son, Carinus, to rule as Augustus in the West while he himself undertook an eastern campaign against the Persians (Sassanians). After driving deep into Mesopotamia and nearly duplicating the earlier successes of Trajan, Carus died under suspicious circumstances, and his younger son, Numerian, led the army back into Roman territory. A year later, in the autumn of A.D. 284, Numerian was murdered in Asia Minor while on the way westward to join his brother, Carinus. The true identity of the assassin of Numerian was never learned, but the troops did not reaffirm their loyalty to Carinus, the western Augustus; instead, they chose an emperor by acclamation: Diocletian, the commander of Numerian's imperial bodyguard. By the spring of A.D. 285, Diocletian had defeated Carinus and come into possession of the whole empire.

Diocletian

Diocletian, one of the greatest Roman emperors, was an uneducated peasant from the Balkans who had joined the Roman army at an early age and risen to the top by sheer ability. Like Augustus, Diocletian was not an outstanding general, but he possessed great administrative

DIOCLETIAN (284–305)

skill and a forceful personality. In an age of disorder, he was able to command respect and obedience; although he would eventually choose to share the empire with three colleagues, Diocletian was always without question *the* senior Augustus.

Diocletian reigned for two decades (A.D. 284–305). Like Augustus, he had time to make changes. With some problems, he had to grope his way toward a solution, although in any case little could be done until the frontiers were secured and internal unity was a fact. The Persians had bounced back after their defeat by Carus, while in the West there was disorder following the defeat of Carinus who had drawn off troops from Gaul in order to force a confrontation with his enemy, Diocletian. This had opened the empire to invasion from across the Rhine as well as reviving Gallic hopes for independence. Unable to conduct simultaneous campaigns in East and West in person, Diocletian took a colleague in A.D. 286. This was Maximian, who was first made Caesar and later Augustus to command in the West as Diocletian concentrated on the defense of the eastern half of the empire. Maximian managed to quiet Gaul, although Britain became independent under a renegade named Carausius, and barbarian tribes played havoc with Roman territory in North Africa. Diocletian in his turn beat back the Persians, but he was harassed by a revolt in Egypt and a barbarian invasion from across the Danube.

Origin of the Tetrarchy.   When it appeared that even a twofold division of the empire was insufficient for control, a fourfold split was made in A.D. 293 with the appointment of two Caesars, Constantius and Galerius. Constantius was assigned to Gaul and charged with responsibility for the reconquest of Britain; Maximian had Italy, Spain, North Africa, and the upper Danubian provinces; Galerius received the Balkans; and Diocletian retained Thrace, Asia Minor, Egypt, and the other parts of the Near East. By A.D. 298 the arrangement had proved its worth: Gaul was secure and Britain restored to the empire; the northern frontiers were quiet; the Persians had been beaten and a revolt in Egypt was put down with great bloodshed. The later years of Diocletian's reign (A.D. 298–305) were relatively peaceful; it was during this period that many of his principal reforms were instituted.

Diocletian's Principal Reforms

Autocracy Founded.   As Augustus had been the founder of the Principate, so Diocletian founded the Dominate, or Autocracy. Under Diocletian the emperor was no longer princeps, first citizen, but rather he was *dominus*, lord, a god-king in the Oriental manner. As a god on earth the ruler was above the law as well as the source of it. His authority was absolute and supreme; even the fiction of responsibility to the Senate was abandoned, and the emperor sought neither its approval nor advice. The ruler did not derive his power from the people; all power now emanated from him to be delegated to the subordinates who assisted him in the business of ruling. The autocracy, then, was a theocracy; the Romans had abandoned their traditional Indo-European theories of government: Politically, they were Orientalized.

Tetrarchy Organized.   For the purposes of administration and defense, Diocletian had organized a tetrarchy, a board of four rulers, each responsible for a part of the empire. There was one Augustus in the East, Diocletian; and one in the West, Maximian. Constantius was Caesar under Maximian, while Galerius was the Caesar of Diocletian; each Caesar married the daughter of his Augustus. There were now four praetorian prefects, one for each ruler. Decrees were promulgated by the tetrarchy as a board, and these measures were supposed to apply to the empire as a whole. Diocletian may also have planned to establish a new pattern for the succession. At any rate, when he abdicated in A.D. 305, he forced Maximian to retire on the same day; Galerius and Constantius were then raised to the rank of Augusti, and two new Caesars were appointed.

Capital Moved.   In the new order, it was significant that Rome was not the residence or capital of any Augustus or Caesar. Diocletian's own

capital was at Nicomedia in Bithynia; Maximian was variously at Milan
or Ravenna in Italy; Constantius ruled from Treves in Gaul, and Galerius
from Sirmium in Pannonia. The Senate, left behind in Rome, was little
more than a municipal council. Furthermore, with the senior Augustus
settled at Nicomedia, the major capital of the empire had thus been
moved from West to East.

Army Reformed; Provinces Multiplied.   Attacks on the frontiers
or internal uprisings were effectively met by the fourfold division of the
empire. Moreover, a gradual reform of the army improved the defenses:
Permanent garrison forces on the frontiers were backed up by powerful
mobile armies that could be rushed to any threatened point. Internal
stability was fostered by a separation of civil and military authorities;
provincial governors generally, for example, ceased to command troops.
This lessened the danger of revolt, and a further deterrent to uprising
was the multiplication of the number of provinces. There were more
than twice as many provinces under Diocletian as there had been under
Hadrian, although the territorial extent of the empire remained approximately the same: The old provinces had merely been divided up into
new and smaller units.

A soldier without civilian administrative experience, Diocletian organized his government as he would have organized an army. As au-
tocrat he was commander-in-chief of both civil and military officials. Authority, the chain of command, began at the top and descended to the
lowest ranks; even the civil officials were put into uniforms. In the army,
in the palace, and in the bureaucracy, militarization and centralization
were the keys to the reforms.

Economy Regimented.   It is hard to know whether Diocletian
might have found better solutions for his problems, but he was right in
feeling that radical and immediate change was necessary. Further, it was
not enough to introduce political and military reform when the economy
was also in need of repair. Here, Diocletian's answer was bold and perhaps predictable: regimentation. A complete census was taken of all
productive land and the manpower on it. Agricultural laborers were
bound to the land, and the land, divided up into taxable units, could be
made to produce its quota. Where lands had ceased to be tilled because
of abandonment, the towns were made responsible for bringing the soil
under cultivation once more. Because of a money shortage, taxes that
had been paid in cash were now collected in kind, and payments to
government employees were also made partly in kind. The state, moreover, began to produce in its own factories many articles that it had
formerly purchased from private industry. As responsibility for the per-

formance of *munera,* or liturgies, was tightened, the areas of activity covered by these forced services were widened.

These reforms were intended to increase production and the tax yield and to cut down the cost of government, but at the same time the military budget was enlarged and much was spent on a vast public works program that was supposed to stimulate the economy. Diocletian also tried to reform the currency by introducing a new silver coinage and attempting to stabilize the ratio between silver and gold. Unfortunately, the new silver coins dropped out of circulation rapidly because Diocletian had undervalued his silver in relation to gold: The silver was hoarded since the pieces were worth more as bullion than the official value given them as coins. These currency problems, combined with overspending, produced a further inflationary trend that the government tried to halt in A.D. 301 with the famous Edict of Prices that set maximum levels for prices and wages. Lacking the proper enforcement machinery, the state was powerless to halt the price rise or the flight of silver so that the attempt at stabilization was a miserable failure.

Edict of Prices: A Note

The Edict of Prices deserves more than a brief mention if only because it illustrates the value of contemporary documents in reconstructing the past. If we had no more than the three certain references to the edict in the ancient authors we should still be ignorant of its contents and purpose as the following quotation will show:

> When he brought about enormously high prices, he attempted to legislate the prices of commodities. (Fourth century A.D.)
> The emperor ordered low prices. (Fifth century)
> Diocletian forbade by law the hoarding of grain, and he established the price of grain and all other things bought and sold lest anyone should export military supplies from the market. (Sixth century)

The first is part of a Christian diatribe against Diocletian. The second is wrongly dated by its author to 302, and the third refers to an oft-repeated situation in Syrian Antioch.

Fortunately for us, today we are able to understand the *De Pretiis* more clearly and fully than even thirty years ago, thanks to the continuing discovery of bits and pieces of the actual edict that was once inscribed on stone and set up for all to see in numerous cities in the eastern part of the empire. Now a fragment in Latin or a few in Greek can be arranged like a jigsaw puzzle to enable us to read the continuous, though still not complete, text of the edict.

The first piece of the puzzle was found, but not recognized, in 1709, and in 1807 a much larger portion came to light in Egypt, but it was not identified and made available for another twenty years. The first formal edition of the edict was published in 1893. This was based on 35 fragments; by 1940 that number had doubled, and today more than 150 are known. Future discoveries may be expected to necessitate reorganization of the form, although we are now in possession of over 1,200 lines of text.

The edict consists of two parts: first, a preamble (now completely restored), and second, a long list of maxima set for commodities, services, and wages. The preamble of the decree, issued in the name of the four rulers, states that numerous wicked and greedy persons have engaged in price gouging and creating shortages of goods to the detriment of the army and the common people. This cannot be endured and so the divine rulers of the empire have intervened to set maxima for prices and wages. Those who do not mend their ways and obey the commands of Diocletian and his colleagues will suffer not fines, but capital punishment. The edict was published in two languages, Latin and Greek, but it is now certain that the preamble was always in Latin, while the price lists were in either Latin or Greek. These lists were long and comprehensive, covering prices, wages, transportation costs, and so on.

On the basis of the extant fragments of the edict, it appears that it applied *only* to Diocletian's part of the empire: Greece, Asia Minor, Egypt, and Cyrene; the one small piece found in Italy a half-century ago is now thought to be an import. The fact that no fragments have turned up in Syria or Palestine is hard to explain.

The heavy spending on public works and the increase of money in circulation could explain the inflation attested in other sources for the closing years of the third century, and the coinage reform financed by the plunder from the victory over the Sassanians could account for new supplies of silver available as well as the fact that the Sassanians had to reduce the percentage of silver in their own coins, but a newly discovered inscription tells us that simultaneous with the edict of prices Diocletian doubled the official (fiat) value of his new silver coins. Once again he had undervalued his silver, but it was too late to make amends.

Several questions remain unanswered. Was the edict mainly intended to benefit the military? The minimum prices and the wages set for civilians would not seem to benefit the common people. If a carpenter or a blacksmith, for example, had to work four days to earn a bushel of wheat or a goose or the cheapest loin cloth or a combination of a pair of boots, two chickens, a dozen eggs, and five heads of lettuce, how did he manage to support a family? A pair of ladies' sandals, a hyena skin, and a quart of olive oil would wipe out the earnings of the next four days!

Subversion.   Even less successful were Diocletian's efforts to curb subversion. His theocracy could hardly be expected to win the acceptance of Jews, Christians, or other monotheists within the empire; they could not accept him and his colleagues as gods. The Manichaeans, for example, members of a new sect which had appeared in the Near East in the third century, proved quite troublesome. Manichaeanism was a hybrid religion combining elements of Zoroastrianism, Judaism, Christianity, and Buddhism with some Neo-Platonism and Gnosticism mixed in for good measure. It had acquired many converts in both the Persian and Roman empires. During the wars between Diocletian and the Persians, the latter had tried to use the Manichaeans as a fifth column, especially in Egypt. This set off a persecution of the Manichaeans within the Roman Empire, but its deterrent effects were slight.

With the Manichaean problem fresh in his mind and with difficulties of all kinds piling up toward the end of his reign, Diocletian was bound to have a showdown with the Christians, for they constituted the largest, and, in his thinking, the most dangerous group among his internal enemies. In A.D. 303 he launched the last and most severe persecution of the Christians, largely confined to the East. A succession of decrees, each one harsher than its predecessor, emanated from the palace at Nicomedia. Churches were destroyed; the sacred books were burned; the Christians were imprisoned, tortured, and executed. Some turned back to paganism to escape punishment, but the majority stood firm. The Christians could not be exterminated as Diocletian had hoped; there were too many of them.

Diocletian Abdicates

Tired, old, and ailing, Diocletian abdicated in the spring of 305. He had done much to create a new way of life in the ancient world. Many of his reforms were to survive and be refined by his successors, but he had not solved the problems of the succession, or inflation, or the Christians. Respected, but not loved, he lived on for nearly a decade in his place of retirement at Salona in Dalmatia on the Adriatic. He died, probably by his own hand, in A.D. 313.

Constantine and Licinius Become Co-Augusti

In the appointment of the new Caesars in A.D. 305, Maxentius, the son of Maximian, and Constantine, the son of Constantius, had been passed over. This was pleasing neither to them nor to their supporters, who had confidently expected their nomination. For this and other reasons, a power struggle soon developed which rent the empire and de-

MODEL RECONSTRUCTION OF DIOCLETIAN'S PALACE

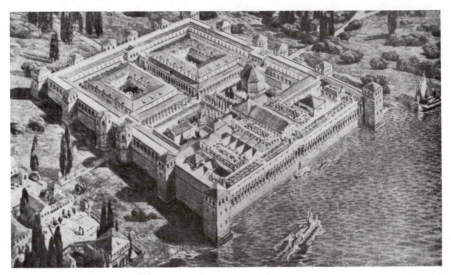

(Courtesy of D. M.)

Diocletian retired to this palace at Split, Jugoslavia, in A.D. 305.

stroyed the tetrarchy. By A.D. 311, there were few survivors; Galerius, Maximian, and Constantius were dead, and Diocletian had refused the pleas of those who begged him to return to public life. The chief antagonists were Constantine and Maxentius; they had never been friends, and now they were bitter enemies. With the loyal support of his father's legions, Constantine had made himself a man to be reckoned with, and he had strengthened his position by an alliance with Licinius, the successor of Galerius.

As the battle for control of the empire progressed, the advantage of an alliance with the Christians began to loom very large in the thinking of the protagonists. Constantine and Licinius were determined to bring the Christians into their camp; as early as A.D. 311 they were promising an end to persecution, and in 313 they went beyond mere "toleration" to put Christianity on an equal footing with the pagan cults. Victorious over their opponents with Christian support, Constantine and Licinius divided the empire and ruled as co-Augusti from A.D. 313–324. As time passed, however, relations between the two emperors became more and more strained until open warfare broke out. Licinius was defeated and executed, and Constantine ruled alone from A.D. 324 until his death in 337.

Constantine's Reforms

Constantine retained and enlarged on a number of the reforms of Diocletian. He continued the reorganization of the army, and he extended the regimentation of the civilian population that Diocletian had begun: Where Diocletian had bound the country people to the land, Constantine turned his attention to the urban dwellers and made membership in the craft guilds hereditary so that a son was forced into his father's vocation. Just as Diocletian's reform was intended to provide an adequate labor force in agriculture, so Constantine aimed at keeping up the strength of the guilds which were charged with performing the liturgies.

Hereditary Monarchy Returned.   Instead of following the mode of succession that Diocletian had tried to establish, Constantine returned to the principle of the hereditary monarchy. There was nothing profound about this—Constantine had sons, and Diocletian did not. At any rate, Constantine himself was the Augustus, while his three sons and two nephews were made Caesars. He thus established a dynasty which, despite family quarrels, was to last until the death of the famous Julian the Apostate in A.D. 363.

Christianity Favored.   Constantine broke sharply with the approach of Diocletian to the Christian problem, and this led to the discovery of a different and more workable basis for the emperor's authority. From his early alliance with the Christians and the equality of

CONSTANTINE THE GREAT (305–337)

treatment which he accorded them after A.D. 313, Constantine moved gradually still farther to the Christian side by favoring Christianity over paganism. He did not take the final step; it remained for his successors to complete the merger of church and state in which Christianity was made the official religion and paganism was outlawed. A Christian emperor could not be a god himself, but he could be the viceroy of God. As far as the Christians were concerned, such an arrangement would not only be acceptable but it would be credible as well. Consequently, the theocratic autocracy acquired a very strong position; theocracy had not been so unassailable since the days of the primary civilizations.

The alliance with the emperor was beneficial to the Christians in some ways, but it did have its drawbacks. The general level of sincerity and devotion to the faith was lowered as the persecutions ceased and many opportunists officially became Christians in order to better themselves in a material way. Moreover, as soon as the pressure of persecution was removed, the Christians began to fight more furiously among

ARCH OF CONSTANTINE IN ROME

(Courtesy of J. M. F.)

themselves over matters of doctrine. Various factions within the Church sought to enlist the support of the emperors against their rivals. Regional antagonisms cropped up in the theological wars; these were based on rivalries that were not doctrinal in origin—they were even pre-Christian. Before long it was Constantinople against Rome, or Alexandria versus Antioch.

Capital Transferred to Byzantium.   Although the move was foreshadowed by Diocletian's choice of Nicomedia for his capital, Constantine is often credited with a major break with tradition through the transfer of his own capital to Byzantium, soon known as Constantinople. The renovation and fortification of Byzantium was begun in A.D. 324, and the city was formally dedicated as New Rome and made the capital of the empire in 330.

The establishment of the chief administrative center of the Roman Empire in the East meant the ultimate abandonment of the West, even though attempts to preserve the unity of the empire continued for the next three centuries. Sentiment notwithstanding, the move was a practical one. The East was the richest, soundest, and economically the most versatile part of the empire. It must be held at all cost, and it could be best defended from dangers looming on the North and East by making Constantinople rather than Rome the imperial center.

Beginning of the End for the Ancient World

The beginning of the autocracy was also the beginning of the end for the ancient world. The autocracy involved, as we have seen, the substitution of Near Eastern political theory for the Indo-European tradition that the ancestors of the Greeks and Romans had brought into the civilized world. The victory of Christianity, which meant the demise of paganism, was another turning point, for it wrought changes not only in religious belief but also in many other phases of thought, art, and even daily life. The political unity of the Mediterranean, despite the stopgap of autocracy, would soon be disrupted, and the society and economy of the West would decline in complexity. Some changes came slowly; others, rapidly. Nevertheless, a new age began with Diocletian and Constantine. There are no precise dates to mark the beginning and the end of the new epoch, but the foundation of Constantinople in A.D. 330 and the fall of that city in 1453 are perhaps convenient boundaries for the limits of the millennium or so that separates ancient from modern times.

THE END OF THE ROAD

Why did the Roman Empire decline and fall? Why did ancient civilization disintegrate? No one knows. Or if someone does, no one else will admit it. These questions have been debated for at least fifteen centuries, but no agreement has been reached.

The Decline and Fall*

The climax reached by ancient civilization in the second century A.D. was followed by a gradual decline in which the political, economic, and cultural unity of the ancient world slowly disintegrated until it ceased to exist. Western Europe reverted to what was almost a new Age of Agriculture, although in the eastern Mediterranean the Byzantine Empire managed to keep alight the flickering torch of ancient culture. We speak of the fall of Rome, but it was more than that: It was the end of ancient civilization.

There was no sudden collapse. Ancient civilization, a complex structure reared to a great height by the toil of ages, subsided slowly, almost imperceptibly, like the ruins of some deserted mud-brick city. Contemporaries saw a changing world, full of invasion and civil war, far different from the quietude and security of the Pax Romana. People were conscious of the economic decline, the intellectual sterility, and the artistic stagnation. The pagans sighed wistfully for the "good old days," but the Christians were more optimistic and looked ahead for something that was "just around the corner."

In modern times there have been numerous attempts to explain the "fall of Rome." In the strictest sense this phrase would apply only to the collapse of Roman world dominion which was but one aspect of the decline of ancient civilization; it might even be called a manifestation of it. Throughout ancient history empires had appeared and disappeared many times before, yet civilization had either been unaffected or had picked itself up and risen to new heights. Thus, while the political and military failure of Rome presents a problem worthy of attention, it must not be allowed to take precedence over the more important question of the decline of ancient civilization. This fact has been recognized by some, but not all, of those who have wrestled with the problem. In addition, many of the explanations which scholars have offered thus far have confused cause and effect, although it is true that an effect that results from one cause may in turn become the cause of another effect. There is also the danger of selecting a single cause as being responsible

---

* This section is from Tom B. Jones, *Ancient Civilization*. Chicago: Rand McNally, 1960, pp. 353–54.

for the whole decline; mature consideration will show that a number of factors, rather than a single one, were important.

It is safe to say that theories attributing the decline of ancient civilization to moral degeneracy, race suicide, "failure of nerve," and miscegenation are patently absurd and may be dismissed without further comment. The barbarian invasions, it is true, administered the *coup de grâce* to the Roman Empire, but it is now recognized that the barbarians were able to cross the frontiers because of the internal weakness of the empire and because the barbarians had attained technological equality with the Romans in the art of war. Some have sought the reason for the decline in political or military factors—the lack of democracy, the development of the autocracy, the great political influence which the army acquired—but these things are superficial, or, at best, results rather than causes of decline. The argument that the fall of Rome was due to social conflict or class warfare is plausible, but the evidence is insufficient to supply adequate proof for a theory that has the additional disadvantage of attributing the decline to a single cause. The blame cannot be laid on the rise of Christianity, since the Christian attitude was prompted by the causes which were also responsible for the decline; one might even say that Christianity provided an answer to problems presented by the decline, but it was a palliative and not an antidote. Soil exhaustion, malaria, capitalism, communism, state socialism, overexpansion, underexpansion, the destruction of Greek initiative (whatever that was!), failure to extend prosperity and culture to the masses scarcely exhaust the long and dreary list of superficial, lunatic, or puerile "explanations" for the decline that have found their way into print. Grandiose and intricate theories evolved by great thinkers on the basis of very little fact are also to be rejected. Many of these theories are intellectually stimulating as exercises in logic and provide a sense of achievement for those who fashion them and those who have the time and patience to follow the argument to its conclusion, but they usually leave both creator and admirer too exhausted to realize that the problem has not been solved. One should especially be on guard against the theory which employs a false analogy; it is a particularly seductive idea that civilizations, like species of plants or animals, have a life cycle.

We might say that in the West civilization declined in complexity because the economy stopped expanding and began to contract. The expansion that had begun in the Near East in the third millennium B.C., spread to Greece and Italy in the first, and reached western continental Europe in the early Christian centuries had terminated in the third century A.D. for lack of additional space in which to grow. Then the movement went into reverse. Trade fell off; as this happened, industry declined, and the cities began to melt away. Complexity of culture in most civilizations tends to vary directly in proportion to urbanization; as "deurbanization" occurred in the West, culture became less complex. In the East, a more diverse and resilient area, economic activity stayed on a relatively high plane, and culture did not drop below the level of civilization.

The decline and fall of the Roman Empire was perhaps hastened by the economic breakdown in the West, but the fall of Rome was almost unavoidable. Like Cyrus and his Persians, or Alexander and his Macedonians, the Romans in the third century b.c. were a "nation" just far enough removed from barbarism and sufficiently touched by civilization to be able to conquer and hold in subjection people more civilized than themselves. As long as the "Romans" were Romans, or even Romans and Italians, they could maintain their position as a ruling minority which held an empire by force. The Romans could assimilate the Italians and "Romanize" the peoples of North Africa, Spain, and Gaul, whose cultures were less complex than theirs. In the East, however, there were two distinct culture areas, one Greek and the other Oriental; they could not be Romanized because their culture was too complex and too firmly established to be much affected by that of Rome. Instead, it was the Romans who became Hellenized and Orientalized; the process was never completed, but it went far enough to weaken the conquerors from the West.

We have already observed that in ancient times a land empire was difficult to maintain. The Persians managed it for two centuries, but it was nip and tuck all the way; the Athenians, Spartans, and Thebans failed utterly, and Alexander's empire did not survive him more than a decade. A maritime empire was possible, as the experience of Athens had shown, and during the late Republic the empire of Rome had been essentially maritime, too. Under the Principate, however, the expansion was inland away from the sea around which the original empire had been built. Yet even the Mediterranean region, although geographically unified, lacked a more essential unity of culture, language, and tradition. The Roman, Greek, and Oriental spheres could be brought together by force, but they could be held together only by the same means; amalgamation would never take place. It is well worth remembering also that the Near East was a natural unit which the Romans had split in half by taking Syria, Palestine, and Egypt but failing to include Mesopotamia and possibly regions farther east. This was bound to make trouble: We have already seen how the Parthians and after them the Persians, groups seeking to unify the Near East, complicated the military problems of Rome.

To sum up, as long as Rome (or Italy) held an empire in subjection, matters went fairly well; but, when there was an attempt to integrate Greeks and Orientals with the Romans—as, for example, by including such non-Romans in the Senate and the army—the result was exactly the opposite of the unity that the integration was designed to promote. Romanization was not possible, and the three basic divisions of the empire began to stand out in even sharper relief. In the end, an emperor was going to have to abandon one, or even two, of them in order to keep the third. Constantine chose to abandon the Romans for the Greeks in the hope that he could also hold the Orientals. By the seventh century A.D. the successors of Constantine held only the Greek portion of what had been the Roman Empire; the West was in barbarian hands, and the banner of Islam waved over the Near East. Where the Parthians and Persians had failed, the followers of the Prophet had succeeded.

A GLANCE BACKWARD

Along with the political and economic disintegration that marked the end of the ancient period, there was an obvious decline in cultural complexity. Particularly in the West, as cities and towns melted away, the political, social, and cultural paraphernalia of urban life were discarded because they had no utility in the new age. Local self-sufficiency became the order of the day, and most aspects of culture were scaled down to fit conditions of existence in small, topographically defined regions. There was a return to the land and to a barter economy; trade and manufacturing slid into lower gear to accommodate local rather than international demands. The microcosm of the village, monastery, or castle constricted the thoughts and aspirations of men whose ancestors had once accepted the concept of the *oecumene,* the unity of the whole inhabited world.

In this process of decline, some (we may never know how much) of ancient civilization was lost, but many of its basic elements survived through the medieval period, and not a little was rediscovered in modern times. This cargo, salvaged from the wreck of antiquity, is even yet of such importance that is is impossible to imagine what our culture today would be like if there had been no civilization in ancient times. We are surrounded by mementos of the past, most of them still more functional than decorative.

Religion and Languages

Geographically speaking, we dwell in the New World, but culturally we live in a world that is very old. Almost from birth we come in contact with two ancient Near Eastern religions, Judaism and Christianity. We learn to speak a language belonging to the Indo-Germanic family, but its vocabulary contains a vast number of words derived from Greek and Latin, especially in the case of nouns, verbs, adjectives, and adverbs. Some indication of this indebtedness to the classical languages may be sensed from the fact that of approximately half a hundred such words in this paragraph, 70 percent are ultimately of classical origin.

The persistence of a language and its influence upon other languages are reliable indicators of the potency of the culture to which the language itself belonged. We have already spoken of the influence of Greek on Latin. Greek is still a living language; it is also a commonplace that Latin lives on in its descendants, the Romance languages. Moreover, Latin did not die with the Roman Empire: It continued to be used for a long time as the language of diplomacy and religion and scholarship; it has been well said that in the Middle Ages whatever men thought and wrote was thought and written in Latin. The language of our modern science of which we are so proud would be greatly impoverished it its working vocabulary of words derived from classical origins were to be deleted. What should we call science itself? What should we substitute for atom, nuclear, mathematics, electricity, and many other words, including the zoological and botanical names we employ?

Classical Sources for Literature

If we turn from language to literature, the situation is unchanged. Vergil's *Aeneid* derived from the epics of Homer and Apollonius, and this was only the beginning of a long tradition: Dante's *Divine Comedy*, Spenser's *Faerie Queen*, the *Lusiads*, and the Chilean *La Araucana* are only a few of the later epics which owed their inspiration to classical sources. Medieval and modern poets who exploited the lyric, elegiac, and other forms developed in Greek and Latin poetry were equally indebted to a past that did not die. The drama, originating with the dramatic poetry of the Greeks, provides another example of the immortality of classical literature. The tragedies of Sophocles and Euripides are still performed, and their plots were adapted by a succession of playwrights from Seneca to Eugene O'Neill. In comedy, the evolutionary line runs from Aristophanes and Menander through Plautus and Terence, the Italian Renaissance and Shakespeare, to our own day; Plautus' *Menaechmi* was of Greek origin, Shakespeare adapted it for the *Comedy of Errors,* and one of its latest manifestations was the musical comedy, *The Boys from Syracuse.*

Prose.   As for prose, the literary types developed in antiquity— history, biography, the essay, the pamphlet, the treatise, the letter, the novel, and many others are still with us. What would history be, or have been, without Thucydides? And what of the giant, Cicero, whose style and mastery of many types of prose have exerted untold influence for centuries? Again, it has been well said that European prose as an instrument of thought was Cicero's creation.

Philosophy.   The contributions of Plato and Aristotle to philosophy do not need to be spelled out; it is enough merely to mention their names. The influence of Plato on the early Church Fathers was prodigious, and that of Aristotle no less so upon the theology of the Middle Ages. As a literary stylist Plato had great influence on Greek literature through the Byzantine period; in the matter of style, both Plato and Demosthenes occupied a position in Greek literature comparable to that of Cicero in Latin. In literary criticism, Aristotle's *Poetics* is still read and debated today; and there is another work well worth reading: Longinus, *On the Sublime*. Gibbon said that he did not truly understand Greek literature before reading this "Golden Book."

Scientific Writing.   For at least eighteen centuries after the death of Aristotle, virtually no one attempted to study natural or physical science without first reading what the great Stagirite had said on the subject; the later Greeks and Byzantines read his works in the original, while others read them in their Latin or Arabic translations. Other scientists of antiquity besides Aristotle continued to be consulted as authorities through the medieval period and into early modern times. The *Natural History* of Pliny the Elder was one of the great encyclopedias of the Middle Ages; after the discovery of the New World and the invention of printing, new editions of this famous work as well as translations appeared with supplementary chapters added to describe the flora and fauna of the Western Hemisphere. The influence of Claudius Ptolemy wa strong even after the time of Columbus, while Vitruvius on architecture and Frontinus on aqueducts were also frequently consulted. In medicine, until the eighteenth century A.D. in some parts of the world, doctors were required to study Galen, Celsus, and the Hippocratic *Corpus*. Euclidian geometry, as we have already noted, is still taught in our schools with the aid of textbooks that are largely translations of his *Elements*.

Education

Until very recently, the elementary school curriculum was not far removed in method and subject matter from the Greco-Roman schools. Ancient education was anything but perfect, and one does not doubt that great improvements have been made; but, while it is often tempting to throw out the baby with the bath, it is not always a procedure to be recommended: Some of the best features of ancient education seem to have been abandoned as, for example, the teaching of grammar and an emphasis on style which once produced people who wrote easily and spoke well. And what of the alphabet, which everyone still learns at a tender age? It has been with us a long time; we got it from the Romans who learned it from the Greeks who in turn borrowed it from the Phoenicians.

Art and Architecture

Our classical heritage in art and architecture is plain for all to see. The government buildings of our national capital and structures on many a college campus remind us constantly of the architecture of Greece and Rome. The column and lintel technique, the gabled roof, the arch, the vault, and the dome are much in evidence. Classic traditions in modern relief sculpture and sculpture in the round have not been completely abandoned, although their influence was stronger in the earlier centuries of the modern period.

Politics and Institutions

Our vocabulary of terms relating to politics and institutions proclaims our debt to Greece and Rome. The very words democracy, diplomacy, republic, senate, census, veto, municipal, and even government itself tell of the origin of the words and institutions they denote. Democracy we naturally associate with the Greeks, but it should not be forgotten that federal and representative government as well as proportional representation began with them, too.

Less tangible things we also owe to these cultural ancestors of ours—our concepts of freedom, justice, beauty, symmetry, wisdom, and moderation—were formulated by the Greeks. We are indebted to them also for formal logic as well as the concept of the general definition and the methods of logical classification. We do not have to subscribe to a literal acceptance of Shelley's dictum that "we are all Greeks" to agree that he had a point.

Near Eastern Contributions

Nor must we neglect the Near East, the source of our basic concepts of morality and monotheism, and more besides. Coined money, the solar calendar, and the idea of codifying the law originated in the Near East. The invention of writing and the alphabet itself are Near Eastern in origin. We still use the sexagesimal system of the Sumerians not only in astronomy and radial measurement but also in a matter so mundane as daily timekeeping as we divide a minute into sixty seconds, or an hour into sixty minutes, or a day into twelve double hours. Words of ultimate Sumerian or Babylonian origin are still in our working vocabulary: copper, cyanide, cotton, and many others for minerals, plants, and herbs. Moreover, as we are debtors to classical civilization, so also the Greeks and Romans owed much to the Near East.

Summing It Up

What has been said here only hints at the size of our present-day mountain of debt to antiquity. We boast of "progress," but it is sobering to reflect that we have not advanced beyond the ancients in many respects. It is difficult to discern great moral improvement; we have conquered many enemies but not ourselves. Advances in science and technology have made it possible to realize, or provided opportunity for us to realize, desirable things of which the ancients only dreamed. Our new sources of power and our machines have abolished slavery; modern methods of production and distribution could banish hunger and poverty; we are conquering disease; better communications and transportation have given democracy a fighting chance; and the economy of the modern world has provided a leisure that might be used for creativity. The ancients would envy us this wealth of opportunity, and it is not comforting to think that they might have made better use of it.

Bibliography

A select list of authoritative, readable works is presented here. Many are paperbacks, easy to obtain and reasonable in price. Hardcover editions are indicated by an asterisk.

1. GENERAL

*Bickerman, E. J. *Chronology of the Ancient World*. Ithaca, N.Y.: Cornell University Press, 1968.

Cambridge Ancient History. 12 vols. Cambridge, England: Cambridge University Press, 1923–39. (A new edition is now in progress. Vols. I, II, III, and VII have already been published.)

Oxford Classical Dictionary. Oxford: Oxford University Press, 1970.

There is a need for a new general atlas of the ancient world. The following are excellent but specialized:

*Barnes, J., and Malek, J., eds. *Atlas of Ancient Egypt*. New York: Facts on File, 1982.

*Cornell, T., and Matthews, J., eds. *Atlas of the Roman World*. New York: Facts on File, 1982.

*Levi, P., ed. *Atlas of the Greek World*. New York: Facts on File, 1980.

May, H. G., ed. *Oxford Bible Atlas*. Oxford, England: Oxford University Press, 1962.

Westminster Historical Atlas to the Bible. Philadelphia: Westminster, 1945.

It should also be noted that there are several periodicals of interest to the general reader. Among these are:

Archaeology, published by the Archaeological Institute of America; *The Biblical Archaeologist* and the *Bulletin of the American Schools of Oriental Research*, both published by the American Schools of Oriental Research. In addition, the *National Geographic* and the *Scientific American* often have useful articles.

2. PREHISTORY, NEAR EAST, AND AEGEAN KINGDOMS (CHAPTERS 1–4)

Archaeology and Prehistory

Bordes, F. *The Old Stone Age.* New York: McGraw-Hill, 1968.

Braidwood, R. J. *Prehistoric Men.* Chicago: Scott, Foresman, 1975.

Clark, G. *Stone Age Hunters.* New York: McGraw-Hill, 1967.

Cohen, M. N. *The Food Crisis in Prehistory.* New Haven, Conn.: Yale University Press, 1977.

Deetz, J. *Invitation to Archaeology.* Garden City, N.J.: Natural History Press, 1967.

*Fagan, B. *In the Beginning,* 5th ed. Boston: Little Brown, 1985.

Jones, T. *Paths to the Ancient Past.* New York: Free Press, 1967.

Piggott, S. *Approach to Archaeology.* New York: McGraw-Hill, 1965.

*Reed, C. A., ed. *Origins of Agriculture.* Chicago: Aldine, 1977.

*Stigler, R., and Gorenstein, S., eds. *The Old World: Early Man to the Development of Agriculture.* New York: St. Martin's Press, 1974.

*Ucko, P. J., and Dimbleby, G. W., eds. *The Domestication and Exploitation of Plants and Animals.* Chicago: Aldine, 1969.

Urbanization

*Adams, R. M. *The Evolution of Urban Society.* Chicago: Aldine, 1966.

*Griffeth, R., and Thomas, C. G., eds. *The City-State in Five Cultures.* Santa Barbara, Calif.: ABC-Clio, 1981.

*Hammond, M. *The City in the Ancient World.* Cambridge, Mass: Harvard University Press, 1972.

*Ucko, P. J., Tringham, R., and Dimbleby, G. W., eds. *Man, Settlement and Urbanism.* London: Duckworth, 1972.

The Near East

*Aldred, C. *The Egyptians.* 2nd ed. New York: Thames and Hudson, 1984.

*Andrews, C. and Faulkner, R. O. *Book of the Dead.* New York: Macmillan, 1985.

*Bermant, C. and Weitzman, M. Ebla: *A Revelation in Archaeology.* New York: Times Books, 1979.

*Brinkman, J. A. *A Political History of Post-Kassite Babylonia: 1158–772* B.C. Rome: Archiv Orientalni, no. 43, 1968.

*Burney, C. *The Ancient Near East.* Ithaca, N.Y.: Cornell University Press, 1980.

*Butzer, E. W. *Early Hydraulic Civilization in Egypt.* Chicago: University of Chicago Press, 1976.

*Cook, J. M. *The Persian Empire.* New York: Schocken Books, 1983.

*Culican, J. *The Medes and Persians.* New York: Praeger, 1965.

*Dothan, T. *The Philistines and Their Material Culture.* New Haven, Conn.: Yale University Press, 1982.

Edwards, I. E. S. *The Pyramids of Egypt.* Harmondsworth, England: Pelican, 1952.

Emery, W. B. *Archaic Egypt.* Harmondsworth, England: Pelican, 1961.

Erman, A. *The Ancient Egyptians.* New York: Harper, 1966.

Frankfort, H. *Art and Architecture of the Ancient Orient.* Harmondsworth, England: Penguin, 1971.

————. *Before Philosophy.* Harmondsworth, England: Penguin, 1949.

Gardiner, A. *Egypt of the Pharaohs.* Oxford, England: Oxford University Press, 1966.

Gelb, I. J. *The Study of Writing.* Chicago: Phoenix, 1963.

*Glanville, S. R. K. *Legacy of Egypt.* Oxford, England: Clarendon, 1942; new edition, 1971.

*Gray, J. *The Canaanites.* New York: Praeger, 1964.

Gurney, O. R. *The Hittites.* Harmondsworth, England: Pelican, 1961.

Harden, D. B. *The Phoenicians.* New York: Praeger, 1962.

Jacobsen, T. *Treasures of Darkness.* New Haven, Conn.: Yale University Press, 1976.

Jones, T. *The Sumerian Problem.* New York: Wiley, 1969.

Kenyon, K. *Archaeology in the Holy Land.* New York: Praeger, 1962.

Kramer, S. N. *Mythologies of the Ancient World.* Garden City, N.J.: Doubleday Anchor, 1961.

————. *The Sumerians.* Chicago: Phoenix, 1963.

Laessøe, J. *The People of Ancient Assyria.* New York: Barnes and Noble, 1963.

*Lambert, W. G. *Babylonian Wisdom Literature.* Oxford, England: Clarendon, 1960.

*———— and Millard, A. R. *Atrahasis.* Oxford, England: Clarendon, 1969.

*Lichtheim, M. *Ancient Egyptian Literature.* 3 vols. Berkeley: University of California Press, 1972–81.

*Macqueen, J. G. *The Hittites.* London: Thames and Hudson, 1986.

*Matthiae, P. *Ebla: An Empire Rediscovered.* Garden City, N.J.: Doubleday, 1971.

Mellaart, J. *Çatal Hüyük.* New York: McGraw-Hill, 1967.

————. *The Neolithic of the Near East.* New York: Charles Scribners' Sons, 1975.

*Michalowski, K. *The Art of Ancient Egypt.* London: Abrams, 1969.

*Moorgat, A. *The Art of Ancient Mesopotamia*. London: Phaidon, 1969.

*Moscati, S. *The Phoenicians*. New York: Praeger, 1968.

Neugebauer, O. *The Exact Sciences in Antiquity*. New York: Harper, 1962.

*Oates, J. *Babylon*. London: Thames and Hudson, 1979.

Olmstead, A. T. *History of the Persian Empire*. Chicago: Phoenix, 1959.

Oppenheim, A. L. *Ancient Mesopotamia*. Chicago: Phoenix, 1964.

*_____. *Letters from Mesopotamia*. Chicago: University of Chicago Press, 1967.

Orlinsky, H. *Ancient Israel*. Ithaca, N.Y.: Cornell University Press, 1954.

*Porada, E. *The Art of Ancient Iran*. New York: Crown, 1965.

*Pritchard, J. B. *Ancient Near Eastern Texts Relating to the Old Testament*. 3rd ed. Princeton, N.J.: Princeton University Press, 1969.

Roux, G. *Ancient Iraq*. Harmondsworth, England: Pelican, 1980.

Saggs, H. W. F. *The Greatness That Was Babylon*. New York: Mentor, 1968.

Smith, W. S. *The Art and Architecture of Ancient Egypt*. Harmondsworth, England: Pelican, 1981.

*Wheeler, J. M. *The Indus Civilization*. Cambridge, England: Cambridge University Press, 1968. (See also *Valley Civilization of the Indus*. New York: Praeger, 1966.)

Wilson, J. A. *The Culture of Egypt*. Chicago: Phoenix, 1956.

Aegean Prehistory

Blegen, C. W. *Troy and the Trojans*. New York: Praeger, 1963.

Carpenter, R. *Folk Tale, Fiction, and Saga in the Homeric Epics*. Berkeley: University of California Press, 1962.

Chadwick, J. *The Decipherment of Linear B*. New York: Modern Library, 1958.

_____. *The Mycenaean World*. Cambridge, England: Cambridge University Press, 1976.

*Doumas, C. J. *Thera*. London: Thames and Hudson, 1980.

Finley, M. I. *The World of Odysseus*. Cleveland, Ohio: Meridian, 1959.

Graham, J. W. *The Palaces of Crete*. Princeton, N.J.: Princeton University Press, 1962.

Hood, M. S. *The Minoans*. New York: Praeger, 1971.

*Mylonas, G. *Ancient Mycenae*. Princeton, N.J.: Princeton University Press, 1957.

Page, D. *History and the Homeric Iliad*. Berkeley: University of California Press, 1963.

Pendlebury, J. D. S. *The Archaeology of Crete*. New York: Norton, 1965.

Samuel, A. *The Mycenaeans in History*. New York: Spectrum, 1965.

*Wace, A. J. B. *Mycenae*. Princeton, N.J.: Princeton University Press, 1949.

3. GREECE (CHAPTERS 5–7)

General Topics

Austin, N. *Greek Historians.* New York: Van Nostrand, 1969.

Biers, W. R. *Archaeology of Greece.* Ithaca, N.Y.: Cornell University Press, 1980.

Boardman, J. *Greek Art.* New York: Praeger, 1964.

Brown, T. S. *The Greek Historians.* New York: Heath, 1973.

*Bury, J. B., and Meiggs, R. *A History of Greece.* 4th ed. New York: St. Martin's, 1975.

*Cook, R. M. *Greek Painted Pottery.* Chicago: Quadrangle, 1960.

Devambez, P. *Greek Painting.* New York: Viking, 1962.

*Dicks, D. R. *Greek Astronomy.* Ithaca, N.Y.: Cornell University Press, 1970.

*Dinsmoor, W. B. *Architecture of Ancient Greece.* 3rd ed. London: Batsford, 1950.

*Jenkins, G. K. *Ancient Greek Coins.* London: Barrie and Jenkins, 1972.

Lloyd, G. E. R. *Early Greek Science.* 2 vols. New York: Norton, 1970–73.

Marrou, H. I. *History of Education in Antiquity.* New York: Mentor, 1964.

*Phillips, E. D. *Aspects of Greek Medicine.* New York: St. Martin's Press, 1973.

Pollitt, J. J. *Art and Experience in Classical Greece.* Cambridge, England: Cambridge University Press, 1972.

Richter, G. M. A. *Handbook of Greek Art.* New York: Phaidon, 1969.

*———. *The Sculpture and Sculptors of the Greeks.* New Haven, Conn.: Yale University Press, 1950.

Scranton, R. L. *Greek Architecture.* New York: Braziller, 1967.

*Semple, E. C. *Geography of the Mediterranean Region.* New York: Holt, 1931.

*Sinclair, T. A. *History of Greek Political Thought.* London: Routledge and Kegan Paul, 1967.

*White, K. D. *Greek and Roman Technology.* Ithaca, N.Y.: Cornell University Press, 1984.

Greece: 1200–500 B.C.

Andrewes, A. *The Greek Tyrants.* New York: Harper, 1963.

Boardman, J. *The Greeks Overseas.* Harmondsworth, England: Pelican, 1964.

*Burn, A. R. *The Lyric Age of Greece.* New York: St. Martin's, 1960.

*———. *The World of Hesiod.* London: Routledge and Kegan Paul, 1936.

Burnet, J. *Early Greek Philosophy.* New York: Meridian, 1957.

*Bowra, M. *Greek Lyric Poetry.* Oxford, England: Oxford University Press, 1961.

*Coldstream, A. N. *Greek Geometric Pottery.* New York: Barnes and Noble, 1968.

*Cook, J. M. *Greeks in Ionia and the East.* London: Thames and Hudson, 1962.

*Desborough, V. R. *The Greek Dark Ages.* New York: St. Martin's, 1972.

Ehrenberg, V. *From Solon to Socrates.* New York: Barnes and Noble, 1967.

Finley, M. I. *Early Greece: the Bronze and Archaic Ages.* New York: Norton, 1970.

*Forrest, W. G. *History of Sparta, 950–192* B.C. London: Hutchinson, 1968.

Freeman, K. *Greek City States.* New York: Norton, 1963.

*_____. *Life and Work of Solon.* London: Oxford, 1926. (Paperback ed., New York: Arno.)

*Graham, A. J. *Colony and Mother City in Ancient Greece.* Manchester, England: Manchester, 1964.

*Huxley, G. L. *Early Sparta.* Cambridge, Mass.: Harvard, 1962.

*Kelly, T. *History of Argos.* Minneapolis: University of Minnesota Press, 1977.

Kirk, G. S., and Raven, J. E. *Presocratic Philosophers.* Cambridge, England: Cambridge University Press, 1960.

*Michell, H. *Sparta.* Cambridge, England: Cambridge University Press, 1952.

*Parke, H. W., and Wormell, D. E. W. *The Delphic Oracle.* 2 vols. Oxford, England: Blackwell, 1956.

*Richter, G. M. A. *Archaic Greek Art.* Oxford, England: Oxford University Press, 1949.

*Snodgrass, A. M. *The Dark Age of Greece.* Chicago: Aldine, 1972.

*Woodhead, A. G. *Greeks in the West.* New York: Praeger, 1962.

Woodhouse, W. J. *Solon the Liberator.* New York: Octagon, 1965.

Greece: 500–336 B.C.

*Camp, J. M. *The Athenian Agora.* New York: Thames and Hudson, 1986.

*Connor, W. R. *New Politicians of Fifth Century Athens.* Princeton, N.J.: Princeton University Press, 1971.

Cornford, F. M. *Origins of Attic Comedy.* Garden City, N.J.: Doubleday Anchor, 1961.

Dodds, E. R. *The Greeks and the Irrational.* Boston: Beacon, 1955.

*Forrest, W. G. *The Emergence of Greek Democracy.* London: Wiedenfield and Nicholson, 1966.

*French, A. *The Growth of the Athenian Economy.* London: Routledge and Kegan Paul, 1964.

Frost, F. J. *Greek Society.* Lexington, Mass.: D.C. Heath, 1971.

*Garner, R. *Law and Society in Classical Athens.* New York: St. Martin's, 1987.

*Hignett, C. *History of the Athenian Constitution.* Oxford, England: Oxford University Press, 1952.

*Hill, I. T. *The Ancient City of Athens.* Cambridge, Mass.: Harvard, 1953.

*Jones, A. H. M. *Athenian Democracy.* Oxford, England: Blackwell, 1957.

*Jones, J. W. *Law and Legal Theory of the Greeks.* Oxford, England: Oxford University Press, 1956.

*Kagan, D. *The Outbreak of the Peloponnesian War.* Ithaca, N.Y.: Cornell University Press, 1969.

Kitto, H. D. F. *Greek Tragedy.* Garden City, N.J.: Doubleday Anchor, 1954.

Larsen, J. A. O. *Representative Government in Greek and Roman History.* Berkeley: University of California Press, 1955.

*Meiggs, R. *The Athenian Empire.* Oxford, England: Oxford University Press, 1972.

*Pickard-Cambridge, A. W. *Dramatic Festivals of Athens.* 2nd ed. Oxford, England: Oxford University Press, 1968.

*Rhodes, P. J. *The Athenian Boule.* Oxford, England: Clarendon, 1972.

Sealey, R. *History of the Greek States.* Berkeley: University of California Press, 1976.

*Thompson, H., and Wycherley, R. E. *The Agora of Athens.* Princeton, N.J.: Princeton University Press, 1972.

Zimmern, A. E. *The Greek Commonwealth.* London: Oxford University Press, 1961.

The Hellenistic Age

Adcock, F. E. *Greek and Macedonian Art of War.* Berkeley: University of California Press, 1957.

*Allen, R. E. *The Attalid Kingdom.* New York: Oxford University Press, 1981.

*Bieber, M. *Sculpture of the Hellenistic Age.* New York: Columbia University Press, 1955.

Borza, E. N. *The Impact of Alexander the Great.* Chicago: Dryden, 1974.

Bury, J. B. *The Hellenistic Age.* New York: Norton, 1970.

*DeWitt, N. W. *Epicurus and His Philosophy.* Minneapolis: University of Minnesota Press, 1954.

*Dickens, G. *Hellenistic Sculpture.* Oxford, England: Oxford University Press, 1920.

Ferguson, J. *Heritage of Hellenism.* New York: Harcourt Brace Jovanovich, 1973.

Forster, E. M. *Alexandria.* Garden City, N.J.: Doubleday, 1961.

Fyfe, T. *Hellenistic Architecture.* Cambridge, England: Cambridge University Press, 1936.

Grant, F. C. *Hellenistic Religions.* Indianapolis: Bobbs-Merrill, 1953.

*Grant, M. *From Alexander to Cleopatra: the Hellenistic World.* New York: Scribners, 1982.

*Griffith, G. T. *Alexander the Great.* Cambridge, Mass.: Heffer, 1966.

*Gruen, E. *The Hellenistic World and the Coming of Rome.* 2 vols. Berkeley: University of California Press, 1984.

*Hansen, E. V. *The Attalids of Pergamum.* 2nd ed. Ithaca, N.Y.: Cornell University Press, 1971.

*Körte, A. *Hellenistic Poetry.* New York: Knopf, 1929.

*Larsen, J. A. O. *Greek Federal States.* Oxford, England: Clarendon, 1968.

*More, P. E. *Hellenistic Philosophies.* Princeton, N.J.: Princeton University Press, 1923.

*Robinson, C. A. *Alexander the Great.* New York: Dutton, 1947.

*Snyder, J. W. *Alexander the Great.* New York: Twayne, 1966.

*Tarn, W. W. *The Greeks in India and Bactria.* Cambridge, England: Cambridge University Press, 1938.

————. *Hellenistic Civilization.* New York: Meridian, 1961.

*Walbank, F. W. *The Hellenistic World.* Cambridge, Mass.: Harvard University Press, 1982.

————. *Philip V of Macedon.* Cambridge, England: Cambridge University Press, 1940.

*Webster, T. B. L. *Hellenistic Poetry and Art.* London: Methuen, 1964.

*Wilcken, U. *Alexander the Great.* New York: Dial, 1932.

*Woodcock, G. *The Greeks in India.* London: Faber, 1966.

4. ROME (CHAPTERS 8–10)

General Topics

*Bailey, C. *Legacy of Rome.* London: Milford, 1923.

Boëthius, A., and Ward-Perkins, J. B. *Etruscan and Roman Architecture.* Harmondsworth, England: Pelican, 1970.

Brilliant, R. *Roman Art.* New York: Praeger, 1974.

Brown, F. E. *Roman Architecture.* New York: Braziller, 1961.

Carcopino, J. *Daily Life in Ancient Rome.* New Haven, Conn.: Yale University Press, 1960.

Grant, M. *Roman History from Coins.* Cambridge, England: Cambridge University Press, 1968.

*Johnson, A. C., et al. *Ancient Roman Statutes.* Austin: University of Texas Press, 1961.

*Jolowicz, A. F. *Historical Introduction to the Study of Roman Law.* Cambridge, England: Cambridge University Press, 1952.

Laistner, M. L. W. *The Greater Roman Historians.* Berkeley: University of California Press, 1963.

Lewis, N., and Reinhold, M. *Roman Civilization.* 2 vols. New York: Harper, 1966.

*Mattingly, H. *Roman Coins*. New York: Dial, 1928; 2nd ed. London: Methuen, 1960.

Rose, H. J. *Ancient Roman Religion*. New York: Harper, 1959.

*Scarborough, J. *Roman Medicine*. Ithaca, N.Y.: Cornell University Press, 1969.

*Schulz, F. *History of Roman Legal Science*. Oxford, England: Oxford University Press, 1946.

*Sherwin-White, A. *The Roman Citizenship*. Oxford, England: Oxford University Press, 1939.

Stenico, A. *Roman and Etruscan Painting*. New York: Viking, 1963.

*Watson, G. R. *The Roman Soldier*. Ithaca, N.Y.: Cornell University Press, 1969.

Wheeler, M. *Roman Art and Architecture*. New York: Praeger, 1964.

*White, K. D. *Roman Farming*. Ithaca, N.Y.: Cornell University Press, 1970.

The Roman Republic

*Adcock, F. E. *Marcus Crassus*. Cambridge, England: Heffer, 1966.

*Astin, A. E. *Scipio Aemilianus*. Oxford, England: Oxford University Press, 1967.

*Badian, E. *Publicans and Sinners*. Ithaca, N.Y.: Cornell University Press, 1972.

*_____. *Roman Imperialism in the Late Republic*. Oxford, England: Blackwell, 1968.

*Baker, G. P. *Sulla the Fortunate*. Rome: L'Erma, 1967.

*Balsdon, J. P. V. D. *Julius Caesar*. New York: Athenaeum, 1967.

*Bloch, R. *The Etruscans*. London: Barrie and Rockliffe, 1969.

*Boren, H. *The Gracchi*. New York: Twayne, 1968.

_____. *Roman Society*. Lexington, Mass.: D.C. Heath, 1977.

Brunt, P. A. *Social Conflict in the Roman Republic*. New York: Norton, 1972.

*Charles-Picard, G. *Carthage*. London: Elek, 1964.

*_____. *Life and Death in Carthage*. New York: Taplinger, 1968.

*Charles-Picard, G., and Charles-Picard, C. *Daily Life in Carthage*. London: Allen and Unwin, 1961. (For Carthage and the Carthaginians, see also Harden and Moscati on Phoenicians noted in Section 2).

Crawford, M. *The Roman Republic*. Cambridge, Mass.: Harvard University Press, 1982.

De Beer, G. R. *Hannibal*. New York: Viking, 1969.

Grimal, P. *Hellenism and the Rise of Rome*. New York: Delacorte, 1969.

Gruen, E. S. *Imperialism in the Roman Republic*. New York: Holt, Rinehart, and Winston, 1970.

*_____. *The Last Generation of the Roman Republic*. Berkeley: University of California Press, 1973.

*_____. *Roman Politics and the Criminal Courts*. Cambridge, Mass.: Harvard University Press, 1968.

Heurgon, J. *Daily Life of the Etruscans*. New York: Viking, 1957.

*————. *The Rise of Rome*. Berkeley: University of California Press, 1973.

Hutchinson, L. *The Conspiracy of Catiline*. London: A. Blond, 1966.

*Huzar, E. G. *Mark Antony*. Minneapolis: University of Minnesota Press, 1978.

*Kaplan, A. *Catiline*. New York: Exposition Press, 1968.

*Kildahl, P. A. *Gaius Marius*. New York: Twayne, 1968.

*Pallottino, M. *The Etruscans*. Bloomington: Indiana University Press, 1975. (Based on 6th ed.)

*Radin, M. *Brutus*. New York: Oxford University Press, 1939.

*Salmon, E. T. *Roman Colonization Under the Republic*. Ithaca, N.Y.: Cornell University Press, 1970.

*Scullard, H. H. *Roman Politics, 220–150 B.C.* Oxford, England: Oxford University Press, 1951.

*————. *Scipio Africanus*. Ithaca, N.Y.: Cornell University Press, 1970.

Seager, R. *The Crisis of the Roman Republic*. New York: Barnes and Noble, 1969.

*Stockton, D. *The Gracchi*. New York: Oxford University Press, 1979.

Syme, R. *The Roman Revolution*. Oxford, England: Oxford University Press, 1960.

Taylor, L. R. *Party Politics in the Age of Caesar*. Berkeley: University of California Press, 1961.

*————. *Roman Voting Assemblies*. Ann Arbor: University of Michigan Press, 1966.

*Volkmann, H. *Cleopatra*. New York: Sagamore, 1958.

*Warmington, B. H. *Carthage*. London: Hale, 1960.

Wellard, J. *The Search for the Etruscans*. New York: Saturday Review Press, 1975.

*Wiseman, T. P. *New Men in the Roman Senate*. Oxford, England: Oxford University Press, 1971.

The Roman Empire

Africa, T. W. *Rome of the Caesars*. New York: Wiley, 1965.

*Balsdon, J. P. V. D. *The Emperor Gaius*. Oxford, England: Oxford University Press, 1934.

*Barnes, T. D. *The New Empire of Diocletian and Constantine*. Cambridge, Mass.: Harvard University Press, 1982.

*Barrow, R. H. *Prefect and Emperor*. New York: Oxford University Press, 1973.

*Birley, A. *Marcus Aurelius*. Boston: Little, Brown, 1966.

*————. *Septimius Severus, The African Emperor*. New York: Doubleday, 1972.

*Bonner, S. F. *Roman Declamation*. Liverpool, England: University Press, 1949.

*Bowersock, G. W. *Augustus and the Greek World*. Oxford, England: Clarendon, 1965.

*_____. *Greek Sophists in the Roman Empire*. Oxford, England: Clarendon, 1969.

"_____. *Roman Arabia*. Cambridge, Mass.: Harvard University Press, 1983.

*Brauer, G. C. *The Age of the Soldier Emperors*. New York: Noyes, 1975.

*Browning, I. *Palmyra*. Park Ridge, N.J.: Noyes, 1979.

*Browning, J. *Petra*. London: Chatto and Windus, 1982.

Cochrane, C. M. *Christianity and Classical Culture*. New York: Oxford Galaxy, 1957.

*Colledge, M. A. R. *The Parthians*. New York: Praeger, 1967.

*Crook, J. A. *Consilium Principis*. Cambridge, England: Cambridge University Press, 1955.

*_____. *Law and Life of Rome*. Ithaca, N.Y.: Cornell University Press, 1967.

Deiss, J. J. *Herculaneum*. New York: Crowell, 1970.

Dill, S. *Roman Society from Nero to Marcus Aurelius*. New York: Meridian, 1956.

Ferrill, A. *The Fall of the Roman Empire: The Military Explanation*. London: Thames and Hudson, 1986.

*Grant, M. *Climax of Rome*. Boston: Little, Brown, 1968.

*_____. *Nero*. London: Weidenfield and Nicholson, 1970.

*Hammond, M. *The Antonine Monarchy*. Rome: American Academy, 1959.

Jones, A. H. M. *Augustus*. New York: Norton, 1970.

Jones, T. *The Silver-Plated Age*. Sandoval: Coronado Press (now of Lawrence, Kansas), 1962.

*Levick, B. *Tiberius the Politician*. Ithaca, N.Y.: Cornell University Press, 1976.

*McKay, A. G. *Houses, Villas, and Palaces in the Roman World*. Ithaca, N.Y.: Cornell University Press, 1975.

*MacMullen, R. *Roman Social Relations*. New Haven, Conn.: Yale University Press, 1974.

*Marsh, F. B. *The Reign of Tiberius*. Cambridge, England: Heffer, 1959.

*Momigliano, A. *Claudius*. New York: Barnes and Noble, 1961.

Ogilvie, R. M. *The Romans and Their Gods in the Age of Augustus*. New York: Norton, 1970.

*Ragette, F. *Baalbek*. Park Ridge, N.J.: Noyes, 1980.

*Reinhold, M. *Marcus Agrippa*. Geneva, N.Y.: Humphrey, 1933.

Richmond, J. A. *Roman Britain*. Harmondsworth, England: Penguin, 1963.

Rowell, H. *Rome in the Augustan Age*. Norman, Okla.: University of Oklahoma Press, 1962.

*Salmon, E. T. *History of the Roman World 30 B.C. to 138 A.D.* London: Methuen, 1968.

*Scramuzza, V. *Claudius*. Cambridge, Mass.: Harvard University Press, 1940.

Seager, R. *Tiberius*. Berkeley: University of California Press, 1972.

Starr, C. G. *Civilization and the Caesars*. New York: Norton, 1965.

*_____. *The Roman Imperial Navy.* Cambridge, Mass.: Heffer, 1960.

*Vogt, J. *The Decline of Rome.* New York: New American Library, 1967.

*Ward-Perkins, J., and Claridge, A. *Pompeii* A.D. *1979.* Boston: Boston Museum of Fine Arts, 1978.

Warmington, B. H. *Nero: Reality and Legend.* New York: Norton, 1968.

*Weaver, P. R. C. *Familia Caesaris.* Cambridge, England: Cambridge University Press, 1972.

*Webster, G. *The Roman Imperial Army.* New York: Funk and Wagnalls, 1970.

*Williams, S. *Diocletian and the Roman Recovery.* New York: Methuen, 1985.

Index

ABOUT THE AUTHOR

Tom Jones is a Professor Emeritus in history at the University of Minnesota. He received his Ph.D. from the University of Michigan. He served on the University of Minnesota faculty from 1935 to 1977. In 1977 he was appointed Regents' Professor of History at the university. His extensive publications include over 125 books, monographs, articles, and reviews. These include *In the Twilight of Antiquity, Ancient Civilization,* and *The Silver-Plated Age.*

A NOTE ON THE TYPE

The text of this book was set 10/12 Palatino using a film version of the face designed by Hërmann Zapf that was first released in 1950 by Germany's Stempel Foundry. The face is named after Giovanni Battista Palatino, a famous penman of the sixteenth century. In its calligraphic quality, Palatino is reminiscent of the Italian Renaissance type designs, yet with its wide, open letters and unique proportions it still retains a modern feel. Palatino is considered one of the most important faces from one of Europe's most influential type designers.

Composed by Compset Inc., Beverly, Massachusetts

Printed and bound by R. R. Donnelley & Sons Company, Crawfordsville, Indiana